Becoming a Brilliant Star: Twelve Core Ideas Supporting Holistic Education

William G. Huitt, Editor

To my Brilliant Stars
Geoff, Katie, and Kevin

Published in the United States by IngramSpark

Print ISBN: 978-1-7326068-0-7
ebook ISBN: 978-1-7326068-1-4
pdf ISBN: 978-1-7326068-2-1

Cover design: Geoffrey Huitt

Image: ID 40101382 © Rawpixelimages | Dreamstime.com

Contents

Figures and Tables

Acknowledgements

The book is the result of many contributors. The co-authors of the individual papers were either colleagues or practicing educators who were working under my supervision. Their contributions made the book possible.

My wife, Marsha, provided invaluable editorial assistance throughout the development of the individual chapters and final editing. John Hummel, David Monetti, and Bob Bauer provided support and encouragement in developing the individual chapters.

Finally, I appreciate the assistance from Valdosta State University for its support in providing support and technical assistance in creating the original website for which the individual chapters were produced.

William G. (Bill) Huitt

Preface

My original college major was business and marketing and I initially worked in the insurance and retail industries. While there, I saw the benefit of setting explicit goals and collecting data for the purpose of measuring success towards meeting those goals.

When I entered education, I adapted that emphasis and focused on goals related to increasing academic achievement as measured on standardized objective tests. After teaching for several years, I joined a team at Research for Better Schools in Philadelphia who had a similar core mission. That work lead to the development of a highly successful program that was the foundation of multiple conference presentations, articles, book chapters, and a book published by ASCD titled *Improving classrooms and schools: A research-based perspective.*

As I worked with that research over the next decade, it became clear that humanity had entered a new era, the digital/information age. Continuing to read business-oriented literature, I noticed a critique of the competencies and capabilities (and the lack thereof) of young people who were entering the workforce as well as concerns about their quality of citizenship. As a result, I became aware that a more holistic approach to schooling and education was necessary.

In response to this growing awareness, I began to develop the Brilliant Star framework that is the focus of this book. The book's chapters reflect the culmination of numerous efforts to organize and communicate to educators and policy makers what theory and research have to offer regarding a more well-rounded conceptualization of a focus of facilitating child and adolescent development. A major goal is to create the elements of a dashboard that can focus attention on a profile that is more reflective of the whole person rather than simply focusing on a single score for academic knowledge and skills.

The purpose of the book is to put all of this knowledge and experience into one volume for easy access. The framework is not intended to be a final, definitive statement regarding human capacities or potential competencies and capabilities, but rather to encourage parents, educators, and policy makers to create a more holistic view of the focus of education, in general, and schooling, especially during childhood and adolescence.

William G. (Bill) Huitt

Introduction

The Brilliant Star framework was developed for the purpose of organizing what is known about human potentials that can be influenced by learning, especially in structured contexts such as schools. A major influence on this approach was Gardner's (1983, 2006) conceptualization of multiple intelligences. However, Gardner's approach focused on intelligences that met certain research criteria while the domains identified in the Brilliant Star framework are considered as potentials that are actualized through experience into competencies and capabilities. The framework was initially conceptualized in the early 1990s and the chapters of the book were written over a 15-year period beginning in 2003. The chapters have been slightly edited and updated for inclusion in this book.

The first chapter provides an overview of the Brilliant Star framework and considers the development of the whole person from the perspective of developing capacities in eight domains: (1) temperament, personality, and self-views, (2) cognition/thinking, (3) affect/emotion, (4) conation/volition (or agency/self-regulation), (5) social/interpersonal, (6) physical/bodily-kinesthetic, (7) spiritual/transpersonal, and (8) moral character. Basic research is considered as well as how interested adults, especially educators, can facilitate development in each of these areas.

Three chapters discuss different aspects of the cognitive domain. Chapter two considers the cognitive domain from the perspective of information processing theories and memory. It includes descriptions and definitions of important terms and models that have been used to depict memory types and processors. The frameworks associated with the stage theory model and schools of thought on pattern recognition and representation models are discussed as well as those on schema, parallel distributed processing, and connectionist models. The chapter ends with discussion on the assessment of cognitive processing in education today and activities for developing instruction that is built on the theories discussed.

Chapter three considers the cognitive domain from the perspective of cognitive development. This chapter provides an overview of the developmental theories of Bruner, Dewey, Piaget, and Vygotsky and the educational application of cognitive and social constructivism, including instruction and assessment activities.

Chapter four uses the theory and research on information processing and cognitive development to explore how people use mental representations as they interact with, and attempt to understand, the environment within which they are embedded. It summarizes the different types of mental representations, from the most general level of worldviews to the most specific level of schema and scripts. The basic perspective is that human beings do not interact with the environment as it exists in reality, but rather do so through mental representations that have been constructed as they have interacted with it. An overview of how the mental representations can be modified is also explored.

Three chapters focus on the affective, volitional, and social domains. Chapter five provides an overview of the affective domain. Mounting evidence supports the position that human beings are inherently emotional beings and that affective/emotional development impacts human development and behavior in a wide variety of important ways. This chapter provides an overview of emotion and the affective domain, including developmental considerations and methods that can be used to facilitate development in this domain. Also discussed are instruments and methods to assess emotional and affective development.

Chapter six provides an overview of the conative domain and the role of agency in human development and behavior. Conation is defined as the mental process that activates and/or directs behavior and action. Various terms used to represent some aspect of conation include intrinsic motivation, goal-orientation, volition, will, self-direction, and self-regulation. Issues are discussed related to various activities and strategies that parents and educators can use to assist children and youth in their development, as well as assessments of conation and its subcomponents.

Chapter seven focuses on social development. Research has shown that human beings are inherently social. Developing competencies in this domain enhance a person's ability to succeed in school as well as positively influencing mental health, success in work, and the ability to be a citizen in a democracy. This chapter outlines research and theories related to the development of social competence and provides a literature review of theory and research supporting the vital importance of social competence, including a discussion of empirically-based interventions and measurement tools that educators can use to facilitate development of social competence.

Three chapters focus on the physical, spiritual, and moral character domains. Chapter eight discusses physical development. It provides an overview of the importance of maintaining physical fitness and proper nutrition as well as an overview of the means by which physical fitness can be obtained and maintained. Cardiovascular endurance, muscular strength, muscular endurance, flexibility, and body composition are components of physical fitness; consuming a healthy diet that includes grains, fruits and vegetables, and lean protein sources are aspects of good nutrition. The chapter also reviews literature related to the assessment of components of physical fitness.

Chapter nine provides an overview of spiritual development and describes the role of schooling in this domain. The first section explains important terms and establishes the importance of spirituality as a component of life success. The second section discusses some important issues regarding the development of spirituality, while the third and fourth sections provide a review of how to stimulate and assess spiritual development, respectively.

Chapter ten provides an overview of moral and character development. This issue has been a topic of concern for thousands of years and was central to the development of American schooling, losing favor in the middle of the twentieth century. Over the last several decades there has been increased attention to the importance of moral character as central to the purpose of schooling. This chapter reviews theories related to moral character development and suggests methods for including it in the school setting.

The last two chapters focus on the integration of the other domains. Chapter eleven considers issues related to self- and self-views with a focus on self-concept, self-esteem, and self-efficacy. These are considered especially relevant because they are constructed by the individual as he or she reflects on personal behavior and interaction with the environment, especially other people. The infant has no conceptualization of self as a separate organism and only develops this concept as he or she becomes more mobile. These self-views are quite flexible throughout childhood and adolescence and are, therefore, open to influence. However, once they become stable in later adolescence or early adulthood, they are quite difficult to change.

The final chapter discusses some ideas related to developing curriculum for glocal citizenship. The concept of glocal comes from the integration of a need to have a global focus while interacting within a local neighborhood and community. The expression "Think global, act local" captures the essence of this concept. Discussed are some practical applications for curriculum development and guiding the teaching/ learning process using the Brilliant Star framework as a guide to thinking about preparing children and youth for life as adults in a rapidly changing, digital, global sociocultural milieu.

1

The Brilliant Star Framework[1]

William G. Huitt

Parents, educators, and concerned citizens around the world are asking questions about how best to prepare children and youth for successful adulthood in the twenty-first century. The issue takes on added importance because humanity is immersed in a social and cultural environment that is changing at an accelerating rate (Kurzweil, 2001). Simultaneously, there is exponential growth in the understanding of human capacities and the potential for human development (Damon, 2004). Though every human society has dealt with issues of preparing children and youth for adulthood, the potential benefits have never been greater for providing the proper learning experiences so that young people flourish as adults.

While it is acknowledged that schools are not the only social institutions responsible for the education of children and youth (Huitt, 2012a), schools are where most will engage in formal, systematic learning experiences rather than the informal and sometimes conflicting learning experiences provided by the home, community, and larger society (Wikeley, Bullock, Muschamp, & Ridge, 2007). Focusing on schools as a means for preparing young people for adulthood is one of the hallmarks of developed countries (The National Commission on Excellence in Education, 1983). On the other hand, when positive connections are made between home, school, and community, the impact can be even more powerful (Epstein & Sanders, 2000; Henderson & Mapp, 2002; Roehlkepartain, Benson, & Sesma, 2003).

A new vision for educating children and youth, both formally and informally, is required if they are to become successful adults in the twenty-first century. Exactly what that means needs to be considered and plans need to be made and implemented (Partnership for 21st Century Skills, 2004; Tate, 2008). This requires the ability to think beyond the actual to the possible through the use of imagination. Liu and Noppe-Brandon (2009) make an excellent point that the use of imagination is the first step towards developing creative solutions to seemingly intractable challenges. It is then necessary to develop innovative products and services that can be used to meet those challenges.

---

[1] Originally published as Huitt, W. (2011, July). *A holistic view of education and schooling: Guiding students to develop capacities, acquire virtues, and provide service*. Revision of paper presented at the 12th Annual International Conference sponsored by the Athens Institute for Education and Research (ATINER), May 24-27, Athens, Greece.

The purpose of this chapter is to provide an overview of research describing innate capacities of human beings that can be actualized through directed school-based experiences and to review the types of curricula, learning experiences, and potential accountability procedures that educators can use to do so. More detailed information will be provided in later chapters. This information is also important to parents and community members who want to facilitate development of a broad range of knowledge, attitudes, and skills related to successful development (Bushaw & Gallup, 2008; Elam, Rose, & Gallup, 1992; Gallup, 1975.) It is intended that readers will be stimulated to provide more of the types of experiences that will allow children and youth to prepare for the challenging times they will face as adults.

Identifying Capacities

The first step in the identification of potential capacities that could be developed via guided learning experiences was to investigate human capacities considered to be intelligences as these refer to an ability or aptitude for learning. A second step was then to investigate whether available research showed that the movement from capacity to competence (ie, an actualized capacity) could be facilitated through guided learning experiences.

Perhaps the most widely accepted approach to identifying a variety of human capacities is Gardner's (1983, 2006) work on multiple intelligences. He initially identified seven intelligences. Three of the intelligences have been labeled Symbol Analytic in that they involve making a conversion from a symbol to a higher-level mental code (ie, *linguistic*—translating letters and words into knowledge and concepts; *logical-mathematical*—converting numbers to quantitative concepts and to think rationally and/or logically; *musical*—translating written musical symbols in timbre, pitch, and rhythm). Two of Gardner's intelligences are considered Personal intelligences in that they are oriented to the person (*intrapersonal*—knowledge of one's self and *interpersonal*—knowledge of others, especially their moods and motivations). Finally, two additional intelligences might be considered as Object-oriented intelligences (*spatial*—the ability to mentally rotate an object in space and *bodily-kinesthetic*—the ability to control one's body and handle objects skillfully).

Gardner (1999) later identified an eighth intelligence which he labeled *naturalist* (an Object-oriented intelligence). He defined this as an ability to discern differences in one's natural surroundings. A ninth intelligence, labeled *existential* (a Transpersonal intelligence) is still under consideration. It involves the ability to search for and connect with universal unknowns.

In the process of investigating other research that might confirm the concept of multiple intelligences, eight domains were identified separately by a variety of researchers: (1) self, including temperament, personality, and self-views, (2) cognition/thinking, (3) affect/emotion, (4) conation/volition, (5) physical/bodily-kinesthetic, (6) social/interpersonal; (7) spiritual/transpersonal, and (8) moral character. Interestingly, five of these relate to terms used by the ancient Greeks to describe different aspects of a human being: body (bodily-kinesthetic), mind (cognition/thinking, affect/emotion, and conation/volition), and soul/spirit. These relatively intrinsic domains are used extrinsically in social interactions, while moral character focuses on issues of right and wrong and the concept of self is considered in terms of how the other domains are holistically integrated and organized.

Figure 1-1. Becoming a Brilliant Star Framework

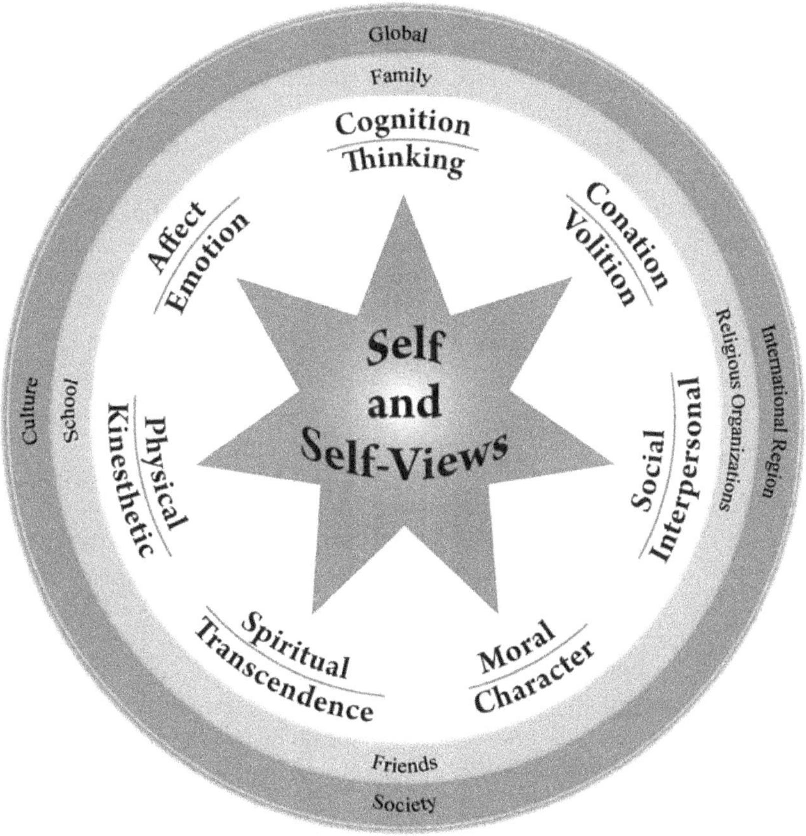

There is considerable overlap between Gardner's (1999, 2006) list of multiple intelligences and the list of intelligences identified separately by others whose research will be discussed below. For example, both lists contain bodily-kinesthetic, social/interpersonal, existential/spiritual, and self/intrapersonal. The domain of cognition/thinking is represented in Gardner's work as a combination of linguistic and logical-mathematical intelligences. However, Gardner does not identify intelligences linked with the domains of affective/emotion, volition/conation, and morality. Likewise, spatial, musical, and naturalistic intelligences are not considered as intelligences by other researchers.

The domains might be considered as points on a star with the self and self-views central to the image (see Figure 1-1). This is a revision of the Becoming a Brilliant Star framework previously developed (Huitt, 2006a). It shows that the domains are developed within a multi-level sociocultural context where family, school, religious organizations, and friends, as well as the connections among them, provide the most direct influence on one's development.

The remaining sections will briefly review capacities represented by these eight intelligences. Discussed first is cognition and thinking, as that is the dominant domain used for identifying the capacity to do well in school through developing academic competence. Next considered are the other two faculties of the mind, affect or emotion and conation or volition (currently discussed primarily in research on agency and self-regulation). The domains of physical or bodily-kinesthetic intelligence, social intelligence, spiritual intelligence, and moral intelligence will then be discussed. Finally, different ideas regarding the development of the knowledge of one's self or intrapersonal intelligence will be considered.

Cognitive Intelligence

While many view cognitive intelligence as inherently fixed (Jensen, 2002), other researchers have demonstrated that learning experiences can impact cognitive processing skills and, therefore, one's ability to learn academic content. For example, Feuerstein and his colleagues (1979; Feuerstein, Rand, Hoffman, & Miller, 1980) showed that measured IQ can be increased through involvement in a two- to three-year program (titled *Instrumental Enrichment*) focused on modifying specific, though non-content related, cognitive processes. Ben-Hur (2000) reviewed research from seven separate studies demonstrating the effectiveness of the program. In general, students who completed the program were more organized in their thinking, more self-sufficient in their learning, and volunteered more in class.

Sternberg (1985, 1996) claimed that traditional measures of intelligence, developed to identify mental capacity related to academic competence, are limited. He identified three separate, though related, categories of cognitive abilities. The first he labeled *analytic*, where the individual uses strategies such as comparing and analyzing to investigate the elements and relationships of an object or situation. The second he labeled *creative*, where the individual uses strategies such as imagining or designing to find different elements or connections to solve non-traditional problems or challenges. Sternberg labeled the third as *practical*, where the individual uses strategies to address problems or challenges as they occur in everyday contexts. Sternberg believed that one's individual profile of successful intelligence is comprised of one's competencies in each of these three areas. While one can have an inherited capacity for each of these types of intelligence, this is relatively less important than how these capacities are developed and used for personal success. Sternberg and his colleagues created specific programs and lessons that focus on the development of the skills related to the different components of successful intelligence (eg, Sternberg & Grigorenko, 2000; Sternberg et al., 2000; Williams, Blythe, Li, White, Sternberg, & Gardner, 1997; Williams, Markle, Brigockas, & Sternberg, 2002).

Wegener (2005) provided another rubric for considering the specific skills used in cognition and thinking. He primarily focused on Sternberg's (1985, 1996) analytic intelligence skills such as making associations, engaging in analysis, drawing implications, and describing correlational and causal relationships. However, he also identified the intellectual skill of synthesis, which is more related to the creative aspect of intelligence described by Sternberg. In all, he described twenty-two cognitive processing skills that provide the foundation for engaging in academic tasks. Most importantly, Wegener provided samples of lessons that can be used to address each of the skills he identifies.

Affective/Emotional Intelligence

Lewis, Haviland-Jones, and Barrett (2008) documented the resurgence of research on emotion and reported on the pervasive influence of emotions on human thinking and behavior. Work done by Salovey and Juneer (1990), and popularized by Goleman (1995), brought this domain to the attention of the public in a manner similar to the impact of work done on cognitive intelligence by Gardner (1983) and Sternberg (1985) a decade earlier.

Unfortunately, Goleman's conceptualization of emotional intelligence, which included a list of twenty-five potential competences, diluted the focus on emotion as only four directly related to other researchers' definitions (ie, the personal competencies of emotional awareness, accurate self-assessment, and self-confidence, and the social-emotional competence of understanding others' emotions.) Juneer and Salovey (1997) provided an update of the research on emotional intelligence, conceptualizing it as comprised of aptitudes in four categories: (1) the ability to perceive emotion; (2) the ability to use emotion to facilitate thought; (3) the ability to understand emotions; and (4) the ability to manage emotions.

Denham (1998), in an excellent overview for educators emphasizing the actualization of emotional intelligence, chose to ignore the component of influencing thought and focused on three aspects of emotional intelligence: (1) *emotional understanding* (of one's own emotions and those of others as well as the ability to relate the two); (2) *emotional expression* (how one uses verbal and nonverbal means to express emotion); and (3) *emotional regulation* (the ability to enhance or dampen one's emotions based one's circumstances.) Maurer, Brackett, and Plain (2004) suggested emotional understanding should be further unpacked into (a) recognizing emotions to obtain valuable information about the environment, (b) understanding how emotions influence attention, thinking, decisions, and behavior, and (c) labeling emotions to describe feelings precisely. This disagreement on a definition of emotional intelligence is only one of many issues that have yet to be resolved (Matthews, Emo, Roberts, & Zeidner, 2006; Matthews, Roberts, & Zeidner, 2004).

There are a number of authors who focused on classroom-based approaches to developing emotional competence. For example, Hyson (2003) and Saarni (1999, 2007) described activities for the early childhood level. Saarni provided an excellent review of research related to developing five emotional competencies: (1) awareness of one's own emotions and discernment of the emotions of others; (2) the capacity for connecting empathically with others; (3) understanding the difference between internal subjective feelings and external expressional expression; (4) self-management when coping with aversive emotions; and (5) awareness of emotional communication and self-regulation in relationships. Maurer et al. (2004) described a middle school program for developing emotional literacy. Additionally, several chapters in an edited volume by Bar-On, Maree, and Elias (2007) review research that schools, parents, and community organizations can use to impact emotional development.

A related area to the development of emotional competence is the issue of subjective well-being, which includes three components. Two are affective components defining everyday happiness (positive affect and negative affect); the third is a cognitive component describing one's overall satisfaction with one's life (Diener, 1984; Diener, Suh, Lucas, & Smith, 1999). Seligman (2002) concluded that there are actually three different orientations to happiness: (1) sensual pleasure (hedonic happiness); (2) engagement (flow, using one's character strengths in challenging situations), and (3) meaning (eudaimonic happiness). Peterson, Park, and Seligman (2005) showed that these orientations could be reliably measured. While a high score on any one of these orientations correlated well to life satisfaction, people with a high score on all three (what the researchers titled "living a full life") showed the highest levels of life satisfaction. Perhaps more importantly, a higher level of meaning-related happiness had a larger effect size than did the other two in predicting life satisfaction.

In a related study, Park, Peterson, and Seligman (2004) found that strengths more related to the affective domain (ie, hope, zest, gratitude, love) and the conative domain (eg, curiosity, persistence, self-regulation) were increasingly likely to be associated with life satisfaction than were strengths more associated with the cognitive domain (eg, perspective/wisdom). Subsequently, Froh and his colleagues (Bono & Froh, 2009; Froh, Miller, & Snyder, 2007; Froh, Sefick, & Emmons, 2008) found that gratitude was a significant component of life satisfaction for adolescents and could be impacted through school-based interventions.

While there are noteworthy challenges to addressing emotional intelligence and emotional competence, including the various components of happiness, these issues continue to attract a great deal of attention. Perhaps that is because emotional development has been tied to cognitive functioning (Isen, 2008; Lazarus, 1999), conative development (Buckley & Saarni, 2009; Saarni, 1999), social development (Goleman, 2006), moral development (Hoffman, 2000), spiritual development (Guela, 2004), and the creation of self-views (Hamachek, 2000). Happiness has been related to outcomes such as higher income, more satisfying and longer marriages, more friends, better physical health, and living longer (Lyubomirsky, 2007). Lyubromirsky also reported research showing that individuals who identified themselves as happier were more creative, helpful, self-confident, and showed greater self-regulation and coping abilities.

One challenge for addressing emotional intelligence and happiness in school is research showing that early experiences, specifically in the home between the infant/child and primary caregiver, are especially important for proper emotional development (Cooper, Masi, & Vick, 2009: Stack, Serbin, Enns, Ruttle, & Barrieau, 2010; Yap, Allen, Leve, & Katz, 2008). A second challenge is that there are relatively few classroom-based programs that focus solely on developing students' emotional intelligence. Rather, focus on emotions is generally embedded in programs such as habits of mind (Costa & Kallick, 2008), social-emotional learning (Zins, Payton, Weissberg, & O'Brien, 2007), conflict resolution (Bodine & Crawford, 1999), or moral development (Narvaez, 2008b). These programs are discussed separately below.

Conative/Volitional Intelligence (Agency)

Central to the concept of conative intelligence is the use of personal agency or volition to use thoughts, emotions, and behaviors to make choices related to goal-directed activities. Although conation has been an area of study in psychology since its beginning as a scientific discipline (Hilgard,

1980), research on this domain, including research on will, volition, and self-regulation, has been fraught with controversy as it highlights discussions of human agency and whether or not it actually exists (Tallon, 1997). However, over the last century, Newton's paradigm of a closed, deterministic universe where human agency was perceived as non-existent gave way to a process ecology or adaptive systems paradigm where the universe, and especially humanity's interaction with it, is viewed as being open and indeterministic (Ulanowicz, 2009). This has led to a philosophical view of human capabilities that allows, even requires, conscious agency. The reappearance of an emphasis on human volition was assisted after a long absence when Wechler included a conative component in his widely-used intelligence measure (Cooper, 1997), Kolbe (1990) developed a reliable and valid measure of conation, and Goleman (1995) included conative components in his definition of emotional intelligence.

Bandura (1986, 1989, 2001a) has been one of the leading researchers in the study of human agency through his investigation of self-regulation. He identified four components that provide the foundation for one's self-regulatory capability: (1) intentionality—the ability to originate a purposeful action; (2) forethought—the ability to think about the future and to make plans; (3) self-reactiveness—the ability to monitor one's actions and make corrections to achieve one's goals; and (4) self-reflection—the ability to evaluate one's purpose, values, and goals with respect to one's plans and actions. Using Bandura's framework, Zimmerman (1998) developed a process approach to self-regulation that included three phases: (1) forethought, including setting goals and making plans; (2) performance, including the use of volition to put plans into action; and (3) self-reflection, including relating performance to goals and taking corrective action.

Huitt and Cain (Chapter 6, this volume) took a slightly different approach by focusing on the self-motivational components of conation, including proactively establishing and maintaining one's goal-directed actions, energizing one's self to action, and persevering in spite of setbacks or obstacles. Proactively establishing one's direction includes at least four sets of skills: (1) becoming aware of human needs in general as well as one's specific needs; (2) articulating a vision for one's life and forming a related statement of long-term desires or aspirations; (3) setting short-term goals related to long-term aspirations; and (4) making specific plans for taking action. Strategies must then be used to put plans into action and one must persevere to bring plans to fruition. Self-directed formative evaluation throughout the process allows one to make adjustments in attainment of goals.

As educators, businesses, and governmental agencies began to address the fast pace of social change, the importance of conative or self-regulation skills related to life-long learning became increasingly apparent (McCombs,

1991). Early research showed that students who scored high in self-regulation had set personal learning goals, engaged in accurate self-monitoring, and thought strategically about their learning activities (Schunk & Zimmerman, 1994). Summaries of research in this field showed that it is intricately linked to cognitive and affective processing (eg, Baumeister & Vohs, 2007; Boekaetrs, Pintrich, & Zeidner, 2000). However, it is distinctive in that it focuses on proactive, goal-directed behavior.

Other research showed that conative or self-regulation skills are significantly related to academic achievement in a wide variety of contexts (eg, Eshel & Kohavi, 2003; Joo, Bong, & Choi, 2000; Neber & Schommer-Aikins, 2002; Pajares & Graham, 1999) and can be modified through classroom experiences (eg, Debowski, Wood, & Bandura, 2001; Perels, Guertler, & Schmitz, 2005; Perry, 1999; Zimmerman, 2002). Additionally, researchers found that classroom teachers could be trained to provide instruction that enhanced student's self-regulation skills (Schunk & Zimmerman, 1994, 1998). Zimmerman and his colleagues published a how-to manual on developing students' self-regulation skills (Zimmerman, Bonner, & Kovach, 1996) and produced a classroom-based program that addressed these skills (Cleary & Zimmerman, 2004; Nelson, Cleary, & Platten, 2008).

Bodily-Kinesthetic or Physical Intelligence

Gardner (1983) stated that bodily-kinesthetic intelligence involves the ability to use the body to complete complex and/or intricate physical tasks. Blumenfeld-Jones (2009) defined bodily-kinesthetic intelligence as an ability to be aware of one's body in space and motion. Visser, Ashton, and Vernon (2008) showed that bodily-kinesthetic intelligence was often differentiated into two components: (1) gross motor ability (eg, extraordinary balance and co-ordination), and (2) fine motor ability (eg, dexterity). As bodily-kinesthetic intelligence is actualized into competence, there are also two categories: basic and advanced. Basic physical competence is often measured in terms of (1) cardiovascular endurance, (2) muscular strength, (3) muscular endurance, and (4) flexibility (Caldwell & Huitt, Chapter 8, this volume) while more advanced competencies are shown in such activities as dance, theatre, and sports (Visser et al., 2008).

Nutrition and physical exercise are the two primary influences on physical development, including health and well-being (Cooper, 1999). With respect to proper eating, a major challenge is that most adults have been taught incorrect information about eating and nutrition (Willett, Skerrett, & Giovannucci, 2001). It does not help that bookstores and magazines are full of competing advice on what and how to eat (Katz, 2005). Fortunately, researchers and practitioners such as Ornish (2007), Sisson (2013), and

Willett et al., (2001) are beginning to provide sound, scientifically-based recommendations on what and how much to eat. Likewise, chefs such as Cooper and Holmes (2006) and Oliver (2009; Smith, 2008) provide guidance in how to put these ideas into practice in schools and homes.

In order to use one's bodily-kinesthetic intelligence, one needs to have a healthy body. In the developed world, approximately two-thirds of adults and one-third of children are overweight (Daniels, Jacobson, McCrindle, Eckel, & Sanner, 2009; Lewis, McTigue, Burke, Poirier, Eckel, Howard…& Pi-Sunyer, 2009). Additionally, as global abundance increases, the epidemic of obesity is spreading rapidly to developing countries (Katz, 2005). Katz (2005) summarized data from the United States National Center for Health Statistics that showed the trends now in place forecast a "shorter life expectancy for children than for their parents" (p. 62).

In a meta-analysis of 21 studies, Cook-Cottone, Casey, Feeley, and Baran (2009) found that programs producing the best results in addressing obesity targeted elementary children, were whole-school oriented (did not just target overweight children), provided children with specific information and activities regarding healthy nutrition and exercise, and had a high level of parental support. This suggests that preventing weight problems is more effective than addressing problems that arise with older children and youth, that providing information and assistance to parents is as important as working with children, and that schools must target both nutrition and exercise while they have children in their care.

Caldwell and Huitt (Chapter 8, this volume) reported on the results of schools spending an increased amount of time attempting to improve academic test scores—a reduction in children's physical activity with a resulting decline in physical fitness and an increase in fitness-related illnesses. Eliminating or even reducing physical activity in schools does not acknowledge research showing that physical activity positively impacts school academic achievement (Trost, 2009). For schools who desire to promote physical competence, it can be done by connecting academic lessons to physical education activities (Huitt, 2009c), involving children and youth in dance, theatre, or sports, or through movement education (eg, Dobbins, DeCorby, Robeson, Hussen, & Tinlis, 2009; Ghassemi & Kern, 2014). Kogan (2004) created a movement education curriculum for elementary students; Carter, Wiecha, Peterson, Nobrega, and Gortmaker (2007) provided a similar approach for middle school students. While there can be specific advantages to having students involved in dance, theatre, sports, or movement education, the most important goal should be to have children and youth develop strong and healthy bodies so that they can use whatever bodily-kinesthetic intelligence they possess.

Social/Interpersonal Intelligence

Human beings are social in their very nature (Aronson, 2007). In fact, Dunbar (1998) hypothesized that the large human brain evolved primarily to adapt to an increasingly complex social environment. Albrecht (2005) and Goleman (2006) provided recent reviews of the literature on social intelligence; their conceptualizations of social intelligence offer an excellent introduction to this topic, even though they focused more on adults than children and adolescents.

As with other domains, there are difficulties with the definitions of social intelligence and social competence. Goleman (2006) identified two basic categories of social intelligence, each with four specific subcomponents: *Social Awareness* (primal empathy, attunement, empathetic accuracy, and social cognition) and *Social Facility* (synchrony, self-preservation, influence, and concern). The School Social Behavior Scales (SSBS), one of the most widely used assessment instruments for students in K-12 classrooms, is actually comprised of two scales: (1) the Social Competence Scale, and (2) the Antisocial Behavior Scale (Merrell, 1993). In turn, the Social Competence Scale is comprised of three sets of skills: (1) *interpersonal skills*, (2) *self-management skills*, and (3) *academic skills*.

The Collaborative for Academic, Social, and Emotional Learning (CASEL, 2003, 2007), one of the leaders in the development of social-emotional learning (SEL), identified five teachable competencies that can provide a foundation for effective personal development:

1. *Self-aware*ness: knowing what one is feeling and thinking; having a realistic assessment of one's own abilities and a well-grounded sense of self-confidence;
2. *Social awareness*: understanding what others are feeling and thinking; appreciating and interacting positively with diverse groups;
3. *Self-management*: handling one's emotions so they facilitate rather than interfere with task achievement; setting and accomplishing goals; persevering in the face of setbacks and frustrations;
4. *Relationship skills*: establishing and maintaining healthy and rewarding relationships based on clear communication, cooperation, resistance to inappropriate social pressure, negotiating solutions to conflict, and seeking help when needed; and
5. *Responsible decision making*: making choices based on an accurate consideration of all relevant factors and the likely consequences of alternative courses of action, respecting others, and taking responsibility for one's decisions.

CASEL and like-minded researchers proposed that school curricula must provide learning experiences that address students' development in the academic, emotional, social, and moral domains (Cohen, 2006; Elias & Arnold, 2006; Zins, Weissberg, Wang, & Walberg, 2004). Notice that the five competencies involved the domains of cognition/thinking (responsible decision making), affect/emotion (self-awareness and self-management—handling one's emotions), and conation/self-regulation (self-management—setting and accomplishing goals; persevering), in addition to the social domain (social awareness, relationship skills). These researchers suggested that by developing a safe and secure environment and directly teaching the above listed social-emotional competencies, students will not only be more academically engaged, thereby learning more academic material, but also less likely to engage in risky behavior that would be detrimental to their development. Additionally, they proposed that when schools form partnerships with the families and community organizations of students they serve, the impact of the school is made even stronger (Patrikakou & Weissberg, 2007; Zins et al., 2007).

Spiritual Intelligence

Huitt and Robbins (Chapter 9, this volume) summarized the views of many researchers in the area of spiritual intelligence and the development of spiritual competence by describing it as: (1) an inherent human component, (2) considered important by a vast majority of people both in the developed and developing world, and (3) extremely difficult to define and assess with any reliability and validity. There are multiple components of a definition of spirituality, including, but not limited to, the ability to connect to the sacred (Pargament & Mahoney, 2002); the ability to generate meaning and purpose for one's life (Frankl, 1997, 1998); self-awareness (Zohar & Marshall, 2000); and the ability to create deep, personal relationships with one's self, with others, with nature, and universal unknowns (Hay & Nye, 1998). Maslow (1971) suggested that human spirituality is an existential, transpersonal quality that is the essence of one's humanity. However, a number of authors have questioned whether spirituality should be considered an intelligence or better thought of as an aspect of another domain of human potential such as cognition or emotion (Emmons, 2000; Gardner, 2000a; Juneer, 2000).

As in the other domains, one of the complexities when investigating spirituality is the attempt to distinguish spiritual intelligence (a capacity or aptitude) from spiritual competence (an expertise or skill). For example, Amram (2007) identified seven dimensions of spiritual intelligence after interviewing 71 individuals from a wide variety of spiritual practices. Amram and Dryer (2008) then developed a self-report instrument, The Integrated Spiritual Intelligence Scale (ISIS), with items in five categories:

1. *Consciousness*: Developed refined awareness and self-knowledge;
2. *Grace*: Living in alignment with the sacred manifesting love for and trust in life;
3. *Meaning*: Experiencing significance in daily activities through a sense of purpose and a call to service, including persevering in the face of pain and suffering;
4. *Transcendence*: Going beyond the separate egoic self into an interconnected wholeness;
5. *Truth*: Living in open acceptance, curiosity, and love for all creation.

Notice that the definitions of each of these indicate that a potential has been actualized at an adult level, at least in a manner that allows the individual to be conscious of its expression. For those working with children and youth, the same difficulty exists with qualitative assessments of spirituality (Hodge, 2001). Roehlkepartain, Ebstyne, Wagener, and Benson (2006) provided an excellent review of the current literature, yet considerable work is needed to identify the developmental sequences for children and youth as they actualize their innate potential in this domain.

Palmer (1998/1999, 2003) has long advocated that spirituality should be part of a classroom teacher's training and practice. McGreevy and Copley (1998/1999) offered a number of suggestions for doing so, including a focus on the arts, making the classrooms and school a place of beauty, taking time to ponder profound issues and questions that students want to address, and involving students in service learning projects. Kessler (2000) identified what she calls seven gateways to the soul that teachers can use as part of their classroom practice. Huitt and Robbins (Chapter 9, this volume) showed that each of the pathways Kessler identified has been considered important by other researchers. However, Kessler stated that if these activities are to address spiritual development, they must be dealt with in ways that are meaningful to each student. If they are dealt with in a perfunctory manner, students will not develop the deep, personal connections required for developing spiritual competence.

Moral Intelligence

Recent research has refocused attention on moral intelligence and the development of moral character. Hauser (2006) provided an overview of the innateness of human moral intelligence; Narvaez (2007, 2008b) proposed that neurobiology bestows a foundation upon which moral character development is built. Coles (1996, 1998) found that the moral development of children is closely intertwined with other domains of development, especially in the cognitive, emotional, social, and spiritual domains. Vessels and Huitt (Chapter 10, this volume) reviewed literature showing that every approach to developmental and learning theory had a theory of moral development. For example, behaviorists (Skinner, 1971; Wynne, 1986) and sociologists (Berkowitz & Grych, 1998; Durkheim, 1961) believed that morality is the direct result of the application of consequences or the intentional transmission of social rules and norms. On the other hand, sociobiologists (Miele, 1996) and nativists (Rousseau, 1979) focused on genetics and maturational influences. Some interactionists, represented by psychoanalytic (Adler, 1995; Freud, 1990), psychosocial (Erikson, 1993), and socio-analytic (Hogan & Emler, 1995) theorists, thought of morality as instinctual and in need of control or socialization while other interactionists, represented by cognitive- and affective-developmental theories (Gilligan, 1977; Kohlberg, 1984; Piaget, 1969) and social cognition theories (Bandura, 1977, 1991b) thought of human morality as essentially good to be developed through interaction with the environment. Finally, there are theorists who see morality as rooted in personality and personal identity (Blasi, 1993; Erikson, 1994).

While there are a number of definitions for moral intelligence, most of them revolve around the habits and patterns of thought, emotions, intentions, and behavior associated with issues of right and wrong, especially in a social context (Vessels & Huitt, Chapter 10, this volume). In the United States, the development of moral character was seen as a fundamental requirement for having a well-functioning society, especially a multicultural democracy (Myers, 2000), and was one of the primary reasons for initially promoting universal, public education (Huitt & Vessels, 2002). A similar expectation provided the rationale for a global expansion of compulsory schooling (Benavot & Resnik, 2007). However, with the increased emphasis on academic learning in the latter half of the twentieth century, moral and ethical education was deemphasized.

There are a wide variety of moral character development programs ranging from moral quality of the month, to the integration of moral character activities into academic lessons, to whole-school programs where instruction is focused on moral character, to service learning programs integrated into the curriculum (Vessels & Huitt, Chapter 10, this volume). In general, research shows that programs work best when they are (1) school-wide, (2) include a school-family connection, (3) include an emphasis on addressing multiple components of moral character (eg, thinking/cognition, affective/valuing, volitional/intending, and behavior described in fairly traditional ways), and (4) provide opportunities for students to demonstrate their development by providing service to others. The goal for these programs is to have students develop an identity of themselves as virtuous people and to build an extensive repertoire of experiences that supports this identity (Borba, 2002).

In my opinion, Narvaez's (2008b) triune theory of moral development and its implementation through the Integrative Ethical Education program (Narvaez, 2006) shows great promise in providing an integrated approach to moral development. While there are certainly many commendable character education programs that are available (eg, Battistich, 2003; Elkind & Sweet, 2004; Lickona, Schaps, & Lewis, 2003), Narvaez's approach not only explicitly makes reference to the neurobiological foundation of moral character, it directly addresses the underlying components related to the domains of affect/emotions (ethical sensitivity), cognition/thinking (ethical judgment), conation/volition (ethical motivation) as well as the actual display of moral behavior (ethical action), especially in service to others (service learning). It, therefore, addresses more of the various viewpoints of moral character development discussed by other researchers.

Self and Self-views (Intrapersonal Intelligence)

Many researchers have demonstrated that the concepts of self and self-views are essential to the study of human behavior. Probably the most fundamental concept is that of temperament, considered an innate or inherited aspect of personality (Derryberry & Reed, 1994; Keirsey, 1998). For example, one's levels of excitability or irritability are considered aspects of one's temperament as well as one's tendency to introversion or extroversion. Temperament has been shown to be related to learning style (Oakland & Joyce, 2004), development of competence and motivation (Rothbart & Hwang, 2005), the type of career one prefers while a student (Oakland, Stafford, Horton, and Glutting, 2001), and the type of career one selects as an adult (Keirsey, 1998).

Personality is another way of conceptualizing how an individual organizes one's thinking, feeling, intending, and behaving. The most widely used description is the 5-Factor model (McCrae & Costa, 1997). The five factors (making the acronym, OCEAN) are (1) openness (an active imagination, a preference for variety, or a display of intellectual curiosity); (2) conscientiousness (being precise and careful or thorough); (3) extroversion (a tendency to look outside the self for stimulation and pleasure); (4) agreeableness (a tendency to be pleasant and accepting in social situations); and (5) neuroticism (a tendency to experience negative emotional states.) These factors have been related to a number of outcomes including political preferences (Carney, Jost, Gosling, & Potter, 2008), tendency to use alcohol or drugs (Flory, Lynam, & Milich, 2002), one's passion for internet activities and willingness to express one's 'true self' online (Tosun & Lajunen, 2009), becoming a 'node' in a social network (Liu & Ipe, 2010), and different aspects of leadership (Judge, Bono, Ilies, & Gerhardt, 2002).

The Myers-Briggs Type Indicator (MBTI) is an alternative view of personality (Myers, 1995). This approach was based on the work of Jung (1971) and proposed that people differ in terms of their preferences related to four dimensions (extrovert-introvert, sensing-intuition, feeling-thinking, and judging-perceiving.) The MBTI has been used in such areas as identifying learning styles (Lawrence, 1984), career selection (Kennedy & Kennedy, 2004), processing social information (Edwards, Lanning, & Hooker, 2002), problem solving and decision making (Huitt, 1992), and leadership styles and working in teams (Kroeger & Thuesen, 1989).

Yet another conceptualization of personality is that of personality traits (Peterson & Seligman, 2004), who identified twenty-four character strengths grouped into six virtues (wisdom and knowledge [cognitive strengths]; courage [emotional strengths]; humanity [interpersonal strengths]; justice [civic strengths]; temperance [strengths protecting against excess]; and transcendence [strengths providing meaning by connecting to something outside of one's self].) Notice that these categories of strengths overlap considerably with the previous descriptions of capacities. Peterson and Seligman's believe that this list of strengths and virtues represents universal positive traits that people use to identify their most important qualities or characteristics.

Finally, there are a number of self-views (eg, self-concept, self-esteem, self-efficacy) that have been explored for their relationship to school achievement and life success. These differ from other measures discussed above in that they are conceptualized as being constructed by the individual through reflection on one's interaction with his or her environment. Initially, it was thought that measures of these constructs related to the cognitive, affective, and volitional domains respectively (Bandura, 1994; Campbell, 1990; Kernis, 2003; Marsh & Hattie, 1996). However, later research showed that there are components of each of these domains in each of the measures (Swann, Chang-Schneider, & McClary, 2007). Swann et al. advocated that a better conceptualization of self-views would relate to the specificity of the view and its relationship to an appropriate level of generalization. For example, if a researcher wanted to predict how an individual's self-view related to a general outcome of life success, then the appropriate predictor would be a general measure of self-concept or self-esteem. One the other hand, if one were looking for a relationship between a self-view and academic achievement, a measure of academic self-concept or self-esteem would be most appropriate. Finally, if one were trying to predict success on a specific task, then a measure of self-efficacy related to the specific task would be best. Most importantly, research over the past two decades has shown that attempting to raise a student's general self-concept or self-esteem through involvement in non-academic tasks bears absolutely no relationship to how well one does academically (Baumeister, Campbell, Krueger & Vohs, 2003).

Summary and Conclusions

A major challenge with traditional approaches to education and schooling is that the focus on academic disciplines leads to an assessment of what children and youth know, not what they can do. However, as adults, what one can do, especially in solving challenging problems, becomes more important. Unless careful attention is paid to actual performance, the same dilemma can trap parents and educators into focusing on competencies in different domains rather than placing children and youth into situations where they must address complex, unstructured challenges that require them to use capabilities from multiple domains. At the same time, it is unreasonable to expect children and youth to develop these competencies and capabilities without specific skills development. One of the benefits of having children and youth engage in group-based activities such as academic service learning, theatre, or sports is that they have the opportunity to use all of their competencies and capabilities in an integrated manner.

One challenge in attempting to focus on the whole person is that often times frameworks that seem to focus on only one domain actually focus on several. For example, Costa and Kallick (2008) developed a framework titled Habits of Mind (see Table 1-2). While this framework is often considered as focused on the cognitive domain, only seven of the 16 actually relate to cognition and thinking (eg, strive for accuracy, think flexibly, and think about one's own thinking). Eight others relate to affect and emotion (eg, listen with understanding and empathy, find humor), conation and volition (eg, manage impulsivity, persist, take responsible risks), and social (eg, effective communication, interpersonal effectiveness). The last habit, metacognition, provides a bridge across the domains as it relates to one's integrated thinking about capacity and competence in the other domains. Combining this framework with ones that would focus on physical development, spiritual development, and moral character development is an excellent way to begin to build a more holistically-oriented set of experiences for children and youth.

An issue that must also be considered is that of assessment. Developing e-portfolios that consist of videos of learners engaging in problem solving as well as examples of completed products that result from that process is one way of enhancing the data compiled from traditional knowledge assessments. Looking through this qualitative and quantitative data, parents and educators can develop a narrative of a child's development across multiple domains. It is this narrative of the whole person that is important, not a score on a single assessment in a single domain.

Table 1-2. Habits of Mind

Domain	Habit	Description
Cognition/ Thinking	Gather data through all the senses	Use all sensory pathways: gustatory, olfactory, tactile, kinesthetic, auditory, and visual.
	Strive for accuracy	Check facts; nurture desire for exactness, fidelity, craftsmanship, and truth.
	Question and pose problems	Consider what data are needed; find problems to solve.
	Apply past knowledge to new situations	Access prior knowledge and transfer that knowledge to new contexts and problems
	Think flexibly	Change perspectives, generate alternatives, and consider multiple options.
	Create, imagine, and innovate	Generate novel ideas, seek fluency and originality.
	Think about one's own thinking (metacognition)	Become aware of own thoughts, feelings, intentions, strategies, and actions and how these affect others.
Affect/ Emotion	Listen with understanding and empathy	Connect cognitively and emotionally with others.
	Respond with wonderment and awe	Be intrigued by the world's phenomena and beauty. Find what is awesome and mysterious in the world.
	Find humor	Look for whimsical, incongruous, and unexpected in life. Laugh at self when possible.
Conation/ Volition	Manage impulsivity	Think before acting.
	Persist	Seeing task through to completion.
	Take responsible risks	Live on the edge of one's competencies.
	Remain open to continuous learning	Be proud of what one knows and humble enough to admit one doesn't know. Resist complacency.
Social	Think and communicate with clarity and precision	Strive for accurate communication in both written and oral form; avoid overgeneralizations, distortions, deletions.
	Think interdependently	Work with and learn from others in reciprocal situations.

* Adapted from Costa and Killick (2008)

Nevertheless, it is important to focus on development within domains and the focus of the next chapters will provide more detailed information about each domain, how competencies within that domain development, how structured learning experiences can enhance the development within that domain, and how competencies and capabilities within that domain can be assessed. A final chapter will discuss how these can be addressed with a focus on developing citizens who can contribute to human civilization, both at the local and global levels.

2

Information Processing and Memory: Theory and Applications[2]

Stacey T. Lutz and William G. Huitt

Educators are very interested in the study of how humans learn. This is because how one learns, acquires new information, and retains previous information guides selection of long-term learning objectives and methods of effective instruction. To this end, cognition as a psychological area of study goes far beyond simply the taking in and retrieving of information. Rather, the focus is on the holistic study of brain functioning and mind. Neisser (1967), one of the most influential researchers in cognition, defined it as the study of how people encode, structure, store, retrieve, use or otherwise learn knowledge. Cognitive psychologists hypothesize an intervening variable or set of variables between environment and behavior—which contrasts it with behavioral theories.

Information Processing and Memory

One of the primary areas of cognition studied by researchers is memory. There are many hypotheses and suggestions as to how this integration occurs, and many new theories have built upon established beliefs in this area. Currently, there is widespread consensus on several aspects of information processing; however, there are many dissentions in reference to specifics on how the brain actually codes or manipulates information as it is stored in memory.

Schacter and Tulving (as cited in Driscoll, 2001) stated that "a memory system is defined in terms of its brain mechanisms, the kind of information it processes, and the principles of its operation" (p. 283). This suggests that memory is the combined total of all mental experiences. In this light, memory is a built store that must be accessed in some way in order for effective recall or retrieval to occur. It is premised on the belief that memory is a multi-faceted, if not multi-staged, system of connections and representations that encompass a lifetime's accumulation of perceptions.

Eliasmith (2001) defined memory as the "general ability, or faculty, that enables us to interpret the perceptual world to help organize responses to

---

[2] First appeared as Lutz, S., & Huitt, W. (2003). Information processing and memory: Theory and applications. *Educational Psychology Interactive*. Valdosta, GA: Valdosta State University.

changes that take place in the world" (p. 1). It is implied by this definition that there must be a tangible structure in which to incorporate new stimuli into memory. The form of this structure has been the source of much debate, and there seems to be no absolute agreement on what shape a memory structure actually takes, but there are many theories on what constitutes both the memory structure and the knowledge unit.

Winn and Snyder (2001) attributed the idea that memory is organized into structures to the work of Sir Frederick Charles Bartlett. Bartlett's work established two consistent patterns regarding recall. First, memory is inaccurate. This finding is not surprising or novel today, but its implications will be discussed later in this chapter. His second finding, though, brought about somewhat of a revolution in traditional thinking about memory. Bartlett suggested that the inaccuracy of memory is systematic. A systematic difference makes allowable the scientific study of inaccuracy, and this suggestion led to an entirely new mode of thought on memory. What accounted for systematic inaccuracies in memory were the intervening influences of previous information and the experiences of the person. This demonstrates that knowledge units are not simply stored and then left alone, but that they are retained, manipulated, and changed as new knowledge is acquired.

Despite disagreement on many levels, there is general agreement among most cognitive psychologists on some basic principles of the information processing system. First, there is the "assumption of a limited capacity." Depending on the theory, these limitations occur at different points in information processing, but it is widely held in all models that there are limitations as to how much and at what rate new information can be encoded, stored and retrieved (eg, Broadbent, 1975; Case, 1978) Most cognitive psychologists also agree that there exists an element of control system for dealing with stimuli (eg, Atkinson & Shiffrin, 1971). Again, exactly how and where the controls operate is a question of some debate, but the actuality a system that requires some processing capacity is generally accepted.

The belief in the interaction of new information with stored information is a third key point of cognitive study. This is usually demonstrated with a bottom-up or top-down system or a combination of the two. A bottom-up system is predicated on the belief that new information is seen as an initiator which the brain attempts to match with existing concepts in order to break down characteristics or defining attributes (eg, Gibson, 1979). A top-down system seems to suggest an opposite approach. The existing information is the initiator and memory representations are evaluated, then matched to the stimuli (eg, Miller, Galanter, & Pribram, 1960).

Finally, there is also agreement that humans have specific genetic traits that dictate the method by which they gain new information. For example, all human infants make the same vocalizations during the first six months, regardless of the language spoken around them (Flavell, Miller, & Miller, 2002). After that, infants begin to vocalize the sounds of the mother tongue and omit sounds not found in that language (Jusczyk, 1997). It has also been discovered that infants begin to lose the ability to discriminate sounds not in the mother tongue at about six to seven months of age (Werker & Tees, 1999). All of these factors play a significant role in the development and understanding of how the mind operates, but they are only the starting point, or maybe more accurately the dividing point, for more in depth models for information processing.

The Stage Model

Traditionally, the most widely used model of information processing is the stage theory model, based on the work of Atkinson and Shiffrin (1968). A key element of this model was that it viewed learning and memory as discontinuous and multi-staged. It hypothesized that as new information is taken in, it is in some way manipulated before it is stored. The stage theory model recognized three types or stages of memory: sensory memory, short-term or working memory, and long-term memory.

Figure 2-1. A Stage Model of Memory

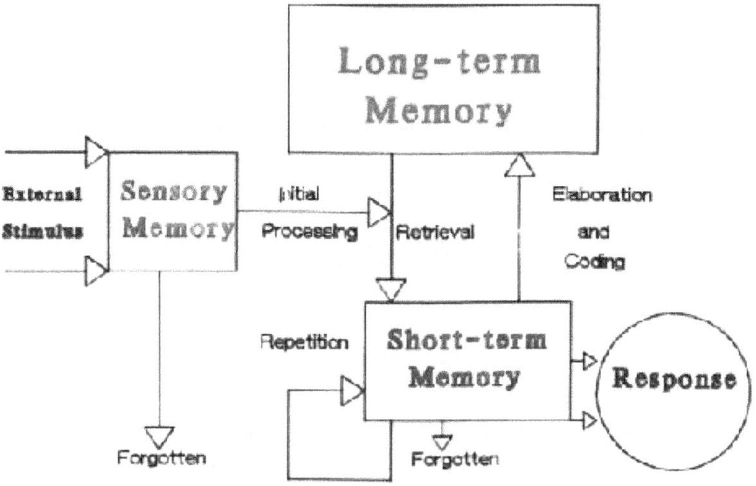

Sensory memory. Sensory memory represents the initial stage of stimuli perception. It is associated with the senses, and there seems to be a separate section for each type of sensual perception, each with its own limitations and devices. Obviously, stimuli that are not sensed cannot be further processed and will never become part of the memory store. This is not to say that only stimuli that are consciously perceived are stored; on the contrary, everyone takes in and perceives stimuli almost continuously. It is hypothesized, though, that perceptions that are not transferred into a higher stage will not be incorporated into memory that can be recalled. The transfer of new information quickly to the next stage of processing is of critical importance, and sensory memory acts as a portal for all information that is to become part of memory. This stage of memory is temporally limited which means that information stored here begins to decay rapidly if not transferred to the next stage. This occurs in as little as ½ second for visual stimuli and three seconds for auditory stimuli. There are many ways to ensure transfer and many methods for facilitating that transfer. To this end, attention and automaticity are the two major influences on sensory memory, and much work has been done to understand the impact of each on information processing.

While attention has been a focus of study for decades, there is still little consensus as to how it operates (Logan, Taylor, & Etherton, 1999). Treisman (as cited in Driscoll, 2001) "showed, however, that attention is not an all-or-nothing proposition and suggested that it serves to attenuate, or tune out, stimulation" (p. 81). Attention does facilitate the integration and transfer of the information being attended, but it is impacted by many factors including the meaningfulness of the new stimulus to the learner, the similarity between competing ideas or stimuli, the complexity of the new information, and the physical ability of the person to attend.

Automaticity is almost the exact opposite of attention. Driscoll (2001) said that "When tasks are overlearned or sources of information become habitual, to the extent that their attention requirements are minimal, automaticity has occurred" (p. 82). Automaticity allows attention to be redirected to other information or stimuli and allows for the ability of multi-tasking without distracting totally from the acquisition of new information.

There are several suggested models of how new stimuli are recognized in sensory memory, and each concerns pattern recognition. The matching of new stimuli to existing memory structures is a crucial factor in the acquisition of new knowledge. If new information is not brought into memory in a meaningful way, it will not be stored as memory. Therefore, the understanding of the patterns by which this information is represented is critical to the proper introduction of new information. Driscoll (2001) said that pattern recognition is "the process whereby environmental stimuli are recognized as exemplars of concepts and principles already in memory" (p. 84). She discussed three models of pattern recognition: template matching, the prototype model, and feature analysis.

The template matching model held that there are exact representations of previous stimuli trapped in the mind. Pattern recognition, then, occurs by matching input with a specific, perfect specimen stored in memory. This model seems to fall short because of the vast numbers of templates that would have to exist in memory for any one type of entity and because it does not account for imperfect stimuli or imperfect templates. The second pattern recognition model is the prototype. This model suggested that the stored unit is a generalized or abstracted form of the knowledge unit, and pattern recognition is based on a comparison of the input to the prototype. If a close match is established, new information can be accepted as the existing class. These two models are very similar in that they each attempt to match incoming information with a whole picture stored in memory. This holistic comparison differentiated them from the third model, feature analysis. In this system, incoming information is judged based on characteristics rather than a whole idea. Individual characteristics are picked out and then grouped to label the new stimulus as an "X". The major difference, simply put, is that these two perspectives seem to work in opposite directions, the first two from top-down and the third from bottom-up.

Short-term or working memory. The second stage of information processing is labeled short-term (STM) or working memory (WM). This stage is often viewed as active or conscious memory because it is the part of memory that is being actively processed while new information is being taken in. STM has a very limited capacity and unrehearsed information will begin to be lost from it within 15-30 seconds if other action is not made. There are two main ways that are effective in processing information while it is in short-term memory. Rote or maintenance rehearsal is the first but less desirable of these methods. This type of rehearsal is intended only to keep information until it can be processed further. It consists mainly of some sort of repetition of the new information and if it is not processed further will be lost. In fact, studies on the limitations of WM have revealed a specific number of units that the mind can process at any given time, and it is now generally accepted that 3 to 7 stimuli is the maximum number that can be processed at once. There are several types of activities that one can perform to encode new information, but the importance of encoding cannot be overstated.

Maintenance rehearsal schemes can be employed to keep information in STM, but, according to the stage theory, more complex elaboration is necessary to make the transfer to long-term memory. It is absolutely necessary for new information to somehow be incorporated into the memory structure in order for it to be retained. There are many suggested models for encoding, but there are basically three ways in which retention occurs. A stimulus can be an almost exact match with existing structures in which case it would be simply added to the mental representation and no change would be made to the structure except its addition. If the new stimulus does not exactly match the existing structure, the structure itself would be adapted to allow for additional characteristics or definitions in which case there would be a fundamental change to the existing structure, which would broaden the defining structures. Finally, if the new stimulus were vastly different from any existing structure, a totally new structure would be created in memory. This new structure could in some way be linked to relevant structures, but it would stand alone as a new unit. At any rate, the incoming information must be acted on and through existing structures and incorporated into those systems in some way for acquisition to occur. The processing of this new stimulus takes place in short-term memory, and the body of knowledge with which the information is integrated is the long-term memory.

The implications of this research are clear. If learning—relatively permanently change—is to take place, new information must be transferred into long-term memory. Therefore, repetition and maintenance rehearsal are not sufficient to produce a lasting effect. This has great relevance to instruction and teaching, for if the aim of education is learning, information must be presented in such a way that learners must work on it so that it can be incorporated into the memory structure.

Long-term memory. As discussed with short-term memory, long-term memory (LTM) stores all previous perceptions, knowledge, and information learned by an individual, but it is not a static file system that is used only for information retrieval. Abbot (2002) suggested that LTM "is that more permanent store in which information can reside in a dormant state – out of mind and unused – until you fetch it back into consciousness" (p. 1). In order to incorporate new information, LTM must be connected with STM and must be dynamic. There are several categories of LTM, and there are many suggestions as to how memory units are represented. While it seems that it might be sufficient to understand simply that there are individual units and structures that exist in LTM, the specific way or ways that information is stored offers extremely important information. If the knowledge unit is pictorial rather than verbal, for example, it would seem to make sense that images would be more easily and readily stored in memory. If the reverse were true, information should be presented in verbal constructs. This oversimplifies the challenge, but it is this question that is at the core of the controversy over memory storage structures. There are two divisions at issue in the discussion of long-term memory: the types of long-term memory and the type of knowledge unit stored in long-term memory.

Organizations of long-term memory. Today cognitive psychologists believe that there are at least two different types of information stored in LTM – episodic and semantic. Each of the memory structures is distinct and serves a different operational function. However, it is evident that some type of very specialized categorization system exists within the human mind. One of the first to make this idea explicit was Bruner (1986, 1990). A basic component of Bruner's theory is that categorization is fundamental to perception, forming concepts, learning, and making decisions.

Tulving (1972) was the first to distinguish between episodic and semantic memory, and all discussions recognize these two distinct types. Most researchers now combine these two in a broader category labeled declarative. Other researchers identified additional organizational types. For example, Abbott (2002) listed declarative and procedural while Pavio (1971, 1986) added imagery to this list. However, Pylyshyn (2002) stated that imagery is not a distinct organizational structure but follows the rules that apply to semantic and episodic memory.

Abbott (2002) defined declarative memory as that which can be talked about or verbalized. It is, then, the sum of stored information that can be readily retrieved and put into words in conscious thought and sharing. As previously stated, declarative memory can be subdivided into both semantic and episodic memories. These two subtypes are radically different although they can each be fairly easily recalled and manipulated. Episodic memory's store is centered on personal experience and specific events. It is entirely circumstantial and it is not generally used for the processing of new information except as a sort of backdrop. "Episodic memories are those which give a subject the sense of remembering the actual situation, or event" (Eliasmith, 2001). This type of memory is somewhat like a personal video of a specific significant day or event, and its parts are not easily disseminated to characteristics or concepts. Semantic memory, in contrast, deals with general, abstract information and can be recalled independently of how it was learned. It is semantic memory that is the central focus of most current study because it houses the concepts, strategies and other structures that are typically used for encoding new information.

Procedural memory can be thought of as "how to" knowledge (Humphreys, Bain, & Pike, 1989). It is the type of long-term memory sometimes associated with information that has reached a state of automaticity, but it is not limited to this. This type of memory is defined in terms of learned skills and the ability to recall instruction-like memory. Paivio (1971, 1986) described imagery as the memory structure for collecting and storing information related to pictures. It captures information much like a photograph and can be extremely useful for context and visual presentation of information.

Memory storage and representation in stage theory model. Theories on the representation and storage of memory units provide the foundation for current trends and beliefs in cognitive psychology and must be examined in order for the more recent models to have a solid foundation. It is not that the models to be discussed here have been dismissed or discounted; some aspects of each have been integrated, broadened or narrowed, but each has contributed its own part to cognitive psychology's development. The first alternative model that became widely accepted and discussed was the network model. Collins and his colleagues (ie, Collins &

Loftus, 1975; Collins & Quillan, 1969) laid the groundwork for this model. It assumed that there are nodes or tabs in memory that store information in sections much like a notebook filing system. When stimuli are introduced, this model suggested that the mind references the incoming data to a chapter or node in memory. One advantage of this model is that it accounts for individual differences in its comprehension and filing system. Each person's nodes would be individualized by the experiences and knowledge that person had gained throughout his or her lifetime. Because this proposed a hierarchical system at work in the mind, integration of new information is shown as a process of moving from stimulus to tab to separate pieces filed behind the tab, a very linear progression. This linear progression later became the center of a bit of controversy and led to new models as this network system began to meet with competition.

Smith, Shoben, and Rips (1974) argued against the network model claiming that instead of being organized in a hierarchal system, information is stored as sets of defining characteristics. In other words, associations are made through the comparison of overlapping features between new stimuli and existing characteristics stored in memory, and in doing this, they differentiated two types of features: defining and characteristic. Several major failures have been found in this model, though. First, there is no allowance here for semantic flexibility, and the world and our perception of it are filled with semantic ambiguities that must be mediated. Also, this system would require vast numbers of collections, but it suggested no concrete organizational system for these collections.

The essential difference between these first two types of encoding and storage systems is related to bottom-up and top-down processing. Network models work on the top-down principle; feature comparison models work from the bottom-up. Klatzky (1980) recognized the similarities between these models and essentially tried to end debate about choosing between them. When she coined the term "mental dictionary", she stated simply that their associations to one another represent concepts. In this light, it is of no material consequence which direction, top-down or bottom-up, the information flows and is connected, it simply matters that associations and connections are made. This effectively merged the two ideas saying that feature analysis is simply an enhanced form of the network model.

Anderson and Bower (1973) proposed the next significant model for how knowledge units are stored. Their model was founded on the belief that knowledge is based on verbal units (consisting of subject and verb constructs) rather than perceptions. This prepositional model moved away from categorization and nodes, but it still held that these propositions are organized in a network structure. Another feature that this model shared with the network and feature analysis models was its serial nature. This model, as both of the previous models, is built on the belief that information is encoded in a linear method; in order for new information to be incorporated, it must pass from point A to point B to integration with X. It is the serial nature of these models that differentiates them from the later models of information acquisition. Later theories suggested that information is not incorporated in a linear fashion, but, rather, they are simultaneously processed at different levels and by different memory categories or structures.

Additional Theories of Information Processing

There are many, more recent theories concerning information processing that differ from the stage theory model, and today, research and study continues to modify existing beliefs in this area of cognitive psychology. Despite the fact that there are commonly accepted pieces, the complete picture of how information is processed continues to change.

Levels of processing. One of the first alternatives to the theories discussed above was developed by Craik and Lockhart (1972) and labeled the levels of processing model. Specifically, the levels of processing theory held that memory is not three-staged which separates it immediately from the stage theory model. Craik and Lockhart argued that stimulus information is processed at multiple levels simultaneously (not serially) depending on characteristics, attention, and meaningfulness. New information does not have to enter in any specific order, and it does not have to pass through a prescribed channel. They further contended that the more deeply information is processed, the more that will be remembered (Kearsley, 2001c). This model was a precursor to the development of schema theory, discussed below. In fact, the two are consistent; Rumelhart and McClelland (1986) found that the larger the number of connections to a single idea or concept was associated with the increased likelihood that it was to be remembered.

Dual coding theory. As mentioned previously, another theory in the information processing debate is Paivio's work in dual coding (Paivio, 1986; Clark & Paivio, 1991). This theory gave equal significance to both verbal and non-verbal processing and suggested there are two separate systems for processing these types of information. Imagens—mental images—are processed by one system, and logogens—verbal entities, chunks or propositions—are processed by a different system. According to Kearsley (2001b), Paivio believed that:

> Human cognition is unique in that it has become specialized for dealing simultaneously with language and with nonverbal objects and events. Moreover, the language system is peculiar in that it deals directly with linguistic input and output (in the form of speech or writing) while at the

same time serving a symbolic function with respect to nonverbal objects, events, and behaviors. Any representational theory must accommodate this dual functionality (p. 1).

Further, Paivio suggested there are three separate types of processing and interaction between these two subsystems: representational, referential, and associative. Representational processing is the direct activation of one system or the other; referential is the activation of one sub-system by the other; and, associative is activation within the same sub-system without the interaction of the other.

Schema theory, parallel distributed processing, and connectionist models. Rumelhart (1980), working in conjunction with others, developed the schema theory of information processing and memory. He proposed that a schema is a data structure for representing generic concepts stored in memory. There are five key components to this view of memory and processing in relation to schema: 1) it is an organized structure that exists in memory and is the sum of all gained knowledge; 2) it exists at a higher level, or abstraction, than immediate experience; 3) its concepts are linked by propositions (verbal constructs); 4) it is dynamic; and 5) it provides a context or structure for new information (Winn and Snyder, 2001). This model is sometimes called the connectionist model or theory; it emphasizes that information is stored in multiple locations throughout the brain in the form of networks of connections. This model is explicitly similar to the levels of processing theory in that it is founded on the belief in parallel processing of information. Therefore, the connections among pieces of information are key, not the order in which connections are made.

Rumelhart later worked with McClelland and the Parallel Distributed Processing Research Group (McClelland & Rumelhart, 1981, 1986; Rumelhart & McClelland, 1986) to expand his initial work and created the connectionist theories. In this enhanced model, it was still proposed that the units of memory are connections rather than any concrete representation of previous information. The latter model goes further, however, stating that the activation of the connections is the knowledge unit. According to Driscoll (2001), there are many advantages to this model, the most prominent of which are that it accounts for the incremental nature of learning, is dynamic, incorporates goals of learning, and has the potential to explain cognitive development.

Development of Memory and Information Processing

As previously stated, cognition is the encoding, structuring, storing, retrieving, using, or otherwise learning of knowledge (Neisser, 1967). There are important developmental aspects for each of these activities. According to Flavell et al. (2002), some of the most important contributions to development theory made by the information processing theories are:

1. Brain changes brought about by biological maturation or experience;
2. Increased processing capacity, speed, and efficiency as a result of both maturation and knowledge development;
3. Modifications of connections in a neural network;
4. New emergent concepts arising from repeated self-organization as a result of adapting to the demands of a changing environment; and
5. Increased capacity for problem-solving and metacognition.

These are discussed further using the steps considered in Neisser's definition.

Encoding

Encoding occurs during the initial processing of a stimulus or event. Maturation and experience influence this process. In terms of maturation, Dempster (1981) hypothesized that the adult capacity for short-term memory of 3 to 7 digits might be as much as 2 digits lower for children aged 5 and 1 digit lower for children aged 9. As for experience, in a series of well-known studies of expertise, novices remembered new information less well than experts (eg, Chi, 1978; Schneider, Korkel, & Winert, 1989). One of the most important differences between novices and experts is the structure and organization of domain-specific knowledge.

Structuring and Organizing

Structuring and organizing information occur as the learner processes and stores information. The learner's ability changes over time as a result of both maturation and experience.

When presented with information they are asked to remember, younger children do not rehearse information in order to remember it. As they get into school, they begin to develop or are taught various strategies. At first these strategies are only used when prompted by someone else, but as the child becomes more competent in their use and uses them more frequently, the child will increasingly use the strategies spontaneously (Flavell et al., 2002).

One of the most important information processing capacities a child develops is the ability to organize information; this is, in turn, influenced by the child's ability to categorize. As is the case with other information-processing capacities, this ability changes with both maturation and experience. One of the basic types of categorization is the grouping of specific events, ideas, people, things, etc. into concepts. Rosch and his colleagues (eg, Mervis & Rosch, 1981; Rosch, Mervis, Gray, Johnson, & Boyes-Braem, 1976) demonstrated two fundamental features to the development of concepts: the ease of identifying similarities of members of the concept and distinguishing differences between members that are not. For example, the development of the concept of animal would be more difficult than developing the concept of dog or cat because it would be easier to identify similarities among dogs or cats and differences between cats and dogs than it would be to identify similarities among all animals or to differentiate all animals from all plants. This has important implications as we design learning activities for children and youth that can help them develop their organizational and storage capacities.

Storage and Retrieval

The amount of information that can be stored and retrieved relative to a stimulus or event also changes over time. For example, prior to about age 7 months an infant will not seek an object that has been shown and then removed from view. The infant has encoded the object (such as a rattle) and will reach for it but seems to lose interest as soon as it is no longer in view. At about 7 months, the infant attains what is called "object permanence" and will begin to seek the object if it is removed from view.

A series of studies by Bauer, Mandler, and associates (as cited in Flavell et al., 2002) demonstrated a child's increasing ability to perform simple multiple-act sequences. By age 13 months infants can reproduce three-act sequences; by age 24 months this has increased to five-act sequences; and by age 30 months to eight separate actions. As children gain language skills, their ability to store and recall more complex events increases. This is shown first in autobiographical accounts of daily activities and then to events they may have witnessed or heard about.

Flavell et al. (2002) made four observations about strategy development:

1. Strategy development is not linear. When developing any particular strategy, development will often stall or even regress before it becomes systematically and correctly used.
2. A strategy will continue to develop after it is first demonstrated in its mature form. This continued development may take months or even years.
3. Children show considerable variability in their use of strategies. Children often go back and forth in their use of strategies, changing strategies even after they have been found to work well.
4. Children differ in their abilities to integrate different strategies into a coherent pattern for successful learning. Children must be given

ample opportunity to create successful learning programs that work for them.

Designing Instruction Incorporating Best Practices for Information Processing

The understanding of how the mind processes and stores information is invaluable to educators as they plan for instruction. If there is little to no understanding of the information processing skills of the students with whom one is working, it would be almost impossible to design instruction that contributes to high levels of learning and achievement. However, attempting to understand the myriad theories of information processing and cognitive development can be overwhelming and contradictory. There are means of structuring instruction, though, that can incorporate the best of all of these ideas, and in order to help students reach higher-level thinking and learning skills, educators must draw from all of these theories.

Information Processing and Memory

If learning is to occur, educators must ensure that new information is processed in such a way that it can be retained in long-term memory. As previously discussed, in order to achieve this, elaboration and connection must occur between previously learned memory and new information. It has been established that the more deeply information is processed and the more connections that can be made between new information and existing memory structures, the more information will be retained in long-term memory. Therefore, in order to make new material meaningful, instruction must be presented in such a way that students can easily access and connect previous learning and experiences with the new material.

One of the most often cited references to levels of elaboration for instructional purposes is the Taxonomy of the Cognitive Domain developed by Bloom and his colleagues (Bloom, Englehart, Furst, Hill, & Krathwohl, 1956) and recently revised by Anderson and Krathwohl (2000).

Bloom et al. (1965) proposed that educational objectives can be classified in six levels, each more complex than the previous (See Table 2-1). The first level is labeled knowing and simply requires a learner to repeat back what was heard or seen. This involves no elaboration. The second level is labeled comprehension and requires some rudimentary levels of understanding that might involve having the student summarize or paraphrase some information. This requires only modest levels of elaboration. The next two levels, application and analysis, involve more elaboration and show a significant impact on long-term learning when they are used during the learning process. Application involves using the concepts or principles to solve a problem, while analysis involves understanding the relationship among the parts and how they are organized into a whole. The last two levels, synthesis and evaluation, are the most complex and require the highest levels of elaboration. Synthesis involves putting the parts or components together in an original manner, while evaluation is the process of making judgments based on comparison to a standard.

Table 2-1. Bloom's Taxonomy of the Cognitive Domain

LEVEL	DEFINITION
Knowledge	Student recalls or recognizes information, ideas, and principles in the approximate form in which they were learned.
Comprehension	Student translates, comprehends, or interprets information based on prior learning.
Application	Student selects, transfers, and uses data and principles to complete a problem or task with a minimum of direction.
Analysis	Student distinguishes, classifies, and relates the assumptions, hypotheses, evidence, or structure of a statement or question.
Synthesis	Student originates, integrates, and combines ideas into a product, plan or proposal that is new to him or her.
Evaluation	Student appraises, assesses, or critiques on a basis of specific standards and criteria.

Research has confirmed that the first four levels are indeed a hierarchy, while there seems to be a challenge with the ordering of the two highest levels. Anderson and Krathwohl (2000) proposed that the ordering is reversed, with evaluation being less difficult than synthesis, while Huitt (2011b) proposed that they are both at the same level of difficulty though they incorporate different types of processing. There seems to be consensus that both synthesis and evaluation are based on analysis or the ability to compare and contrast parts of a whole and understand the relationship among parts. The type of thinking involved in synthesis is often labeled "creative thinking," while that involved in evaluation is often called "critical thinking." Research confirmed that both are necessary for successful problem solving (Huitt, 1992).

In order to create an environment in which high levels of elaboration are taking place, the educator must build background knowledge and link previously learned material to new. This does not simply mean that he or she should rely on the classes students have had in the past. Connections must also be made thematically between units, lessons, theories, or concepts. One of the writing standards for the Common Core State Standards for grades 9-10 learners, for example, stated students must "draw evidence from literacy or informational texts to support analysis, reflection, and research" (Common Core State Standards Initiative, 2018, p. 46). This is a theme that can be carried through all lessons, units, and literary works, and it can be a thread that helps students connect new ideas and works to ones previously discussed. In addition, this type of thread structure can make the literature more meaningful—at once strengthening and increasing the connections that can be made and the opportunities for elaboration.

If in British Literature students first learn about the qualities the Old English society valued in a hero, could not the same discussion be held when the concept of the hero changes in Middle English literature? And, does this question not require students to draw from information learned in the previous material in order to find an answer? The larger question could certainly then become what does the current literature (popular or academic) tell students about what society today values in its heroes. Even in this simple example, there are tremendous opportunities to allow students to actively integrate new information with old by combining new information with existing knowledge, by building or expanding structures, or by creating new and more diverse structures.

Once the background is established, the new information on the topic can be presented in a variety of ways, but again, in order to ensure understanding and retention, the new material must be connected to concrete examples. For example, if the teacher organized a lesson about the satire in literary terms, it would be absolutely important to follow up the classroom activity by examining an example of a satire and walking students through an evaluation process of the example showing them how and where the example conforms to the characteristics named in the lecture.

When the teacher and learners have examined a satire together, the students could be asked to go through the evaluation process individually or in groups. This allows learners to demonstrate their competencies or deficiencies in a safe environment in which the teacher can guide, refocus, or assist. The important aspect of the activity is that learners are forced to begin to synthesize and evaluate new information based on their previous experiences and any new skills they are developing. To take this lesson full circle, the teacher could ask the learners to create their own satire based on a current social problem, perhaps developing a skit or video in the process.

When a learner creates, either individually or in a group, an original satire at the end of the lesson, the learner has connected with all levels of elaboration in Bloom et al.'s (1956) taxonomy. At the beginning of the learning experience, the class could discuss possible topics as a whole and why certain ideas would or would not be appropriate for satire. In order to bring along learners who might still be having problems, starter sentences or paragraphs could be provided or the teacher could provide more examples of satires for the students to evaluate. Additionally, learners have begun to process information at the formal operational stage (see chapter four for a discussion of Piagetian theory) if they can make the abstract connections required to complete the activities of the lesson.

Another theorist firmly grounded in the information processing approach is Sternberg (1988). Sternberg's theory was focused on cognitive intelligence; he advocated that cognitive development is skills-based and continuous rather than staged and discontinuous as stage theorists proposed. This focus on intelligence separated his ideas from stage theorists because it rejected the idea of incremental stages, but rather hypothesized that development occurs in the same way throughout life differentiated only by the expertise of the learner to process new information. First, and very importantly, Sternberg's model did not differentiate between child and adult learning. Also, he dealt solely with information processing aspects of development and did not incorporate any facets of biological development into his theory. Cognitive development was viewed as a novice to expert progression; as one becomes better at interaction and learning, one is able to learn more and at higher levels. Sternberg proposed that cognitive development occurred as a result of feedback, self-monitoring, and automatization. In this theory, intelligence is comprised of three kinds of information processing components: metacomponents, performance components, and knowledge-acquisition components.

In Sternberg's (1988) model, each of these three components works together to facilitate learning and cognitive development. Metacomponents are executive in nature. They guide the planning and decision making in reference to problem solving situations; they serve to identify the problem and connect it with experiences from the past. There is, however, no action directly related to metacomponents, they simply direct what actions will follow. Performance components are the actions taken in the completion of a problem-solving task. Performance components go beyond metacomponents in that they perform the function also of weighing the merit and/or consequences of actions in comparison to other options rather than simply identifying options. Sternberg's third proposed type of intelligence is the knowledge-acquisition component. This type is characterized by the ability to learn new information in order to solve a potential problem. This type is much more abstract and may or may not be directly related to a current problem-solving task (Driscoll, 2001). This three-leveled view of intelligence comprised the componential aspect of Sternberg's theory, but this is only one of three parts to his larger triarchic theory of intelligence (Kearsley, 2001e).

Sternberg's (1988) theory added the components of feedback to theories of cognitive development; this suggested that an individual's social interaction has some impact on cognitive development. In fact, one of the three parts of his theory was based on the context in which learning takes place; this subpart of the theory "specifies that intelligent behavior is defined by the sociocultural context in which it takes place and involves adaptation to the environment, selection of better environments, and shaping of the present environment" (Kearsley, 2001e). The addition of social context as a factor in cognitive development linked Sternberg to the interactional theories of development of Bruner (1977a, 1986) and Vygotsky (1978). These theories, and others of this type, are premised on the assumption that learning does not occur in a vacuum. Therefore, one must discuss the social and cultural contexts of learning. Driscoll (2001) stated, "Of central importance is viewing education as more than curriculum and instructional strategies. Rather, one must consider the broader context in how culture shapes the mind and provides the toolkit by which individuals construct worlds and their conceptions of themselves and their powers" (p. 221).

Assessment and Evaluation Concerns

The understanding of how information is stored in memory and the developmental process of learning leads naturally to the issue of how one can best understand a learner's developmental progress and what he or she knows. It is important to address domain-specific knowledge and processing capacities as well as capacities that are non-domain specific.

Dietel, Herman, and Knuth (1991) provided some important guidelines regarding assessment and evaluation. One of the most important points is that data gathered during the assessment process, which in turn, will be used for evaluation purposes, is guided by one's beliefs in regard to learning. As one can surmise from the review of literature on information processing and memory, this can be a very complex task. They reported that "From today's cognitive perspective, meaningful learning is reflective, constructive, and self-regulated. People are not seen as mere recorders of factual information but as creators of their own unique knowledge structures" (p. 3). Therefore, creating accurate assessments for individual learners becomes troublesome.

One might think that a traditional area of strength for the educational system has been the assessment of knowledge and cognitive skills. However, as previously discussed, the cognitive taxonomy of educational objectives developed by Bloom et al. (1956) and revised by Anderson and Krathwohl (2000) showed there are significant differences between lower- and higher-level thinking and knowing. Unfortunately, the testing process now used in the United States overemphasizes lower-level knowing (Stiggins, 2002). The fact that standardized test scores seem to dictate most educational practice identified a direct conflict of interest for ensuring that students are taught and assessed in higher-level cognitive skills. Stiggins argued that the failure to balance classroom assessment of higher-level skills with standardized assessments has drastically hurt the educational system. More recently, "most of the national curriculum standards expect teachers to create active learning environments that stimulate higher-level student thinking" (Freiberg, 2002, p. 56). In view of the demands of modern society, it seems that additional effort must be placed on the assessment of higher-level cognitive skills and information processing (Hummel & Huitt, 1994).

Fortunately for educators, there are many constant themes of information processing regardless of the specific theory to which one subscribes. Almost all ideas related to how information becomes stored in memory agree that the more deeply and meaningfully a learner processes information that is presented in a context-rich manner, the more readily available that information will be. It has been demonstrated that when new information is presented within a context of knowledge that a learner possesses, he or she has background knowledge with which new information can be compared and categorized. This categorization is also a critical piece of information processing at high levels.

These theories all work under the assumption that new information can most effectively be learned if the material can be matched to memory structures already in place (Winn and Snyder, 2001, p. 3). Most theories hold that the mind contains some type of framework into which new information is placed. This structure is multi-leveled and has varying degrees of specificity. New information can be matched with, compared to, joined with, or modified to fit with existing structures. This in-place structural system allows for differing levels of complexity of information processing. The formation of and continual building of these structures, then, is critical in order for learners to process information in various ways and at higher levels. Again, though, the question becomes how to assess this development.

What, then, should cognitive assessments look like? If one argues that current methods are inappropriate, why are they so? What should these assessments do differently to accommodate the best theories of development and help move students to higher-level thinking and information processing?

Stiggins (2002) said, "Clearly, over the decades, we have believed that by checking achievement status and reporting the results to the public we can apply the pressure needed to intensify – and thus speed – school improvement" (p. 3). This has not occurred. He argued, though, that there are ways that assessment can directly improve schools. "If assessments of learning provide evidence of achievement for public reporting, then assessments for learning serve to help students learn more. The crucial distinction is between assessment to determine the status of learning and assessment to promote greater learning" (p. 4). The factor that he views as most important for this more formative view of assessment is to involve students in the process and help them to be accountable for their learning.

Summary and Conclusions

In summary, there are many different theories of information processing that focus on different aspects of perceiving, remembering, and reasoning. One of the most important agreements is that elaboration is a key to permanently storing information in a way that facilitates its quick retrieval when it is needed. Bloom et al. (1956) and Anderson and Krathwohl (2000) provided some excellent suggestions as to how we can encourage increased elaboration among our students. However, as advocated by Hummel and Huitt (1994), if students are not required to demonstrate the results of elaboration on meaningful tasks such as examinations or projects, they are not likely to adequately develop the skills required for higher-level thinking. It is, therefore, imperative that educators and parents require the development and use of these skills as a normal process of students' lives. If we do that, the amounts and types of student knowledge will increase dramatically and students will be better prepared for life as adults in this rapidly changing, global, digital sociocultural milieu in which humanity finds itself (Huitt, Chapter 12, this volume).

3

Connecting Cognitive Development and Constructivism: Implications from Theory for Instruction and Assessment[3]

Stacey T. Lutz and William G. Huitt

A review of the last fifteen years of literature reveals the attempt to consolidate the findings of a number of cognitive psychologists and philosophers who contend that several major assumptions of the information processing approach to cognition are incomplete. For example, one of the assumptions of this approach is that knowledge and competencies of thinking are situated within the individual and can be studied independently of the situation within which they are used (Bruner, 1990). Alternatively, Greeno (1989), a leading proponent of situated learning, proposed that thinking is a result of interaction between the individual and the environment. Greeno argued that person/environment interactions are of such complexity as to make attempts to discover generalized cognitive processes quite irrelevant. Rather he suggested a need to study how a student's innate abilities are used to develop knowledge and thinking competencies through interaction with specific environments. This position hypothesized that the information processing model may be adequate to explain current understandings of how memory operates, but it does not fully describe or predict differences in cognitive development. Situated models like Greeno's serve to highlight an ecological model for cognitive development (Huitt, 2012a) that focuses on how individuals construct meaning from interactions with their environments.

As in every domain of human development, there are three major questions that are addressed: what is the role of biology, what is the role of experience, and how can the environment be arranged so as to best address the interaction between these two factors? John Dewey, Jean Piaget, Lev Vygotsky, and Jerome Bruner, researchers who provide the theoretical underpinnings for the increasingly popular constructivistic approach to the teaching/learning process, have different responses to these questions. However, the group of theorists discussed in this chapter would subscribe to this questioning of assumptions. While they may disagree as to the emphasis

---

[3] Lutz, S., & Huitt, W. (2004). Connecting cognitive development and constructivism: Implications from theory for instruction and assessment. *Constructivism in the Human Sciences,9*(1), 67-90.

on the individual or environment, they would all recognize the importance of studying person/environment interactions. This acknowledgment increases the complexity of their findings, making them that much more difficult to understand and use in guiding and assessing students' cognitive development. Consequently, there are many questions that remain unanswered. This chapter provides an overview of theories fundamental to the constructivistic approach, as well as practical suggestions for classroom practice and methods of assessment and evaluation germane to the constructivistic approach.

John Dewey

John Dewey (1998) was an American psychologist and philosopher who promoted the value of personal experience in learning. He placed relatively little emphasis on maturational factors and taught that human beings understand the world through interaction with their environment and, thus, knowledge is constructed by the individual. Dewey (1944) proposed that a primary function of schooling was to prepare young people to live in a democratic society and that one's reflection on personal experiences would provide the foundation for the development of the necessary attributes for successful living. He believed the dualistic conceptualization of thinking and doing to be false. Rather he proposed a reciprocal, continuous relationship between thinking and doing that is reflected in the work of the other researchers discussed in this chapter (Vanderstraeten & Biesta, 1998). As a leader in the progressive education movement in the early twentieth century, his work set the stage for an acceptance of the work of later researchers.

Jean Piaget

Jean Piaget (2001) was a Swiss biologist, philosopher, and behavioral scientist who developed one of the most significant theories in cognitive psychology. His stage theory gained wide acceptance in the 1960s and 1970s as a result of the translations of his work into English and its promotion by influential American psychologists (eg, Flavell, 1963). His impact on the field of cognitive development cannot be overstated, even though many of the precepts he developed have been criticized by subsequent evidence (Parent, Normandeau, & Larivee, 2000).

Piaget described himself as a genetic epistemologist. His work focused on developing a general theory of knowledge, how a child develops a knowledge of his or her world, and the role that biology plays in that development. To Piaget, intelligence is represented by how an organism interacts with its environment through mental adaptation. This adaptation is controlled through mental organizations or structures that an individual uses to represent the world; it is driven by a biological impulse to obtain balance (homeostasis or equilibrium) between those mental organizations and the environment.

Piagetian theory can be discussed in two parts: 1) his theory of adaptation and the process of using cognitive schemes and 2) his theory of cognitive developmental stages (Huitt and Hummel, 2003).

The process of coming to know, the first aspect of Piaget's (2001) theory, starts with the fact that individuals are born with reflexes that allow them to interact with the environment. These reflexes are quickly replaced by constructed mental schemes or structures that allow them to interact with, and adapt to, the environment. This adaptation occurs in two different ways (through the processes of assimilation and accommodation) and is a critical element of modern constructivism. Adaptation is predicated on the belief that the building of knowledge is a continuous activity of self-construction; as a person interacts with the environment, knowledge is invented and manipulated into cognitive structures. When discrepancies between the environment and mental structures occur, one of two things can happen. Either the perception of the environment can be changed in order for new information to be matched with existing structures through assimilation, or the cognitive structures themselves can change as a result of the interaction through accommodation. In either case, the individual adapts to his or her environment by way of the interaction. It is clear that Piaget believed that cognition is grounded in the interface between mind and environment. The result of this interplay is the achievement or working toward a balance between mental schemes and the requirements of the environment. It is a combination of maturation and actions to achieve equilibration that advances an individual into a higher developmental stage.

Piaget (2001) proposed four sequential stages of cognitive development. Other researchers have critiqued his theory, using four criteria implied by it (Driscoll, 2001). First, if each stage is progressive, as he asserted, then each must represent a qualitative (discontinuous) change in cognition, or there must be an obvious, substantial improvement or change when a child moves from one stage into the next. Second, the stages of progression must be consistent for all children across all cultures and societies. If Piaget's theory is true and cognitive development is biologically based, cultural and societal factors should not impact that development. Next, preceding stages must be integrated into later stages of development. As growth occurs in a stage theory model, the abilities and structures from all previous stages should be present and operational at all higher stages. Finally, at any point in development, a child's mental structures or schemes and his or her physical operations join to form a whole unit, and as development occurs, this unit becomes more complex. These four criteria form the backdrop for Piaget's four-staged theory of cognitive development. Because his theory asserts that the stages are age dependent and based on cognitive readiness, the approximate ages for each stage are included in the discussion of each.

Piaget differentiated three types of knowledge that must be present at all stages of cognitive development: physical, logical-mathematical, and social (Driscoll 2001). Physical knowledge is gained through hands-on interaction with the environment. It deals directly with experience and perception of objects and is very concrete in nature. This type of knowledge can only be gained from personal, direct contact with environmental elements. Logical-mathematical knowledge is an abstract reasoning that is applicable beyond physical interaction with a concrete stimulus. While physical knowledge is discovered, logical-mathematical knowledge is created through actions. It can only be gained by repeated exposure and interaction with multiple objects in multiple settings in order for mental structures to be modified and created. Here, it is the manipulation of objects in different patterns and contexts that allows for generalizations and abstractions to be created. Likewise, social knowledge can only be gained through interaction with others. This type of knowledge is culture specific and its acquisition is based on actions rather than physical perception of objects. These types of knowledge are at work at all stages of cognitive development and are not necessarily hierarchical in nature—as are Piaget's proposed stages of development.

The first stage suggested by Piaget is the sensorimotor stage. In general, this stage lasts from birth to about two years of age. At this point intelligence is based on physical and motor activity but excludes the use of symbols. Mobility, crawling, and walking facilitate knowledge acquisition, and progress is shown through the modification of reflexes in response to the environment. One important milestone of this stage is the development of object permanence. Beginning at about 7 months infants start to understand the concept that objects continue to exist even though they cannot be seen. The end of this stage is marked by the immature use of symbols and language development that signals the progression to the second stage.

The second stage, labeled pre-operational, lasts from about two years of age until approximately seven. It is marked by the demonstration of intelligence through the use of symbols, especially the maturation of language. Children in the pre-operational stage are able to mentally represent objects and events, and at this point in development, memory and imagination are developed. An important signifier of this stage is the ability of a child to do monological, nonreversible thinking; children in this stage can deal with or determine only one aspect of a problem at a time, and they cannot think or process information in a multidimensional fashion. A child's thinking at this stage is also highly egocentric, and even in conversation, he or she will fail to recognize any duality in the exchange of information and certainly will fail to comprehend any perspective other than their own. The end of this stage is marked by the child's ability to conserve number (ie, the child knows that spacing of objects does not impact their quantity).

The reaching of Piaget's third stage, the concrete operational, is evidenced by a child's ability to demonstrate logically integrated thought, and the typical age span for this stage is from seven to eleven. At this point in development, the child's exposure to, and integration of, knowledge has matured such that all three types of knowledge (physical, logical-mathematical, and social) can be used by the child to interact with the environment to a relatively high degree. At this point, intelligence is based on logical and systematic manipulation of concrete objects and related symbols. The child can engage in reversible mental operations (ie, the child can interact with the environment from more than one perspective). Subsequently, egocentric thinking declines. The major milestone yet to be reached by the concrete operational child, however, is the ability to make abstractions and hypothesize. At the concrete operational stage, his or her development is still limited to the application of knowledge to concrete objects and stimuli.

From eleven years onward, Piaget presumes that the preadolescent begins the process of attaining the formal operational stage of development. At this stage, intelligence is shown through the logical use of symbols related to abstract concepts. There is typically a return to egocentric thinking early in the period, but the abstractions that this type of thought allows eventually move the individual to a much broader perspective and thinking beyond himself or herself. Siegler (1991) suggested that an important ability of people who reach this stage is that they are able to think abstractly about such issues as truth, morality, justice, and the nature of existence and to provide alternative, competing beliefs about these. Thus, cognitive development becomes a pre-requisite for the acquisition of morality based upon abstract principles.

It is important to note that empirical evidence indicates the formal operations stage is not necessarily reached because of physical maturity (Eylon & Lynn, 1988; Renner and others, 1976). Eylon and Linn (1988) categorized the percentage of high school students at Piaget's developmental levels as shown in Table 3-1. As is evident most students have not attained the formal operations stage by the time they get out of high school, let alone at age 15 when Piaget stated that most young people should have attained it.

Piaget's stages have come under significant scrutiny in the years since they were introduced, and many theories have added to the scope or particularities of his ideas. Kagan (as cited in Stanton, 1993, p.1) pointed out that "Piagetian theory fails to account for how and why a child passes from one stage to another, and second, it fails to provide a systematic description of the conceptual structures possessed by the child at each stage." While the theory has often been amended or refuted, its impact is unquestionable, and many of Piaget's ideas continue to validly describe the process of mental change. Dasen (as cited in Suizzo, 2000) said that "There may be some discussion about the age at which particular concepts are attained, the possibility that for some individuals this type of reasoning may, in some conceptual areas, remain a potential rather than a performance applicable to all contexts, but it remains that concrete operational reasoning has been found world-wide" (p. 847). Further, although new theories of cognitive development have gone beyond Piagetian thinking, they all seem to agree with at least the spirit of Piaget's work that children are spontaneously and actively processing their interactions with the environment in a self-directing manner, using a wide variety of information processing processes to construct a view that is unique to each individual (Flavell, Miller, & Miller, 2002).

Table 3-1. Percentage of Students in Different Piagetian Stages

Age	Grade	Pre-operational	Entry Concrete	Advanced Concrete	Entry Formal	Middle Formal
14	8-9	1	32	43	15	9
15	9-10	1	15	53	18	13
16	10-11	1	13	50	17	19
16-17	11-12	3	19	47	19	12
17-18	12	1	15	50	15	19

One modern extension of Piagetian theory may be found in Case (1985), who provided an excellent example of research that continues to develop Piaget's original framework. He agreed with Piaget that there are developmental stages and that increasingly sophisticated structures develop at each, but he preferred to model mental structures using afen information processing approach. Relying on this model, Case hypothesized that as automaticity increases and more structures are developed, new developmental stages could be reached. He focused on the demands on memory for task performance and suggested that at all levels a person's capacity for gaining knowledge is divided between operating space and storage space. Although he names automaticity in particular, it is suspected that other factors, including biological ones, contribute to developmental increases. Also, he subdivided each of Piaget's stages into four substages. He first introduced these levels in 1980, but in 1985 revised and renamed them as operational consolidation, operational coordination, bifocal coordination, and elaborated coordination (Stanton, 1993).

Lev Vykotsky

The inclusion of society and culture as impactors of cognitive development is most evident in the work of Lev Vygotsky (1978). His work uses social interaction as the framework for all learning and development. To Vygotsky, "the development of the mind is the interweaving of the biological development of the human body and the appropriation of the cultural/ideal/material heritage which exists in the present to coordinate people with each other and the physical world" (Cole and Wertsch, 1996, p. 2). There are three major principles underlying Vygotsky's social development theory (Kearsley, 2001d; Wink & Putney, 2002). First, social interaction plays a critical role in cognitive development in relation to what is learned and when and how learning occurs. This principle asserts that "Without the learning that occurs as a result of social interaction, without self-awareness or the use of signs and symbols that allow us to think in more complex ways, we would remain slaves to the situation, responding directly to the environment" (Nicholl, 1998, p. 1). The second principle associated with this theory is "the idea that the potential for cognitive development is limited to a certain time span" (Kearsley, 2001a, p. 1). Finally, Vygotsky asserted that the only way to understand how humans come to know is to study learning in an environment where the process of learning rather than the product that is the result of learning, is studied.

The impact of society and culture are central to social development theory. Vygotsky (1978) believed that all higher mental functions must first be filtered through an external stage in the form of social occurrences. They are then integrated into an individual's thinking through the use of language. This "dialectical discovery" is a continuous process that becomes increasingly complex over time (Wink & Putney, 2002, p. 10). Therefore, all higher functions originate as actual interpersonal relationships between individuals.

Vygotsky (1978) believed that two levels of mental functions exist: elementary and higher mental functions. The first are functions that individuals are born with (ie, no learning is required for their use). These functions require no thought and are naturally occurring such as hunger and sensing. Conversely, higher mental functions include the creation and use of self-generated stimulation such as memory, attention, thinking, and language (Kozulin, Gindis, Ageyev, & Miller, 2003). The transition from elementary to higher mental functions is made through the use of cultural tools. Vygotsky's view is that human beings create cultures through the use of tools and symbols. Culture (and in turn society) then dictates what is valuable to learn and how it is learned. Society, then, is the driving force behind cognitive development. This is a departure from theories that contend that cognitive development proceeds in order to prepare a person to interact with society in a meaningful way. Instead, cognitive development is the internalization of social functions and the conversion of social functions into mental functions (Driscoll, 2001).

The concept in Vygotsky's (1978) theory that each person has an individual range of potential for learning is called the zone of proximal development. This zone indicates that at any point in development, there are three levels of ability that are possible: that which a person can do without guidance or help, that which a person cannot do even if helped, and that which a person can do with help. The measurement of cognitive development, then, cannot be accomplished by a simple evaluation of a task completed by one person. In this theory, it is the potential for development that is important, not the snapshot that can be provided by simply asking a child to complete a task independently. The zone itself is the distance between the actual developmental level as determined by independent problem solving and the level of potential as determined through problem solving under adult guidance or in collaboration with more capable peers (Kozulin et al., 2003). These potential changes as an individual continually actualizes potential; the zone is a sliding scale throughout life, and, in theory, full development can never be reached. This idea, also, is radically different from stage theorists because it delineates no final destination or developmental stage.

With respect to Vygotsky's (1978) belief that one must study the process of learning rather than the product, he was interested in how a person mediates or actively modifies the stimulus situation as a part of learning. His observations focused on how children go about the process of problem solving and what societal tools are employed in their solutions. In order to assess development, he studied the interaction of subjects with a problem-solving task but was not necessarily concerned with whether or not a correct solution was achieved. Different developmental levels were demonstrated by the elements such as use of symbols, abstractions, and past experiences. In addition, Vygotsky would often add additional problematic circumstances to a problem-solving task such as mixed language groups in order to understand more about the process of finding solutions (Driscoll, 2001).

Jerome Bruner

Bruner's (1986, 1990) constructivist theory incorporated many of the ideas offered in previous theories. First, he included the Piagetian notion that cognitive development occurs in progressive stages and that each stage is incorporated and built upon by succeeding stages. Bruner also agreed with Piaget in arguing that categorization and representation are keys to an individual's cognitive development. His ideas can also be linked to those who propose information processing models in that he hypothesized development occurs as mental structures become more elaborate and sophisticated through interaction and experience: "learners construct new ideas or concepts based upon their current/past knowledge. The learner selects and transforms information, constructs hypotheses, and makes decisions, relying on a cognitive structure to do so" (Kearsley, 2001a, p.1). In addition, his work is considered interactional in a manner similar to that proposed by Dewey and Vygotsky. He is concerned with the sequence of representation (ie, the stages), but he is equally concerned with the role of culture on cognitive development.

There is one fundamental difference between Bruner's (1986) theory and Piaget's (2001) theories. First, stage theories maintain that cognitive readiness is key to learning and development. According to these, age or biological state dictates what can be learned and how learning can occur. Constructivist theory says that it is the translation of the information that dictates what type of information can be processed and how learning can occur. Piaget would say that an individual cannot process certain types of information at certain ages or stages, but Bruner disagreed, stating that certain aspects of any content or principle can be taught to any child. It will likely be necessary, however, to revisit these as the individual acquires more knowledge and capacity.

The other critical piece of the equation for Bruner (1986, 1990) was the impact of culture on learning, and it is with this element of Piaget's theory that he takes issue. According to Piagetian theory, all individuals pass through exact stages and progress in the same ways regardless of cultural or societal differences. This idea, however, is not supported in empirical research (eg, Renner and others, 1976). It has been shown that "Members of different cultures, because of the specific and unique demands of living in their societies, make sense of their experiences in different ways" (Driscoll, 2001, p. 236), and these differences manifest themselves at variant stages of development. This would seem to indicate, then, that culture and social structure do in fact play a role in cognitive development. Bruner (as cited in Driscoll 2001, p. 236) stated that "Intelligence is to a great extent the internalization of 'tools' provided by a given culture". If a society's tools are different, their categorization structures would also be different, and their representations would be different. Different skills and types of knowledge would be necessary at different ages, and this alone calls into question stage-theorists proposals that the stages of development are invariant.

Bruner believed that the ability to compare new stimuli with existing structures is critical to learning and development. In fact, the inability to interpret information based on existing mental structures would lead to a failure to adapt higher, more sophisticated mental structures and, hence, to fail to develop cognitively. In regard to this comparison, Bruner's theory suggested that children must develop ways to represent recurrent regularities in their environment. This representation system is developed through the building and establishment of progressively more sophisticated and specific mental schemes or structures (Driscoll, 2001). To this end, Bruner (1986) recognized three modes of representation that must be present at all stages of development. These three modes of representation (enactive, iconic, and symbolic) are not necessarily hierarchical, but some learning can only be achieved by passing through each type in a specific developmental order. Enactive representation can only demonstrate the past through appropriate motor experiences. If the enactive mode is the only one being employed, the learner could only demonstrate knowledge by using motor activity to demonstrate thinking. He or she could demonstrate how to do a particular task but could not explain or use any symbolic medium to express knowledge. Iconic representation employs the use of organizational structures, spatial signifiers, or images to represent past experiences. Someone using this type of representation could relate an experience to images or concrete symbols like maps or diagrams. The third mode of representation is symbolic. In this mode, design features that can include remoteness or arbitrariness represent the past. Language is the most common tool used for this type of representation, but the characterizing feature of this type of representation is that the symbols being used do not have to have a concrete correlation to what is being described. The representation goes beyond a concrete connection to the information. It is at this level that analogies could be used to refer to past experiences.

Impacting Classroom Practice

It is important to understand that there is no single set of recommendations as to how to incorporate a constructivistic approach to learning into the classroom. Each of the major theorists has specific recommendations and they do not always agree with each other. The common thread that runs throughout a constructivistic approach is that the development of meaning is more important that the acquisition of a large set of knowledge or skills that are easily forgotten (Black & McClintock, 1995; Moshman, 1982). Two of the most important concepts for applying these theories relate to matching learning experiences to a student's level of readiness and providing for social interaction during the learning process.

Student Readiness

One of the most important considerations to be made in designing instruction from the constructivistic perspective is Dewey's (1944) view that education and schooling should be done for the purpose of preparing the student to live in a democratic society. His advocacy of experiential learning as the basis of the curriculum leads to a set of readiness requirements for those experiences. One of the most important is curiosity or interest in the task to be learned (Dewey, 1998). Students also need to understand the practical applications of the knowledge or skills (Dewey, 1997). A student is therefore ready to learn when the student has the necessary prerequisite experiences that allow him or her to be curious or interested in the learning and to have some understanding about its usefulness.

Piaget's (2001) theory also advocated the importance of the readiness of the student to learn new information. This readiness is based on one of two main factors. Stage theorists hold that the developmental stage or age of the child is the determining factor while interactionalists would argue that it is the child's expertise level (Driscoll, 2001). Regardless of the theory, the result is the same: educators must activate previous experiences, knowledge, and learning strategies in order to effectively present new information in a context that students can readily process.

Although Piaget's framework stated that students begin moving to the formal operational level in early adolescence (Huitt and Hummel, 2003), data provided by Eylon and Linn (1988) and Renner and others (1976) showed that most high school students do not reach the formal operational stage and some are still only moving into the concrete operational. Therefore, instructional activities should be structured in such a way as to mediate between where students are and the cognitive level that schools wish for them to achieve. In addition, from an information processing perspective, students must receive instruction that moves them from the knowledge and comprehension levels of the cognitive taxonomy to the higher levels of evaluation and synthesis (Bloom, Englehart, Furst, Hill, and Krathwohl, 1956). This can be done with concrete objects for students in the concrete operations stage and then connected to abstract concepts to help students move to the formal operations stage.

To this end, educators must develop lessons that build from the concrete level to the formal operational level and that require students to use both lower-level and higher-order thinking. This can be consistently achieved if lessons are constructed in such a way that new information draws from previous experience and knowledge and then builds to higher-level thinking. This framework emphasizes making connection among ideas and activities and requires considerable planning to be successful. For example, if at the end of a lesson on satire, one wanted students to be able to pen their own satires, the structure of the lesson might look something like the following.

First, in order to form some connections to concrete interactions and experiences students have previously had, the teacher might bring in examples of comic strips familiar to students. Before talking about any new information - the satire – the teacher might lead a discussion on what makes the comic strips humorous. The examples would be chosen based on their likeness to satire so that the discussion could lead to another concrete tool, the political cartoon. Even though the comic strip and the political cartoon are very similar, the transition is an easy one to make, and the students should be very comfortable. It is highly likely that every child in a high school classroom has seen some type of comic strip, and, hopefully, most would have even been exposed to political cartoons at some point in a government or history class. Also, Vygotsky (1978) stated that student readiness is an important factor in learning but would emphasize observing how a student works independently and then attempting to teach the student a new concept in order to ascertain the student's "zone of proximal development." All instruction would then take place within this zone.

Once the concrete connection has been established, students must begin making metaphorical connections between the ideas expressed in the cartoons and the intent of the writer. What do you think the writer hoped to gain by creating this cartoon? What might be some other reasons people create cartoons like these? This connection must be made if the students are to understand the motivation behind satire in general and must be understood if students are later to evaluate and create satires based on their new information on the topic.

Bruner (1990) made another case for the importance of readiness. He suggested that children need social and cultural experiences that prepare them to understand the meaningfulness of their actions as well as those of others. Bruner distinguished between behavior, whether mental or physical, and action, which he defines as intentional behavior displayed within a specific cultural setting that includes the reciprocal actions of other participants. Bruner therefore advocates providing children with the kinds of experiences that would allow them to create meaning through their interaction during instructional activities and to assist students in creating that meaning. This then creates the readiness for the next learning experience.

Social Interaction

Dewey's (1944) emphasis on the preparation of children and youth for living in and supporting a democratic society led him to advocate social interaction as a primary source of instruction. Interactions between adults and children are of primary importance as they are the means of the transmission of culture from one generation to the next. Social communications are a critical feature of a democracy and children must be allowed and encouraged to develop their skills in this area. It is the continuous experience of interacting in groups to achieve a practical purpose that provides the foundation on which these skills develop.

Vygotsky's (1978) theory focused on the learner's utilization of the signs and symbols of the culture as a basis for knowing. To the extent that his theory is valid, it is imperative that parents and educators provide students with a worldview that both matches reality and incorporates valid formulas for success in the adult world. A major problem facing educators and parents today is that the world is rapidly changing and a worldview that propelled nations to greatness in the twentieth century needs to be replaced by one that is more appropriate for the world in which children and youth will spend their adult lives (Huitt, 2017a). One of the most important skills is the ability to get along with a wide variety of people of different backgrounds, ethnicities, personalities, etc. Cooperative learning provides a method for addressing this vital aspect of schooling (eg, Holt, 1993). At the same time, cooperative learning provides a strategy whereby students can learn from one another.

There are four major components of successful cooperative learning strategies (Slavin, 1994):

1. There must be cooperative interaction among groups. Merely assigning students to groups does not have an impact on students; they must have an opportunity to work together on a project or learning assignment.
2. Group incentives must be provided. This works as a cohesive factor in getting individual students to operate as a group. This also provides an incentive for the more capable students to assist those less capable in the learning process.
3. There must be individual accountability. If only group incentives are provided, it allows some students to do nothing and still earn the group incentive. By holding each individual responsible for his or her work, the teacher can encourage all students to participate.
4. There must be an equal opportunity for all students to earn high scores and contribute to the group effort. This is often done by calculating gain scores as well as absolute scores. For example, if a student scored above 90 on an exam that would contribute 4 points to the group's score. However, a student with a 60 average could also earn 4 points by scoring 10 points above her average. The group would then receive an incentive for obtaining a specific average gain score.

Two additional components of cooperative learning that have been demonstrated to be successful in some situations are task specialization (eg, Aronson, 2000) and team competition (eg, Slavin, 1994). While these are not absolutely necessary, their inclusion often adds an important element to the overall success of cooperative learning strategies.

Instructional Example

Desetta and Wolin (2000) provided an excellent example of a constructivistic approach to teaching writing skills. Teenagers who had attended a writing workshop were asked to write stories about their lives with the best selected for publication in one of two magazines for youth (see http://www.youthcomm.org/). A review of the organization's mission statement reveals many of the principles of a constructivistic approach to learning such as the need to relate learning directly to the individual's life experiences, to provide a realistic audience where students can demonstrate their learning, and to provide opportunities for social interaction during the learning process (Youth Communication, 2004):

- Teens need a public forum for sharing their experiences, exploring the issues that affect their lives, and identifying their common concerns. Our magazines are designed to provide that forum.
- Teens who read little else are more likely to read and heed stories which accurately reflect their experience and concerns. The stories we publish provide a rich source of information and peer perspectives and influence many teen readers to change their attitudes and behavior.
- For young writers and artists, producing a magazine for their peers is a powerful learning experience. Through a rigorous process that begins by reflecting on their own experiences and place in the world, our students acquire a range of skills and develop the self-awareness necessary to effect change in their lives and in society at large.
- To grow and change, young people need to interact and bond with their peers. We provide an environment in which teens from diverse backgrounds learn to support and respect each other.
- Reading and writing remain the best ways to encourage reflection and discussion and stimulate the imagination. Literate, thoughtful citizens are essential to the survival of a diverse, democratic society.

For the book, Desetta and Wolin selected writing examples that related to one of the major resiliency themes identified by Wolin and Wolin (1993): insight, independence, relationships, initiative, creativity, humor and morality. The stories can be read by youth, some of whom are not regular readers, to encourage them to be resourceful and struggle to solve their own problems. The book also serves as a guide for educators who are looking for ways to make the communication processes of reading and writing more relevant to their students.

Summary

In summary, it is important to realize there are a variety of recommendations from constructivist theorists as to how instruction should be organized and implemented. These range from Dewey (1991) who proposed that educators should not impose a curriculum on students but rather act as a guide or assistant to Vygotsky (1978) who advocated that teachers provide direct learning experiences to the child as needed. Bruner (1986, 1990), in attempting to synthesize the recommendations of constructivist theorists, suggested that educators should go beyond attending to readiness and social interaction, and should require students engage in deep learning and fill in the gaps in their knowledge through exploration and inquiry. This can best be accomplished using a concept he described as a spiral curriculum, where the same topics are addressed at ever increasing levels of abstractness and complexity. On the surface, this recommendation might look quite similar to one advocated in a standard curriculum. The major difference is that new concepts are introduced by tying them to previous learning rather than their being considered as separate and independent. The practical implication of this approach is that fewer concepts are covered, but the ones that are covered are explored in greater depth.

Assessment and Evaluation

There are number of implications for how to assess cognitive development using the perspective of the stage-theory models of Piaget and Bruner. First, these models of development contend that growth occurs in a serial, sequential manner and that developmental stages are biologically driven and correlate to a specific range of ages. If these theories are correct, assessment should take into account what is developmentally appropriate to each stage. With the ever-increasing pressure to raise standards and expect higher-level processing, how students are assessed is of critical importance, and stage-theories create conflict between what can and should be taught. Some researchers argue that it is pointless to present certain types of information to learners at developmentally inappropriate levels and that attempted assessment of higher-level thinking skills is pointless. Orlich (2000) said, "One could argue, as many naïve reformers do, that American students just don't work hard enough…. It will do little good to make 9- and 10-year-olds work harder if their cognitive development has not reached the level that allows them to engage in formal operational thinking" (p. 4).

In contrast, children of all ages show information processing skills at each of the six levels of Bloom et al.'s (1956) cognitive taxonomy, though certainly maturational factors play a role in the complexity of their use. For example, children acquiring their first language exhibit the natural ability to use analogies between the ages of 3 and 4. When a 4-year-old inappropriately uses a phrase like "I goed to my bedroom," she is using application and analogy skills. Although no one has explicitly explained the grammatical rule of creating past tense forms, she has analyzed that one typically uses an –ed suffix to indicate a past action. In addition, she has made the assumption, albeit incorrectly, that, in order to express the past action of going, she would apply the same rule. One could even argue that her production of this new form exhibits synthesis level thinking because she has integrated the rule and created a new speech pattern. At the very least, she has gone through the computational model's first three stages: observation/experience, generalization, and rule formation.

However contradictory these ideas may seem many researchers believe that developmental stages must be considered in assessment. In order to appropriately assess the pre-operational child, activities must be based on the physical environment and focus on hands-on interaction. The egocentric nature of the pre-operational child suggests that activities and assessments should be limited to the personal perspective of the individual, and the pre-operational child will probably be unable to take into account the opinion or perspective of others. Green and Gredler (2002) advocated that, in accordance with Piagetian theory, "the material world should be the starting point for learning because it is both accessible and contains complexities of which children have never dreamed" (p. 3).

Once a child has reached Piaget's third stage, concrete operations, the assessments should be vastly different. At this point in development, students can recognize and evaluate the views of others. This alone adds great dimension to the types of assessments that would be appropriate because students can now be asked to evaluate and critique differing viewpoints and discuss perspectives other than their own. Another attribute of the concrete operational child is that he or she can participate in logical reasoning and use symbolic representations to solve problems using operations, applications, and generalizations. There are limitations to this stage as well. The major limitation of children in the concrete operational stage is the inability to think hypothetically (Driscoll, 2001), and they continue to have difficulty solving problems that are multi-faceted. Understanding and appropriately assessing this developmental stage is critical for educators because "the majority of students in middle schools and high schools are still in the concrete operational stage" (Orlich, 2000, p. 3).

When a learner reaches the formal operational stage, the range of assessments is almost endless. These young individuals can incorporate value judgments and problems of social and cultural scope as part of their processing.

While considering a child's current developmental stage is important in creating appropriate assessments, it is important at all levels to continue to have students use skills and information processing techniques from all previous developmental stages in the acquisition of new information. Assessments at every stage should also be concerned with all previous stages. This is crucial because "if individuals maintain access to preceding stages of cognitive ability, a pattern of seemingly lower level responses may be an integral part of processing new information and developing abilities beyond their current optimal level" (Stanton, 1993, p. 3).

A second group of developmental theories is associated with interactive theories of development, primarily those of Dewey (1991) and Vygotsky (1978) who focused on the development of children in relation to their social interactions. The key element of assessment for this school of thought is that it should be done in a socially context-rich environment. Suizzo (2000) said, "a child's performance level on a given cognitive task will vary according to the level of social support he or she is accorded" (p. 846). This possible variance suggests that for assessments to be valid, they must be conducted in a socially supportive setting because "With modeling or memory prompting by an adult, children will be able to perform at their optimal level, but without that support, they may perform only at their 'functional' level and show no evidence of competence at the higher level" (Suizzo, 2000, p. 846).

A significant advocacy of Dewey's (1944) theory is that assessments and evaluations should be done in the context of practical, real-world applications of knowledge, dispositions, and skills. If possible, learning should result in products that would be recognized as useful by the society. For Dewey, traditional assessments that rely on measuring a student's knowledge or skills outside of the context within which they would be used misrepresent what the student knows as knowing is equated with doing.

Summary and Conclusions

In summary, the work of Dewey, Piaget, Vygotsky, and Bruner present a powerful case that human beings seek meaningful interactions with the environment and construct knowledge of themselves and the world around them through these interactions. Collectively, these theorists provide the foundation for an approach to learning called constructivism (Schunk, 2000). Moshman (1982) stated there are three competing forms of constructivism: exogenous, endogenous, and dialectical. Those subscribing to an exogenous viewpoint are heavily influenced by Vygotsky (1978) who proposed that the individual first adopts social and cultural artifacts and then adapts these to his own knowledge structures. Those more oriented to the endogenous viewpoint are more influenced by Piaget (2001) who proposed that knowledge structures come first and guide one's interaction with the environment. The dialectical position purports that both are correct (as well as incorrect): knowledge and cognitive processing competencies derive from the interaction of the individual and environment. However, they would not subscribe to the position that all knowledge is inextricably tied to specific environments nor are specific structural capacities necessary for learning to occur. Bruner (1986) and Dewey (1998), as well as Bandura (1986), are examples of researchers who would support this perspective.

Brooks and Brooks (2000) stated there are at least four guiding principles for educators and parents who desire to put a constructivistic viewpoint into practice. First, because learning is a search for meaning, learning objectives should be established that connect to issues important to the student. These issues might arise from biology and maturation, one's sociocultural environment, or some combination of both. The precise origin is less important than the fact that the individual perceives some meaning in the learning task. Sometimes educators will need to place students in situations that will create disequilibrium or curiosity in the learner before beginning a learning task. Other times the learner will come to the task with a set of questions that he or she wants answered. In either case, to begin a learning task without establishing that the student perceives a "need to know" what is being taught will produce frustration on the part of both teacher and student and little learning.

A second principle of constructivism is that meaningful learning requires an understanding of wholes as well as parts. To constructivists, the inductive approach advocated by behaviorists whereby pieces of a process are taught separately and then combined into a complete process is the opposite of a sound instructional process (Ertmer & Newby, 1993). A constructivistic process involves having the student engage in the complete process, first in a simplified manner and then in more complex ways (eg, the spiral curriculum process advocated by Bruner, 1977b). For example, students would engage in the process of writing by first writing sentences, then simple paragraphs, then more complex paragraphs, etc. Correct punctuation, parts of speech, spelling and other specifics would be taught as they were needed to complete these holistic tasks.

A third principle discussed by Brooks and Brooks (2000) is that educators must understand students' mental models or representations of the world in order to help them learn and integrate new understandings. To a constructivist, learning is the process of adjusting mental models to better adapt to the world around us. As previously discussed, these models can be impacted by our biology and our experiences. It is not enough to understand these principles in general; we must understand each individual's mental model if we are to successfully guide learning. That requires that we become intimately involved with learners in the teaching/learning process. It also means that we must provide ample opportunities for students to demonstrate and/or express their mental models, preferably in the process of learning rather than in a high-stakes testing environment. This is difficult, if not impossible, to do in a standardized curriculum and implies that teachers must provide different kinds of learning experiences for students based on their mental models.

This then leads to a fourth principle of the constructivistic approach. Assessment, measurement, and evaluation should be a natural part of the learning process rather than an activity completed at the end of the learning process. The focus is on the use of projects and portfolios as means of demonstrating competence rather than tests given at the end of a unit, semester or year. Additionally, students should be involved in making judgments of learning and these judgments should be combined with judgments of teachers or other experts when making decisions about grades. While there are a variety of viewpoints as to the viability of constructivistic methods (Phillips, 2000), there is little doubt that this approach is gaining in popularity (Marlowe & Page, 1998). What is currently needed is more work on both the validity of specific components or principles as well as methods of documentation that can accurately describe the benefits of this approach to student learning. Many principles of learning from the behavioristic and cognitive paradigms have proven quite valuable (Cooper, 1993; Ertmer & Newby, 1993) and should not be completely abandoned in a continuing search for better methods of guiding student learning.

4

Understanding Reality: The Importance of Mental Representations[4]

William G. Huitt

Human beings have an innate ability and desire to understand the world in which they live (Frankl, 1998; Wong, 2012). As they interact and organize their experiences with the world, as described in the previous two chapters, they do so through the construction and use of mental representations (Markham, 1999) or mental models (Johnson-Laird, 1983). These are cognitive representations of the real or imagined world as it supposedly exists; they are a map rather than an exact replica of the territory they represent (Koltko-Rivera, 2004). Because they are merely constructed representations they are not necessarily accurate nor do they include all of the critical features of reality. However, they are very useful in that they serve to highlight important features of experience and facilitate the use of one's intelligence to adapt to, modify, or select environments in which one is embedded (Sternberg, 2003). Without them, experience would be perceived as a chaotic set of stimuli, making it very difficult, if not impossible, to interact with the world.

These mental representations are created at a variety of levels, from general ideas about the nature of reality to specific steps about how to accomplish tasks such as getting ready to go to work, ordering food at a restaurant, or interacting with others in a social situation. Quite often these mental representations are implicit, having been developed within a specific sociocultural context (McClelland, 1995). A variety of terms associated with mental representations—worldviews, paradigms, frameworks, models, schema, and scripts—will be discussed in the following sections.

Worldview

The term worldview is often used as the most encompassing mental representation (DeWitt, 2010) and has been defined as "the set of beliefs about fundamental aspects of Reality that ground and influence all one's perceiving, thinking, knowing, and doing (Funk, 2001). This mental construct includes thoughts related to such issues as "human nature, the meaning and nature of life, and the composition of the universe itself..."

[4] Huitt, W. (2017). *Understanding reality: The importance of mental representations* (revised). Valdosta, GA: Valdosta State University.

(Koltko-Rivera, 2004, p. 3). Indeed, Sire (2010) stated that a well-constructed worldview should address seven questions:

1. What is prime reality – the really real?
2. What is the nature of external reality – the world around us?
3. What is a human being?
4. What happens to a person at death?
5. Why is it possible to know anything at all?
6. How do we know what is right and wrong?
7. What is the meaning of human history?

While it is certainly possible to systematically develop a worldview that explicitly addresses these questions, it is more common that a person's worldview is constructed implicitly within a specific sociocultural experience (Webb, 2009; Wilkens & Sanford, 2009). In fact, Webb (2009) went so far as to state that

> No one comes to adult consciousness without first having passed through a cultural gestation, and no one begins to think by constructing a worldview on his or her own. Every human being is endowed with one from the start by the mere fact of having been born into a milieu where language is spoken and stories are told (p. 5).

As it is likely the case that one's worldview is only partially formed and hidden from conscious thought, those who want to make it more explicit can systematically address Sire's (2010) seven questions. A first step might be to complete an instrument developed by Ai, Kastenmüller, Tice, Wink, Dillon, and Frey (2014) that focuses on one worldview question—what happens to a person after death—as a means of identifying an individual's connection with one of three major cultural orientations: (1) a secular/materialistic worldview which holds no conception of an afterlife; (2) a cosmic-spiritual worldview which proposes that a spiritual soul exists in an abstract, ill-defined space; and (3) a God-centered view which advocates that a spiritual soul inhabits a well-defined "Heaven" under the control of a Creator. It should be noted that this latter view most often includes the concept that both the material and spiritual components of the universe or cosmos are under the control of a Creator.

Using the seven cultural/religious perspectives they explored, Ai et al. (2014) stated that followers of Confucianism and Daoism (Taoism) would likely hold a secular/materialistic worldview, those following Hinduism and Buddhism would likely hold a cosmic-spiritual worldview, and those following one of the Abrahamic religions of Judaism, Christianity, Islam, and Bahá'í would likely hold a God-centered worldview. It seems reasonable that an individual with an atheistic orientation would likely be associated with the secular/materialistic worldview, even though that orientation was not included in the construction of the instrument.

Although the secular/materialistic, cosmic-spiritual, and God-centered worldviews can be identified, there is extensive diversity within each of these categories. For example, Barrett, Kurian, and Johnson (2001) discussed how some countries, such as Australia, Canada, the United States, and South Korea have a wide variety of religions with which people identify; this multi-religious sociocultural experience can impact how people think about each of Sire's (2010) questions. On the other hand, one might expect less variety in countries such as Egypt, with a population of 90% Sunni Muslim, or Iran, with over 90% Shia Muslim (Central Intelligence Agency, 2013). Additionally, in countries with a higher standard of living, a higher percentage of people identify as secular/materialistic and/or cosmic-spiritual (McCleary & Barro, 2006). However, in countries with a higher level of education, more people report converting to a different religion rather than changing their God-centered worldview (Barro, Hwang, & McCleary, 2010). Therefore, worldviews must be interpreted within a specific sociocultural milieu (Hofstede, 2001) and even within a specific generation (Strauss & Howe, 1997). Nevertheless, these broad categories can be useful in delineating important similarities and differences about how people think, value, and behave.

The modern and post-modern examination of the relationship between science and religion (eg, Clayton, 2012; Polkinghorne, 2011) has implications for a discussion of worldviews. Kluge (2003) suggested that a review of the four causes identified by Aristotle can contribute to this component of the concept of worldviews. He defined these four causes as

a. Material – substance from which something is derived; made out of (bowl from clay).
b. Formal – form from which something is derived; sample to be an exemplar (dress from pattern).
c. Efficient – producer or initiator of change; produces (carpenter makes table).
d. Final – the end result for which something will be used; purpose, teleos (driving a nail is the cause of a hammer)

Kluge stated that within this differentiation among causal explanations lays the foundation for the unification of science and religion in a single, coherent scheme. Science restricts itself to the study of the material and efficient causes of all phenomena whereas religion studies formal and final causes. In this sense, they complement, that is, complete, each other and, thereby, help us make complete sense of the phenomenal world (p. 31).

The investigation of worldview is made somewhat more complex as the current formulation of the secular/materialistic worldview that dominates scientific investigation is undergoing revision because of recent discoveries in the relationships among brain, mind, and behavior in living organisms (Nagel, 2012). Nagel's reasoning is that science has yet to explain the existence of conscious minds and when it does that will most likely change the current version of the secular/material worldview. Another challenge to the current secular/materialistic paradigm comes from researchers who study near-death experiences (Long & Perry, 2011; Moody, 2001). While the evidence is anecdotal, the sheer volume of the data and the congruence of findings across researchers and cultures suggests the need for serious consideration of some of the basic tenets of at least a cosmic-spiritual worldview. It may be that in the near future, science provides the pathway to an integration of what now appear to be quite separate worldviews.

The possibility of using science and religion as two fundamental, complementary sources of information presents additional opportunities for scholarly interaction. For example, while each started from a different religious tradition, Bertrand (2007), Gosling (2011), Guessoum (2010), Harrison (2010), and Phelps (2009) all advocated a rapprochement between science and religion. Additionally, Peterson and Seligman (2004) took religious teachings into account when they developed their descriptions of personal strengths. The boundaries among sources of information used to generate worldviews as well as the worldviews themselves are being constantly deliberated and deserve additional consideration.

Maxwell (2016) proposed an emerging worldview, that he labeled as integrative, that combines the modern or mental/rational orientation that forms the foundation for a secular/materialistic worldview with earlier worldviews described as archaic, magical, and mythical (using the nomenclature developed by Gebser). He proposed that this emerging worldview identifies the partial truths from each of the previous worldviews that can be demonstrated as correct using both the methods of philosophy and science. More importantly Maxwell hypothesized there is a teleological aspect of the cosmos that is pulling all of its components to greater novelty and consciousness. This integrates the qualitative dimensions of form and final causation with the quantitative material and efficient causation that is the foundation of modern science and technology. Maxwell concluded that the basic principle of the physics of entropic disorder must be synthesized with a syntropic teleological principle of an impulse towards novelty, consciousness, and order. Finally, he proposed that the great world's religions anticipated this integrative worldview in their scriptures.

As one's worldview is the most comprehensive mental representation and as it impacts all other representations, it is worthy of study. This brief overview indicates there are many aspects that need further consideration and that everyone needs to put effort into identifying one's own worldview as many aspects are likely unconscious for most people.

Paradigms

Cutting across these major worldviews are different paradigms that offer more precise statements about how reality works (Huitt, Chapter 1, this volume; Baker, 1992); that is, paradigms can be thought of as "a subset of a shared worldview" (DeWitt, 2010, p. 352). Kuhn (1970) described the importance of paradigms for scientific investigation as they define:

1. What phenomena are to be investigated?
2. What are the parameters of the questions that can be asked?
3. How should the questions be structured and organized?
4. What types of data should be collected?
5. What methods should be used to collect data?
6. How will the data be organized and interpreted?
7. What legitimate theories can be developed from the data and interpretations?

Four paradigms currently used in science include a mechanistic/reductionistic paradigm based on Newtonian physics; an existential/phenomenological paradigm based on the philosophers Kierkegaard, Heidegger, and Husserl; an organismic/holistic paradigm based on Darwinian biology and systems theory; and a process paradigm based on the philosopher Alfred North Whitehead (Crowell, 2015; Smith, 2013; Ulanowicz, 2009). These categories are quite similar to the world hypotheses presented by Pepper (1942, 1967). See Table 4-1 for an overview of basic principles associated with each paradigm.

In general, the mechanistic/reductionistic paradigm assumes interchangeability and a linear relationship among parts, and a deterministic relationship among parts that is consistent at multiple levels. The existential/phenomenological paradigm focuses on the qualitative and subjective perceptions of an individual's concrete experiences. The organismic/holistic paradigm focuses on the dynamic changes of a whole system or organism as it interacts with its environment. A basic assumption is that the whole emerges from the interaction of parts at a lower level and cannot be reduced to the parts on which it is based. The process paradigm assumes that the dynamic relationships among parts are more important than the temporary stable structures that might define the whole at any given point in time.

Table 4-1. Identification of Worldview Paradigms

Paradigm	Worldviews		
	Secular/ Materialistic	**Cosmic-Spiritual**	**God-centered**
Mechanistic	A focus on parts and the functioning of a machine-like organization. If parts and mechanisms are known, prediction and control are possible. It is important to study cause/effect factors one at a time. Physics and chemistry are the foundation-al sciences for investigating how the world works. Empirical observations should be the basis for making decisions.	Interaction of material and spiritual operate in deterministic manner. If parts and mechanisms of material and spiritual are known, prediction and control are possible. A spiritual practice will have a positive impact on one's life. Regular meditation will be beneficial to uplifting one's spirit. One's spiritual practice is the most significant impact on one's happiness.	God's actions determine reality; reality is deterministic emanations from God. If God's laws are known, prediction is possible. Asking God for assistance is always beneficial. Following God's laws is the best way to live a good life. Whatever happens in the universe is determined through God's will.

Table 4-1. Identification of Worldview Paradigms (continued)

Paradigm	Worldviews		
	Secular/ Materialistic	Cosmic-Spiritual	God-centered
Existential/ Phenomenological	Phenomenological explanations are critical Subjective experience is reality Human needs and understanding are the foundation for investigating reality Asking people about their lived experiences provides the best information about how the world works. Context makes it difficult, if not impossible, to generalize scientific findings.	Human beings are spiritual beings engaged in a material experience. There are many different paths to spiritual development. It is important to select a spiritual practice that feels comfortable. Spirituality is uniquely experienced by each individual. There is ample scientific evidence to support human spiritual existence.	Human prayers are answered. Human beings have the potential to understand God's methods. God directly interacts with human beings.

Table 4-1. Identification of Worldview Paradigms (continued)

Paradigm	Worldviews		
	Secular/Materialistic	**Cosmic-Spiritual**	**God-centered**
Organismic/ Systems	Biology and living systems are the foundational sciences for understanding reality. Parts cannot be understood completely in isolation from the whole. Investigating organism/ecology interaction is critical for understanding development. Emergence and self-organization are critical principles to understand reality.	Connect to spiritual reality. The process of spiritual development can be explained. There are both unique and universal aspects of human spiritual development. Spiritual potential is actualized in much the same was as biological potential. Human spiritual development is a naturally occurring process.	God created the context within which material and spiritual evolution occurs. Everything in the universe is connected and emanates from God. God has created the potential for the establishment of observed patterns of material and spiritual aspects of reality. God establishes laws; human beings have choice as to whether to follow.

Table 4-1. Identification of Worldview Paradigms (continued)

Paradigm	Worldviews		
	Secular/ Materialistic	**Cosmic-Spiritual**	**God-centered**
Process	Reality is comprised of coordinated collections of occurrences, all of which are relational in nature. Processes are arranged holarchically. Becoming (coordinated change in processes over time) and being (processes occurring at one time) are equally relevant.	Everything (physical and non-physical) is connected to everything else in vast web or network. There is an essential unity between the concrete, physical aspect of reality and the abstract, non-physical aspect of reality. The material and spiritual are connected via processes.	God is sum of all past actual events and future possible events. God actively draws nature towards greater organization and complexity. Panentheism – An impersonal God is in all events and relationships which, in turn, comprise God.

Each of these paradigms can be seen in guiding research and theory development in the behavioral and social sciences. For example, the mechanistic/reductionistic paradigm is seen in psychology in the research of Skinner (1953), in sociology in the work of Coleman (1969, 1988), in anthropology in the work of Malinowski (2014), and in economics in the work of Samuelson and Nordhaus (2009). While this paradigm is considered the dominant scientific paradigm today (Ulanowicz, 2009), significant work has been done within other paradigms as well. The existential/phenomenological paradigm is well represented—in psychology, Rogers (2003) is an excellent exemplar as are Schutz (1967) in sociology, and Sartre (1993) in anthropology. The organismic/systems paradigm is seen in psychology through the work of Piaget (1952, 2000); other representatives include Bowen (1994) in sociology, Bateson (1987) in anthropology, and Daly and Farley (2011) in economics. While the process paradigm has yet to gain much acceptance in the sciences (see Hibberd, 2014, as an excellent example), there is a large body of work related to process theology (Mesle, 1993). An analysis of paradigms is especially useful in an analysis of approaches to education and schooling (Huitt, 2011b).

Combining concepts derived from the worldview and paradigm orientations provides the opportunity for more detailed analyses (see Table 4-1). It is hypothesized that each of the paradigms is seen in each of the worldviews. However, as most people have not developed their thoughts on worldviews and paradigms through explicit analysis, it is likely that research will find that actual categories are not as clearly differentiated as this analysis might project (Bencivenga, 2012; Kosko, 1993).

Framework

While a worldview provides an overall picture of reality and a paradigm provides some detail about how the worldview should be investigated, a theoretical or conceptual framework provides a more focused presentation of the factors to be studied, the relationship among factors, and the importance or strength among those factors (Maxwell, 2013). Though the terms theoretical framework and conceptual framework are often used interchangeably, they are overlapping, but different, terms. A theoretical framework is connected to one specific theory that provides an explanation of the relationship among factors that one is investigating. Any research or anecdotes are selected for review because they fit within a particular theory. As such, it will be connected to one of the paradigms described above. Skinner's (1953) operant conditioning theory, Freud's psychoanalytic theory (Gay, 1989), Roger's (2003) humanistic theory, and Piaget's (1952, 2000) cognitive development theory are exemplars that have provided a variety of theoretical frameworks. On the other hand, a conceptual framework is more based on personal experience and research support and the construction of important factors and their relationships will likely cross theoretical (and therefore, paradigm) boundaries. The World Health Organization's (2010) framework for action on the social determinants of health and McCurry and Hunter Revell's (2015) partner's in family caregiving framework are two exemplars of conceptual frameworks.

As an example of how worldview, paradigm, and framework might interact, two people may adopt a secular/materialistic worldview and mechanistic paradigm, and even a behavioral theory of human behavior, but have different conceptual understandings of exactly what factors to observe and why (Graham, 2015). Or two people may adopt a cosmic-spiritual worldview and existential paradigm and have similar conceptual understandings even though these are derived from different theories (Webster, 2004). The Brilliant Star framework is an example of how a theoretical and conceptual approach might be combined (Huitt, Chapter 1, this volume). It was developed from an organismic/systems theoretical paradigm approach (Huitt, 2012a) while the specific domains or categories included in the framework were identified from research. Diener and his colleagues (Diener, 2012; Diener & Dierner, 2008; Diener, Suh, Lucas, & Smith, 1999) as well as Seligman and his colleagues (Peterson & Seligman, 2004; Seligman, 2011; Seligman, Railton, Baumeister, & Sripada, 2013) review much of the same literature but organize the concepts differently because they start from different theoretical perspectives. Diener and his colleagues developed measures of positive and negative emotions, positive thinking, and psychological wellbeing while Seligman and his colleagues focus on five factors (PERMA: Positive emotions, Engagement, Relationships, Meaning, and Achievement). Much work remains in the development of frameworks for each of the worldview/paradigms shown in Table 4-1.

Model

A model is an even more specific mental construction. The Merriam-Webster Online Dictionary (Model, 2012) defined a model as

> usually small copy of something; a particular type or version of a product (such as a car or computer); a set of ideas and numbers that describe the past, present, or future state of something (such as an economy or a business).

Within the behavioral and social sciences, whereas a framework describes the concepts and principles that would be included in a depiction of reality, a model provides a more explicit statement about factors or variables to be included, methods of measuring those, and precise statements about the relationships among those variables. A model is specific enough to allow for the development of simulations so that the performance of the model can be analyzed.

Models are especially important in the study of complex adaptive systems (which includes any systems involving human beings) because the realities involving humans are so complex that they are difficult to study in real time (Miller & Page, 2007). Running simulations (for which a model is required) has become a viable alternative to the traditional statistical investigations of systems (Hegyi & Garamszegi, 2011). This is especially important as many of the traditional statistical procedures used in the behavioral and social sciences are built on assumptions from a mechanistic paradigm that are limited when it comes to studying phenomena from an organismic/systems paradigm (Ulanowicz, 2009, Yackinous, 2015).

A wide variety of examples of the use of models are available in the behavioral and social sciences. For example, Savery and Duffy (1996) developed a model of instruction focused on problem-based learning that was derived from a constructivist paradigm which, in turn, was developed from Piagetian and Vygotskyan theories of learning and development. Bures and Tucnik (2014) used systems theory in their development of agent-based economic models. Garamszegi (2011) described how information theory was the foundation for multiple explorations of behavioral ecology models. In each of these instances (and many more could be cited), the development of theory within a worldview and paradigm led to the development of a framework within which models could be developed and explored as to their efficacy in making predictions of future performance. These were then investigated using actual or simulated behavior.

Schema and Scripts

The terms schema and scripts are mental constructions that people use daily as they think about themselves and their interactions with the world around them. Use of the term schema (plural, schemata) has a long history, dating to Kant's (1993) use of the term in the late eighteenth century. It has been part of the terminology in the study of memory and information processing for at least eight decades (Bartlett, 1995) and has received considerable attention in the investigation of reading (Bransford, 1979, 1985) and the development of network and connectionist theories of memory (Rumelhart, 1980). From this perspective, a schema is a generalized, somewhat abstract, organization of knowledge that provides a structure for receiving and organizing new information. For example, in the process of reading, the text is understood in the context of the schema one brings to the reading process. If one reads about cold or snow, but has lived in the tropics all one's life, those terms do not have the same meaning as someone who has grown up in an area where cold and snow are annual occurrences. Or if one has lived exclusively in a rural environment, comprehending stories about living in an urban environment is a difficult process. An important principle of schema theory is that the schema must be activated in order to be utilized properly; therefore, the process of activation is as important as the process of construction (Bransford, 1985).

Piaget (2000) used the term schema (and, alternately, scheme) somewhat differently. From his perspective as a genetic epistemologist who studied children's thinking extensively, a schema is an organized pattern of thought that allows an individual to interact with, and adapt to, the demands of the environment. More specifically, whereas investigators using information processing theory consider a schema as a set of propositions (Corcoran, 2012), for Piaget (1952) a schema is "a cohesive, repeatable action sequence possessing component actions that are tightly interconnected and governed by a core meaning" (p. 240). For Piaget, the ability to meet the requirements of the environment using these cognitive structures is central to cognitive development. Whenever that does not occur (ie, when disequilibrium or imbalance occurs), the individual will first change the stimuli extracted from the environment (called assimilation) or, if that does not work, change the cognitive structures (labeled accommodation) (Lutz & Huitt, Chapter 3, this volume). This activity of adapting to the environment adds a dimension not found in a traditional information processing approach.

The last mental representation to be discussed, scripts, are similar to schemas; in fact, script theory was derived from schema theory by Tompkins (1979, 1987) as part of his theory on affect and emotions. A script is a simpler version of a schema with the additional condition that repetitive events are expected or steps are followed within a specific context called a scene or vignette (Abelson, 1981; Schank & Abelson, 1977). The specific expectations or action patterns of a script are activated when triggered by thoughts and emotions generated in specific contexts. As an indication of how widespread is research on the use of scripts, just a few of the topics include emotion regulation (McRae, Misra, Prasad, Pereira, & Gross, 2012), monetary wealth (Klontz, Saay, Sullivan, & Canale, 2015), personal transformation (Erskine, 2010), projections of machoism (Ihanus, 2014), social anxiety (Lau, Wang, Fung, & Namikoshi, 2014), and weight loss (Hartmann-Boyce, Jebb, Fletcher, & Aveyard, 2015).

An important component of a script is that it allows one to automate certain behaviors by simply following a narrative of how a story should unfold. To the extent that the script makes it more efficient to achieve a goal, it is considered as positive. However, to the extent that it thwarts goal achievement, especially a feeling of happiness or wellbeing, it is considered as negative. The challenge in the latter case is that once a script is activated, it is very difficult to alter because it is often implicitly developed and, therefore, unconscious (Schank & Abelson, 1977; Tompkins, 1979, 1987).

Altering Mental Representations

Even though, historically, sociocultural worldviews and paradigms can take decades, even centuries to change (DeWitt, 2010; Van Belle, 2013), it is possible for change to happen much more quickly. As the brain demonstrates a remarkable amount of plasticity (Schwartz & Begley, 2002), individuals can modify mental representations once they are developed. However, it generally requires more energy and effort than constructing correct representations of reality during childhood and adolescence

(Gardner, 2004). Once developed, mental representations take on a life of their own and resist alteration. An excellent example is Einstein's refusal to adopt quantum theory even though he was one of its originators (Bohr, 1949). Einstein could never accept the probabilistic version of the universe that is foundational to quantum theory.

DeWitt (2010) suggested that mental representations change when they are no longer held to be true in the sense that the facts, concepts, and principles on which they are based are not coherent (ie, there are unresolvable conflicts in the relationships among the parts) or they do not correspond to reality as it is believed to exist. In his theory of cognitive dissonance, Festinger (1957, 1962) showed that when there is conflict among thoughts or between thoughts and behavior, friction occurs and the individual is motivated to take action to reduce that conflict. This is especially true when the thoughts or behavior involve personal experience (Salti, El Karoui, Maillet, & Naccache, 2014). Because mental representations, more often than not, are developed out of personal experience embedded within a specific society or culture, they are implicit and unconscious. Nevertheless, they have a powerful impact on how people live their lives, reflect on past events, and plan for the future. This indicates that an important component of the transformation of mental representations is to make implicit representations more explicit so that conflicts can be identified.

Schlitz, Vieten, and Amorok (2008) proposed that changing one's view of reality as described by a worldview and/or paradigm is most readily accomplished through a process of transformation in consciousness or perception of reality, including one's own reality. More specifically, "It includes self-awareness, your relationships to your environment, the people in your life, and your worldview or model of reality" (Schlitz et al., p. 16). This change in consciousness can be quick through a transformative experience or occur more slowly through diligent, mindful practice. For example, many individuals having a near-death experience report an immediate alteration in how they view bodily death which alters their perceptions of reality (Long & Perry, 2011; Moody, 2001). Alternatively, individuals who engage in mindfulness exercises experience heightened self-awareness and corresponding positive changes in self-regulated behavior and wellbeing that occur gradually over time (Brown & Ryan, 2003).

With respect to frameworks, theoretical frameworks can be very difficult to change unless underlying theory changes. As is the case with worldviews and paradigms, a well-established theory can take decades or more to change. However, conceptual frameworks are more readily changed as they are explicit conceptualizations based on understandings derived from empirical analysis and personal experience. For example, a comparison of the frameworks for identifying important knowledge, attitudes, and skills needed for success in the twenty-first century (eg, Partnership for 21st Century Skills,

2009; Wagner, 2012) could provide opportunities for modification as different viewpoints are analyzed and as new data becomes available that might change important factors and their relationships.

Models are also more readily changed when used in simulations; empirical validation is required to continue to use a model. An excellent example is work done by RTI International as they use a variety of models to simulate the relationships among economic factors and environmental policies (https://www.rti.org/impact/economic-analyses-environmental-regulations). They regularly publish their findings and seek peer review of their models. The models are constantly changed based on experience and feedback.

In general, schema are constructed based on one's experiences in specific situations. This highlights the importance of the relationship among environment, behavior, and mental representations (a basic principle of Bandura's (1986) social cognitive theory). The reciprocal influence of these three factors has been studied extensively over the past several decades in such areas as personality (Bandura, 1999), learning and teaching (Zimmerman, 1989), leadership (Ibarra, 2015), and cultural differences (Bandura, 2002). A basic principle is that change in mental representations best occurs through reflections on personal experience in a variety of contexts, but all three elements must be present if mental representations are to be transformed.

Finally, while changing scripts (patterns of thought and behavior in specific contexts) is difficult, recent work in the area of prospection supported the recognition that scripts can be modified. That is, positive scripts can be strengthened and negative scripts can be weakened so as to allow one to better achieve goals and higher levels of wellbeing (Seligman et al., 2013). A key concept for script transformation is that when mentally activating a future script, it must feel real, providing validation for the concept of triune consciousness—the idea that thoughts, feelings, and intentions are naturally integrated in conscious thought (Tallon, 1997). This idea of bringing unconscious mental representations into consciousness in order to change them is an area requiring further exploration (Christian, Miles, Hoi Kei Fung, Best, & Macrae, 2013).

In summary, mental representations can be modified and transformed. Many of the methods and techniques for doing so can be categorized as a form of metacognition (ie, strategic knowledge, knowledge of cognitive tasks, and self-knowledge; Krathwohl, 2002). Some key principles for explicitly modifying mental representations include having a wide variety of experiences while engaging in a wide variety of contexts and then reflecting on those in a way that implicit mental representations are made explicit. It is also beneficial to change one's language and manner of speaking as one engages in different environments. Coordinating and sustaining these components is no easy task, but the possibility for doing so should provide hope as human beings learn to cope with an environment that is rapidly changing.

Summary and Conclusion

This brief overview of different types and levels of mental representations cannot do justice to this burgeoning field of cognitive psychology. Entire books have been written on the topic, with no single text able to cover the whole field. However, it is important that people begin to think about how the mind works as it is widely recognized that the world is rapidly changing, moving in ways never before experienced by humanity (Brynjolfsson, & McAfee, 2011; Diamandis & Kotler, 2012, 2015), and this is producing significant discomfort (Rushkoff, 2014). Add to this the fact that America (and likely the entire developed world) is in the middle of a winter season of economic downturn (Strauss & Howe, 1997), and the need for accurate mental representations to guide individual decisions and social policy has never been greater.

Just considering these two, somewhat conflicting, sociocultural challenges supports the importance for having a set of mental representations that provide a correct map of reality. On the one hand, there are major changes that are accelerating exponentially as a result of forces such as globalization, increased digitalization, population growth, and climate change while at the same time there is an economic downturn influenced by demographic changes (Dent, 2014) and the increase in global debt relative to economic activity (Duncan, 2012). It is easy to become paralyzed when confronted with these complexities and simply rely on incremental adaptation. However, rapid sociocultural and technological change requires that time is spent on stating and analyzing mental representations to insure they can be used to attain one's goals. Otherwise, one could engage in behaviors that, on the surface seem reasonable, but are not ultimately successful because they did not accurately depict reality.

As Piaget (1952, 2000) demonstrated, people are more likely to change their perceptions of reality and use already developed schemata to adapt to the world (assimilation) than create new, more accurate, schemata (accommodation) that can be used to adapt to the demands of this new environment. Wagner (2012) proposed that developing innovators who can create new approaches to all aspects of modern life is an extremely high priority. I propose that engaging in systematic analysis of created mental representations can begin the process of achieving that objective. A good place to start is to systematically teach the skills associated with meta-cognition (Bartsch & Estes, 1996). Making the implicit representations explicit and providing the opportunity to modify those will provide learners with the skills necessary to be systematically creative.

It is not easy to develop a coherent worldview and paradigm that corresponds to reality, but it is necessary if one wants to be something different than a dead fish floating down the stream of the twenty-first century. As Wallerstein (2000) pointed out, humanity is in a sociocultural transition that will result in a completely different manner of living for children and youth living today. Increasing the likelihood that individuals and their offspring can build a more positive living experience should be reason enough to put time and effort into examining and modifying one's mental representations. Not doing so means that humanity will simply continue to use mental representations that have yet to produce high levels of life satisfaction and wellbeing for all of humanity and increase, rather than decrease, anxiety and low levels of happiness and wellbeing.

5

Overview of the Affective Domain[5]

Amy M. Brett, Melissa L. Smith, & William G. Huitt

Life in America at the dawning of the 21st century exhibits a complex tapestry of distressful social and cultural problems, including public school and church shootings, racial and ethnic tensions, apathy and cynicism in the political sphere, grave challenges to the family unit, and disturbing levels of youth violence, drug abuse, alcoholism, and teen pregnancy. All of these problems have an important feature in common – they are heavily influenced and, in some cases, dominated by the power of human emotions (Goleman, 1995; Greenspan, 1997; LeDoux, 1996). Most psychologists agree that the study of emotion and the affective domain is one of the most perplexing topics in the field of psychology (Plutchik, 2001). However, even the somewhat confusing picture produced to date has led researchers to conclude that one's emotional awareness and ability to manage emotions may be even more important than IQ in determining success and contentment throughout all areas of life (Gardner, 1995; Sternberg, Wagner, Williams, & Horvath, 1995).

A variety of definitions have been provided for emotion and its relation to the affective domain. Aristotle gave one of the earliest when he described emotions as "all those feelings that so change [people] as to affect their judgments, and that are also attended by pain or pleasure" (Jenkins, Oatley & Stein, 1998; p. 7). However, Plutchik (2001) estimated that more than 90 different definitions of emotion were proposed throughout the twentieth century. One of the most well-known was provided by Goleman (1995) who defined emotion as, "a feeling and its distinctive thoughts, psychological and biological states, and range of propensities to act" (p. 289).

The affective domain refers to emotions as well as their outward expression. As with the concept of emotion, descriptions of the affective domain are rather vague, lacking a universal, operationalized definition. While emotion is at the core of the affective domain, it spreads quickly from there. This is because emotion is often seen as involving three subcomponents: feeling, cognition, and behavior. Feeling is the physiological sensation one experiences. Cognition is the subjective thoughts that accompany the sensation. Behavior, which might be facial display, body positioning, or a variety of other actions, is related to both feelings and

---

[5] Brett, A., Smith, M., & Huitt, W. (2003). Overview of the affective domain. *Educational Psychology Interactive*. Valdosta, GA: Valdosta State University.

accompanying cognitions. Thus, the affective domain encompasses physiological, cognitive, and behavioral processes related to emotion. It also encompasses our awareness or discernment of our and other's emotions, the ability to connect our emotions to those of others, the display of emotion, and the ability to manage or regulate one's emotions.

While the affective domain has been a subject of research for centuries, there are three individuals who are typically considered the founding fathers of research on emotions: Charles Darwin (1998), William James (1884), and Sigmund Freud (1960). Darwin founded his concept of ethology with observations of emotional expression in natural settings and connected them to human evolution. James emphasized physiological changes in the body and showed that emotions are involved in monitoring our bodies. Freud offered the method of listening to what people said about their emotional lives and people may need to discuss their emotions with others in order to be understood. More recently the concept of appraisal has become an important influence on research in the affective domain.

Theories of Emotion

As with any concept, researchers and theorists have differing views as to the function and importance of the affective domain. Some see it as a regulatory system whereas others see it as an activation system. Some see emotion as a precipitating event whereas others see it as a resulting event. This section will discuss some of the current theories and models.

In the Communicative Theory (Oatley & Johnson-Laird, 1995), emotions were viewed as caused by conscious or unconscious cognitive evaluations. Each evaluation produces a signal that is transmitted through multiple processors of cognitive architecture to produce a basic emotion. This signal functions to control organization of the brain in order to ready the mechanisms of action and bodily resources, to direct attention, to set up biases of cognitive processing, and to make the issue caused the emotions salient in consciousness. The phenomenological experience of the signal is a distinctive feeling, or emotion (eg, happiness, sadness, anger, etc.). Thus, in essence, emotions are seen as managing goals.

The Feedback Theory (Parkinson & Manstead, 1992) assumed that emotions arise as a consequence of a bodily reaction, rather than cognitive appraisals of a presenting situation. This theory dates to William James (1884), who drew attention to the fact bodily responses, including facial, postural, motor, and autonomic changes, are central aspects to our idea of experiencing emotion. Our relationship with an object evoking the emotion is expressed through the body (eg, turn away from unpleasant sights, approach pleasant sights). Thus, part of experiencing emotion is to feel oneself expressing a physical attitude toward an object. Furthermore, James proposed that feelings are a result, rather than cause of emotional behavior (eg, we are happy because we smile).

A similar theory, the Discrete Emotion Theory (Fogel, Nwokah, Dedo, Messinger, Dickson, Matusov, and Holt, 1992) suggested that emotions organize and motivate action such that a discrete emotion can be defined as a particular set of neural processes that lead to a specific expression and a corresponding specific feeling. The emotion program is believed to be phylogenetically adapted with respect to the basic function of survival. This theory breaks down each emotion, indicating that patterns of neural stimulation cause associated changes in feeling, and are associated with distinct sets of facial, vocal, respiratory, skin, and muscle responses. These theorists focus primarily on the face in expression of emotion, and believe emotional development is controlled by maturation of the central nervous system (CNS), and that the organism must learn rules that modify and modulate expression. An example of research that supports this position had participants hold a pencil between their teeth for a period of time, a task that uses the facial muscles involved with smiling. Results showed that the participants reported feeling happy.

According to the Functionalist Model (Campos, Mumme, Kermoian, & Campos, 1994), emotion is "the attempt by the person to establish, maintain, change, or terminate the relation between the person and the environment on matters of significance to the person" (p. 285). This model is closely aligned with Lazarus' (1991) Relational Model discussed in more detail below. Emotional development begins with a core set of CNS emotions programs, which are defined with respect to basic functional or survival relationships between the individual and environment and involve tendencies of the entire body. Emotions are part of innate routines for social communication and serve to initiate and maintain contact with others.

Lastly, the Social-Constructivist Model of Emotion (Jenkins et al., 1998), similar to the functionalist model, also views emotional experience as embedded in the conditions that justify it. This perspective emphasizes that we learn to give meaning to our experiences through our social exposure and cognitive developmental capacities. Thus, one's emotional experience is contingent upon specific factors, which contribute to our learning what it means to feel something and then do something about it.

Appraisal and Viability

Magda Arnold introduced the concept of appraisal into emotions research around 1954 (Jenkins et al., 1998). Building on the ideas of Aristotle and St. Thomas Aquinas, Arnold developed the view that emotions are judgments of the relation of objects and events to goals. Since then, there has been a host of research on the issue of appraisal in emotion research.

In describing his Relational Model of emotion, Lazarus (1991) wrote that appraisal involves an appreciation of a particular harm or benefit in the relationship with the environment and carries with it implications for well-being, action, and coping. Simply put, emotions can be viewed as reactions to events perceived as significant by the individual. However, a reaction must include recognition that the event carries significance for one's personal well-being in order to count as emotional. Thus, one's reaction is generated as a consequence of evaluation of the situation and the individual's relation to it.

Lazarus (1991) identified three aspects of appraisal: primary, secondary, and reappraisal. Primary appraisal concerns whether something of relevance to one's well-being has occurred (ie, does the person have a personal stake in an encounter). Secondary appraisal concerns coping options (ie, whether a given action may prevent, ameliorate, or produce harm or benefit). Finally, all encounters with the environment are in a continual state of change. Primary and secondary appraisals are continually changing, and feedback from the environment and one's actions constitute new information that must be evaluated. Lazarus termed this third process of evaluation reappraisal. Therefore, in reappraisal, the original encounter is reevaluated in terms of the success or failure of implemented coping strategies.

Lazarus (1991) elaborated on both primary and secondary appraisal, breaking each down into three subcomponents. Primary appraisal includes goal relevance, goal congruence or incongruence, and type of ego-involvement. Goal relevance refers to whether or not one cares about or has a personal stake in an encounter. Goal congruence or incongruence refers to the extent to which a transaction foils or facilitates one's personal goals. Type of ego-involvement refers to aspects of one's ego-identity.

Secondary appraisal includes the subcomponents blame or credit, coping potential, and future expectations. Blame and credit deal with the process of determining who is accountable or responsible for an emotion resulting from an encounter. Coping potential refers to an evaluation of one's ability to manage the demands of an encounter. Future expectancy deals with whether things are likely to change psychologically for the better or worse (ie, become more or less goal congruent).

In the ongoing story of each human life, inside the brain of every individual, there are complex systems that are making an appraisal, moment by moment, both unconsciously and consciously, of whether or not there are threats or opportunities confronting the individual (Damasio, 1999). The inputs to the appraisal mechanism are both internal and external. Internal threats and opportunities can originate from the organs and physiology of the body or from processes occurring within the mind. External threats and opportunities can originate in the physical environment or in the realm of social interaction. However, the affective domain's importance does not end with appraisal. Once a situation is appraised, one must make a decision as to what course of action should be taken to respond to the situation. Thus, cognitive processing and accompanying behavior are seen as embedded with affective domain.

Mechanisms of emotion. In the appraisal/viability theory of human emotions, the affective system in every person is simultaneously the home of the most sublime human experiences and darkest impulses. To achieve the goal of enhancing personal viability, the affective system integrates the highest and most advanced regions of the human brain with ancient parts that evolved at a time when reptiles ruled the earth. The appraisal mechanism is operating constantly and utilizes diverse processes (LeDoux, 1996). Depending on the situation an individual is facing, to make the viability determination, the appraisal mechanism uses either rapid stimulus or pattern recognition processing (Goleman, 1995; LeDoux, 1996; Niehoff, 1999) or complex, personal and cultural rules that can be labeled as emotional schemas (Greenberg, Rice, & Elliott, 1993; Nathanson, 1992; Omdahl, 1995; Ortney, Clore, & Collins, 1988). These two aspects of the affective appraisal system interact constantly and are actually identified with different parts of the brain (Carter, 1998; LeDoux, 1996). The rapid stimulus or pattern recognition aspect of the appraisal mechanism depends upon the amygdala, the hypothalamus, and the brain stem, brain structures active at an exclusively unconscious level and the home of emotional memory, the mind-body link, and the fight-or-flight mechanism (Carter, 1998; Damasio, 1999; LeDoux, 1996; Rossi, 1993). The portion of the appraisal mechanism processing emotional schemas does so in the prefrontal cortex of the brain, which is the home of conscious emotions, rational planning, and decision-making.

A threat situation is often experienced with a concurrent and negative emotion such as fear, anger, hostility, envy, disliking, hatred, guilt, shame, sadness, pain, or surprise. Depending on the situation, the intensity level and duration of the emotion can vary (LeDoux, 1996; Ekman and Davidson, 1994; Ortney et al., 1988). Perceptions of threats originate from either internal or external sources. When they are perceived, either consciously or unconsciously, the general human response is avoidance.

Threats are the opposite of opportunities. An opportunity situation is often experienced with a concurrent, positive emotion such as love, joy, liking, enthusiasm, interest, affection, flow, pleasure, satisfaction, confidence, or surprise. As with threats, the intensity level for opportunities may be very mild or overwhelmingly strong and the duration may be long-lasting or very brief. Perceptions of opportunities also originate from either internal or external sources. When they are perceived, either consciously or unconsciously, the general human response is to approach.

Combined states, such as fear and courage, indicate the push and pull of multiple emotions going on simultaneously. Conflicts between perceived threats and opportunities arise when attraction and repulsion are experienced simultaneously, as in when a much-loved parent does something hurtful to a child or when achieving some long-desired goal requires finding the inner courage with which to vanquish an overwhelming fear. Regardless of the situation, in general, if it is perceived as enhancing viability, an individual tends to move towards it, either physically or psychologically. Likewise, if a situation is perceived as a threat to well-being, an individual tends to move away from it, all the while internally experiencing the complex fabric of concurrent, matching, and sometimes conscious human emotions.

The Relationship of the Affective Domain to Other Domains

The affective domain provides a unique arena of human behavior, involving complex information processing, fundamentally unlike, but intimately related to, all the other domains of human development. As stated above, the affective domain combines body sensation of feelings, a perception of positive or negative well-being, the activation of related emotions, and an arousal for action, such that people tend to approach opportunities which they perceive as helping their viability and to avoid dangers which undermine it (Carney and Jordan, 1976; Damasio, 1999). And while development in the affective domain has been related to such disparate topics as moral character development (Hoffman, 2000), motivation (Gollwitzer & Bargh, 1996), performance appraisal (Hirt, Levine, McDonald, & Melton, 1997), reasoning and problem solving (Isen, 1993; Murray, Sujan, Hirt, & Sujan, 1990; Russ, 1999), self-regulation (Aspinwall, 1998), and spiritual development (Hay & Nye, 1998), it is probably most closely associated with social behavior (Nathanson, 1992; Pinker, 1997). The affective domain is seen as contributing to social interactions through a concept often referred to as social-emotional learning (SEL) skills. SEL can be defined as "the process through which people learn to recognize and manage emotions, care about others, make good decisions, behave ethically and responsibly, develop positive relationships, and avoid negative behavior" (Fredericks, 2003).

Emotions and related SEL skills are important in social interactions because emotional knowledge and expression function to guide social interactions, both directly and indirectly. Denham and Weissberg (2003) reported that emotion knowledge yields not only information about emotional expressions and experience in self and others, but also about events in the environment. Additionally, emotion can play a role in guiding goal-directed behavior, as well as providing social information to others, thereby affecting their behavior as well (Denham, 1986; Denham & Couchoud, 1991; Denham, McKinley, Couchoud, & Holt, 1990; Strayer, 1980). There is accumulating evidence that children who understand and are able to balance their positive and negative emotions tend to be more prosocially responsive to their peers, are rated as more likable by their peers, and are rated as more socially skilled by teachers.

Emotional competence is also useful in determining motives and states in others. Human beings are also biologically hardwired to consciously and unconsciously answer the viability question as it applies to other people, especially those who are close. People notice the physical signs of distress in others. Expressive facial movements, tone of voice, and body language are all observed, though often unconsciously. Individuals listen for signs of anger or happiness, sadness or joy, in their conversations with others. Just as people are perceiving and inferring the emotional states of others, so also does each person either broadcast or conceal his or her own conscious or unconscious affective states through the same channels of communication (Ekman and Davidson, 1994; Pinker, 1997). Thus, the viability question becomes elaborated in the social arena as, "How well are others doing right now," and self-reflexively as "How well do others think I'm doing right now?" This, in turn, can also affect how others respond in a non-ending, recursive manner.

When the answer to the viability question is negative, an emotional state such as repulsion motivates an individual to either move away from a threat or to make it move away from them. When the answer to the viability question is positive, an emotional state such as acceptance motivates an individual to move towards that which is helping him to feel good or to find ways to bring it closer. In either case, the issue is distance (interpreted either physically, psychologically, or socially, depending on context). No doubt human ancestors long ago learned that viability would be increased if threats prompted an increase in distance and opportunities prompted a decrease.

Summary

Basic emotions have evolved to deal with fundamental life tasks. In the continuous, complex, and moment by moment flow of daily existence, the affective system enables human beings to answer the most fundamental question of survival: "How well am doing I right now?" In the ongoing story of each human life, inside the brain of every individual, there are complex systems which are making an appraisal, moment by moment, both unconsciously and consciously, of whether or not there are threats or opportunities confronting the individual (Damasio, 1999). The inputs to the appraisal mechanism are both internal and external. Internal threats and opportunities can originate from the organs and physiology of the body or from processes occurring within the mind. External threats and opportunities can originate in the physical environment or in the realm of social interaction. Taken together, the viability criterion, the appraisal mechanisms, the dimensions of affective expression, and the approach/avoidance response tendencies are the essence of the affective domain.

Developmental Issues

Child development is typically viewed through an organizational, biological lens. As such, development is seen as going through specific stages, with transitions to new stages being influenced by, or contingent upon accomplishments attained in earlier stages. Just as children's language or mental capabilities develop as a result of maturation and experience, so too does children's affective development. Affective development is often seen as progressing in the same manner, and as being impacted by both internal (biological predispositions, within-child abilities) and external (physical and social environment) influences. Additionally, there are stable differences among children that impact development in the affective domain. For example, a small percentage of children are highly active while another small percentage are slow to warm up (Kagan, 1994). Additionally, Plomin (1990) presented research indicating a genetic basis for empathy by showing that identical twins are more alike in their empathetic responses than fraternal twins.

Greenspan and Greenspan (1985) identified six emotional milestones that infants and young children go through as they develop. The first milestone is to feel peaceful despite the inundation on the newborn's senses by stimulation and to reach out to that stimulation during the first few weeks after birth. In the second stage, the infant takes an interest in the human world, as well as the sights and sounds that encompass it. The third milestone is met when the infant realizes that the world is cause-and-effect. For example, this might be demonstrated when a baby's movement produces a corresponding movement in a mobile. The infant shows his or her preparedness for the fourth stage by taking the "emotional dialogue with the world one step further and learning to connect small units of feeling and social behavior into large, complicated, orchestrated patterns" (Greenspan & Greenspan, 1985, p. 6). During the fifth stage, children are able to hold an image (their mother, for example) in their minds even when that object, person, etc. is not present. In the sixth and final milestone, young children are better able to understand the ideas of "pleasure and dependency, curiosity, assertiveness, anger, self-discipline or setting their own limits, even empathy and love" (Greenspan & Greenspan, 1985, p. 6).

While children may be able to understand these concepts in early childhood, they have a narrow vocabulary for communicating their feelings (Denham, 1998; Vernon, 1999). During this stage of life, children have a hard time comprehending that it is possible to feel many different emotions concurrently about a particular event, even though they do understand that it is possible to have different feelings at different times. By the end of the preschool period, children begin to respond to other people's emotions, though they usually concentrate on the most evident characteristics of an emotional experience, such as being angry or happy.

Young children are typically amateurs in utilizing the affective domain. In everyday interactions, children are constantly attempting to understand both their own and others' behavior. Emotions play a significant role in this understanding by conveying crucial interpersonal information that can guide interaction. In social interactions, the child uses information conveyed through the behavior, emotions, perceived intentions, and the likely effect of others' behavior to help guide their own response or behavior. A child who is able to regulate emotions is more likely to be able to utilize a problem-solving process that allows him or her to generate and focus on adaptive goals that will build and enhance a relationship (eg, avoid conflict, not hurt others' feelings). Those who are less skilled may focus on more external and self-serving goals, which lead them to react in less adaptive ways that do not promote successful interaction (eg, revenge, spite).

The development SEL skills are thought to be of particular importance during the preschool period, when children are learning to interact with their peers. Denham and Weissberg (2003) reported that children who enter kindergarten with positive SEL profiles also develop positive attitudes about school, successfully adjust to the new experiences they encounter in the school setting and demonstrate good grades and achievement. Conversely, they reported that children with specific SEL deficits are more likely to experience difficulties in social relationships. There is accumulating evidence that SEL components contribute to overall success in interacting with others. Children who understand and are able to balance their positive and negative emotions tend to be more prosocially responsive to their peers, are rated as more likable by their peers, and are rated as more socially skilled by teachers (Denham, 1986; Denham & Couchoud, 1991; Denham et al., 1990; Strayer, 1980).

During middle childhood, children are capable of more complex emotionality (eg, guilt, shame, and pride), and recognize that it is possible to experience different emotions simultaneously. Children of this age are also more cognizant of other people's emotions and can camouflage their feelings to prevent upsetting someone else. Finally, those in middle childhood may begin to experience school or peer-related anxiety.

Impacting the Affective Domain

Although it would be extravagant to hypothesize that schooling by itself has the power to solve all these problems, it is difficult to imagine any effective long-term solutions that exclude it. Well-conceived, systematically designed learning experiences, utilizing well-chosen techniques, technology, and media, can lead to significant gains in resolving important social and personal issues. Additionally, research shows that child do better academically when schools attend to emotional and social development (Gewertz, 2003).

Unfortunately, despite the potential, educational efforts aimed at these problems have not always been successful (Kilpatrick, 1992; Sonnier, 1989). In fact, some attempts to utilize the affective domain, such as the so-called "affective education," "self-esteem" and "values clarification" approaches, have actually caused harm, leading to increases in the incidence of illicit drug usage, alcoholism, teen pregnancy, and sexually transmitted diseases among youths exposed to these approaches (Kilpatrick, 1992).

This failure of schooling to effectively address the affective domain is in sharp contrast to the successes achieved in other arenas. For example, the cognitive-behavioral, the person-centered, and other schools of psychotherapy have devised increasingly effective ways to help people recover from specific emotional problems (Corey, 1996; Martin, 1999; McMullin, 1986). Likewise, marketers have built a multi-billion dollar global advertising industry by learning how to systematically and effectively evoke those human emotions that prompt consumers to buy their products (Ries and Trout, 1993; Schoell and Guiltman, 1992). Whereas specialists in these disciplines have articulated concepts of the affective domain suited to the purposes of their specific disciplines, those in schooling have mostly avoided it (Krathwohl, Bloom, and Masia, 1964; Martin and Briggs, 1986).

Difficulty in the field of schooling with the affective domain may be a result of several influences. First, one must consider the cognitive-structuralist and deontological theories that underlie much of the schooling system. In these theories, moral education and emotions are typically seen as conflicting concepts. Proponents of these theories suggested that the central aim of moral education is a desirable state of mind (Roebben, 1995), an autonomous and free-thinking person (Smeyers, 1992). Moral learning is considered to be a matter of developing innate intellectual capacities, and not one of supplying missing emotions and motives (Spiecker, 1988, p. 44). The involvement of emotion is often considered detrimental to the attainment of these qualities. It is believed that every emotion has a specific paradigmatic scenario, which, once learned, is applied to situations which are relevantly similar to the paradigm scenario in which it originated (Roebben, 1995). In this view, emotions can act as a barrier, which disturbs the ongoing process of moral reasoning, and works against critical thinking, leading to a potentially biased or flawed view of one's environment.

One the other hand, Hoffman (2000) proposed that empathy is foundational to moral development. His research showed that empathy, the connecting of one's feelings and emotions to another's, can be discerned in infants and develops in readily identifiable stages. He proposed that justice, a core value in Kohlberg's (1984) theory of moral development, has two components, care and equity, and that empathy provides a foundation for both. Hoffman, therefore, advocated that adults encourage children to share the feelings of those he or she has mistreated as essential for moral development. Peil (2000) went even further, hypothesizing that emotions are an individual's moral compass, evolutionarily developed to guide one's self-regulating and adaptive behavior.

A second potential influence in the dearth of emotionally-focused school programs may lie in the fact that, to date, researchers have developed no comprehensive conception of usefulness of emotion for purposes of academic learning and instruction (Goleman, 1995; Price, 1998; Salovy & Sluyter, 1997; Sonnier, 1989). In past affective education approaches, young people were taught to treat all social values as equally acceptable; they were led to believe that there are no right answers in ethical situations; they were encouraged to invent their own value systems without reference to accepted standards or the needs of society at large; they were encouraged to get in-touch with their feelings regardless of what those feelings might be; and they were convinced to claim self-esteem through self-talk even while test scores and other measures of academic achievement were falling (Kilpatrick, 1992). Yet, educators could not continue in this direction once longitudinal studies became available which indicated an increase of youth violence, teen pregnancy, alcoholism, and drug abuse among students exposed to these affective education approaches.

This brings schooling into the horns of a dilemma. Any approach to learning in the affective domain that smacks of indoctrination, that is too touchy-feely, or that promotes self-esteem at the expense of accomplishment has been rejected and will continue to be rejected by parents and educators. But the problems that are tearing at the fabric of society and shattering individual lives are almost certainly unsolvable without recourse to education and training involving the affective domain. Somehow, new steps must be taken towards a revised view of the affective domain as it applies to the field of education.

Fostering Emotional Functioning

Denham (1998) proposed three categories of emotional functioning: emotional understanding, emotional expression, and emotional regulation and management. In terms of emotional understanding, she stated that students need to be able to discern one's own emotional states as well as those of others and properly use emotional vocabulary.

In terms of emotional expression, Denham (1998) included the use of gestures to display emotional messages nonverbally, demonstrating empathy by connecting one's emotions to those of others, displaying both self-conscious as well as complex social emotions, and realizing there are differences between experiencing an emotion and how one acts.

The category of emotional regulation and management includes coping with both pleasurable and aversive/distressing emotions as well as the regulation of those situations that elicit them. This category also includes the ability to use this experience to strategically organize the experience in terms of setting goals and learning to motivate oneself and others.

As in the other domains, parents play a crucial role in a child's development before he or she begins school. One of the most important ways to get children off to a good start in this domain is through a secure attachment relationship with caring adults (Denham and Weissberg, 2003). Consistent and sensitive caregiving, particularly during the first years of life, can foster such attachment. Early experiences and interactions with caregivers form the basis from which children develop their view of the world. Positive and meaningful interactions can lead children to develop a positive world view (ie, The world is a safe place; Others are predictable and readable; I am important and worthy of care.). Research has shown that secure relationships with caregivers predict not only concurrent emotional development, but also later ability to relate to peers (Howes, 1997). In contrast, emotional insecurity can cause a child to be resistant to learning about emotions and more apt to experience aversive emotions.

Modeling of appropriate behavior is also an important influence in children's learning. Research on the impact of vicarious learning has led us to accept the implications of the old saying "Do as I say, not as I do". Children constantly observe the behavior of others and often incorporate this learning into their own behavior. Children use such information to determine what is and is not acceptable or appropriate, and in which contexts. Thus, through their emotional displays, adults are sending a powerful message. Therefore, adults who model adaptive and appropriate emotional responses can help guide their child's learning of emotional regulation.

Positive guidance by parents and early caregivers is a third way to foster effective and appropriate emotional and related social skills. From a very young age, children are learning what it means to be part of a group. Children need assistance in learning appropriate rules for behavior in group and social settings. Young children learn best when they have clear rules and limits set for them, and when they receive both direct and indirect guidance (Denham and Weissberg, 2003). Direct guidance refers to concise rules as to appropriate behavior. Indirect guidance refers to providing an environment that is conducive to positive emotion and behavior. In providing positive guidance, there are three specific socialization techniques considered as crucial: teaching about emotions and behaviors, modeling positive emotional expression and behaviors, and demonstrating accepting and helpful reactions to children's emotions and behaviors.

Positive guidance also includes reaction to children's emotions. Contingent reactions to child behavior by adults should be linked to the child's emotional development (Denham & Weissberg, 2003). This includes behavioral and/or emotional reinforcement or discouragement of specific behaviors and emotional responses (Tomkins, 1991). The dismissing or ignoring of emotions may be perceived by children as punishment for showing emotion, which can cause confusion and interfere with the development of adaptive and effective SEL skills. However, positive reactions by adults (tolerance, comfort, validation, empathy) can convey the message that emotions are not only manageable, but also even useful (Gottman, Katz, & Hooven 1997).

Coaching about emotions can be done through discussing children's feelings, thoughts, and behaviors. Central to this is providing reasons or explanations for events, including correction of inappropriate behavior. For example, alerting children to potential consequences of behaviors can be effective (ie, Johnny may not want to play with you anymore if you do not share.) Additionally, helping children to consider the viewpoint of others is also important (ie, That hurt Johnny's feelings. Look at how sad he looks.) Adults who demonstrate an awareness of emotions and discuss them with their children can assist in development of self-management skills and help in formulating other-awareness (for developing empathy).

Thus, the four main components for contributing to the development in the affective domain for young children are secure attachment, modeling, positive guidance and coaching. There are specific techniques that parents and early caregivers can use for facilitating learning in this domain. These techniques include: distracting the child and assisting him/her in choosing a more appropriate substitute behavior, ignoring inappropriate behavior (when there is not threat of harm to self or others), telling the child what to do (as opposed to what not to do), and stating expectations clearly and in a manner suitable to the child's cognitive level. Such techniques can help guide children toward appropriate emotional and behavioral responses.

While it is known that individuals raised in a loving, caring environment have been found to have a substantially lower incidence of major illness and disease in mid-adulthood (Russek & Schwartz, 1997), educators can also have a significant impact on affective development. The same approaches laid out for parents and early caregivers can be applied by teachers: attachment, modeling, guidance, and coaching. As mentioned previously, development of a positive, consistent, and emotionally supportive relationship with important adults is crucial to development in the affective domain. As such, children who have not experienced secure attachments with other caregivers may seek such attachment with teachers. Therefore, teachers can also utilize techniques to foster a secure attachment relationship with students.

Teachers can also provide positive behavior management and guidance to students. For example, Bergin and Bergin (1999) advocated the use of persistent persuasion to increase compliance and help instruct and guide students toward appropriate behavior and emotional displays. Teachers can also utilize inductive guidance techniques that focus on the consequences of the child's behaviors on others, including the feelings of others.

Finally, teachers can help children develop better knowledge and understanding of their own and others' emotions by utilizing emotion language. Children, especially young children, may not have much experience in using language to express their feelings. Being able to attach a label to emotions and feelings can bring them to consciousness, which, in turn, assists in emotional regulation (Denham and Weissberg, 2003).

Assessment and Measurement

There are three primary areas of development in the affective domain that need to be addressed: emotional understanding (including discernment of emotions in both self and others), emotional behavior (including demonstrating empathy), and emotional self-regulation and management (including warming oneself up or cooling oneself down).

Emotional Understanding

According to Saarni (1999), for emotional discernment in self to occur, the child must be cognizant that he or she is the one feeling something. It has also been proposed that for one to be emotionally self-aware, one must be able to recognize that emotionally-related bodily sensations are inherently different from other bodily sensations, such as feeling hungry.

Researchers have found that children at a relatively young age are able to discern the emotions of others (Saarni, 1999). According to Saarni (1999, p. 109), the following characteristics must be present in children to encompass sophisticated insight into others' emotions: "they need to be able to decode the usual meanings of emotional facial expressions; they need to understand common situational elicitors of emotion; they need to realize that others have minds, intentions, beliefs, or what has otherwise been referred to as 'inner states;' they need to take into account unique information about the other that might qualify or make comprehensible a nonstereotypical emotional response or a response that differs from how oneself would feel in the same situation; and they need to be able to apply emotion labels to emotional experience so that they can verbally communicate with others about their feelings."

Gottman (1997) suggested that parents can help their children discern emotions by providing labels for different feelings that their children might have. When children know the uncomfortable feelings, they are having has a name, it seems more manageable and more like a part of everyday life. This process of labeling emotions for children can also help in the child's development of empathy. For example, if a parent notices a child is feeling down and says, "You're feeling sad, aren't you," the child then feels both understood by the empathic statement and comforted by knowing that there is a word to describe how he or she is feeling.

Emotional Expression

Denham (1998) discussed items from the Hawaii Early Learning Profile (HELP; Parks, 1992), which includes lists of behaviors considered appropriate development of children from birth to three years of age. Denham (1998, p. 210) specifically listed items from several different subscales of the HELP pertaining to the expression of emotions and feelings that are developmentally appropriate for children aged 18 to 36 months, including (Parks, 1992, pp. 280-321):

- Expresses affection
- Shows jealousy at attention given to others, especially other family members
- Shows a wide variety of emotions (eg, fear, anger, sympathy, modesty, guilt, joy)
- Feels easily frustrated
- Attempts to comfort others in distress
- Tantrums peak
- Dramatizes feelings using a doll
- Fatigues easily
- May develop sudden fears, especially of large animals
- Demonstrates extreme emotional shifts and paradoxical responses

Parents and educators can also use the aforementioned developmentally appropriate behaviors to appraise where their children are compared to what is considered average for that particular age group.

Emotional Regulation

While school psychologists may conduct most assessments on children with special needs, parents and early childhood educators can conduct their own informal assessments on children to see where they are developmentally.

There are formal tests used by psychologists that judge emotional discernment by showing children pictures of faces with different expressions then asking the child what emotion that particular face is displaying. Parents and teachers can easily replicate this but must remember that young children will most likely not answer correctly all the time, particularly when shown more complex emotions, such as guilt and shame.

It is typically the school psychologist who has been assigned the responsibility of assessing emotional regulation in school-aged children. Historically, the approach exemplified in federal guidelines, and thus most commonly used in assessment, has been a deficit-focused approach (Buckley, Sorino, and Saarni, 2003). However, the tides do seem to be turning, and strength-based assessment is beginning to receive more attention in literature. Yet there remains a great need for additional psychometric attention in the area of emotional assessment.

In the following section, we will outline several existing measures that can be used in assessing some of the skills associated with emotional competence. However, it is important to note that these measures were not designed to measure emotional competence, and thus have not been validated for this purpose. However, by attending to aspects of the measure that address specific emotional competence skills, results of such assessment instruments can be useful in overall assessment.

Emotion Regulation Checklist (ERC; Shields and Cicchetti, 1997). The ERC is a survey measuring affective behaviors in school-aged children. It contains two subscales considered as useful in assessment of emotional competence: Lability/Negativity and Emotion Regulation. The Lability/Negativity subscale examines mood swings, angry reactivity, affective intensity, and dysregulated positive emotions. The Emotion Regulation subscale captures emotional understanding, empathy, and equanimity. Internal consistency for these two subscales was .96 for Lability/Negativity and .83 for Emotion Regulation (Buckley et al., 2003).

Emotion Regulation Q-Sort (Shields and Cicchetti, 1997). The Q-Sort is related to the ERC, both of which are directly applicable to the measurement of emotional regulation. The Q-Sort measures reactivity, empathy, and socially appropriate expressions. Though administration is somewhat cumbersome, it is suitable for a wide age range, and is useful for longitudinal research.

The Behavior Emotion Rating Scale (BERS; Epstein and Sharma, 1998). The BERS is a survey measuring behavioral and emotional strengths of children ages five to 18. It provides an overall strength quotient, and addresses five dimensions. The dimensions most relevant to emotional competence are the interpersonal, intrapersonal, and affective strength domains. The BERS has strong content validity, moderate to high reliability, consistency among raters, stability overtime, and adequate convergent validity with several measures (Epstein, Harniss, Pearson, & Ryser, 1999).

The Multifactor Emotional Intelligence Scale - Short Version (MEIS; Mayer, Salovey, and Caruso, 2008). The MEIS was used to measure emotional intelligence prior to implementation and again after the conclusion of the Connecting program. The MEIS consists of eight tasks that are divided into components representing three levels of emotional reasoning ability: perceiving, understanding, and regulating emotions. The scale yields four scores: and overall score reflecting general emotional intelligence and a score for each of the three emotional reasoning abilities. The short version of the MEIS consists of 258 items, and is scored by an expert scoring method, in which each response is compared with an expert answer, or one that MEIS experts believe is the most accurate assessment of a particular ability.

Mayer-Salovey-Caruso Emotional Intelligence Test (MSCEI; Mayer, Salovey, and Caruso, 2008). The MSCEIT is an extension of the MEIS. This test also an ability test designed to measure aspects of emotional intelligence. However, it was designed for use with individuals 17 years old and up. The MSCEIT measures the following four branches of emotional intelligence:

1. Identifying emotions - the ability to recognize how you and those around you are feeling. The examinee is presented with faces and situations and are asked to pick out the extent to which certain feelings are present.
2. Using emotions - the ability to generate an emotion, and then reason with this emotion. Examinees are asked to imagine specific events that trigger particular feelings - while feeling each feeling, the examinee is asked to indicate the extent to which the feeling is for instance light or dark, warm or cold.
3. Understanding emotions - the ability to understand complex emotions and emotional 'chains', how emotions transition from one stage to another. Examinees are assessed through definitions of emotions and also through presenting specific situations.
4. Managing emotions - the ability which allows you to manage emotions in yourself and others. Examinees are presented with a range of scenarios and are asked to determine the effectiveness of taking particular actions.

The Social Skills Rating Scale (SSRS; Gresham and Elliott, 1990). The SSRS has two forms, one for use with children grades three through six, and another for use with children grades seven through 12. The measure yields scores on three scales, Social Skills, Problem Behaviors, and Academic Competence. However, it is questions within the Social Skills scale that appear to capture several emotional competencies, such as capacity for empathetic responses, affective expression, and emotional regulation and coping (Buckley et al., 2003).

Existing research has indicated the importance of emotional competence in multiple areas of functioning, including academics. Furthermore, research continues to provide support for the role of systemic, ongoing social-emotional education in optimal cognitive and behavioral development. Thus, it is certainly arguable that additional research attention to the area of emotion and emotional competence is warranted. Nevertheless, empirical studies investigating emotional competency programs are rather limited. Furthermore, intervention programs typically emphasize broad social competencies rather than emotional competencies.

Summary and Conclusions

The promotion of emotional and related social competence is essential for the development of informed, responsible, and caring individuals (Richardson, 2000). Competence in recognizing and managing feelings and social relationships are crucial for success across settings, including home, school, and the workplace. Furthermore, emotional competence is considered a central predictor of later mental health and well-being (Denham, Blair, DeMulder, Levitas, Sawyer, Auerbach-Major, & Queenan, 2003). Young people who lack social and emotional competence tend to have more discipline problems and are frequently unsuccessful in their academic pursuits (Richardson, 2000). Similarly, poorly managed emotions and emotional reactions can lead to behavior problems as well as create physiological conditions that inhibit cognitive processes involved learning and potentially increase the risk of certain diseases later in life (McCraty, Atkinson, Tomasino, Goelitz, & Mayrovitz, 1999).

Goleman's (1995) theory of emotional intelligence rests on the notion that self-awareness and the ability to control how we respond to our own moods or feelings are keys to achieving success. By gaining knowledge of one's own emotional state and associated labels, an individual acquires the ability to handle his or her responses in a productive manner, which, in turn, allows the person to motivate oneself, to solve problems, to make moral decisions, and to interact successfully with others. Thus, through the acquisition of this knowledge and ability, other skills can be further developed. Goleman argued that the ability to delay gratification is a skill representative of self-awareness, which he refers to as metamood, and that exhibiting such awareness is a sign of emotional intelligence and potential success (Kaschub, 2002).

If this brief description of the affective domain is valid, what does it mean to speak of educating the emotions? Is the affective domain unteachable, as some have alleged, or is the affective domain within the potential scope of education, as others have asserted? As recent findings in psychology, neuroscience, and other disciplines are beginning to demonstrate, the answer to both of these questions is "yes" (Goleman, 1995; Keller, 1987; Krathwohl et al., 1964; Martin and Briggs, 1986; Price, 1998; Salovy and Sluyter, 1997).

Humans appear to be biologically predisposed to rapidly react to certain things, such as large looming animals with big teeth, slithering creatures on the ground, sharp objects flying through the air, extremely sour tastes, foul odors, and sudden booming sounds (Pinker, 1997). No doubt the viability of humanity's distant ancestors was greatly enhanced by obeying such inborn instructions. Little or no thought was involved, training was not needed, and precision was not required (Goleman, 1995). The creature moving on the grass might not be a poisonous snake, but there is no cost in avoiding it. Errors made on the side of caution generally produced positive viability results.

Pattern recognition involves making approximate and rapid judgments that are able to generate sudden feelings, though they are frequently unconscious. These are then instantly processed in terms of emotional memories of past experiences. In general, these responses are engaged rapidly, the memories formed are likely to become permanent, and the response tendencies are not easily modified by new learning (LeDoux, 1996).

On the other hand, rules of culture (D'Andrade, 1995), emotional schemas (Greenberg et al. 1993; Nathanson, 1992; Ortney et al., 1988), and environmental situations are highly variable. No genetic pattern could code for them rapidly enough to be passed on to subsequent generations. Even if they could, such genetic instructions would not add to viability because conditions will probably be changed by the time the next generation is born.

Human beings are known for a relatively long childhood period (Pinker, 1997) and a remarkable plasticity of the brain (that is, the power to learn new responses from life experiences; Bruer, 1997; Driscoll, 2001). Together, these provide a context in which a growing human being can learn the appropriate approach/avoidance responses to life's infinitely diverse situations. Thus, although the smile response itself appears to be universal (Ekman and Rosenberg, 1997; Darwin, 1889/1998), the young child learns gradually whose smiles are to be trusted and whose are not (Greenspan, 1997). Children learn to be shy or outgoing depending upon whether the smile is coming from an adult never seen before or from a parent, sibling, or other close relative. Perhaps never explained in exact words, but unceasingly coded as emotional memories, as he matures, the child unfailingly learns through direct experience and parental training what situations bring benefits and which ones bring harm (Greenspan, 1997; LeDoux, 1996).

Some emotional learning is astoundingly fast, permanent, and precise (LeDoux, 1996). For instance, anyone who has accidentally received a shock while working with an electrical appliance or been the victim of a mugging never has to repeat the experience. Once is enough. The brain takes care of that - right down to the cellular level. An emotional memory is created instantly, complete with context, arousal, thoughts, and feelings. The entire experience is deeply encoded due to a brain process at the cellular level known as long term potentiation (LTP) (Carter, 1998). Thus, some emotional learning comes about through rapid stimulus and response conditioning and once learned cannot be easily extinguished.

Other emotional learning is slow, accumulative, and ill-structured in nature. As noted, since there are many variations along the friend/stranger continuum, the human mind must form over many experiences a general image of whom to approach and whom to avoid. Similarly, values, such as citizenship, morality, good-character, motivation to learn, and self-esteem must be embedded in a near infinite diversity of situations and examples before a complete picture emerges. In this arena, conscious thought becomes the ally of emotional memories (Greenspan, 1997; LeDoux, 1996). Personal emotional schemas are built up over time and combined with society's rules which are also gradually acquired. As they become blended together in each individual, one's unique attitudes, beliefs and personality take shape.

The unconscious, rapid emotional systems and the conscious, slower ones interact constantly, generally in a manner similar to a car's accelerator and brake. For instance, an individual walking on a city street hears a loud cracking sound at night and ducks down instantaneously, without any conscious planning. Then, the mind of the individual, finding itself suddenly hugging the pavement and observing a car with a smoking tail pipe speeding away, quickly analyzes the situation and realizes that the loud sound was not gunfire, but rather an engine backfiring. The individual breathes a sigh of relief because a perceived danger has been avoided. Likewise, when a friend says words that are hurtful, the first instinct is to feel anger, but in a few seconds most people are able to realize it was just an unfortunate choice of words and are able to mute their anger.

In both of these examples, the rapid emotional systems are engaged instantly while the conscious mind rushes to catch up (LeDoux, 1996; Zajonc, 1984). The conscious mind makes a more precise judgment of whether or not the sudden reaction is justified. If not, it acts upon the body and mind like a brake, quieting the internal alarm and controlling impulses to react (Goleman, 1995). On the other hand, the conscious faculties may identify the danger as real and thus further prime the automatic fight-or-flight systems to keep going, like an accelerator (LeDoux, 1996). The point is that, although the affective system is biased towards preserving safety with its rapid stimulus or pattern recognition and approximate reactions, both the conscious and the unconscious systems work together, interacting literally on a second-by-second basis to modulate the appraisal and adjust the individual's responses based on the viability criterion.

In sum, then, affective experience is largely unconscious and partly conscious. Some emotional learning is extremely rapid and based on single experiences, occurring primarily through priming or stimulus-response conditioning. However, other incidences of it is slower and cumulative, resulting from the gradual acquisition of emotional memories and the elaboration of complex emotional schemas, interacting with other cognitive schemas as well. Some of the learning is quite precise, as in "Don't put your finger in the electric outlet," while other experiences are ill-structured, as in learning whom to approach as a friend and whom to avoid as a stranger. All aspects of the affective domain are organized around the principle of maintaining viability and well-being, generating an arousal to approach that which is perceived as positive to personal well-being and to avoid that which is perceived as negative to well-being.

It is clear that there is much of the affective domain that may be susceptible to training, particularly involving learning outcomes which aim to enhance the effectiveness of the appraisal mechanisms or which promote positive interaction between intelligent thought processing and affective reactions. Some obvious examples include: a) Learning to discern the emotional states of others as expressed in their words, their tone of voice, their body language, and in the deeds they do; b) Learning ways of expressing emotions that improve the amount and quality of mutual understanding between oneself and others; and c) Learning to coherently apply one's affective experience, intellectual abilities and coping mechanisms in order to enhance viability, to resolve approach/avoidance conflicts, to generate moral behaviors, and to solve problems in the social or personal context. Each of these learning outcomes, and many others, when understood in terms of the viability framework described herein, can be susceptible to a teaching and learning process. Not only can specific component skills be identified in the case of each learning outcome, but, within the viability framework, the goal and purpose of the teaching and learning experience can be more easily articulated and understood. This sets the stage for constructive analysis of specific learning outcomes and the initiation of instructional design activities within the affective domain.

Empathy is a core skill that benefits virtually all human relations, whether professional or personal. Think about any significant relationship – parenting, teaching, counseling, friendships, business relations and so on – and one finds empathy at the foundation. Speaking of the empathy that counselors must develop, Martin (1999) defined empathy as follows:

> Empathy is "communicated understanding of the other person's intended message, especially the experiential part." …It is not enough to

> understand what the person said; you must hear what he or she meant to say, the intended message. It is not enough to understand, even deeply; you must communicate that understanding somehow. It is absolutely essential that the other person feel understood–that the understanding be perceived... The part of the intended message that will be critical is the emotional or experiential part of the message... You will be listening for what your client is trying to say, and one way you will be doing this is to hear the feelings implicit in his or her message" (p. 11).

According to Goleman (1995), those who lack empathy have a serious shortfall in emotional intelligence. He stated that this lack of empathy can be found in "criminal psychopaths, rapists, and child molesters" (p. 96) and points out that people rarely express to others in words what they are feeling. Rather, we must read and understand nonverbal cues to understand another's emotions. Psychologists have found that babies only a few months old will start crying when they observe another child crying. Furthermore, young children's empathic capabilities appear to be influenced by their observations of how people react to the distress of others.

Crucial to empathy is that it involves understanding and communication "as if" from the other person's point of view, taking the other person's perspective, while at the same time not losing sight of the fact that the feelings and thoughts in fact belong to the other person. Empathy is multidimensional in the sense that the understanding of the other person may be either cognitive or affective or both. Empathy may go beyond understanding of the other person to include emotional responsiveness or resonance such that an individual comes to experience the same or compatible emotions of the other person. Thus, along with understanding the situation as if from the other person's perspective, an aspect of empathy may include feeling distress when confronted with the distress of others, or it may include pity in response to another's sorrow and loss. Empathy is thus a complex process that involves both cognitive and affective abilities such as listening to key ideas and discerning core emotions in emotion stories; being able to recognize the facial display of emotion; identifying emotion in verbal statements, tone of voice and body language; carefully selecting appropriate emotion words when preparing a response; emitting appropriate emotional responses; internally "resonating" with compatible feeling; offering sensitive reflection statements; and generalizing emotional content to new or comparable situations (Goldstein & Michaels, 1985; Martin, 1999).

6

Human Agency and the Conative Domain[6]

William G. Huitt and Shelia C. Cain

Traditionally, psychology has identified and studied three components of mind: cognition, affect, and conation (Hilgard, 1980; Huitt, 2010b; Tallon, 1997). Cognition refers to the process of coming to know and understand; of encoding, perceiving, storing, processing, and retrieving information. It is generally associated with the question of "what" (eg, what happened, what is going on now, what is the meaning of that information.)

Affect refers to the emotional interpretation of perceptions, information, or knowledge. It is generally associated with one's attachment (positive or negative) to people, objects, ideas, etc. and is associated with the question "How do I feel about this knowledge or information?"

Conation refers to the connection of knowledge and affect to behavior and is associated with the issue of "why." It is the personal, intentional, planful, deliberate, goal-oriented, or striving component of motivation, the proactive (as opposed to reactive or habitual) aspect of behavior (Baumeister, Bratslavsky, Muraven, & Tice, 1998; Emmons, 1986). Atman (1987) defined conation as "vectored energy: i.e., personal energy that has both direction and magnitude" (p. 15). It is closely associated with the concepts of intrinsic motivation, volition, agency, self-direction, and self-regulation (Kane, 1985; Mischel, 1996).

Some of the conative issues one faces daily are:

- What is my life's purpose and are my actions congruent with that purpose?
- What are my aspirations, intentions, and goals?
- On what ideas, objects, events, etc. should I focus my attention?
- What am I going to do, what actions am I going to take, what investments am I going to make?
- How well am I accomplishing what I set out to do?

At the beginning of modern psychology, both emotion and conation were considered central to its study; however, interest in these topics declined as overt behavior and cognition received more attention (Amsel, 1992; Ford, 1987). While desired outcomes associated with these latter domains are

[6] Huitt, W., & Cain, S. (2005). An overview of the conative domain. *Educational Psychology Interactive*. Valdosta, GA: Valdosta State University.

deeply enmeshed in attempts to prepare children and youth for adulthood (eg, basic skills, critical thinking), the Brilliant Star framework (Huitt, Chapter 1, this volume) advocates this list be expanded.

Many researchers believe volition, defined as the use of will, or the freedom to make choices about what to do, is an essential element of voluntary human behavior and human behavior cannot be explained fully without it (eg, Bandura, 1997; Donagan, 1987; Hershberger, 1988). Campbell (1999) suggested that human beings should be viewed primarily as agents who possess a power to "get things done" (p. 15), to transform themselves and/or their environments in conflict to behavioral resistance from their own conditioning or environmental resistance. Both Bagozzi (1992) and Miller (1991) proposed that conation, a term that includes volition, but also includes additional aspects such as planning and perseverance, is especially important when addressing issues of human learning and that failure to adequately predict behavior was because the construct of conation had been omitted. Therefore, helping students develop the conative attitudes and skills associated with self-direction and personal efficacy is one of the most critical tasks presently facing parents and educators (Barell, 1995).

Developing knowledge, attitudes, and skills associated with conation, especially self-regulated learning skills, will be increasingly important to success as the twenty-first century continues (Huitt, 2017a). Educators, who frequently insist that students strive to be their very best, must be aware of the volitional strategies students need to be able to reach their potential. McMahon and Luca (2001) pointed out that the movement to the information age and the subsequent availability of employment opportunities through the Internet requires children and adults to use self-regulated learning skills in an unprecedented frequency and manner. They also need to be aware that the use of these conative skills requires energy and subsequent behavior is prone to deteriorate when volition is activated (Baumeister et al., 1998).

The purpose of this chapter is to briefly review some of the research in the area of conation, volition, and self-regulation, giving examples of how these issues can be addressed in the learning process.

Overview

The study of intentionality is common to the behavior of both animals and human beings. However, Frankfurt (1982) proposed that human intentionality is different from animal intentionality in that human beings can desire to contravene their conditioning. Bandura (1997, 2001b) suggested this is possible because of the singularly human ability of self-reflective evaluation and that studying human learning without considering human agency is unproductive. In the last several decades the terms executive function (Baumeister et al., 1998) and self-regulation (eg, Bandura, 1991a; Schunk & Zimmerman, 1994) have often been used as synonyms for conation, adding an additional dimension to the study of self (eg, self-concept, self-esteem, self-reflection, self-determination, self-control).

One reason the study of conation has lagged behind the study of cognition, emotion, and behavior is that it is intertwined with the study of these other domains and often difficult to separate (Snow, 1989). Conative components are often considered when measuring cognition or emotion. For example, the Wechsler scales of intelligence include a conative component (Cooper, 1997; Gregory, 1998), while Goleman's (1995) construct of emotional intelligence includes both affective (eg, empathy, optimism, managing emotions) and conative (eg, setting goals, self-regulation) components. Likewise, considerations of conation have included cognitive and affective, as well as volitional, components (eg, Gollwitzer, 1990; Snow & Swanson, 1992).

One of the critical factors in the successful use of volition, conation, or self-regulation is to realize that one has the ability and the freedom to choose and control one's thoughts and behavior (Kivinen, 2003). Volition has two subcomponents: (1) covert—referring to the controlling of one's own actions, and (2) overt—referring to the controlling of the environment that impacts one's actions (Corno, 1989, 1993). Conway (1975) suggested that, at a minimum, volition includes the processes of attention, goal-setting, and will. Glasser (1998) stated that in order to fully exercise one's autonomy it is important to direct volitional processes: (1) to control and regulate one's own behavior and (2) to select environments that are congruent with one's choices. Huitt and Dawson (Chapter 7, this volume) added that it is equally important to influence the development of those aspects of the environment that nurture one's own development as well as that of others (often referred to as developing social capital).

A variety of researchers who believe that volition ought to be the cornerstone of the psychological study of human behavior hypothesized that while animals are controlled mainly by instincts and reflexes, the impact of these processes is greatly reduced in human beings through learning and choice (eg, Ford, 1987; Hershberger, 1987; Howard & Conway, 1987). This allows human beings greater latitude in their range of behaviors, which can allow behavior that is both more adaptive and less adaptive, more moral and less moral (Vessels & Huitt, Chapter 10, this volume). Lacking the relatively restricting boundaries of animal instincts, individual choice, along with widely adopted social and cultural mores, become the chief protection against degradation in human behavior and provide the opportunity for creativity and ingenuity. This situation elevates the importance of volition, especially in an increasingly chaotic social and cultural milieu (Huitt, 2017a).

There are a variety of ways to discuss the domain of conation. One is to describe the preferred approaches of putting thought into action or interacting with the environment. Kolbe (1990) described this as one's conative style. This approach can be compared to the study of temperament or personality type that attempts to identify general patterns of thinking, feeling, and behavior or to learning style (eg, Huitt, 1988; Keirsey, 1998; McFarland, 1997; Myers, 1995). This perspective will be discussed in more detail below.

A second approach is to describe a taxonomy of the conative domain (Atman, 1987). She proposed five conative stages:

1. Perception: an openness to multiple forms of sensory and intuitive stimuli. It is important at this stage for the individual to be able to perceive relationships and flow among phenomena.
2. Focus: the ability to distinguish a particular stimuli or pattern from the background. This is the stage at which the individual establishes a goal or desired end result.
3. Engagement: the individual begins to more closely examine the goal and its features, beginning to develop an action plan as to how the goal can be accomplished.
4. Involvement: the individual begins to implement the action plan. Depending upon the level of attention shown in each of the previous stages, this involvement can range from minimal to absorbed.
5. Transcendence: the individual is completely immersed in the task "in such a manner that the mind/body/task become one" (p. 18). A variety of researchers such as Maslow, Assagioli, and Csikszentmihaly have described this stage as *peak experience*; *joyous*, *transpersonal will*; and *flow*, respectively.

The major benefit of describing conation in terms of taxonomy is the potential to describe the specific skills associated with each stage, thereby providing a foundation by which educators can facilitate the development of conation.

A third approach to the study of conation is to describe the processes of conation as an approach to the study of internal motivation. A major benefit of this approach is to distinguish internal from external motivation, again as a guide to facilitate the development of competencies necessary to successfully develop conation. The following discussion presents research findings on conation related to each of the three aspects of motivation: directing, energizing, and persisting.

Directing

Research has identified at least five separate components of the directing aspect of conation: (1) defining one's purpose; (2) identifying human needs; (3) aspirations, visions, and dreams of one's possible futures; (4) making choices and setting goals; and (5) developing an action plan.

One of the principal issues related to the purposeful directing of one's energies is to consider one's life purpose, both in relationship to a general purpose of a human life and a specific purpose of one's own life, given a set of strengths and the particular requirements of the time and culture in which one is living (Millman, 1993). No issue calls into question one's philosophy or worldview more than when one considers one's life purpose. A materialistic or naturalistic worldview may lead one to focus on contributing to the DNA pool and acquiring possessions. A humanistic worldview may lead one to authenticity (Irvine, 2003) or focusing on developing one's personal strengths (Seligman, 2002). A pantheistic worldview may lead one to get in touch with one's intuition and to become aware of moments of synchronicity (Adrienne, 1998). A theistic view is likely to lead one to get in line with God's purpose for humankind (Hickman, 2003; Warren, 2002). Whatever the case, it is safe to say that one must address one's worldview, either previous to or simultaneous with, one's statement of personal purpose. There is no more significant issue in Becoming a Brilliant Star than this task, as every perception, thought, feeling, commitment, or action will be influenced by one's belief about the purpose of one's life.

A second aspect of volition is to become aware of one's human needs (Franken, 1997). Maslow's (1954) hierarchy of human needs, with its categorization of deficiency needs (physiological, security, belongingness, esteem) and growth needs (self-actualization, transcendence), is probably one of the most well-known approaches. Although not supported by empirical research, it is hard to argue that individuals do not have these needs, even if they are not arranged in the hierarchical order hypothesized by Maslow (Huitt, 2011e). There are other specific formulations of human needs that have been the focus of research such as the need for optimal arousal or flow (Csikszentimihali, 1991), the need for achievement (McClelland, 1992), the need for cognitive balance (Festinger, 1957), the need to find meaning in life (Frankl, 1997, 1998), the need for power (Murray, 1938), and the need for social affiliation (Sullivan, 1968). The perspective of the Brilliant Star framework is that there are needs within each of the identified core elements and domains that develop simultaneously and interactively. That is, physical does not come first, followed by social, and growth needs; rather spiritual, moral, perceptual, cognitive, affective, conative, and social needs exist at birth and develop interactively throughout life. Development is defined as the increasing differentiation and integration of these needs in an ever-increasing complexity that generalizes over a growing number of situations. However, certain components are more important for a specific individual at a specific time because of temperament, personality, strengths, etc. Therefore, it is necessary to provide experiences designed to help the individual identify what is important to him or her as one of the first and recurring steps in the development of conation.

A third aspect of direction is to become aware of the "possible self." Markus and Nurius (1986) hypothesized that the perception of this possible self provides the bridge to action; without something being considered as possible for the individual, goals will not be set and plans will not be made. Levenson (1978) suggested that aspirations, visions, and dreams define and expand the possible self. However, these long-term, often vague statements must be turned into goals (short-term, specific, personal statements) if they are to impact immediate behavior (Markus & Nurius, 1986). Additionally, Epstein (1990) stated that aspirations and goals must have visual and emotional components in order to be effective.

A fourth aspect of the direction component of conation is the setting of goals for the aspirations or dreams that have been chosen. Dweck (2000) differentiated two types of goals: (1) mastery goals that focus on developing competence or on the process of learning, and (2) performance goals that focus on the outcome, winning, or attaining credentials. Urdan and Maehr (1995) suggested a third alternative: (3) social goals that focus on performance of the group or the individual fitting in with others. The importance of working in groups in the modern era (eg, Bridges, 1994; Toffler & Toffler, 1995) highlights the importance of the ability to set and achieve social goals. Prawat (1985) demonstrated that affective goals should be included as an additional type of goal, at least in elementary classrooms. Goleman (1995) cited an extensive literature showing that the ability to manage one's emotions is as important, or perhaps even more important, than one's cognitive ability to acquire and process information quickly. Therefore, children and youth must develop the ability to set goals in all these areas if they are going to be adequately prepared for adulthood in the modern era.

Ames (1988, 1992) showed that in school settings students with mastery goals outperformed students with performance goals. However, it must be considered that in the highly-structured school setting, goals are largely chosen by the system. It is the individual's adoption of the importance of those goals that is reflected in a mastery orientation. In the less structured environment outside the school, it is likely that one must focus on both process (mastery) and outcome (performance) goals if one is to be successful. In fact, Dweck (1986) suggested that mastery and performance goals are two ends of an ellipse that students recycle through on a continuous basis. Mastery goals relate to the development of competence, whereas performance goals relate to the confirmation of that competence. Both types of goals must be used; each pertains to a different stage of the learning and evaluation process. Mastery goals are more related to the process of learning and formative evaluation; performance goals are more related to the product of learning and summative evaluation.

There are several important issues to consider when setting goals. First, goals must be difficult, but attainable (Franken, 1997). Following the Yerkes-Dodson law (Yerkes & Dodson, 1908), moderate amounts of difficulty lead to optimal performance. Setting goals that are perceived as too easy or too difficult does not increase appropriate behavior. Second, goals must be in agreement (or at least not in conflict) with one's principles and personal vision (Conway & McCullough, 1981; Waitley, 1996). An individual will simply not persist in a behavior that is in conflict with deeply held values. Third, the emotional state of an individual can influence the setting of goals. Higher goals are set when the individual is emotionally aroused (Lazarus, 1991) and lower goals are set when the individual is depressed (Beck, 1976). Likewise, individuals with increased levels of optimism (which grow out of a person's explanatory style) set higher goals (Seligman, 1990) as do individuals with increased levels of self-efficacy (Franken, 1997). The spiraling connection of goals and self-efficacy are demonstrated by research that shows higher levels of self-efficacy are obtained when mastery goals are met (Bandura, 1997). Like the setting of goals, self-efficacy can also be impacted by mood (Kavanaugh & Bower, 1985).

A fifth aspect of successful self-direction is to develop action plans that can turn aspirations, visions, dreams, and goals into reality (Herman, 1990). Plans must be written and specific, starting with a clear description of desired outcomes. Two activities are very useful in this process: backwards planning and task analysis (see Huitt, 1992). In backwards planning, one starts with the desired end results and then identifies the most immediate state and required procedures to meet that result (ie, if I am here and do this, then these results will be obtained.) To be successful, backwards planning must be accompanied by a task analysis that will identify the skills and knowledge that are prerequisite to learning and are required to learn or perform a specific task. By systematically completing a task analysis as one works backwards from the desired end results, one arrives at the starting point with a clearly delineated plan for obtaining them.

Energizing

Energizing behavior towards established goals is a complicated matter involving a wide variety of factors. Most importantly, minds and bodies have a natural tendency towards equilibrium or homeostasis (eg, cognitive consistency, Festinger, 1957; the development of intelligence, Piaget, 2001;

emotion, Solomon, 1980; and eating, Woods & Schwartz, 2000). When moving in new directions, there is always some discomfort involved because of the unfamiliarity of the new thoughts and behaviors. In general, if inertia is to be overcome and action taken, the potential for pleasure resulting from striving and obtaining dreams, desires, and goals must outweigh the discomfort of change or fear of failure (Corno, 1993). Goals that are in one's self interest (Sansone & Harackiewicz, 1996) or are congruent with self-identified personal convictions (Brunstein & Gollwitzer, 1996) have the strongest impact because these are most integral to a definition of self.

McCombs and Whisler (1989) proposed that human beings have an innate need for self-development and self-determination which can be enhanced or thwarted by one's self-concept and self-esteem, or, as stated above, one's possible self (Markus & Nurius, 1986). It is therefore important to consider developmental and environmental factors that can enhance, or at least not inhibit, this natural predisposition.

The domains and core elements of the Brilliant Star framework provide a way to categorize the various factors that can impact one's energy levels (Huitt, Chapter 1, this volume). For example, being physically fit produces energy to engage in demanding tasks. Focusing attention on aspirations and goals while managing thoughts and emotions are essential elements of the energizing component of conation (Conway, 1981). Putting oneself in a position to perceive positive thoughts and emotions, such as reading positive books, listening to positive messages, and engaging in positive self-talk can be important daily activities that prepare one to expend energy on new tasks. Social interactions with family and friends can also be powerful sources of energy (Bandura, 2001a).

Persisting

Persistence is increasingly recognized as an important component of conation, as well as for success. For example, Goodyear (1997), in a review of literature regarding the success of professional psychologists, found that while there are "threshold levels" of intellectual and interpersonal skills, motivation and persistence were even more important in predicting levels of expertise. There are a number of skills associated with persistence such as engaging in daily self-renewal activities; monitoring one's thoughts, emotions, and behaviors; self-evaluation based on the monitoring data collected; reflection on progress made; and the completion of tasks.

Although it is true that certain personal characteristics such as level of achievement motivation (McClelland, 1985), expectations for success (Atkinson & Birch, 1978; Hayamizu & Weiner, 1991), and level of self-esteem (Tafarodi & Vu, 1997), as well as environmental factors such as amount of failure experiences (Miller & Hom, 1990), being praised for effort rather than ability (Brophy, 1981; Mueller & Dweck, 1998), the public display of summative, but not formative, assessments (Seijts, Meertens, & Kok, 1997), and the use of variable reinforcement schedules (Plaud, Plaud, & von Duvillard, 1999) can impact task persistence, the student's use of self-regulation processes can mediate these influences when the learner does not possess the desired characteristics or is not in a conducive environment (Bandura, 1991a; Koonce, 1996). For example, learners who matched goals to enduring interests and values (Sheldon & Elliott, 1999) or who perceived tasks to be important (Seijts et al., 1997) persisted longer. Miller, Greene, Montalvo, Ravindrann and Nichols (1996) reported that students who had learning goals, desires to obtain future consequences, and wanted to please the teacher persisted longer in academic work. Students who were able to produce well-elaborated, specific, vivid pictures of possible future selves persisted more and had higher levels of achievement than those who did not (Leondari, Syngollitou, & Kiosseoglou, 1998).

In summary, the appropriate use of conation, volition, and self-regulation require the individual to take personal responsibility for his or her own motivation (ie, directing, energizing, and persevering toward self-selected aspirations and goals.) There is significant overlap among the conative domain and the other core elements and domains of the Brilliant Star model. However, it deserves to be considered as a separate domain because of its importance in self-direction and self-regulation. All of the other domains can develop and operate effectively, but if the person does not display competence in the conative domain he or she will always be controlled by the circumstances of the situation or environment. This would be a significant omission in the actualization of one's full potential.

The Development of Agency and Conation

While there is a dearth of research on the development of the specific term "conation," there is an abundance of research on related concepts such as intrinsic motivation, volition, self-regulated learning, and self-direction. For example, Bronson (2000) compared the numerous theories concerning the development of self-regulation in early childhood. According to the psychoanalytic theory, self-regulation comes from the ego as the individual learns to deal with the environment. Behavioral theorists propose that self-regulation is learned through experiencing consequences in interactions with the environment. The information processing theory purports an interest in problem-solving as the reason for self-regulation and adds the desire to be in control. Piagetians support the theory that the cognitive abilities of the individual allow logic to determine the level of self-regulation. Neo-Piagetians believe interest and ability are the primary qualities used to solve problems. According to the Vygotskian theory, intrinsic independent curiosity leads to self-regulation. Social learning theorists believe self-regulation is realized through self-evaluation of personally established standards. The reality is that the conative domain is so intertwined with the cognitive, affective, and psychomotor domains that it is difficult to separately analyze it.

Self-regulated learning represents one area in which conation has been studied relative to the learning process. Ponton and Carr (2000) identified two categorizations of self-directed learning: (1) the process perspective and (2) the character perspective. Process researchers focus on topics such as setting goals, establishing strategies, using resources, and monitoring progress. This has been the focus of the literature review for this chapter. However, the character perspective suggests that an important human need related to conation is a desire for autonomy (Chene as cited in Ponton & Carr), a human need also considered important by Lumsden (1994) and Pink (2009). Attributes that lead to becoming autonomous and self-directed include initiative, resourcefulness, and persistence; these all influence whether or not an individual's desires and initiatives will be successful.

Kolbe (1990) provided additional information on the character perspective of self-regulation. As stated above she advocated that each individual has a biological, instinctive approach to putting energy into action which she labeled one's modus operandi (MO). Kolbe developed the Kolbe Conative Index (KCI), that identified the level of intensity in which one operates in each of four Action Modes; Fact Finder, Follow Thru, Quick Start, and Implementer. Although each person is endowed with conation, many are unaware of the importance of learning how to channel the conative energy as they strive to become successful in their lives. According to Kolbe, participants are unable to predict their results 50 percent of the time. However, participants are in agreement with the results of the KCI 98 percent of the time. Results do not change significantly with additional administrations of the KCI, within a five percent margin of error.

Kolbe (1990) was adamant in urging people to use the information gained through the KCI to channel their conative energy to be more productive, rather than trying to change their orientations. Parents are urged to assist their children in identifying conative instincts and then committing to using those talents to realize goals. According to Kolbe, conative bias often prevents children from realizing their natural potential because parents try to change and mold children to fit a preconceived image or pattern. Children need the opportunities to be individuals who are allowed to accomplish tasks through their own designs in order to maximize their conative talents. Parents and teachers often prevent children from developing and using their conative instincts by expecting the same results through the same processes that work for them. Adults also often fail to recognize that insisting that a child go against instinctive conative nature is unnecessary and potentially damaging to the child. Lack of skills and values can be limitations in realizing conative goals even after the MO is realized. Other factors that may lead to interference in using conative potential are monetary limitations, dependency, and stereotypes. Children may be denied use of their conative instincts based on the perceptions that opportunities are not available. Kolbe suggested mentors as guidance and encouragement for the child who may have a conative nature that is incompatible with the parent(s). However, there is some controversy over whether providing materials congruent with one's conative style actually improves learning (Wongchai, 2003).

Alternatively, other theorists support the theory that managing one's conative energy is a learned behavior, operating through processes of self-regulation. As mentioned earlier, Bandura (1986) believed self-evaluation is a basic component of self-regulation. Effects of behaviors are observed as the individual gains insights as to which behaviors lead to internal or external desired or undesired consequences. Self-regulation is then an intrinsically learned behavior based on the individual's established standards regarding appropriate action in specific situations or contexts. The ability to practice self-regulated behaviors enables the individual to develop self-guided activities. This involves monitoring the cognitive, affective, and social processes involved in interacting with the environment (Garcia & Pintrich, 1996). Barkley (as cited in Bronson, 2000) proposed that self-regulation is not taught, but learned through the interaction of the neurological abilities of the brain and the environment. He stated that a child is born with a self-regulatory process, memory, internal self-regulatory language, motivational system, and a behavior analysis process. Environmental factors then influence the individual's ability to self-regulate, but self-regulation is instinctive due to the genetic composition of the neurological system.

In summary, a diverse set of specific characteristics or skills of conation and self-regulation have been identified by a wide variety of researchers. Among these are having an achievement orientation, developing autonomy and curiosity, setting goals and strategies for success, self-monitoring and self-evaluation, and being persistent. While there is some discussion as to whether conative abilities are innate or learned, there is ample evidence to suggest that both views have merit and parents and teachers need to monitor children and youth from both perspectives as they develop during the school years. While it may not be practical or reasonable to develop a single index of conation, parents and educators can certainly make some holistic judgments about a student's preferred pattern for energy use and progress on the process attributes.

Activities to Promote Agency and Conation

While specific perceptual, cognitive, affective, and volitional components of goal-oriented motivation have personal style and maturational influences, they can also be impacted via the social environment (Heckhausen & Dweck, 1998). It is important that parents, educators, and other individuals concerned with the development of children and youth work towards developing the conative components of mind that enhance self-direction, self-determination, and self-regulation. Specifically, young people need to imagine possibilities in their lives, set attainable goals, plan routes to those goals, systematically and consistently put goals and plans into actions, practice self-observation, reflect on results, and manage emotions. These need to be addressed in a spiraled curriculum because of the developmental aspects of their successful utilization.

The relationship between intrinsic motivation and conation plays an important role in the educational life of a child. Lumsden (1994) attributed a child's primary attitude toward learning to the influences from the home and school environments. She encouraged questioning, exploration, and exposure to resources as ways to nurture the child's feelings of self-worth, competence, autonomy, and self-efficacy. White (cited in Bronson, 2000) found that young children develop feelings of competence when given opportunities to explore and investigate their environment. Competence leads to motivation, in which the child gains internal rewards through self-efficacy. Corno (1992) suggested that allowing the child to engage in interesting activities without formal evaluation is one way that teachers and parents can encourage student responsibility for learning. Deci and Ryan (1985) described the development of autonomy as an important component of this exploration. Autonomy can be defined as the initiation and regulation of behaviors based on experiences with the environment and people who have this ability use information and experiences to make choices and become self-regulated.

Covey, Merrill, and Merrill (1994) suggested the development of a mission statement as one way to help think about one's priorities. Developing this statement provides an opportunity for the individual to explicitly consider and state important values and beliefs. In addition, Waitley (1996) advised imagining what one's life would be like if time and money were not a limiting factor. That is, what would you do this week, this month, next month, if you had all the money and time you needed and were secure that both would be available again next year. Developing vivid, specific images of these and then relating them back to the important values in one's mission statement can impact one's commitment and persistence toward those desired end results.

Seligman (1996) suggested children be taught to "capture" their automatic thoughts, which are often negative, evaluate them for accuracy, and replace them with more positive and optimistic thoughts (similar to Cognitive Therapy, eg, Alford & Beck, 1998). Helmstetter (1987) and Ziglar (1994) proposed adults adopt a more proactive approach and teach the use of self-talk techniques. In this approach, statements are developed specifically for an individual and/or situation and the learner recites the self-talk statement at regular intervals (see http://www.edpsycinteractive.org/brilstar/affstate.pdf for an example:).

As previously stated, self-efficacy is an important influence on conation. Bandura (1986, 1997), in his social cognitive theory, suggested that providing mastery experiences is one of the best ways to help students develop self-efficacy. In turn, self-efficacy predicts future success in tasks related to that mastery. Corno (1992) suggested that providing students the opportunity to revise work allows students the ability to move towards mastery through successive iterations. Parents and educators can also use social persuasion, being careful to praise the effort and striving, not the learner's ability (Brophy, 1981; Mueller & Dweck, 1998). Providing opportunities for learners to experience success vicariously through the success of others (perhaps thorough peers) is also important, as it can impact a learner's perceptions of what is possible.

Lumsden (1994) stated that the classroom environment must be supportive and every member must feel valued and respected in order to benefit fully and create and maintain a high degree of motivation to learn. While teachers may be tempted to use external rewards, Lumsden warns that the expectancy of external rewards may decrease instinctive intrinsic motivation. Deci and Ryan (1985) stated that external rewards may interfere with higher-level thinking due to emotional stress. These researchers found intrinsic motivation was promoted when students are given the opportunity to choose to participate in activities that develop competence.

Unfortunately, in today's school environment, there is not a lot of opportunity for student choice if students are required to show content mastery via a standardized test of basic skills. One way that may be productive in addressing both issues is to develop teaching strategies that allow students to be responsible for and to control their own learning through setting goals, planning, acting on the plans, and evaluating progress (Bandura, 1986). When given the freedom to make choices about their learning, to set individual goals based on a prescribed curriculum and held to standards, children receive intrinsic rewards and become self-regulated learners. Lepper (1988) suggested using challenging, yet achievable, tasks that are relevant to the learners and implementing multiple teaching styles to accommodate a variety of learning modalities. However, Baumeister et al. (1998) suggested that adults need to be careful regarding how much volition they require individuals to use—expending energy for volitional activities depletes the resources necessary to make those decisions. For example, resisting the temptation to eat a piece of chocolate reduces the energy available to make similar decisions. Considering this research, it may be important to balance constructivistic (Lutz & Huitt, Chapter 3, this volume) and direct instruction (Huitt, Monetti, & Hummel, 2009) lessons during the learning process.

Jones, Valdez, Nowakowski, and Rasmussen (1995) recommended a four-step process in putting these suggestions into practice. The first step is to gain the commitment from administrators and the school district to allow students to be more responsible for their own learning. Second, parents must be informed about the process and benefits of self-regulated learning. The third phase is to ensure that teachers give students the opportunity to participate in controlling their learning by allowing them to set goals and monitor their individual progress. Finally, students must take advantage of their ability to have some degree of control of their own learning through implementation of strategies, setting goals, monitoring, reflection, and evaluation.

Specific activities for helping students become more self-directed include the use of class discussions, reflection journals, graphic organizers, personal portfolios, reciprocal teaching, and KWHL (What do I **K**now? **W**hat should I learn? **H**ow will I learn it? What did I **L**earn?) strategies. The KWHL strategy is often referred to as a metacognitive strategy (Blakely & Spence, 1990). Additional metacognitive strategies include discussing the processes used when thinking, journaling, planning, reflecting on how the thinking process led to the outcome, and self-evaluation.

Reflection journals enable the student to develop and assess the cognitive processes used during problem-solving. Personal portfolios are not only a collective way of displaying a student's work, but when the student is allowed to evaluate pieces of the portfolio and instructed to give evidence for choosing certain items as their best work, self-directed skills are used. Using graphic organizers allows students to visualize the whole situation at one glance before beginning to focus on problem solving strategies. Through reciprocal teaching, the student and the teacher reverse roles periodically and the student is given opportunities to practice higher-level skills by summarizing, posing questions, and predicting. KWHL strategies promote higher level thinking. Through this method, students reflect upon and share prior knowledge, making valuable connections with the new knowledge gained.

Assessing Agency and Conation

Studies and information on instruments that measure multiple aspects of conation are rare. Rather, there is a tendency to focus on one aspect of conation (eg, intrinsic motivation, goal-setting, volition). Likewise, most studies do not focus exclusively on conation; they combine measurement of one aspect of conation with one aspect of cognition, affect, or behavior.

As previously mentioned, the Kolbe Instinct Index (Kolbe, 1990) measures individual's innate predispositions to activate behavior. Participants respond to thirty-six questions by marking their most likely and least likely reaction to various situations; results are reported in narrative and graphic form. The index has been administered to thousands of people world-wide and Kolbe found that even though cultural, economic, and political factors influence or limit opportunities for the individuals, the index is a genuine indicator of the drive and talents of individuals in the global community.

Several instruments are available which measure volition, self-regulation, motivation, and self-directed learning skills and strategies. Concerned about the lack of knowledge of volitional strategies when faced with academic problems, Husman, McCann, and Crowson (2000) conducted a study using a modified version of the Academic Volitional Strategies Inventory (AVSI). Questions were divided into three areas of strategies; thoughts involving negative consequences, stress reduction behaviors, and the use of positive motivational behaviors. Results indicated undergraduate college learners most frequently use strategies considering the consequences of behavior when faced with academic obstacles. This instrument could be used as a pre- and post-measure for programs that focus on improving students becoming more consistently responsible for their own learning.

In a study by Kivinen (2003), the Motivated Strategies for Learning Questionnaire (MSLQ) was administered to both European and University of Michigan students in an effort to find correlations between motivation and self-regulated learning skills. Three types of behaviors were determined to be associated with volition: practicing attention control, self-instruction, and self-helping strategies. The results supported Kivinen's proposal that self-regulated learning incorporates motivation, cognitive learning, and resource management when performing academically. Additionally, Kivinen showed that the volitional skills of attention control, self-instruction, and self-helping strategies could be reliably and validly assessed.

Self-regulation may be assessed with several instruments including the Connell-Ryan self-report questionnaire (Deci & Ryan, 1985). The scale, developed for 8-to-12-year-olds, is designed to identify reasons for students' performance in school. The questions distinguish between external motivational reasons (eg, potential for praise, guilt-avoidance behaviors, and knowledge acquisition) and internal factors (eg, performing based on the belief that school assignments are fun.) After administrating the questionnaire in a study of fourth through sixth grade students, Connell and Ryan (as cited in Deci & Ryan, 1985) found a negative relationship between external motivation factors and mastery motivation. Students who were more extrinsically motivated felt less confidence in their intellectual abilities, learned material on a lower level, and had lower achievement scores. The results of the study indicated a relationship between the ability to use positive coping skills and self-esteem, confidence in personal cognitive abilities, and mastery motivation.

McMahon and Luca (2001) reported that The Learning and Study Strategies Inventory (LASSI) is used by 2000 institutions world-wide to assess students' learning strategies. Available to be taken on-line, the LASSI consists of three domains; effort, goal orientation, and cognition with ten scales measuring attitude, motivation, time management, anxiety, concentration, information processing, selecting main ideas, study aids, self-testing, and test strategies. Immediate feedback of the LASSI includes suggestions for interventions in addition to scores.

In summary, while there is not an extensive array of available instruments to measure various components of conation, there are enough to get started. Simultaneously collecting data on multiple aspects of conation will likely provide the most valuable information. For example, Kivinen (2003) collected both quantitative and qualitative data on 18 strategies that students used in learning academic material. The most often used strategies (motivation regulation, time management, and affect regulation; used by 51.0%, 37.9%, and 36.9%, respectively) did not predict either high or low grades. Rather high grades were predicted by two conative strategies (encoding control and attention control) and four cognitive and metacognitive learning strategies (rehearsal, elaboration, organization, and critical thinking). The organization, critical thinking and encoding control strategies were used by a small percentage of students (11.6%, 9.1%, and 8.1%, respectively), yet were effective in predicting high performers.

Summary and Conclusions

Although often overlooked as a significant factor in an individual's success, conation, also discussed as volition or self-regulation, has a significant role in the development of educational process. As discussed in this chapter, there are a wide variety of knowledge, attitudes, and skills that comprise the conative domain (see Table 6-1). Among these are having an achievement orientation, establishing a life vision, setting goals, and regulating one's behavior. Each of these has a developmental sequence or an appropriate level of expectations given the age and/or experience of the individual. Educators must have a long-term program that addresses the various aspects of conation if children and youth are to develop successfully in this domain.

Table 6-1. Considering Style and Process Aspects of Agency and Conation

Conative Style	Fact Finder	Gathers data and probes for more information; "most oriented to activities that encompass defining, calculating, formalizing, and researching"
	Follow Thru	Seeks patterns for known information; "most oriented to such acts as arranging, coordinating, integrating, and implementing"
	Quick Start	Seeks to be creative and innovate; "most oriented to activities that involve brainstorming, intuiting, inventing, and risk taking"
	Implementer	Desires to demonstrate knowledge and skills: "most oriented to such acts as building, crafting, forming, and repairing"
Process	Directing	1. Defining one's purpose 2. Identifying human needs 3. Aspirations, visions, and dreams of one's possible futures 4. Making choices and setting goals 5. Developing an action plan
	Energizing	1. Overcoming inertia 2. High self-esteem 3. Physical fitness, high physical energy 4. Focus attention 5. Positive self-talk 6. Ability to manage emotions (arouse and dampen) 7. Gets started, initiates task 8. Positive social interactions with family and friends
	Persevering	1. Engaging in daily self-renewal 2. Monitoring thoughts, emotions, and behavior 3. Self-evaluation using data collected in the monitoring process 4. Reflection on progress 5. Completing tasks

Parents, as a child's first teachers, must be made aware of the importance of acknowledgement and acceptance of their child's conative nature. Schools must provide opportunities for students to learn intrinsic motivational, volitional, and self-regulatory skills through experiences in which they are given choices and options. Teachers are in need of staff development focusing on the strategies that are needed to assist students in becoming more self-directed. At each level, the importance of goal development, commitment, and action must be stressed in order for students to realize their conative potential. Additionally, human beings are "happiest when they are striving for 'something larger' than themselves (Sheldon & Schmuck, 2001), especially when using personal strengths to do so (Seligman, 2002).

In today's unstructured and chaotic environment, children and youth will need the conative skills discussed in this presentation if they are to be successful as adults. Recognizing that there is limited time in the school day, educators must stack activities that can develop these attitudes and skills into an already crowded curriculum. While this may be a Herculean task, to not attempt to do so is to send our youth into the 21st century woefully ill-prepared.

7

Social Development[7]

William G. Huitt and Courtney Dawson

When Aronson (2007) first published *The Social Animal* in 1972, he confirmed scientifically what people knew experientially: Human beings are social in their very nature. In fact, Dunbar (1998) hypothesized that the large human brain evolved primarily to adapt to an increasingly complex social environment. As Goleman (2006) put it: "[W]e are wired to connect" (p. 4).

The domain of social intelligence and development is a critical component of descriptions of human ability and behavior (Albrecht, 2005; Gardner, 1983, 2006). Social skills are important for preparing young people to mature and succeed in their adult roles within the family, workplace, and community (Ten Dam & Volman, 2007). Elias, Zins, Weisberg, Frey, Greenberg, Haynes…, & Shriver (1997) suggested those involved in guiding children and youth should pay special attention to this domain: social skills allow people to succeed not only in their social lives, but also in their academic, personal, and future professional activities. For educators, it is increasingly obvious that learning is ultimately a social process (Bandura, 1986; Dewey, 1944; Vygotsky, 1978). While people may initially learn something independently, eventually that learning will be modified in interaction with others.

Defining Social Intelligence

As with other domains, there are inconsistences within and between the definitions of social intelligence (a capacity or potential) and social competence (an achievement or actualization of potential). For example, Gardner (1983) defined social intelligence (labeled interpersonal intelligence) as the "ability to notice and make distinctions among other individuals and, in particular, among their moods, temperaments, motivations, and intentions" (p. 239). Goleman (2006) defined social intelligence as "being intelligent not just *about* our relationships but also in them" [p. 11, emphasis in original]. His definition includes both the capacity to be *socially aware* (with components of primal empathy, attunement, empathetic accuracy, and social cognition) as well as the ability to develop *social skill or facility* (including components of synchrony, self-preservation, influence, and concern). The

[7] Huitt, W. & Dawson, C. (2011, April). Social development: Why it is important and how to impact it. *Educational Psychology Interactive*. Valdosta, GA: Valdosta State University.

latter is Albrecht's (2005) primary focus—he defined social intelligence simply as "the ability to get along well with others and to get them to cooperate with you" (p. 3). We believe that Albrecht's definition is closer to defining social competence rather than social intelligence. A definition of intelligence should focus on the ability to learn to do something rather than being competent at it.

In each of these definitions, cognitive/thinking, affective/emotional, and conative/volitional components are considered important because they provide the foundation for the establishment and maintenance of interpersonal relationships. Therefore, any attempt to develop social capacity (ie, intelligence) into social competence will need to consider these other domains as well.

There is some controversy about whether social intelligence really exists in a manner similar to cognitive intelligence and the extent to which it can be developed through learning experiences (Weare, 2010). There are similar controversies when discussing other domains such as emotion (Brett et al., Chapter 5, this volume) and conation or agency (Huitt & Cain, Chapter 6, this volume). However, there is no debate about whether people vary in their ability to learn and develop social skills.

Defining Social Competence

Bierman (2004) defined social competence as the "capacity to coordinate adaptive responses flexibly to various interpersonal demands, and to organize social behavior in different social contexts in a manner beneficial to oneself and consistent with social conventions and morals" (p. 141). Broderick and Blewitt (2010) identified four categories of foundational social competencies: (1) affective processes (including empathy, valuing relationships, and sense of belonging), (2) cognitive processes (including cognitive ability, perspective taking, and making moral judgments), (3) social skills (including making eye contact, using appropriate language, and asking appropriate questions), and (4) high social self-concept.

The Collaborative for Academic, Social, and Emotional Learning (CASEL, 2003, 2007), one of the leaders in the development of social-emotional learning (SEL), identified five teachable competencies that they believe provide a foundation for effective personal development:

1. **Self-awareness**: knowing what one is feeling and thinking; having a realistic assessment of one's own abilities and a well-grounded sense of self-confidence;
2. **Social awareness**: understanding what others are feeling and thinking; appreciating and interacting positively with diverse groups;

3. **Self-management**: handling one's emotions so they facilitate rather than interfere with task achievement; setting and accomplishing goals; persevering in the face of setbacks and frustrations;
4. **Relationship skills**: establishing and maintaining healthy and rewarding relationships based on clear communication, cooperation, resistance to inappropriate social pressure, negotiating solutions to conflict, and seeking help when needed; and
5. **Responsible decision making**: making choices based on an accurate consideration of all relevant factors and the likely consequences of alternative courses of action, respecting others, and taking responsibility for one's decisions.

Based on extensive research over the past two decades, many investigators proposed that school curricula must provide learning experiences that address students' development in the cognitive/academic, emotional, social, and moral domains (Cohen, 2006; Elias & Arnold, 2006; Narvaez, 2006), Zins, Weissberg, Wang, & Walberg, 2004).

As with the definitions of social intelligence, the different components of social competence provided by Broderick and Blewitt (2010) and CASEL (2003, 2007) involve the domains of cognition/thinking (perspective taking, making moral judgments, responsible decision making), affect/emotion (empathy, valuing relationships, self-awareness, and handling one's emotions), and conation/self-regulation (self-management—setting and accomplishing goals; persevering), in addition to the social domain (social awareness, relationship skills such as making eye contact and using appropriate language). Broderick and Blewitt's inclusion of social self-views provides an insight into the complexity of addressing social competence. Therefore, an effective social development program will include elements of developing the foundational competencies in other domains that support and enrich it and will do so in a way that the child or adolescent has high social self-esteem in a variety of social situations.

Based on the discussion above, a comprehensive definition of social competence would include a person's knowledge, attitudes, and skills related to at least six components: (1) being aware of one's own and others' emotions, (2) managing impulses and behaving appropriately, (3) communicating effectively, (4) forming healthy and meaningful relationships, (5) working well with others, and (6) resolving conflict.

The remainder of this chapter outlines research and theories related to the development of social competence and how it is directly related to education and schooling. The next section offers a literature review of theory and research supporting the vital importance of social competence to academic achievement as well as successful adulthood. The final two sections provide a discussion of empirically-based interventions and measurement tools as well as additional resources for teachers and administrators.

Understanding Social Development

This section is organized around two different perspectives on understanding social development: theories and research.

Theories Related to Social Development

According to Bowlby (1982, 1988), an infant's attachment to a caregiver serves as the foundation for all future social development. He suggested that attachment is biologically-based and is intended to ensure that infants and children have enough support and protection to survive until they are able to function independently (Gilovich, Keltner, & Nisbett, 2006).

Ainsworth, Blehar, Waters, & Wall (2015) found four distinct categories of attachment: *securely attached* (about 65%), *avoidant-insecurely attached* (about 20%), *anxious-ambivalently* attached (about 10%), and about 5% whose attachment was categorized as *disorganized-disoriented.* According to Ainsworth et al., the attachment patterns developed in infancy and toddlerhood are fairly stable throughout the lifespan. In a study of children attending summer camp at age 10, Sroufe, Egeland, Carlson, and Collins (2005) found that securely attached children tended to have more friends and better social skills. Likewise, in a cross-sectional study using self-report data, 15-18-year-olds with good parental attachment had better social skills and, subsequently, better competence in developing friendships and romantic relationships (Engles, Finkenauer, Meeus, & Dekovic, 2005). Ainsworth et al. found that the *anxious-ambivalently* attached are especially at-risk for later behavioral problems, including aggressive conduct. These data suggested it is vital for the one-third of children who do not develop a secure attachment as infants be provided opportunities to repair the original attachment relationship or construct some form of attachment outside the home, perhaps through interaction with a teacher or mentor.

Erikson (1993) provided another important theory related to social development; his *psychosocial theory* of personality development emphasized the interplay between the social and emotional domains. Erikson highlighted the importance of the person resolving a series of conflicts where interpersonal relationships play an important role. In infancy, the conflict is *Trust versus Mistrust.* Erikson hypothesized that an infant will develop trust through interaction with a warm, available, and responsive caregiver or the infant will develop mistrust through interaction with a negative or unresponsive and unavailable caregiver. Subsequently, it is this development of trust in infancy that allows an individual to succeed in the next stage of toddlerhood called *Autonomy versus Shame and Doubt.* In this stage, the toddler is more likely to develop a sense of independence and control over the toddler's own behavior and environment if a base of trust in a caregiver is developed in the first stage. The next two stages, the development of *Initiative versus Guilt* and *Industry versus Inferiority* are especially critical for educators. Early childhood is quite often the age when children first begin their involvement in formal education. Children must learn to integrate their interest in personal exploration and the use of their imaginations with working with others involved in the same task. For elementary-aged children, the task of integrating personal interests and needs with those of others becomes even more complex. They must learn to follow rules and "get things right" while at the same time learning to take the perspective of others and work with others in group projects. Failing in either of these stages leads to children being at-risk for an inability to take action on their own and/or developing a sense of inferiority, unproductiveness, and feelings of incompetence in regards to their peers and their social roles and abilities.

Vygotsky (1978), another well-known theorist in the areas of social development and education, argued that cognitive functions are connected to the external (or social) world. He viewed the child as an apprentice guided by adults and more competent peers into the social world. Vygotsky explained that children learn in a systematic and logical way as a result of dialogue and interaction with a skilled helper within a *zone of proximal development* (ZPD). The lower boundary of the ZPD are activities the learner can do on his or her own without the assistance of a teacher or mentor. Similarly, the upper limit of the ZPD are those learning outcomes that the learner could not achieve at this time even with the assistance of a competent teacher or mentor.

Another of Vygotsky's (1978) concepts for guiding learning is *scaffolding,* by which he meant the process by which the teacher constantly changes the level of assistance given to the learner as the learning needs change. When engaged in scaffolding a teacher or coach is involved in every step during the initial stage of instruction. As the teacher observes the child correctly demonstrating partial mastery of the skill or task the teacher provides increasingly less support, with the child eventually demonstrating independent mastery of the task or skill. Both of these constructs are important in describing how a child becomes socially competent.

In his theories of social learning and social cognition, Bandura (1965, 1977, 1986) theorized three categories of influences on developing social competence: (1) behaviors children and adolescents observe within their home or culture, (2) cognitive factors such as a student's own expectations of success, and (3) social factors such as classroom and school climate. Bandura's *reciprocal determinism model* stated that these three influences are reciprocally related. That is, each factor influences others equally and changes in one factor will result in changes in the others. In the classroom, for example, a child's beliefs about himself and his competence (*self-efficacy*) can affect social behavior which, in turn, will have an impact on the classroom environment. At the same time, changes in the classroom that lead to a change in competence will have an impact on self-efficacy. Many researchers support this reciprocal view of the construction of a variety of self-views (Harter, 1999).

Bronfenbrenner (1979) provided an expanded view regarding the impact of the environment on human development. His *ecological theory* stated that people develop within a series of three environmental systems. At the core of his theory are *microsystems*, which include the few environments where the individual spends a large part of his time. According to Bronfenbrenner, the school and the classroom represent a significant microsystem of social development for children. His theory also emphasized the importance of the *macrosystem*, including the factors that are impacting all individuals such as the movement from the agricultural age to the industrial age to the information/conceptual age (Huitt, 2007). Bronfenbrenner also highlighted the importance of the *mesosystem* which he views as the link between various microsystems (eg, the link between family experiences and school experiences) as well as the interpreter of the macrosystem to the individual child or youth. Bronfenbrenner's work adds support to the importance of communication and collaboration between the family and school in a child's social development.

Research Support for Developing Social Competence

Researchers have been studying the connection between social development and academic achievement for decades and have come to a startling conclusion: the single best predictor of adult adaptation is not academic achievement or intelligence, but rather the ability of the child to get along with other children (Hartup, 1992). Additionally, Wentzle (1993) found that prosocial and antisocial behavior are significantly related to grade point average and standardized test scores, as well as teachers' preferences for the student. These studies, and others like them, indicated that a socially adjusted child is more likely to be the academically successful child.

As an explanation for why social development is important to the academic learning process, Caprara, Barbanelli, Pastorelli, Bandura and Zimbardo (2000) noted that aggression and other maladaptive behaviors detract from academic success by 'undermining academic pursuits and creating socially alienating conditions' for the aggressive child. Studies show also that if children are delayed in social development in early childhood they are more likely to be at-risk for maladaptive behaviors such as antisocial behavior, criminality, and drug use later in life (Greer-Chase, Rhodes, &

Kellam, 2002). In fact, Kazdin (1985) noted that the correlations between preschool-aged aggression and aggression at age 10 is higher than the correlation between IQ and aggression.

Studies done with students at the ages of middle childhood and adolescence support the notion that those social skills acquired in early education are related to social skills and academic performance throughout school-aged years. One such longitudinal study conducted with third- and fourth-grade students found that social skills were predictive of both current and future academic performance (Malecki & Elliot, 2002). Mitchell and Elias (as cited in Elias, Zins, Graczyk, & Weissberg, 2003) found similar results; they showed that academic achievement in the third grade was most strongly related to social competence, rather than academic achievement, in the second grade. Similarly, Capara et al. (2000) found that changes in achievement in the eighth grade could be predicted from gauging children's social competence in third grade. At the high school level, Scales, Benson, Roehlkepartain, Sesman, and van Dulmen (2005) measured students' level of 'developmental assets', (positive relationships, opportunities, skills, values and self-perceptions) and its relationship to academic achievement. In this study, seventh, eighth, and ninth grade students with more increased 'developmental assets' had higher GPAs in tenth through twelfth grade than those with less assets. These findings support the view that a broad focus on social and emotional development promotes academic achievement throughout middle and high school.

A study completed by Herbert-Myers, Guttentag, Swank, Smith, and Landry (2006) provided a glimpse into the complexity and multidimensionality of developing social competence. They found that "social connectedness, compliance, and noncompliance with peer requests were predicted by concurrent language skills, whereas concurrent impulsivity and inattentiveness were important for understanding frustration tolerance/flexibility with peers" (p. 174). They also found that language and skills used in toy play at age three were directly related to language competence and attention skills at age eight. Their conclusion was that early social and language skills influenced later social competence through both direct and indirect means.

Summary

This short review of theory and research related to social development highlights the following issues:

1. Social intelligence and social competence, while defined differently by various theorists and researchers, all point to a definition that includes multiple components (at the very least, self-views, social cognition, social

awareness, self-regulation, and social facility or skill). Some researchers would add moral character development to this list.

2. An individual's self-views are (1) constructed in social settings, (2) an important component of developing social competency, and (3) vary depending upon the social situation in which the individual is engaging.
3. The relationships between early social development, the concomitant foundational competencies, and later social development are complex and not always direct and linear. This suggests a systems approach would provide the best framework to describe how best to influence the development of social competency; both in terms of a view of individual human beings as well as the environment or ecology within which that development occurs

Fortunately, research on social and emotional interventions in the early childhood years showed the potential to positively impact maladaptive social behavior. Hemmeter, Ostrosky, and Fox (2006) summarized research showing that the outcomes of early childhood interventions included decreased aggression and noncompliance, improved peer relationships, increased academic success, and increased self-control, self-monitoring, and self-correction. These issues will be discussed in the next section.

Impacting Social Development

As discussed previously, the initial development of social competency takes place within the home and is initiated with the infants' attachment to his or her primary caregiver. As such, the quality of the parent-infant interaction is an important influence on the development of a quality level of attachment. A key issue for infant attachment is the sensitivity of the primary caregiver to the infant's psychological and behavioral processes and states (De Wolff & van IJzendoorn, 1997). While there is evidence to support a genetic link to sensitivity levels (Scarr, 1993), there is also evidence that sensitivity has a learning component (Baumrind, 1993).

As the infant becomes a toddler and then moves into early childhood, Baumrind (1989, 1993) as well as Parke and Buriel (2006) found that other dimensions became important. These included such factors as parental warmth (eg, being aware and responsive to a child's needs) and demandingness (eg, limiting inappropriate behaviors and reinforcing socially acceptable behaviors). Brooks-Gunn, Berlin, and Fuligni (2000) suggested that these skills neither come naturally nor are developed automatically by all parents and, therefore, it is necessary to include the education of the family in any effective early childhood development program.

Much of the current research on the importance of social-emotional learning (SEL) points to the years of pre-kindergarten through first grade as the *sensitive period* for social development. Not only are young brains still developing rapidly during these years (Sigelman & Rider, 2006), but normally children are having their first social interactions outside of the home. Most often, those programs focus on developing school readiness to learn in formal learning environments (Shonkoff, 2000).

However, critics suggest that society should not expect schools to make up all deficits in home and community functioning. Fox, Dunlap, Hemmeter, Joseph, and Strain (2003) advocated developing a school-wide approach to developing social and emotional competence in young children that includes links to families and community. They presented their model in the form of a pyramid with activities designed for all stakeholders at the bottom and activities targeted to specific individuals with particular challenges at the top. The four levels are: (1) building positive relationships with children, families and colleagues; (2) designing supportive and engaging environments both at the school and classroom level; (3) teaching social and emotional awareness and skills, often in short, explicit lessons, and (4) developing individualized interventions for children with the most challenging behavior, such as children with Attention Deficit Hyperactivity Disorder or Autism Spectrum Disorders.

Home and Community

Brooks-Gunn et al. (2000) suggested that, at the very least, schools need to have a parent education component for their early childhood programs. In a review of 800 meta-analyses of factors related to school achievement, Hattie (2009) found that the home environment and parental involvement with the child's school are two of the 66 most significant variables predicting academic achievement (see Huitt, Huitt, Monetti, & Hummel, 2009, for a review of this research). A wide variety of other researchers concluded that positive connections among the home, school, and community establishes a sociocultural climate that is conducive to any number of desired developmental outcomes (Epstein & Sanders, 2000; Henderson & Mapp, 2002; Roehlkepartain, Benson, & Sesma, 2003). CASEL (http://www.casel.org/) as well as The Search Institute (http://www.search-institute.org/) are two excellent resources for material on how to establish these connections.

Supportive and Engaging Environments

Even though the home environment is a powerful influence on social development, Sroufe (1996) provided evidence that the quality of the social interactions after infancy can modify early attachment experiences. An important component of that influence is to have a learning environment that students perceive as safe and supportive (Caprara et al., 2000). Bub (2009) showed specifically that children had better social skills and fewer behavior problems when enrolled in preschool, first-, and third-grade classrooms that were more emotionally supportive rather than academically focused.

As previously mentioned, activities and programs focused on impacting social development generally also focused on emotional development, referred to as social emotional learning (SEL). Proponents of SEL are not arguing for a reduced focus on academic learning, but rather a balanced curriculum that incorporates academic *and* social/emotional learning (Merrell & Guelder, 2010). A variety of researchers have demonstrated that a focus on SEL can aid in the academic learning process and lead to increased scores on academic tests. For example, Wang, Haertel, and Walberg (1990) examined 28 categories of variables that influence learning. They found that 8 of the 11 most influential categories predicting improved academic learning were related to social and emotional factors such as social interactions, classroom climate, and relationships with peer groups. Elias et al. (1997) supported that finding: "[W]hen schools attend systematically to students' social and emotional skills, the academic achievement of children increases, the incidence of problem behaviors decreases, and the quality of relationships surrounding each child improves" (p. 1). Ryan and Patrick (2001) found that

> When students believe they are encouraged to know, interact with, and help classmates during lessons; when they view their classroom as one where students and their ideas are respected and not belittled; when students perceive their teacher as understanding and supportive; and when they feel their teacher does not publicly identify students' relative performance, they tend to engage in more adaptive patterns of learning than would have been predicted from their reports the previous year (p. 441).

Relatively simple actions teachers can use to impact the classroom climate include greeting each child at the door by name, posting children's work at their eye level, praising students' work, encouraging students who are not immediately successful, and sending home positive notes about students' classroom behavior (Fox et al., 2003).

The next sections will address the development of social competencies. However, this research and theory in this domain should be integrated with a focus on developing cognitive, affective, conative, and moral competencies as these are interwoven when social competencies are being developed and demonstrated.

Integrating a Focus on Developing Academic and Social Competence

There are basically four different categories of approaches to developing social competencies in a school setting: (1) integrate a focus on social development within traditional methods of teaching; (2) develop academic lessons and units utilizing an instructional approach that highlights a focus on developing social competence; (3) develop a holistic approach to instructional design with corresponding connections to curriculum and assessment that identify social development as one of several domains that will be the focus of competency development; and (4) directly teach social skills. Examples of these four approaches will be discussed below. There will also be a short discussion of the necessity to develop a classroom management system that complements the selected approach to instruction.

Integrate a focus on social development within traditional methods of teaching. There are quite a number of lesson plans available that integrate a focus on developing social competency within a traditional direct instruction lesson format. For example, Huitt (2009d, 2010a) worked with practicing PreK-5 classroom teachers to develop lessons that integrate academic reading lessons with more holistic objectives identified in the Brilliant Star framework. Lessons dealing with developing social competencies focus on making friends and interacting with family members. An excellent set is provided by Lesson Planet (go to http://www.lessonplanet.com using the search terms "social emotional development").

For the most part, a focus on developing social competency utilizes instructional methods associated with cooperative learning. One of the most widely used is referred to as Think-Pair-Square-Share (Kagan, 1991). In this method, the teacher asks a question and has each student write down his or her thoughts. The students then work in pairs to discuss their thoughts; at a minimum this means that every student is involved in a conversation on the topic. Next, students get in groups of four and share the ideas they discussed while in pairs, working on building a set of shared ideas. Finally, one member of the group shares the group's thinking with the class while the teacher integrates and organizes the different viewpoints.

Develop socially-oriented academic lessons and units. Another approach to integrating a focus on developing social competence with academic competence is to use a method of instruction that imbeds developing social competence into the events of instruction. For example, the 4MAT system developed by McCarthy (2000) included eight steps designed to address different learning styles and brain lateralization dominance of students (see Huitt, 2009b, for an overview.) Each lesson is comprised of two instructional events that answer the primary question of four different types of learners: (1) Why?; (2) What?; (3) How?; and (4) If?

The developer advocates extensive social interaction throughout each lesson and has resources showing exemplary lessons for all academic areas in K-12 classrooms available at her website (see http://www.aboutlearning.com/).

The Character Through the Arts program is an excellent example of reorganizing instruction so that it focuses both on academic learning as well as developing more holistic competencies. It has as its foundation the Artful Learning Model developed by Leonard Bernstein (see https://leonardbernstein.com/artful-learning) and adds to that an integration of skills associated with a holistic view of human development similar to that of CASEL (eg, Cohen, 2006; Elias & Arnold, 2006; Zins et al., 2004) and Narvaez (2006). Each lesson has four different steps: Experience, Inquire, Create, and Reflect. These are very similar to those used in 4MAT system but are more constructivistically-oriented rather than using direct instruction.

Develop a holistic approach to instructional design. There are a variety of programs that take a more holistic approach to developing children and youth; these programs not only advocate developing lessons and units, but also advocate assessing the development of competencies across a wide range of domains. For example, the Habits of Mind program developed by Costa and Kallick (2000, 2008; Costa, 2009) described 16 habits of mind that all children and youth need to develop. Three of those relate to competencies in the affect/emotion domain (listen with understanding and empathy, respond with wonderment and awe, and find humor) and two relate to competencies in the social domain (think and communicate with clarity and precision; think interdependently). Their approach is very similar in many ways to the SEL approach developed by CASEL (eg, Cohen, 2006; Elias & Arnold, 2006; Zins et al., 2004) and the moral character development program developed by Narvaez (2006). Sample lesson plans are provided through Costa's website (see http://www.artcostacentre.com/).

One of the most complete school-based approaches to developing the whole person is the International Baccalaureate (IB) program. Central to each of the three programs (Primary Years Program, Middle Years Program, and Diploma Program) is the Learner Profile (International Baccalaureate Organization, 2010) that lists nine desired attributes. In addition to two that focus on the social domain (communicators and open-mindedness), two focus on the self (balanced and reflective), two are categorized in the cognitive/thinking domain (knowledgeable and thinkers), one in the affective/emotion domain (caring), one in the conative/volitional domain (risk-takers), and one in the moral/character domain (principled).

A foundational principle of all IB programs is "learner as inquirer" and the inquiry units have collaboration in groups as a primary activity. For teachers in an IB program there are a wide variety of lesson plans and units for all subjects in all grade levels.

Directly teach social skills. There are times when it is necessary to directly teach social skills in order to prepare students to work successfully in cooperative groups. The Department of Education in Contra Costa County, California has provided an excellent resource with lessons covering a wide range of topics (see http://www.cccoe.net/social/skillslist.htm). There are lessons addressing basic skills such as introducing one's self and reading body language, social skills used in the classroom such as listening to others and being in a group discussion, skills used in interacting with peers such as expressing empathy and arguing respectfully, and skills used in interacting with adults such as completing agreements and proper theater behavior. This website would be a good place to start when looking for ideas on directly teaching social and emotional skills.

Another excellent resource is provided by Teacher Vision (see http://www.teachervision.fen.com/emotional-development/teacher-resources/32913.html). In addition to lessons focused directly on teaching social and emotional skills, there are also many that integrate these issues with academic content.

Classroom management. Designing lessons that address the development of social and emotional skills must be done within the context of providing a learning environment that supports the instructional lessons. Norris (2003) made the case that developing a school-wide classroom management program focusing on the social and emotional skills identified by CASEL (Elias et al., 1997) is the best way to address these issues. Not only does classroom management set the climate for learning, it is also where the need for developing social and emotional skills is seen most directly. Her major point, as a principal of an elementary school, was that developing these skills must be seen as a year-long process and that one should not expect to see instant results. Teachers need to be trained, parents need to be involved, and children need to systematically develop and practice the skills over an extended period of time. At the same time, teachers found that when they took the time to directly teach these skills, less time was needed to attend to classroom management issues and more time was provided for teaching necessary academic content. Zins et al. (2004) made much the same case in their review of the connection between social and emotional learning and school academic success.

Bailey's (2001) conscious discipline program is an excellent example of directly teaching the skills necessary to developing a classroom climate that allows academic learning to flourish. Two principles provide the foundation for the conscious discipline program: (1) classroom discipline must be focused on developing community rather than compliance with rules; and (2) the human brain is structured to process information in certain, specific ways. Most importantly from the perspective taken in this chapter, there must be a focus on developing student's thinking, emotional, conative, and social skills in the context of the individual person taking responsibility for his or her own behavior and contributing to positive social interactions. The program emphasizes that everyone has seven powers (perception, unity, attention, agency, love, acceptance, and intention); the teacher and students are both responsible for setting the conditions and making the effort to develop these powers.

Developing Individualized Interventions

Despite all the best efforts that a school and classroom teachers can make to develop a positive and engaging environment, provide opportunities to develop social skills within academic settings, and teach these skills directly to all students, there will always be children and youth who need additional learning opportunities to develop these skills. Most likely these will be students with challenging mental, emotional, and/or behavioral issues that stem from a particular diagnosis associated with Autism Spectrum Disorders (ASD) or emotional and behavioral disorders (EBD) (Quinn, Kavale, Mathur, Rutherford , & Forness, 1999). However, White, Keonig, and Scahill (2007) make a case that social cognition is such an important process that special effort must be made to create the types of environments and provide the support that will result in even the most challenged students developing social competency.

Autism Spectrum Disorders (ASD). Winner (2007) reviewed research on three separate theories that describe social competencies that most children will learn as a matter of normal development, but that must be addressed specifically for students with ASD: (1) central coherence theory; (2) executive dysfunction theory; and (3) theory of mind. Firth (as cited in Winner) defines the primary issue of central coherence as the ability to "conceptualize to a larger whole…to relate their information back to a larger pattern of behavior and thought" (p. iv). People with ASD will often become so focused on a specific, concrete detail that they are unable to relate that detail to other details or to a larger whole. There is a tendency to isolate each and every stimulus into its own separate category. This makes establishing social relationships very difficult because they simply do not perceive a back and forth connection between their thoughts and actions and those of others.

McEvoy, Rogers, and Pennington (as cited in Winner, 2007) defined the primary issue of executive dysfunction theory as the "ability to create organizational structures that allow for flexibility and prioritization" in moment-to-moment and day-to-day activities (p. v). Students who have difficulty in this area simply follow a step-by-step procedure for doing whatever needs to be done. If anything changes from the pattern they have memorized, they get very upset and confused. Again, this makes it difficult to form and engage in social relationships because they seldom follow a set pattern.

Baron-Cohen, Leslie, and Frith (as cited in Winner, 2007) stated that the major issue in the theory of mind is the ability to "intuitively track what others know and think across personal interactions" (p. vi). Pelicano (2010) suggested that one's theory of mind is a somewhat abstract concept and dependent upon one's level of central coherence and executive functioning. He suggests that those two areas should be the focus of interventions.

Emotional and behavioral disorders (EBD). In a review of the literature on teaching social skills to students with symptoms of EBD, Maag (2006) found that literally hundreds of studies had been published on developing their social skills. He discussed the difference between developing social skills (the learning of specific behavioral practices) and developing social competence (a more general term describing the ability to establish and maintain relationships and work in groups). He concluded that social skill development does not automatically mean the development of social competence.

The interventions Maag (2006) reviewed represented selections from a wide variety of different learning theories: operant conditioning (rehearsal, reinforcement), information processing (goal setting, problem solving), observational (modeling), and social cognitive (group discussions, self-monitoring, self-evaluation). In general, meta-analyses showed interventions had only a moderate impact on behavior (effect size = 0.35). His overall conclusion was that the impact of social skills training on EBD students ranged "from dismal to guarded optimism" (p. 14). It would appear that the best advice for classroom teachers is to develop very targeted interventions for specific individuals based on what they believe to be the most important deficits that the student needs to address. Whatever success they may have will likely be as good, but no worse, than what the experts have devised.

Assessing, Measuring, and Evaluating Social Competence

Those interested in developing students' social competencies must address the existing pressure on schools to be accountable for student learning as measured by scores on standardized academic tests and the lack of attention paid to other aspects of the developing student (Braun, 2004). The No Child Left Behind (NCLB) Act (U.S. Department of Education, 2001) and the more recent *Race to the Top* legislation (U.S. Department of Education, 2009) have codified an emphasis building for over three decades since the publication of A *Nation at Risk* (National Commission on Excellence in Education, 1983) which, in turn, was a restatement of a concern stated two decades earlier (Carroll, 1963; Coleman et al., 1966). Fortunately, there is ample evidence to show that a focus on SEL increases academic test scores rather than causing then to drop (Durlak, Weissberg, Dymnicki, Taylor, & Schellinger, 2011; Payton et al., 2008; Zins et al., 2004). In addition, a wide variety of researchers have shown that SEL is important for mental health, success in work, and living in a democracy (Berkowitz, 2007; Cohen, 2006: Goleman, 2006; Payton et al.,2000). However, one result of the focus on academics has been that areas of schooling such as art or music, and even recess, where students would more likely focus on components of social and emotional development, have been reduced (Center on Education Policy, 2007).

It is vital that parents, educators, and community members who value the development of competencies in the social domain recognize that efforts to do so must be held accountable for success. This means that evidence must be collected, organized, analyzed, and programs evaluated using the best information available.

Gresham (1983) made the case that there is a difference between assessing social skills (thought to be discrete components of social competence) and social competence itself. He suggested there are three types or categories of measures focused on social development: socially-valued goals, observations in natural environments, and standardized measures. Each of these types will be discussed in the following sections.

Socially-valued Goals

Gresham (1983) provided examples of socially-valued goals that are of concern to the general public as well as parents and educators; these would include such school related factors as school attendance, disciplinary referrals, and school suspensions. He also included such non-school related factors as interaction with law enforcement. Other researchers have identified such factors as engaging in less risky behavior (Zins, Payton, Weissberg, & O'Brien, 2007) and knowledge of community and national affairs, involvement in volunteering, voting, or engaging in leadership in youth organizations that should be desired outcomes of schooling and education (Moore, Lippman, & Brown, 2004).

While social competence has been shown to be related to these indicators and could certainly point to desirable outcomes for children and youth, these types of indicators are not very sensitive when evaluating the relatively short-term school-based programs discussed in this chapter. Additionally, there are many other factors that could influence these types of measures such as home environment (Roehlkepartain, Scales, Roehlkepartain, & Rude, 2002) and community interactions (Devaney, O'Brien, Tavegia, & Resnik, 2005). Therefore, while they may be valuable in investigating the overall mental health and well-being of a community, they should not be used for evaluating programs focused on addressing the development of social competencies.

Observations in Natural Environments

Gresham (1983) identified a number of measures derived from observations in natural environments that could better serve as indicators of social competence in school-related settings. These include such factors as peer acceptance (or rejection), making and maintaining friendships, and successfully working in groups. Other researchers would add reports of bullying or being bullied, engaging in nonviolent conflict resolution, resisting negative peer pressure, and self-report measures on attitudes towards school to this list (Moore et al., 2004; Roehlkepartain et al., 2003; Zins et al., 2007).

It is also possible to collect evidence directly on the social competencies discussed previously such as social awareness and relationship skills (Collaborative for Academic, Social, and Emotional Learning (CASEL), 2003, 2006; Goleman, 2006). For example, in a study of peer social status during middle childhood and adolescence, Cole, Dodge, and Coppotelli (1982) identified five groups: (1) popular, (2) average, (3) neglected, (4) rejected, and (5) controversial. In a follow-up study by Dodge, Schlundt, Schocken, and Delugach (1983), students categorized as popular had high levels of perspective taking skills, self-regulation, and communication and language skills. They also had higher levels of cognitive and social problem-solving abilities and were assertive, but not deliberately antagonistic or disruptive to others. In general, students in the average group had lower levels of social competence than did those classified as popular. They also showed less aggression than did those classified as rejected. The neglected group had these same characteristics with the addition of being less likely to be visible in a social group. On the other hand, those classified as rejected displayed higher levels of aggression, were more likely to behave in ways that were potentially embarrassing to peers and were more likely to be socially withdrawn. These students also had lower levels of perspective taking and self-control as well as less well-developed social interaction skills. Finally, those students classified as controversial had higher levels of cognitive ability and social interaction skills, but also had higher levels of aggressive behavior.

There are at least two challenges that must be of concern when collecting these types of data. First, social competence is a composite of many different types of skills, attitudes, and knowledge. Guiding students to developing new knowledge or changing an attitude or a skill, may or may not impact social competence as defined in such activities as making and maintaining relationships and working in groups. Gresham, Sugai, and Horner (2001) suggested measures of skills displayed in role-play tests and assessments of problem-solving or social cognition might be especially vulnerable to a lack of predictive validity.

A second challenge in collecting these types of data is the necessity of training educators and parents to collect data that are both reliable and valid. Chan, Ramey, Ramey, and Schmitt (2000) found that teachers and parents made quite different assessments of children's developing social skills in kindergarten through third grade. Parents saw their children as developing social skills in an absolute sense, although teachers judged children as not meeting their expectations of appropriate social behavior for their age group. Therefore, while these types of data are potentially useful in determining the success or failure of interventions, care must be taken to provide adequate training for the observers and to determine the relationship of discrete measures of knowledge, attitudes, and skills to social competence.

Standardized Measures

There are a wide variety of standardized instruments that have been used to assess both social skills and social competence (Elias et al., 1997; Sosna & Mastergeorge, 2005; Yates, Ostrosky, Cheatham, Fettig, Shaffer, & Santos, 2008). Some instruments, such as the Ages and Stages Questionnaire (ASQ), the Social Emotional section of the ASQ (ASQ: SE), the Denver Developmental Screening Test, and the Parents Evaluation of Developmental Status (PEDS) are used more for screening purposes in order to identify at-risk children (Ringwalt, 2008). These types of instruments are used frequently at the behest of state and local governments to identify those who may be delayed, or at risk for delay, in social emotional development (p. ii, Rosenthal & Kaye, 2005). While these might be useful for describing student characteristics upon entering school, they do not provide the opportunity to assess change over the full range of years a child or youth would likely be in school and, therefore, are of limited use for assessing the development of social competency. An important caveat when using these screening instruments is that they should not be used as the sole criterion for making a judgment regarding a child's readiness for school. Rather they should be used in conjunction with other approaches, such as observations in naturalistic environments, in order to increase the validity of any placement decisions. A second issue is that they should be administered by trained and qualified personnel. There are nuances in collecting and analyzing data that are not obvious to an untrained practitioner.

There are three widely accepted standardized assessments used regularly in research on social and emotional competence for K-12 (ages 5 to 18) children and youth. These include the School Social Behavior Scales (SSBS, Merrell, 1993; SSBS2, Merrell, 2008), Home and Community Social Behavior Scales (HCSBS, Merrell & Caldarella, 2008), and the Social Skills Rating System (SSRS). There are also a variety of new instruments that focus on social competence such as the Social Skills Improvement System (SSIS,

Gresham & Elliott, 2009), meant as a replacement for the SSRS and the Initiation-Response Assessment (IRA, Cummings Kaminski, & Merrell, 2008). Each of these will be briefly discussed in this section.

School Social Behavior Scales (SSBS2). The School Social Behavior Scales (SSBS), developed by Merrell (1993) and recently updated (Merrell, 2008), is one of the most widely used assessment instruments for students in K-12 classrooms. It is a rating scale designed to be used by classroom teachers or other educators and takes less than 10 minutes to complete. The SSBS2 is actually comprised of two scales: (1) the Social Competence Scale, and (2) the Antisocial Behavior Scale. In turn, the Social Competence Scale is comprised of three subscales: (1) interpersonal skills, (2) self-management skills, and (3) academic skills.

Taub (2001) provided an excellent example of research using the SSBS. She evaluated the implementation of a violence prevention program in a rural elementary school. The instrument was sensitive to change in social competence and anti-social behavior over the duration of the one-year program and matched results of observations of actual classroom behavior. No published data beyond that of validating the revision of the SSBS2 is available at this time.

Home and Community Social Behavior Scales (HCSBS). The Home and Community Social Behavior Scales (HCSBS) is a 65-item instrument designed for use by parents and caretakers. It is seen as a compliment to the SSBS/SSBS2 (Merrill, Streeter, Boelter, Caldarella, & Gentry, 2001; Merrell & Caldarella, 2008) and is comprised of the same two subscales: Social Competence and Anti-social behavior.

Zion and Jenvey (2006) provided an example of how the HCSBS (as well as the SSBS2) are used in research. They studied intellectually challenged children aged 9-12 and children with average IQ children in two types of school environments—a regular school and a special education school. The differences they found between ratings of parents and teachers confirmed previous research (Chan et al., 2000) in that parents tended to rate their children higher on social competence and lower on anti-social behavior than did their children's teachers. This is a very important issue when implementing programs designed to address social development in school-aged children, especially when educators attempt to communicate with parents regarding their children's classroom and school behavior.

Social Skills Rating System (SSRS) and Social Skills Improvement System (SSIS). The Social Skills Rating System (SSRS) was developed by Gresham and Elliott (1990). It is comprised of three separate questionnaires to be completed by teachers, parents, and children with third-grade reading skills and generally takes 15-25 minutes to complete.

The SSRS comprises three subscales: Social Skills, Problem Behaviors, and Academic Competence. Of most interest to educators focused on developing social competence, the Social Skills subscale includes five subscales: Empathy, Assertion, Responsibility, Self-control, and Cooperation. Notice that these overlap quite well with Goleman's definition of social intelligence (social awareness and social skills) as well as the conceptions of social competence developed by Broderick and Blewitt (2007) and CASEL (2003, 2007).

McKown, Gumbiner, Russo, and Lipton (2009) provided an excellent example of research completed using this instrument. They used a number of different instruments to assess different factors thought to be related to social competence. They found that SEL Skill level (a combination of three latent variables—nonverbal awareness, social meaning, and social reasoning) was a relatively good predictor of the score on the SSRS social competence subscale. However, measures of self-regulation were even more strongly related, confirming that this conative/volitional component must be addressed in addition to social awareness, social competence, and social skills in order for social competence to be demonstrated in natural environments such as home and school.

The Social Skills Improvement System (SSIS) was developed by Gresham and Elliott (2009) as a replacement for the SSRS. While little research has been conducted using this instrument, a school-based intervention program has been developed using the research that lead to its development (Elliott & Gresham, 2007). Those interested in using one of these instruments should consult with the authors as to which one would be most appropriate for a specific application.

Initiation-Response Assessment (IRA). The Initiation-Response Assessment (IRA) is a classroom behavior observation process used to collect data on social competence while students engage in prescribed cooperative learning tasks (Cummings et al., 2008). This approach provides an opportunity to collect data on classroom behavior using a standardized process. First-grade students were videotaped while they engaged twice in four activities in an 8-week period. The videotapes were then coded for children's engagement in four categories of social interaction: (1) frequency of social interactions (were the interactions goal-directed or non-goal directed), (2) helpful/encouraging/facilitative (HEF), (3) overall level of task engagement (on/off-task or cooperative), and (4) negative behavior (either weak or strong). Scores on these categories were compared with SSBS developed by Merrell (1993). Four summary scores were then developed using the behavioral data. The authors reported that "Correlations between scores on the IRA and the SBSS "tended to correlate in expected directions with the SSBS and its subscales" (p. 939). However, the authors stated these correlations are difficult to interpret and a great deal more work is needed in this area.

An advantage of developing observation protocols for social skills and social competence is that teachers trained as observers become more sensitive to the specific behaviors for which they are trained to observe (Huitt, Caldwell, Traver, & Graeber, 1981). Developing videos of children and youth engaging in standardized social interaction activities and then using those to train educators to collect reliable and valid data on important knowledge, attitudes, and skills related to social competence could be one of the most effective and efficient methods for addressing the development of social competence in the classroom.

A caveat. In a comparison of 19 instruments used to assess social skills and social competence, Caldarella and Merrell (1997) found three dimensions were covered about half the time (Peer Relations, Self-management, Academic Success) while two more were covered about one-third of the time (Compliance and Assertion.) The specific behaviors that comprised these dimensions varied widely. Therefore, it is critical that project implementers carefully compare specific behaviors assessed in any given instrument with behaviors addressed in the project to make sure there is adequate overlap. It is very possible to have changes in social knowledge, attitudes, skills and competence that are not demonstrated in the assessment process.

Warnes, Sheridan, Geske, and Warnes (2005) provided another important warning when using standardized assessments to study social behavior. They used qualitative methodology to identify important social skills for second- and fifth-graders. A major finding was that the social behaviors considered important by children as well as their parents and teachers changed for those two age groups. Second-graders (and their parents and teachers) focused more on rule-governed behaviors when defining social competence such as "being respectful of others and their property, following and respecting rules, being fair, and having manners" (p. 183). Just three years later, there was more of a focus on factors dealing with verbal communication such as "communicating verbally about problems and frustrations, being a good listener, giving praise and compliments to others" (p. 183). While the overall definition of social competence did not seem to have changed in that time period, the underlying discrete behaviors used to make that judgment did change. This is similar to assessing academic competencies involved in reading and mathematics. The specific skills used to define competencies in those academic subjects will change as the child progresses through school.

Summary and Conclusions

A common question asked by parents and educators alike is: "If there is so much research to support the importance of social development in academic performance and personal success, why has it not in the mission statements and primary activities of educational institutions?" There are several common arguments against promoting social development in schools (Weare, 2010).

One critique is that a focus on SEL is not the role of the educators; rather it is the parents' responsibility. Critics argue that parents do not want educators involved in the social and emotional development of their children. This critique does not acknowledge that not all students have the support they need from their parents. Even children from families who are not battling factors that increase the likelihood of abuse or neglect such as low socio-economic status, single-parenthood, parental mental health or criminality are likely to benefit from further guidance in the classroom. Knitzer and Lefkowitz (2005) stated that parents play the most vital role in a young child's life, but parenting is a challenge even in the best of circumstances. School and community organizations can provide support even when parents are appropriately guiding the development of SEL in the home (Roehlkepartain et al., 2002).

Some administrators amay believe they already have a school-based social competence program. The challenge is that these are most often targeted at specific individuals in Fox et al.'s (2003) pyramid discussed above. The view taken by Greenberg et al. (2003) is that the impact of such programs has a 'splinter' effect and limits their effectiveness. Greater impact could be made by a school-wide intervention program that addresses social development for all children and connects with families and community for increased support.

Teachers argued that there is not enough time in the day, and teaching and measuring social development will take valuable time away from making sure their students can pass their standardized tests for academics. Again, this is not a question of teaching one or the other, rather it is training educators to address them both, simultaneously. As seen in the research cited in the previous section, putting social skills education into the curriculum does not detract from academic learning time, it makes it more efficient.

Another criticism of SEL implementation is that empirically-based interventions have not been available and measuring progress or delay in social development is not as easy as documenting change in academic achievement. However, research reviewed in this chapter have identified a number of very promising approaches. While more research is certainly needed, there is ample evidence to support an approach addressing multiple domains which contribute to the development of social competency (CASEL, 2003, 2007) and the need to include connections among families, schools, and community in such programs (Epstein & Sanders, 2000).

One the other hand, surveys completed by such groups as Gallup, Metlife, and Public Agenda found that most educators, parents, students, and members of the public support an educational agenda that facilitates the social-emotional development of students (Greenberg et al., 2003). Given the importance of social development for life success and its positive influence on academic learning, it seems the relevant question should no longer be "Why?", but "How?".

One of the most important findings is that successful programs are more likely to focus on multiple domains, include all students in a school rather than just a subset of "problem" students, and involve parents and community in at least the implementation, if not the development of the program (Brookes-Gunn et al., 2000; Fox et al., 2003; Patrikakou & Weissberg, 2007; Weare, 2010; Zins et al., 2007). Another important finding is that developing social competency is done best within social interactions, not in teaching students cognitively about social competency (Zins et al., 2007). The practical implication of this finding is that social and emotional learning activities must be incorporated into the day-to-day instructional and classroom management strategies of the school. At the same time, Durlak et al. (2011) found that "programs are likely to be effective if they use a sequenced, step-by-step training approach, use active forms of learning, focus sufficient time on skill development, and have explicit learning goals" (p. 408). These four components are used to make the acronym SAFE and are highlighted by four questions:

1. Does the program use a connected and coordinated set of activities to achieve their objectives relative to skill development? (Sequenced, step-by-step)
2. Does the program use active forms of learning to help youth learn new skills? (Active)
3. Does the program have at least one component devoted to developing personal or social skills? (Focused)
4. Does the program target specific SEL skills rather than targeting skills or positive development in general terms? (Explicit) (p. 410)

Not only must the program meet specific requirements, but implementing change requires training and expert support for teachers as well as administrative supports and policies (Hemmeter et al., 2006). Because of the necessary time investment in successful program implementation, faculty and staff turn-over is another obstacle that must be considered. Elias et al. (2003) stated that it can be a 5- to 10-year process to implement a program effectively and in this time, there is likely to have been a dramatic change in administration, teachers, and leaders of the program.

Having several school leadership teams involved in implementing reform, rather than one primary 'change agent', will limit the effects of turn-over. Senge (1990) described this as an important component of developing a learning organization. Senge, Scharmer, Jaworski, and Flowers (2004) expanded on this fundamental concept and describe the process of a learning organization emerging from the interactions of its component parts (e.g, administrators, teachers, parents, students). Their view is that learning takes place through cycles of reflection-action-reflection and that consultation among group members is essential to developing a shared understanding of the needs of the present moment.

Losada (2008a & b) described flourishing teams as the foundation for a learning organization. He stated that high flourishing teams have high ratios of inquiry to advocacy, positive statements to negative statements, and other to self when engaging in group consultation. One of his most important findings was that average (languishing) teams have a ratio close to 1:1 for positive versus negative statements, whereas flourishing teams have a ratio between 3:1 and 11:1. An interesting research study might investigate the relationship between classroom teachers' demonstration of these consultation skills and their impact on the development of social competencies among their students. It is certainly conceivable that teachers who participate in flourishing teams will be more likely to model these behaviors in the classroom and be more sensitive to their expression in their students.

8

An Overview of Physical Development[8]

Michelle Caldwell and William Huitt

The education of children and youth today encompasses much more than the traditional reading, writing, and mathematics seen in years past. There is a need to consider the education of our young people from a more holistic perspective (Huitt, Chapter 1, this volume). This chapter will address the importance of considering the physical development of children and youth.

Booth, Chakravarthy and Spangenburg (2002) proposed that the human body is genetically prepared for a higher level of physical activity than is current among most people in post-industrial societies and that physical functioning of the body influences all other domains of the individual. This relationship is best described through the concept of wellness, referring to the total health of the individual including the mental, physical, emotional and spiritual domains (Edlin, Galanty, & Brown, 2002). From the perspective of wellness, each aspect of one's health must be viewed with equal importance because they are all intertwined. If one area of health is neglected, other domains suffer as well.

At the same time that there is a concerted effort to raise test scores (Rebora, 2004), there is a steady decline in the overall physical health of our nation (U.S. Department of Health and Human Services, 2001). Two diseases in particular are increasing in epidemic proportions: obesity and Type 2 diabetes. This rise is linked with two major factors: physical inactivity and poor nutritional habits.

The Surgeon General reported that nearly 50 million adults between the ages of 20 and 74 are obese. Overall, more than 108 million adults are either obese or overweight. That is an astounding 61% of the U.S. population. Though previously considered an adult disease, Type 2 diabetes has increased dramatically in children and adolescents. Laino (2003) reported that one in three American children born in the year 2000 will develop diabetes if they adopt the nation's inactive and overeating lifestyle.

---

[8] Caldwell, M., & Huitt, W. (2004). An overview of physical development. *Educational Psychology Interactive*. Valdosta, GA: Valdosta State University.

One way to address these issues and curb these trends is to better educate our children and youth about the importance of regular physical activity and proper nutrition. Exposure to these topics beginning in early childhood is crucial to the healthy development of our youth. Throughout the remainder of this chapter, more specific issues regarding physical development will be explored, suggestions will be made as to what parents and educators can do to help promote physical development, and measurement issues will be considered that can help educators, parents, and the community take more responsibility for the health of our nation.

Fitness Component

When discussing the physical domain of the human body, it is important to consider five health-related fitness components: cardiovascular endurance, muscular strength, muscular endurance, flexibility, and body composition.

Cardiovascular endurance is defined as the ability of the lungs, heart, and blood vessels to deliver adequate amounts of oxygen and nutrients to the cells to meet the demands of prolonged physical activity. The American Heart Association (2004) reported that cardiovascular disease is the number one killer in America. Therefore, activities promoting cardiovascular fitness are extremely important in the prevention of this life-threatening disease as well as other degenerative illnesses that can be related to poor cardiovascular endurance.

The second and third components of health-related fitness are muscular strength and muscular endurance. Muscular strength is the ability of the muscle to exert a single maximum contraction, whereas muscular endurance is the ability of the muscle to work for long periods of time without getting tired. Muscular strength and endurance are extremely important for everyday living. Daily activities such as climbing stairs, carrying groceries, as well as manual labor, require both strength and endurance of the muscles.

Although it is often times overlooked, flexibility is yet another key component to health-related fitness. Flexibility is defined as the joints ability to move through a full range of motion. Excellent flexibility provides various health related benefits, which include improved physical performance, greater freedom of movement, improved posture, an increase in physical and mental relaxation, and a decrease in the risk of injury. Although an individual's level of flexibility is primarily due to genetics, gender, and age, it is important to recognize that the level of physical activity plays an important role as well. In simple terms, the less physically active we are, the less flexible we are likely to be.

Probably the most outwardly visible sign of an individual's level of physical activity is body structure or body composition. Body composition is the percentage of fat and muscle that makes up a person's body (Rimmer,

1994). For good health, an individual should maintain a proper ratio of one to the other. When levels of body fat are high, an individual is at greater risk for a variety of health problems. High percentages of body fat are strongly correlated with arthritis, heart disease, hypertension, and diabetes. There are many different ways to find body composition; however, not all are accurate. Height and weight charts are probably one of the least accurate means of finding body composition. An individual's muscle mass is not taken into consideration; therefore, someone may be considered obese when in reality they have a large amount of lean muscle in the body. Body mass index (BMI), another commonly used measure of body composition, assesses one's body weight relative to height. A person with a BMI under 18.5 is considered underweight. BMI values of 18.5-25.9 is considered normal, 25-29.5 is considered overweight, and 30 or over is considered obese. The National Center for Chronic Disease Prevention and Health Promotion (2004) provided an easy-to-use, web-based process for calculating BMI.

Understanding the importance of body composition is essential when considering issues regarding overall health. In most schools, when fitness testing is administered, the body composition component of the test is removed because it is considered embarrassing to the child if the percentage of body fat is too high. However, as educators, it is necessary to provide this information to the student and parents, taking the same care with physical data as with academic achievement data. Dealing with the issue while the student is still in school could actually save the individual's life later.

Influencing Factors

There are two major factors that influence each of the health-related fitness components: physical activity and nutrition. Education in both areas is critical in helping an individual to develop overall physical health.

The benefits of physical activity have been viewed as important in our society for many years. However, it was not until the second half of this past century that evidence from a scientific standpoint began to support these beliefs (Cooper, 1991,1999). There is an accumulating body of evidence to support the fact that young children are becoming less physically active and more overweight and obese. For example, the Centers for Disease Control and Prevention (CDC; 2000) reported that physical inactivity has contributed to the 100% increase in the prevalence of childhood obesity in the United States since 1980. In addition to issues regarding obesity, many studies on physical activity have shown that the body responds to exercise in ways that have positive effects on the cardiovascular, respiratory, endocrine, and musculoskeletal systems. More specifically, physical benefits of exercise such as increased muscle strength, range of motion, flexibility, posture, and endurance, all promote self-sufficiency and decrease feelings of depression, dependence, and lack of control. Regular participation in physical activity also appears to reduce anxiety, improve mood, and enhance an individual's ability to perform daily tasks. Also, emerging research in animals and humans alike suggests that physical exercise may boost brain function, improve mood, and otherwise increase the capacity for learning (Kong, 1999).

Proper nutrition is the other major factor that influences physical development. Many adults have been taught incorrect information about nutrition and are teaching this to their children (Willett, Skerrett, & Giovannucci, 2001). For the well-being of children, adults need to become more aware of what proper nutrition encompasses and attempt to instill proper nutritional habits in children from an early age. Unfortunately, some of the information coming from respected sources is inaccurate (Willett, 2001). For example, the Dietary Guidelines for Americans published by the United States Department of Agriculture (1995) suggested that the daily diet should contain 6 to 11 servings of foods high in carbohydrates such as bread, cereal, rice, and pasta. However, the suggestions from faculty at the Harvard School of Public Health (Willett, et al., 2001) proposed these foods should be used sparingly. While both suggested eating healthy foods such as grain products, fruits and vegetables, low-fat dairy products, beans, lean meat, poultry, fish, or nuts, the recommended portions of each are often quite different (see Willett, 2001 for a detailed comparison).

It is also important that adults teach children healthy eating by example. Children should not only hear educators and other adults telling them how they should eat, but they should also see those around them eating these same healthy foods. There is a caveat in the recommendations from experts: dietary guidelines are intended for children over the age of two years. Infants from birth to the age of two need a higher amount of fat intake in their diet because of their rapid growth rate. The American Heart Association (2004) stated that beginning around the age of two, toddlers can be moved on to the recommended dietary guidelines recommended for adults. Parents should consult their family pediatrician for more specific dietary guidelines for an infant. Staying up-to-date on current information regarding nutrition and following recommended dietary guidelines are important factors in being able to help properly educate our youth.

Educational Programs

There needs to be a concerted national effort to curb the current trends of cardiovascular disease, obesity, Type 2 diabetes, and other degenerative illnesses related to physical inactivity and improper nutrition. In order to take a step in the right direction, the first priority must become stressing a greater importance in the area of physical development in our educational system. One of the most distressing statistics of all in the relationship of disease and physical inactivity are the statistics that show physical education programs throughout our nation are being placed on the back burner. The CDC (2000) reported that nearly half of young people 12-21 years of age are not vigorously active. For most children, physical education class is the only place they will have any type of exposure to physical activity. Yet, only one state, Illinois, requires daily physical education in all grades K-12. In Georgia, only one semester of health and physical education combined in high school is required for graduation. If this is the case, what can educators and parents do to help children and youth in the area of physical development?

Physical Education Programs

From an educational standpoint, it is imperative that standards be established that will guide the physical development of children and youth throughout their years of formal schooling. Effective physical education programs should set clear expectations of students, specifically designed as age appropriate. Expectations should not only cover the development of motor skills, they should include aspects of the cognitive and affective domains as well. Those in charge of setting standards, such as those implemented in South Carolina (South Carolina Department of Education, 2018), should be applauded for showing a commitment to the overall health of their children.

In South Carolina, seven different standards must be met if an individual is to be considered physically educated. All standards are addressed at each grade level, though each is modified so that it is age appropriate. In addition, all standards at each grade level are given an example of assessment that are used to monitor student learning and development. For example, physical education standard number one states that students should be able to demonstrate competency in many movement forms and proficiency in a few movement forms. The standard is then modified for age appropriateness so that, in preschool and kindergarten, the standard specifies that students should be able to display most fundamental movement patterns (eg, throwing, receiving, jumping, and striking) in simple conditions and demonstrate control of the varied use of these patterns.

Each standard includes several benchmarks so that student learning can be monitored. An example of a benchmark for preschool and kindergarten is: the student will travel with control forward, backward, and sideways using a variety of locomotor patterns and change directions quickly. In addition to the benchmarks, an example of assessment is given which includes teacher observation along with criteria for assessment of the movement patterns. If the task is to demonstrate a locomotor skill (eg, slide, hop, skip, or gallop), the teacher assesses the task and three points are given if the student demonstrates each pattern at a level of mature form. If the student demonstrates the beginnings of each pattern but it is not fully developed, two points are given. Finally, one point is given if there is no evidence that the student can demonstrate the pattern at the time. This is just one example of the format used for students in the state at each grade level. The South Carolina Department of Education (2018) website provides further information regarding effective physical education programs and a complete list of state standards. It is of utmost importance that all educational systems adopt these kinds of standards and make a more concerted effort to hold educators accountable for teaching and measuring them. These issues will be addressed later in the chapter.

Age-appropriate Activities

As educators and parents consider how to help children develop the five health-related fitness components it is important to consider the age-appropriateness of activities. Obviously, one would not expect a young child in the first or second grade to participate in the same type of muscular strength and endurance training as a senior in high school. It is necessary to develop exercise prescriptions for both the elementary, middle grades, and secondary levels. The goal of the prescriptions is to increase the activity level of all students to at least 60 minutes per day by suggesting activities which students can engage in outside of the classroom. Within this prescription, detailed instructions must be given for activities that are age appropriate for the development of each health-related fitness component; students can chart the time spent engaged in the various activities for their math classes and write about their exercise in their language arts classes. It is important to consider that fitness activities need to be made fun for children or they will not want to participate. For most individuals, giving a direct command to go out and run two laps will not be an interesting activity in which to participate.

In the area of cardiovascular endurance some fun activities for elementary age and middle school students might include: flag tag, a 15-minute fun circuit, or a family fun walk. In a game of flag tag, each student puts a flag in their back pocket. On the signal the students begin chasing others around the designated area, attempting to grab as many flags as they can. At the end of 1 minute, stop the game; the person with the most scarves is declared the winner for that round. The 15-minute fun circuit includes stations for jump rope, jumping over a hoop, jumping jacks, and mountain climbers. Adding music to the fun circuit makes the activity even more appealing. The family fun walk is an activity that can take place at home. With the family, students are encouraged to take a brisk 20- minute walk throughout the neighborhood. A list of items to be found along the walk can be compiled to make the walk into a scavenger hunt type of activity.

For middle grade or secondary age students, flag tag can be modified into rollerblade flag tag. The same directions would apply with the exception that the students are rollerblading instead of jogging. Jumping rope is another cardiovascular activity that older students can enjoy. Creating task cards and routines as well as setting the activity to music is an excellent way to engage students in a cardiovascular workout. It is also important to consider that basic activities such as jogging, walking, swimming, and aerobic dance are also considered excellent activities for people of all ages that promote cardiovascular endurance.

When most people think of muscular strength and endurance training, they immediately think of weight training in the weight room. However, educators should be aware that weight training is not a feasible activity for younger children. There are many activities that students of all ages can engage in without ever entering a weight room facility. For elementary age children, activities like tug-of-war, push-up routines, and the use of a stability ball can all assist in the development of muscular strength and endurance. Middle school and secondary level students can also use the stability balls, yet they may also safely begin workouts within the weight room environment. It is crucial for educators and parents to understand that teaching proper technique as well having proper supervision are key elements in a successful weight lifting program.

Body composition can be developed through a variety of activities. The stability ball can be used to perform sit-ups and crunches for students of all age levels. Each activity can be modified to fit the ability level of all students. For example, level one would consist of sitting on top of the ball, lying back and performing a certain number of sit-ups. In level two, there is a slight increase in the difficulty of the task. At this level, the student slides down the ball with their back at a slight angle. The student then attempts to perform the set number of sit-ups. Level three would be the most difficult. The student would lie down with their back on the ground, and their legs on top of the ball while performing the sit-ups. Older students can also use weight training as a method of developing body composition. Educators and parents need to also consider the importance of proper diet along with these methods of exercise when attempting to develop body composition.

The development of flexibility is mainly acquired through stretching programs. Stretches can be categorized on a continuum from static (no motion) to ballistic (rapid motion) (Kurz, 1994). Static stretching involves stretching a muscle to the farthest point and holding the stretch. Isometric stretching is a type of static stretching which involves resistance of muscle groups through the tensing of the muscles. This type of stretching is considered one of the best ways to increase flexibility. Passive stretching is sometimes referred to as relaxed stretching. During a passive stretch, an individual would assume a position and hold it using another part of the body, a partner, or an apparatus of some type. This type of stretching is good for cooling down after a workout because it helps to reduce muscle fatigue and soreness. Active stretching includes assuming a position and holding it there with no assistance other than using the strength of your agonist muscles. Active stretches are usually very difficult to hold for more than ten seconds and should not be held any more than fifteen seconds. One would find this type of stretching in an activity such as yoga. Dynamic stretching involves moving parts of one's body and gradually increasing reach, speed of movement, or both. Dynamic stretching can be useful as part of a warm-up for an aerobic workout. Ballistic stretching uses the momentum of a moving body part or limb in an attempt to force it beyond its normal range of motion. This type of stretching is not considered useful and it has also been known to lead to injury.

As mentioned earlier, any physical activity designed for young children needs to be made fun. Although stretching routines can be very monotonous, they can be made more exciting for young children by simply adding music and giving each stretch a unique name.

Classroom-based Activities

Although the physical education classroom is a critical area for the development of the physical domain, the push for more physically active students should not end there. Educators need to be aware that young children learn about the world through movement and physical activity. Classroom teachers should keep in mind that physical activity can be integrated within other subject areas to give children opportunities for more movement throughout the day.

One way to incorporate this physical activity would be to use a thematic approach to teaching units within the curriculum. An example of a thematic approach would be an Olympic Games theme. In the area of Language Arts, students can read books, write reports, and perform skits that pertain to the games and athletes of the Olympics. Students can be shown maps in Social Studies, where they can compare the geographical locations of where they live and the place where the games are being held. A scale could be made up that shows the number of steps taken that are equal to a certain number of miles. Students could be given pedometers to calculate how many steps they have taken since the last class period. Each day when the students enter the classroom, they would go to the map and chart their "distance traveled" toward the sight of the Olympic Games. In math class, students can be introduced to the use of stopwatches. Teachers can have the students' time each other in a few physical skills and the data collected can be analyzed and graphs can be made using the results. Finally, in physical education classes, students could participate in activities similar to those of the Olympic Games. Through the use of this theme, each subject area teacher will have then done a small part in incorporating some type of physical activity into their classroom.

Parent Involvement

In addition to introducing children to physical activity through physical education programs and integrated curriculum parents can be encouraged to become involved in this aspect of their children's development. Children today are leading a more sedentary lifestyle than ever before (U.S. Department of Health and Human Services, 2001). The days of coming home from school and playing outside until dark have been replaced with activities such as watching television, surfing the internet, and playing video games. However, there are many things that parents can do to get children out of the house and involved in some type of physical activity (New York Online Access to Health, 2004). Some of these activities may include taking family walks or bike rides, going to the park or other recreational facilities, encouraging participation in extracurricular activities, and encouraging playtime outdoors. Parents should also get involved in school activities. They can ask their children what they are doing in physical education or better yet, visit them in class. Encouraging them to practice skills learned or practicing with them can be an effective way to keep them turned on to physical activity.

Assessment and Evaluation

The final issue that must be addressed is how appropriate development of children and youth in the physical domain can be addressed. It is our belief that the answer is simple. Fitness testing within the educational system must be required and educators must be held accountable if standards are not met. Testing is required in all other areas of education and physical development should not be held to any lower standards.

There are three different programs that provide excellent examples of effective tools for measurement within physical education: FITNESSGRAM, Physical Best, and the President's Challenge Physical Activity and Fitness

Awards Program. FITNESSGRAM is a health-related physical fitness assessment that was developed in 1982 (The Cooper Institute, 2001). The goal of this program is to develop an easy way for physical educators to report the results of physical fitness assessments to parents. Each student is assessed in three areas of health-related fitness: aerobic capacity, body composition, and muscular strength, endurance, and flexibility. Activities within the category of aerobic capacity include The Pacer (a 20-meter progressive, multi-stage shuttle run set to music), a one-mile walk/run, or a walk test which is commonly used for secondary students. In the area of body composition, percent body fat can be calculated by taking skin fold measures from the triceps and calf or through Body Mass Index which is calculated from height and weight. Muscular strength, endurance, and flexibility can be measured in one of several ways. Abdominal strength is evaluated through a curl-up test. Trunk extensor strength and flexibility is evaluated by means of the trunk lift. Upper body strength can be measured by either the 90-degree push-up, the pull-up, flexed arm hang, or modified pull-up. Finally, flexibility can be measured by the sit-and-reach test. When testing is complete, students are compared on an individual basis to health-related fitness standards that were carefully established for age appropriateness and gender. Each student tested receives a report which contains objective, personalized feedback and positive reinforcement. This is critical in changing behavior patterns and it also serves the purpose of essential communication between educators and parents. In order to obtain the maximum benefit of the fitness test, a pre-test and post-test should both be administered. This is the only way to tell if progress has been achieved throughout the student's time in physical education.

Physical Best is considered to be a companion product of FITNESSGRAM (American Fitness Alliance, 2001); it is a complete educational program for teaching all areas of health-related fitness. It was developed by the American Alliance for Health, Physical Education, Recreation, and Dance (AAHPERD) and includes learning activities for aerobic capacity, muscular strength, endurance, and flexibility, and body composition. The Physical Best program contains materials, books, computer software, as well as hands on training through workshops that attempt to assist physical educators in impacting the long-term health of their students.

Summary and Conclusions

With the health of our nation in its present state, those who are concerned about the development of children and youth can no longer keep the focus of overall education solely on increased scores on standardized tests of basic skills. The importance of physical activity and proper nutrition must be emphasized as well. From an educational standpoint, our nation can no longer afford to consider physical education merely a place for athletes to excel. Educators in every aspect of schools must make a more concerted effort to focus on the physical development of each and every student irrespective of one's discipline. If the present disturbing trends continue, educational systems that do not give appropriate emphasis to physical development may continue to turn out intelligent and competent workers; however, the life spans of these children and adolescents will steadily decrease in adulthood. As you think about the issues proposed in this chapter, ponder over this one last thought: how effective is the most intelligent and successful person in the world, if that person dies at an early age or has his or her productivity cut short because of debilitating disease. It is our hope is that through the information presented in this chapter, educators and parents alike will begin to take notice of the importance of the physical development of children and youth and will begin to advocate a focus on this domain in schools as well as the home and community.

9

Spiritual Development: Meaning and Purpose[9]

William G. Huitt and Jennifer L. Robbins

Spirituality is a difficult concept to define. While it has been explored throughout human history as one of the three fundamental aspects of human beings (ie, body, mind, spirit) (Huitt, 2010b), there is widespread disagreement as to its origin, functioning, or even importance (Huitt, 2000). However, in a broad perspective, spirituality deals fundamentally with how human beings approach the unknowns of life, how we define and relate to the sacred.

Spirituality is considered by many psychologists to be an inherent property of the human being (Helminiak, 1996; Newberg, D'Aquili, & Rause, 2001). From this viewpoint, human spirituality is an attempt to understand and connect to the unknowns of the universe or search for meaningfulness in one's life (Adler, 1980; Frankl, 1998). Likewise, Weaver and Cotrell (1992) proposed that spirituality "refers to matters of ultimate concern that call for releasing the passions of the soul to search for goals with personal meaning" (p. 1). Other definitions include a relationship with the sacred (Beck & Walters, 1977), "an individual's experience of and relationship with a fundamental, nonmaterial aspect of the universe" (Tolan, 2002). Others view soul or spirit as a description of the "vital principle or animating force believed to be within living beings" (Zinn, 1997, p. 2) or "the very source of energy" that lives within each person (Chee, 2002, p. 11). Danesh (1994) suggested that when individuals study their human spirituality it provides an opportunity to connect to a larger source of energy and power, thereby impacting our ideas of who we are. It is this exploration of the meaningfulness of our lives and our relationships to ourselves, to others, to nature, or to a higher power that is considered the essence of spirituality (Hamilton & Jackson,1998; Hay & Nye, 1998). One can engage in a search in any or all of these areas simultaneously (Collins, 1998). This may or may not involve a relationship with God, Goddess, Creator, Great Spirit, Universal Mind, etc. However, it does involve a quest for a relationship with, or understanding of, the essential or non-material as compared to the concrete or material.

---

[9] Huitt, W., & Robbins, J. (2003). *An introduction to spiritual development.* Paper presented at the 11th Annual Conference: Applied Psychology in Education, Mental Health, and Business, Valdosta, GA, October 3.

There are essentially three broad categories of belief regarding humankind's spirituality: naturalism, pantheism, and theism (Copan, 2001). Naturalists believe spirituality and definitions of what is sacred exist as a natural operation of the human mind and that our spirituality ceases to exist along with our physical body (Maslow, 1983). Pantheists believe that God exists in everything and that the entire universe is either God or an expression of His nature (Levine, 1997). Theists believe that humankind's spirituality results from a non-material soul, created by God, and destined to continue to exist after the material body ceases to function (Collins, 1998). Solomon (2002) suggested that a belief in a Creator or Great Spirit is not necessary as atheists or skeptics can express their spirituality through a philosophical inquiry that is demonstrated in a thoughtful love for life.

This discussion of the essence of human spirituality links the topic to religion. However, there is an important distinction. Whereas spirituality is a consideration of meaning or ultimate purpose, religion refers to the organized, institutionalized set of beliefs, teachings, and practices that are established to connect groups of individuals to a particular expression of spirituality (Tolan, 2002). One can be spiritual without being religious (eg, a seeker of a relationship with the Creator without belonging to a particular practice of that relationship). Alternatively, one can be religious without being spiritual (eg, practicing a particular set of rituals or attending a specific worship service without establishing a relationship with the sacred, non-material aspects of the universe). This distinction is an important part of the discussion of spiritual development in the context of schooling. Coles (1990) provided extensive detail on the differences between children's interpretation of the signs, symbols, and rituals of their religious upbringing and their quest to provide personal meaning in their lives. He emphasized, however, that children's religions experiences and their creation of meaning are not independent, as a child's spiritual journey is accomplished within the context of an individual's religious (or non-religious) education.

Meeting the directive of the United States Constitution to maintain neutrality between secular and religious views (Segars & Jelen, 1998) does not mean that all discussions of human spirituality must be omitted within public institutions. That is hardly neutral. It does mean, however, that those leading discussions in these institutions must be careful to allow a full discussion of spiritual development that includes the views of both those who believe in a Supreme Creator, God, or Great Spirit and those who do not. It also means that the wisdom found in the various religious scriptures must be treated with equality, rather than in a parochial, biased manner. Wilson (2000) suggested this is possible by focusing on those spiritual and moral goals that are needed for lasting human happiness using findings from both science and religious scripture.

While this discussion of connecting spiritual development to a belief in a God or Universal Spirit may be an important issue to the majority of scientists who identify themselves as unbelievers (Larson & Witham, 1998), it is certainly not an issue for the majority of the American public. Gallup (1993) reported that 94% of adult Americans believe in God or a universal spirit, although less than 50% attend religious services on a regular basis (Gallup International, 2017). Similar results are found throughout the industrialized world (Huddleston, 1993). The number of people who identify themselves as believers but express no specific religious identification almost doubled in the U.S. in the 1990s (from 8% to 14%) (Gallup International, 2017). This now makes the unchurched 29.4 million American adults the third largest group of believers in America, after Roman Catholicism (50.9 million) and Baptists (33.8 million). It is interesting to note that measures of interest in spirituality have increased at the same rate as leaving organized religion (Marler & Hadaway, 2002). This discrepancy between beliefs and practice may be one reason that people seem to be seeking spirituality (Taylor, 1994). Hout and Fischer (2002) believed this growth of unchurched believers in the U.S. is a result of dissatisfaction with the manner in which Christian views have been expressed in the public discourse.

What is clear is that whether the topic of spirituality and its various interpretations is addressed from the perspective of science, religious observers, or unaffiliated believers, it is considered important by the American public. In addition, spirituality and related processes of spiritual development such as a profession of faith, prayer, or regular attendance at religious services have been related to a wide-range of important outcomes such as:

- lower blood pressure (Koenig, 1999),
- improved physical health (Koenig, McCullough, Larson, 2001; Levin, 2001),
- healthier lifestyles and less risky behavior (Koenig, 1999),
- improved coping ability (Pargament, 1997),
- less depression (Koenig, 1999),
- faster healing (Dossey, 2002; Koenig, 2002),
- lower levels of bereavement after the death of a loved one (Walsh, King, Jones, Tookman & Blizard, 2002),
- a decrease in fear of death (Ardelt, 2008), and
- higher school achievement (Ginsburg & Hanson, 1986).

Similarly, Kass (2007) indicated that a lack of spiritual development leads to serious issues, such as overeating, risky behavior, low self-esteem, and poor health. In fact, Koenig (2002) reported that the data on the relationship of spirituality and health are so conclusive that nearly two-thirds of American medical schools taught required or elective courses on religion, spirituality, and medicine in 2001.

Educators today know the impact that issues such as health, levels of self-esteem, and choices in non-academic behavior can have on a student's ability to learn. Based on the connection between one's spiritual development and these various outcome measures, it might seem obvious that spirituality should be a topic addressed in schools. However, many activities normally associated with spiritual development are not those that educators can advocate in a most public-school settings.

Fortunately, there are alternatives by which spiritual development can be addressed without crossing the critical line separating religion and public activity. We need only to look to modern business practices to see that this can be done. For example, businesses in this country are facing the need to address meaningfulness and important relationships with their employees (Gooden, 2000). Today's more educated and skilled workforce is increasingly demanding

> "more autonomy in work, more satisfaction from work, and more meaningful engagement at work. Those leaders who understand and are sensitive to the need for meaning, and who value environments that help workers realize their potential, are likely to be more in tune with the new environment than are those who are insensitive to these trends" (p. 47).

Page and Wong (2013) reported that the most successful companies develop a vision for the business that is holistic and congruent. These companies advocated an inclusive approach that included the church, the family, the community, and the institution.

Educators would do well to learn from these experiences. Attempts by schools to develop an approach to spirituality that does not consider all of the relevant influences on the lives of children and youth are doomed to failure as a result of conflicts among values and purposes that are certain to arise (Kessler, 2000). Fowler's (1995) faith development theory addressed the impact that spirituality has on learning. This aspect of the total being has been historically neglected in education theory and practice. Neglecting the spiritual nature of humans is to "ignore an important aspect of human experience and avenue of learning and meaning-making" (Tisdell, 2001, p. 3). The implication is that learning must be made meaningful if it is to be relevant. The challenge lies in identifying what is meaningful for individual human beings and addressing it in a manner in our public institutions that is acceptable to all strands of our society.

In summary, spirituality addresses such human-centered questions as:

1. How can we increase meaning in our lives, in general, and my life, in particular?
2. Who are we as human beings? Where did we come from? How are we related?
3. Are we in control of our lives or is our destination a result of fate?
4. Where did the universe come from? What are its origins?
5. Is there a God (in whatever way we define or know a Supreme Being)?
6. What is our relationship to God or the Creator, if there is one?
7. Is there a continuity of life after this life? If so, what is it like?

These questions are fundamental to understanding human beings and our relationships to each other and the rest of the universe (Moody & Carroll, 1998). To the extent that we carefully consider these questions and answer them to our ability and satisfaction, we can say that we are in the process of developing in the spiritual domain. Of special importance, from the perspective of this paper, is the role of science in addressing these questions. At a minimum science should be able to identify the available choices in addressing human spirituality and provide evidence as to the impact of making different choices on the lives of individuals and groups.

The Development of Human Spirituality

As with every other area of human development there are diverse viewpoints on how spiritual development occurs. Hay (2007), a zoologist, stated that spiritual experiences are a part of natural selection because they hold some type of survival value. He cited data showing a spiritual dimension in every known human society or culture.

Alternatively, Sullivan (1993) believed that one component of spiritual development is the intimacy with which people are involved with their life experiences. "Many of the so-called larger-than-life people…are profoundly present to the continuum of their lives…Thus some die at seventy with an experiential age of seventeen while others are closer to a hundred and seventy, so intimate are they with the happenings of their lives" (p. 1). This theme has been studied extensively from the perspective of existential psychology (May, 1958). Some of the most important qualities of a well-developed adult are a willingness to take intentional control over one's life and to have the courage to put intentions into action. The development of these qualities must be addressed in early childhood (Erikson, 1993).

There are numerous outlines of spiritual development from specific religious traditions (Wilson, 1991). Differentiating the process of spiritual development from any specific religious development is challenging, but not impossible. A number of researchers have developed generic descriptions of spiritual (or faith) development that can be used in public schools (Moody & Carroll, 1998; Peck, 1998a, 1998b). Perhaps the most well-known description is by Fowler (1995). He used the term faith which he defined as "a person's way of seeing him- or herself in relation to others against a backdrop of shared meaning and purpose" (p. 4).

Fowler (1995) took an analytical approach to the development of spirituality with clear progressive divisions. While these six stages parallel Piaget's cognitive-development stages and Kohlberg's stages of moral-development, progression through each stage is not a chronological guarantee (Gathman & Nessan, 1997). The attractive aspect of Fowler's theory for our purpose is that, while no specific higher power is the defining factor of whether one can apply these stages to one's life, a connection to something greater than self is a must (see Table 9-1).

According to Fowler (1995), prior to the development of faith, an infant has an undifferentiated faith where he or she is beginning to interact with adults and learn about the social, built, and natural environment. Stage I typically begins around age three to seven years, and involves the imagination of the inner-child, which is filled with fantasy and free of logic. An early awareness of life's mysteries (i.e. death, sexuality, and cultural taboos) exists at this stage, which is referred to as intuitive-projective faith. Ironically, the inner child concept promotes listening to one's inner thoughts. Nurturing this type of simplistic self-actualization is one aspect of spiritual development. The increase in the ability to think concretely is what brings this stage to a close. The image of a divine power being parent-like is symbolic of the child's limited experiences.

As cognitive abilities increase with the development of concrete operational thinking, the child has the potential to evolve to stage II, the mythic-literal faith stage. It is in this stage that the world is viewed in terms of opposites like good and bad. In addition, authorities have unquestionable knowledge, and truth is provided in the simple form of stories that instill core beliefs (Gathman & Nessan, 1997). The focus on acknowledgement of authority indicated a low functioning of self-awareness and an increase in focus on the relationship with others.

Table 9-1. Fowler's Stages of Faith

Stage	Typical Age	Defining Qualities	Influences	Major Antecedents to Transition
0. Undiffer-entiated Faith	Infancy	Mutuality, trust, and preimages of the background of life	Interaction with important adults and environment	Development of language and imagination
I. Intuitive-Projective Faith	3-7	Fantasy-filled, imitative phase; free of logic; focus on episodic interactions	Interaction with important adults through stories, role playing, etc. providing episodic knowledge	Development of concrete operational thinking
II. Mythic Literal	7-15, although some adults remain in this stage	Concrete operational interpretation of beliefs and observances of community; worldview of good and bad	Authorities, including parents, teachers, religious and community leaders	Development of critical thinking
III. Synthetic Conven-tional	15-21, plus some adults	Formation of personal identity and shaping of personal definition of faith	External sources such as school, work, friends, media and personal reflection	Internal conflict between personal beliefs and social expectations

Table 9-1. Fowler's Stages of Faith (continued)

Stage	Typical Age	Defining Qualities	Influences	Major Antecedents to Transition
IV. Individ-uative-Reflective	Young Adult	Unique, individualistic worldview	Independent critical thinking; beginning of balance of self, others, and higher power	Desire to integrate worldviews of self and others
V. Conjunc-tive	Mid-life and beyond	Value direct experience while affirming others' beliefs	Increasing appreciation of symbols and myths; meaningful learning experiences	Desire to reconcile the untransformed world and the personally-developed transforming vision and loyalties
VI. Univers-alizing Faith	Few ever reach	Disciplined activist seeking to make tangible impact on transforming the social order	Consciousness of complex universal issues; loss of egocentric focus	

Stage III, or the synthetic-conventional faith stage, is marked by the impact of external forces, such as school, work, friends, and media. Balancing these influences is the focus of this stage. The push to conform causes internal conflict, as conformity can mean going against core beliefs. Ironically, critical examination of beliefs and values does not exist. The aspect of spirituality that is being addressed in this stage is the relationship to others. The conflicts between self and the newly introduced relationships lead to the end of stage III, due to the development of critical thinking skills (Fowler, 1995). As one breaks away from authority, the need to think independently creates a search for validation by others who have similar views. Self-actualization and increased connection to others is required in order to determine the similarities between self and sub-groups of society.

Individuative-reflective faith, stage IV, is a highly intellectual stage (Fowler, 1995). This marks the beginning of a unique and quirky worldview. The potential to be influenced by others is diminishing as thinking independently means the desire for peer approval has narrowed to a specific subgroup. Symbols have lost their mythical meanings as the person evolves into an abstract thinker, which leads to an understanding of just how complex life is. The newfound appreciation for the gray areas leads to the completion of this stage. It is the beginning of balancing the relationships between self, others, and a higher power.

The kind of understanding that is present in stage V is conjunctive faith. A second naïveté exists as an increased appreciation for the power of symbols and myths develops. A return to the inner-child that values direct experience, while learning to affirm other's beliefs, is indicative of conjunctive faith. The motivating factor at this level of faith is acquiring the rewards for personal dedication and obedience to the spiritual rules, or the carrot-at-the-end-of-the-stick (Gathman & Nessan, 1997). A new level of understanding leads to the resolution of black-and-white thinking; this leads to a realization that there being correct in one's perception does not mean that others are wrong. The characteristics that a person possesses at this level of spiritual maturity are parallel with the type of maturity that comes with age. For example, according to Jung (1981), the first half of life is influenced more by biology whereas the second half of life is more influenced by culture. The cultural aims of mid-life and beyond strive to create a world of peace, justice, and beauty–a world fit for future generations–and have come to fruition by the maturation of the spirit (McFadden & Gerl, 1990). This is similar to Erikson's (1993) contention that generativity is an important issue in midlife. Again, the recurring theme of meaning motivates learning. Fowler (1995) stated that few individuals attain the kind of consciousness of complex issues such as social justice and loss of egocentric focus that is needed to spiritually progress to universalizing faith, or stage VI. The above stated consciousness, plus a life dedicated to those issues, is what distinguishes those in stage six from stage five. Examples given by Fowler are Mother Teresa, Martin Luther King, Jr., Mahatma Gandhi, and Thomas Merton.

Several researchers such as Coles (1990) as well as Hay and Nye (1998) believed that Fowler's (1995) approach was too cognitive in its orientation. They supported an approach that would put more emphasis on emotion and awareness. In fact, Hay and Nye suggest that "relational consciousness" describes the essence of spirituality. Relational consciousness is a type of metacognitive activity that describes ever increasing consciousness of growth and opportunity consequences for the individual. In this context, development is considered moving from simple to complex, from naïve to sophisticated, or from insecurity to confidence in terms of the relational aspects of self, others, nature, God, or universal unknowns. This is a continuous, rather than discontinuous, process as described by Fowler (1995). There is a similar discussion of continuous versus discontinuous development in cognition (Piaget, 2001; Vygotsky, 1978) and emotion (Erikson, 1993; Plutchik, 1980) and it is no surprise that we see it in the discussion of spiritual development.

Spiritual Development Activities

There is little doubt that the development of the human spirit is an important issue to be addressed if we consider the individual in a holistic perspective. Palmer (1998/1999) proposed that the place to start is with the teacher's spiritual development. As with any other topic, one cannot teach what one has not developed.

Where should educators start in this process? One approach may lie in an analysis of one's development of faith as described by Fowler (1995). A second might be a consideration of the contexts of spiritual development defined by Hay and Nye (1998) [self, others, nature, God/Creator] or to the elements of spirituality defined by Hamilton and Jackson (1998) [self-awareness, interconnectedness, and a relationship to a higher power]. These are relatively complex tasks and likely to require some assistance from a knowledgeable mentor or at least involvement in a study group. This means that educators will require some specialized training to address the demands of developing and implementing a spiritual development curriculum. Teacher training institutions should consider making a course in spiritual development a part of the preservice teacher training program. For teachers who are already in the field, school districts need to provide inservice training programs through workshops or conference attendance.

One of the first steps educators can take to address the spiritual development of their students is to build an environment conducive to learning (Kessler, 2000). This would call for educators to reassess the ultimate goal of education. It would also require that schools coordinate with families, religious organizations, and other community institutions to provide a full range of spiritual development activities appropriate for the individual's developmental readiness.

Requirements of neutrality in public institutions suggests a division of spiritual activities into two categories, non-school and school. For children and youth, non-school activities can vary widely, depending upon one's parents' beliefs. As stated previously, Coles (1990) showed a child's spiritual journey is done within the context of an individual's religious (or non-religious) training. For the vast majority of Americans, this would mean a focus on building a connection between the individual and a Greater Being.

Activities such as prayer, meditation, reading of sacred texts, singing songs, and rituals all enhance knowledge of the relationship between a person and the Creator (Stonehouse, 1998). While prayer, meditation, and rituals cannot be implemented into the public school setting, time and space can be allotted to allow the students to practice these activities if they wish. Silence (Kessler, 2000) is an excellent example of providing students with an opportunity to reflect on their accomplishments, lessons learned, personal moments, people served, or communicate with a higher power, all of which help the student develop the conscious relationships.

Activities that increase self-awareness, strengthen relationships with others, and build a connection to the universe, while remaining free of religious doctrine, are more appropriate for a school setting. Alternatively, it might be appropriate to include study of scriptures from major world religions as part of sociocultural diversity lessons. Due to the current demands on educators, appropriate activities can and should be incorporated into all classrooms, regardless of subject area, rather than developing courses specifically focused on spiritual development.

Kessler (2000) suggested there are seven pathways to the soul that express a particular yearning on the part of the individual. Each individual is likely to express at least one of these yearnings if provided an opportunity in a conducive environment. Table 9-2 shows these seven pathways. As shown in the table, each separate pathway has been discussed by other authors. What makes Kessler's approach unique is that she advocates establishing an environment where a person's most intimate questions and desires can be addressed. While group activities can be implemented, it is more important to provide a wide range of activities that will allow the individual student preferences to emerge. From Kessler's perspective, we should be guided by individual expressions of students rather than focused on a particular theory. She also suggested that spirituality can be seen in a number of different curriculum areas when issues of meaningfulness and connectivity are addressed.

Each of the pathways described by Kessler (2000) can be used to address the different levels of faith development described by Fowler (1995) or the contents of spirituality described by Coles (1990) or Hay and Nye (1998). A key is to address each of the pathways in a manner appropriate for the developmental level of the individual. This can be done through implementation of a "spiral approach" as shown in Figure 9-1. Each of the pathways can be used at the intuitive- projective level, again at the mythical-literal level, and so on. As the individual explores the different pathways at increasingly progressive levels, the core pathway of deep personal meaning becomes more developed.

Table 9-2. Pathways to the Soul

Pathway	Description	Found in Other Theories
Yearning for Deep Connection	Describes a quality of relationship that is profoundly caring, is resonant with meaning, and involves feelings of belonging, or of being truly seen and known; may experience deep connection to themselves, to others, to nature, or to a higher power.	Erikson (1993) — Need for Belongingness (especially to something larger than oneself) Gardner (2000b) —Inter-personal Intelligence (connection to others)
Longing for Silence and Solitude	As a respite from the tyranny of "busyness" and noise, silence may be a realm of reflection, of calm or fertile chaos, an avenue of stillness and rest for some, prayer or contemplation for others.	Gardner (2000b) —Intra-personal Intelligence
Search for Meaning and Purpose	Exploration of big questions, such as "Why am I here?" "Does my life have a purpose? "What is life for?" "What is my destiny?" and "Is there a God?"	Gardner (2000b) — Existential Intelligence
Hunger for Joy and Delight	Can be satisfied through simplistic experiences, such as play, celebration, or gratitude; also describes the exaltation felt when encountering beauty, power, grace, brilliance, love, or the sheer joy of being alive.	Csikszentmihalyi (1998) — Flow in Consciousness
Creative Drive	Is part of all the gateways; students feel the awe and mystery of creating, whether developing a new idea, a work of art, a scientific discovery, or an entirely new lens on life.	Sternberg (1988) — Creative Intelligence

Table 9-2. Pathways to the Soul (continued)

Urge of Transcendence	The desire to go beyond perceived personal limits; includes not only the mystical realm, but experiences of the extraordinary in the arts, athletics, academics, or human relations.	Maslow (1983) — Transcendence
Need for Initiation	Deals with rites of passage for the young—guiding adolescents to become more conscious about the irrevocable transition from childhood to adulthood.	Campbell (1972) Schlegel & Barry (1980) – Initiation

For example, if the teacher were addressing the pathway of creativity at the intuitive-projective level she could tell simple stories of connecting to self, others, nature, the Creator, or unknowns and have the child draw a picture and explain it. It is especially important to connect with the child's imagination at this stage. At the mythical-literal level the teacher could have children read more complex stories that address children's specific concerns. The teacher would ask the child to look for logical consistencies and inconsistencies and try to explain them.

Another activity that might be useful at this stage is "gratitude-in-a-jar." Gratitude-in-a-jar can be purchased or created as a quick method for aiding students to show appreciation for personal talents, positive experiences, or awareness of environmental issues. The jar contains small slips of paper that have comments printed on them designed to generate discussion, reflection, and curiosity. An example of a gratitude-in-a-jar comment is "Today I make a distinction between what I can control and what I can let go of." Language arts teachers can create gratitude-in-a-jar comments that utilize terms that will be covered during the year, or literary quotations from novels that will be read. Environmental Science teachers could create gratitude-in-a-jar comments that create an appreciation for elements of nature. Again, it is important to address the different contexts of spirituality at each stage.

The thought for a day activity developed by Huitt (2005) is another lesson that could be used at this stage. The concept behind the thought for a day is "to demonstrate that our cultural/historical and religious backgrounds provide us with generic knowledge about how to think and behave in our modern world, and to practice learning to apply these in specific situations in our daily lives" (p. 1). Quotations from a variety of sources, both secular and religious, can be discussed at the beginning of each day as a stimulus to encourage students to focus on developing a particular virtue or value for that day. This can be supported by discussions at home or in the community by having similar thoughts or quotations presented on billboards, on marquees, in newspapers, etc.

Figure 9-1: A Spiral Approach to Spiritual Development

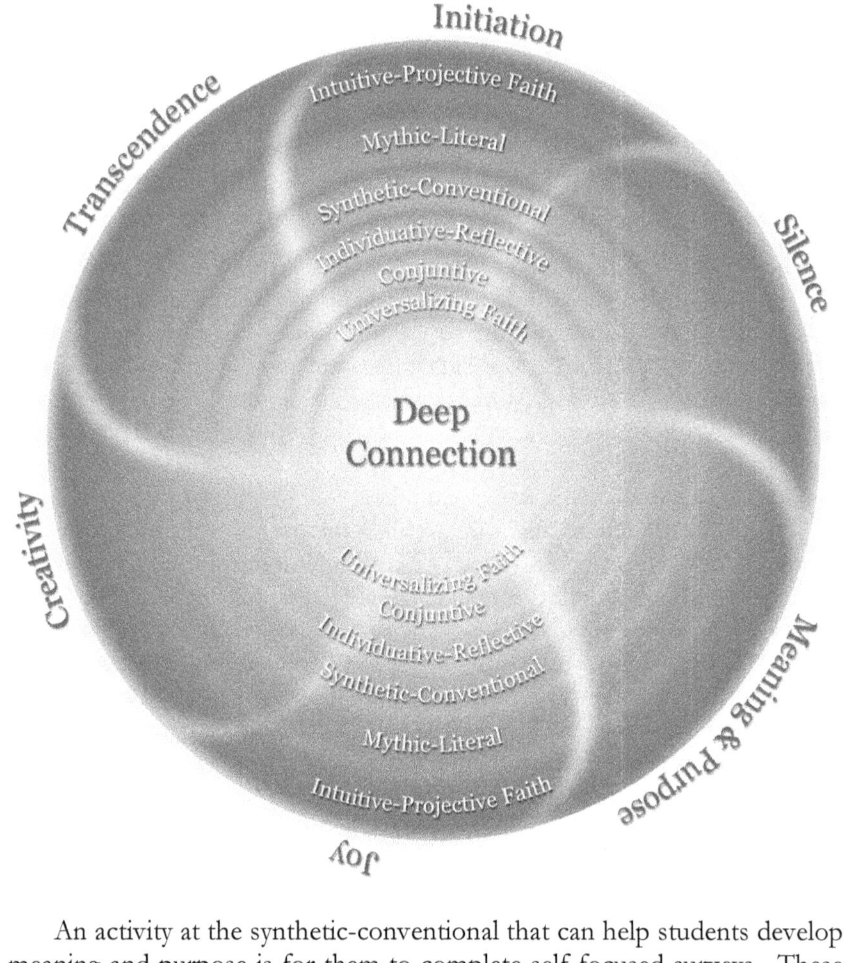

An activity at the synthetic-conventional that can help students develop meaning and purpose is for them to complete self-focused surveys. These can be fun while provoking the student to evaluate his or her self-knowledge. The Index of Core Spiritual Experiences (INSPIRIT) online evaluation is an excellent example (Kass & Kass, 2000). As the name indicates, this questionnaire measures the experiences of the spiritual core. In addition to the survey, students can review the spiritual boosters that are made available at the INSPIRIT website.

Another assessment that can provide insight into one's inner self is the assessment of signature strengths described Seligman (2002). Peterson and Seligman (2004) identified 24 strengths related to 6 categories of virtues found in all cultures: (1) wisdom and knowledge, (2) courage, (3) love and humanity, (4) justice, (5) temperance, and (6) spirituality and transcendence. Adult and youth versions of the assessment instrument are available.

Spiritual journaling, whereby students are encouraged to write their beliefs and experiential knowledge of themselves, can be used at any stage to increase and/or document spiritual progress. Ideally, this can be done in an English or Language Arts class to afford the educator an opportunity to assess writing skills. Integrating a spiritual journal into a career class could be a technique for increasing the student's awareness of personal tastes, views, and talents all of which are needed for making a career choice. The educator should guide the student by listing the purposes and grading criteria for the journal, providing the student with clear expectations. Questions such as, "What do you like most about yourself," can stimulate self-reflective critical thinking while providing the educator a view of how the students see themselves. Limiting or prohibiting classroom sharing may be necessary in order to create an environment conducive to meaningful contribution in the journal.

Individuative-reflective, conjunctive, and universalizing stages would normally be addressed in adulthood (Fowler, 1995). However, the same concept applies. Different activities can be provided that encourage the individual to address increasingly complex issues to resolve (ie, require increased levels of differentiation and integration). While it is important to provide opportunities for all children and youth to experience activities in all pathways, it is likely that mature adults will begin to select those pathways with which they have had some sort of positive experience. If parents and educators have done their job well, adults will be able to make their selections based on their own experiences rather than on only those promoted by their society or culture. Hopefully, this will result in the individual continuing to select activities that can impact spiritual development. If not, there is likely to be little growth beyond the mythical-literal or synthetic-conventional stages of childhood and youth.

All activities appropriate for use in the educational setting are meaningless if the climate is not conducive to learning. Having educators, administrators, and school boards that understand the impact a student's spiritual status can have on the student's ability to meet the school's objectives is crucial. If these activities are implemented without a commitment and desire to truly touch the student in a meaningful way, then the activities are not likely to have the desired impact. Thus, prior to integrating any type of spiritual development program into the classroom, the foundation must be laid for a solid understanding of the value of, and the need for, spiritual development.

Measuring, Assessing, and Evaluating Spirituality

It is important to address the question "Are students making progress in the spiritual domain?" Fortunately, Lucas (1999) showed that "...spiritual growth [has] the same basis as any other form of growth... life" (p. 3), including the issues of measurement, assessment and evaluation.

Understanding the difference between assessing, measuring, or evaluating any aspect of learning is the precursor to implementation (Dietel, Herman, & Knuth, 1991). For the purposes of this discussion, assessment refers to any type of data collection process, whether qualitative or quantitative. On the other hand, measurement refers to the quantifying of data, and evaluation addresses the comparison of that data to a standard. All have a place in spiritual development and will be discussed.

One of the most important aspects of assessing spiritual development is making certain that there is a true representation of the full range of knowledge, attitudes, and skills that comprise the domain. That is, it is important to provide children and youth with opportunities to engage each of the pathways discussed by Kessler (2000) and having students consider all of the contexts described by Coles (1990) and Hay and Nye (1998). If students are not provided an opportunity to express themselves in a pathway or context that truly interests them, understanding of any particular individual will be severely restricted.

Another important issue relates to evaluating student progress. While we might expect that most children would begin to move from the intuitive-projective level to the mythical-literal at some time during the early elementary grades (Fowler, 1995), if some do not they should not be considered developmentally delayed. If Fowler is correct, and human beings evolve spiritually at different rates, then assessment must be based on individual progress rather than achieving a minimum milestone. It is, therefore, more important to establish methods of data collection and feedback that provide the student and parents with meaningful data to guide further progress than to use the data for comparison to a normative standard.

While Fowler (1995) did not write *Stages of Faith* to serve as a spiritual assessment tool, the very nature of the stages provides a framework for assessment. Spirituality can be assessed by documenting the stage at which a student is currently functioning. Methodologies to be used with Fowler's stages could include spiritual essays, stage-specific questions, or a combination of both. If the goal is for the student to advance through the stages, then assessing the current stage of faith could actually be a motivator for advancement to the next stage (Hodge, 2001).

There are several instruments developed by experts for assessing one's spirituality in a manner other than that described by Fowler (1995). Paper/pencil instruments are the most widely used methods of collecting data on spiritual development (Hodge, 2001). The dilemma with many assessment tools is that they can alter the reality of the person's perspective due in part to the limitations of the questions asked. In addition, questionnaires function under the premise that the participant has the literary ability to process the terms and understand the concept posed.

One example of a quantitative spiritual assessment tool is the previously mentioned INSPIRIT (Kass & Kass, 2000), developed to study the impact of spirituality on health. INSPIRIT is a self-test that provides quantitative results of a connection with one's spiritual core. While there are concerns with this type of assessment tool, the instrument is widely used and can bring the participant to a greater level of self-awareness. The test refers to a Supreme Being but provides the participant with a definition that can be applied to other belief systems. It also addresses the relationship between self and others. Integrating INSPIRIT into the classroom setting would be simple and the results possibly meaningful to the participants. However, the scope of the participant's spiritual knowledge may be limited.

Another established quantitative assessment tool is the Spiritual Well-Being Scale (Buffor, Paloutzian, & Ellison, 1991; Paloutzian & Ellision, 1982). This assessment tool has two dimensions: religious and existential. It is a 20-item self-administered test that yields a total score, a religious well-being summed score, and a summed score for the existential well-being. It has a test-retest reliability of .93; the internal consistency coefficients ranged from .94 to .89 in 7 different studies (Bufford et al., 1991).

Berg (1997) developed an online assessment instrument based on the work of McSherry (1987). The instrument provides scores for strength of religious belief, spiritual injury, and a series of scores for types of stress. No reliability data are available for the instrument.

Qualitative measures more oriented to open-ended questions and focused more on process can be used to supplement forced-choice data. Kessler (2000) suggested having students anonymously ask "mystery questions" dealing on personally-related topics. A first step when working with groups is to spend some time developing a sense of trust among the students. Rules must be established and practiced so that, when the facilitator reads an anonymously-provided question and solicits students' thoughts, others show respect and consideration. A review of student questions provides the facilitator with an overview of the types of issues that are of interest to a particular group. Having students reflect what they have learned about these important questions at the end of unit or course that deals with these topics can be a valuable resource for evaluating student learning.

Hodge (2001) provided an overview of qualitative assessment tools developed by Fitchett (1993), Nino (1997), and Pruyser (1976). Fitchett's approach also focuses on seven areas: beliefs and meaning, vocation and consequences, experiences and emotion, courage and growth, ritual and practice, community, authority and guidance, which provide an understanding of the student's spirituality in a broader context. Nino's spiritual quest is based on 10 items that lead the participant to create a detailed autobiographical story. Pruyser's model includes seven categories: things that are sacred, hope and trust, commitment, thankfulness, guilt, connectedness, and purpose in life and work. When utilizing this instrument, the instructor listens to students' stories, asking questions that relate to the seven themes. In each case, the authors include items that relate to the three domains discussed by Hamilton and Jackson (1998): a relationship to one's self, a relationship to others, and a relationship to a Higher Power.

Hodge (2001) proposed a spiritual framework for the purpose of counseling. His two-dimensional framework has a narrative and an interpretive aspect. The narrative framework is composed of three questions providing information on the subject's religious or spiritual tradition and experience. The interpretive anthropological framework is multidimensional and provides data on the subject's understanding of his or her spiritual beliefs and activities. The interpretive portion is made up of six topical questions that focus on affect, behavior, cognition, communion, conscience, and intuition. The use of this framework requires a significant amount of time and commitment to explore the strengths of an individual as a spiritual being. However, the collection of the data and a person's identification of spiritual strengths is, in itself, a potentially successful intervention.

Hummel and Huitt (1994) used the phrase "what you measure is what you get" to convey an important relationship between assessment and instruction. If specific data are not collected, reviewed, and shared, it is unlikely that the outcomes related to the data will continue to be viewed as important. It is therefore critical that educators think about the type of data related to spiritual development that is both pertinent and available for sharing with others. Deciding exactly what is to be measured of a person's spirituality is challenging. Referencing the assessment to the five aspects of spirituality (self, others, nature, unknowns of the universe, and Creator) is a logical choice. Measuring a person's self-knowledge can be done with a self-administered survey or a one-on-one interview. This aspect of spirituality is likely related to the domains of personal style and affect or values. Assessing the development of the second aspect, relationships with others, can be more varied. Observing how a student interacts and having the student reflect about those observations or utilizing surveys asking about an individual's views of one another are just two examples of tools that can be created to capture the development of that part of spirituality. This aspect is likely related to development in other domains described in the Brilliant Star framework (Huitt, Chapter 1, this volume) such as family, friends, and social/cultural. The third aspect, relationship to nature, and the fourth, relationships to the unknowns of the universe, can be assessed in similar ways through observation and personal reflection.

The last aspect (relationship to God, Creator, Supreme Being, Great Spirit, etc.) is far more difficult to address. Due to what has been interpreted as the constitutional demand of maintaining neutrality between organized religious and public policy as well as the reality of respecting diverse religious backgrounds in the United States (Eck, 2001), focusing on the development of a relationship between the human being and a higher power may be seen as inappropriate. However, the essence of this relationship can be addressed by looking at the connection between self and the unknowns. The teacher might organize surveys or interviews, or have students compose essays that can be used to foster an awareness of how a person perceives his or her personal fate or the future. Examining the relationship to a Greater Being could be an option for those individuals who have a desire to express that conviction.

A primary benefit of stating a desired outcome in measurable terms is for the teacher to stay focused on the goal and for the student to understand what is important. An example of this might be to have each student identify one new attribute or personality characteristic about him- or herself that was not previously identified and document how this quality affects the individual's self-concept. There are myriad issues to consider at this point. For example, does a measurable term mean an obligation to provide a score? Is it more appropriate to simply document thoughts, attitudes, and behavior using qualitative data?

After collecting all the information, what do the data mean to the process of spiritual development? One activity might be for the teacher to provide students and parents with data on student consideration of spiritual issues. For example, an instructor can demonstrate an impact on self-knowledge if it can be documented that 98% of all students completing the spiritual development assessment were able to identify one new quality of their personality of which they were not previously aware. Statements of how the self-actualization affected the student's perception of self, treatment of others, and a new-found ability to deal with the future could be indicators of how valuable spiritual education can be. Examples of behavioral outcomes of this consideration is the number of students who become involved in spiritually-related activities such as prayer, joining a group, or selecting and supporting social causes.

In summary, there are a wide variety of approaches to assessing, measuring, and evaluating children's and youth's spiritual development that can be used in a public school setting. Probably more of an issue is whether there are appropriate activities that can be used in schools to address development in this domain.

Summary and Conclusions

Humankind's spirituality has been an element of every known society and culture. This chapter provided an overview of empirical research demonstrating that attending to one's spiritual development is connected to a variety of positive outcomes and its neglect can have a detrimental effect. Fowler (1995) indicated spiritual advancement is conducive to becoming more accepting of others, more confident, and more caring. The development of student's level of faith or spirituality can be documented and assisted using classroom-based activities that are neutral with respect to any specific religion or belief system. Other social institutions, such as private businesses, are seeing a need to address worker's spiritual needs in the workplace and are finding ways to do so.

If one of the goals of education is to stimulate the desire of the pupil to continue seeking knowledge after leaving the formal school setting, connecting the need for that knowledge to one's essence and existential meaning is an important activity (Weaver & Cotell, 1992). Postman (1995) believed that engaging in learning activities without meaning has no purpose and it is our spirituality that provides the meaningful need to learn. Reaching the spirit of a person during the formal educational process would increase the chances that the individual would make learning a custom spanning the entire lifespan.

To omit the topic of human spirituality completely from our public institutions separates those institutions from the very people who support them. Addressing spiritual development in a manner that is constitutionally appropriate and acceptable to a wide variety of parents will require much wisdom and tact. However, the potential impact on the preparation of children and youth for successful living in the 21st century would suggest a need to get started immediately.

10

Moral and Character Development[10]

Gordon Vessels and William Huitt

The development of moral character has been the subject of philosophical and psychological investigation since Aristotle theorized three levels of moral character development: an ethics of fear, an ethics of shame, an ethics of wisdom (Kraut, 2001). Philosophers, psychologists, and educators as diverse as John Locke, John Stuart Mill, Herbert Spencer, Emile Durkheim, and John Dewey, and as ancient as Confucius, Plato, and Aristotle have viewed the development of moral character as the primary purpose of schooling (Purpel & Ryan, 1976). From the beginning of American public education in the 1600s until the first third of the twentieth century, our nation's educators, working closely with parents and the community, performed this moral-educational role with commitment (McClellan, 1992). In the middle of the twentieth century, moral character education in the schools (hereafter used interchangeably with the term character education) began to decline as a result of increased cultural diversity, perplexing and seemingly prohibitive First Amendment decisions, uncertainty about what values to teach and how to teach them, a preoccupation with social movements, and a Cold War emphasis on increasing academic achievement (Vessels & Boyd, 1996; Wynne & Ryan, 1997). A few variants emerged out of social necessity including civic education, global education, multicultural studies, prudential education, social skills training, and values clarification. But as Heslep (1995) points out, these variants continued without moral education providing the "unifying context of principles" that is central to character education.

A renewed interest in character education and a willingness to find legal and culturally sensitive ways to carry it out emerged in the late 1970s and early 1980s among educators who were interested in promoting all aspects of child development, and among most American citizens who believed their lives were being negatively impacted by decades of too little emphasis on moral values (Bennett, 1993; Elam, Rose, & Gallup, 1993; Gallup, 1975, 1980). The public was out in front of the educational establishment on this issue and gave the new generation of instructional pioneers enough support to rekindle educators' interest in moral and character education. Programs like the Basic

---

[10] Vessels, G., & Huitt, W. (2005). *Moral and character development.* Paper presented at the National Youth at Risk Conference, Savannah, GA, March 8-10.

School, the Child Development Project, the Character Counts Coalition, Character First, the Cooperating School Districts, and the Responsive Classroom gave renewed life and a new methodological diversity to character education (Vessels, 1998).

Since the early 1990s, the need to educate for character and community has been viewed as critically important by a majority of Americans, ranking ahead of concerns about academic achievement or other social pressing issues such as racial and gender equality (Myers, 2000). In spite of (a) extensive public support, (b) a variety of successful programs around the country, and (c) both politicians and educational administrators calling for character education in addition to higher test scores, most schools and school systems have adopted reform models that (a) paradoxically narrow the curriculum, (b) largely ignore critical areas of development besides academic, and (c) fail to effectively educate for character (Damon, 2002). Rather, most current approaches to whole-school reform reflect the current political push to accelerate students' academic learning and to raise test scores while failing to adequately promote other important aspects of child development including social, moral, intellectual, artistic, emotional, and personality (Huitt & Vessels, 2002).

Sommers (2002) stated that in order for education to fully address (1) public concerns about decency and literacy, (2) students' developmental needs, and (3) political pressures to improve schools, a K-12 curriculum infused with moral content is needed. We concur and believe that the road to success with character building is paved with (1) content that conveys universal moral principles and virtues, and (2) instructional methods that ensure their internalization and the cultivation of moral emotions, moral commitments, and moral reasoning that necessarily underlie moral action. In order to set these cornerstones of socially conscious and effective educational reform in place, we must (1) define moral character, (2) explain the known developmental pathways to moral maturity, (3) use any and all strategies thought to be effective at any point in time, and (4) use methods of assessment that will determine the most effective strategies. Stated simply, we must know the qualities of character we want to promote and must determine through research how they emerge and what can be done by parents, teachers, and other concerned citizens to ensure that moral potential is fully realized. The remainder of this chapter will address these issues.

Moral Character Defined

Damon (1988) identified six ways that social scientists have defined morality: (1) an evaluative orientation that distinguishes good and bad and prescribes good; (2) a sense of obligation toward standards of a social collective; (3) a sense of responsibility for acting out of concern for others;

(4) a concern for the rights of others; (5) a commitment to honesty in interpersonal relationships; and (6) a state of mind that causes negative emotional reactions to immoral acts. This categorical scheme may not accommodate all useful definitions, particularly the more substantive definitions offered by philosophers and theologians, but they reflect the wide variety of definitions and the need for an explicit operational definition that can guide programming and research.

A number of authors proposed definitions of moral character in rather traditional terms. For example, Wynne and Walberg (1984) wrote that moral character is "engaging in morally relevant conduct or words, or refraining from certain conduct or words" (p. 1). Others, such as Piaget (1969) focused on the source of one's behavior as being especially important. He said that the essence of morality is respect for rules and that acting on internalized principles (autonomy) represents a higher level of morality than performance based on rules imposed by others (heteronomy). Others, such as Pritchard (1988) focused on moral character as a personality construct: "a complex set of relatively persistent qualities of the individual person, and the term has a definite positive connotation when it is used in discussions of moral education" (p. 471). Berkowitz (2002) said that moral character is "an individual's set of psychological characteristics that affect that person's ability and inclination to function morally" (p. 48). Still others, such as Havighurst (1953) equated morality with altruism. Lickona (1991) attempted to connect psychological and behavioral components when he said that "Good character consists of knowing the good, desiring the good, and doing the good—habits of the mind, habits of the heart, and habits of action" (p. 51).

While most researchers support a multidimensional aspect to moral character, especially Lickona's (1991) advocacy of cognitive, affective, and behavioral components, several authors support additional components. For example, Narvaez and Rest (1995) suggested that the skills of moral and character development should be considered in terms of four psychological components. They said that the focus should be on the internal processes and behavioral skills that are required for moral behavior and propose that sensitivity, judgment, and motivation emerge from the interaction of cognitive and affective processes.

1. Ethical Sensitivity—the perception of moral and social situations, including the ability to consider possible actions and their repercussions in terms of the people involved;
2. Ethical Judgment—the consideration of possible alternative actions and the rationale for selecting one or more as best;

3. Ethical Motivation—the selection of moral values most relevant in the situation and the commitment to act on that selection;
4. Ethical Action—the ego strength combined with the psychological and social skills necessary to carry out the selected alternative.

Moral character incorporates the underlying qualities of a person's moral or ethical knowledge, reasoning, values, and commitments that are routinely displayed in behavior (Huitt & Vessels, 2002). Character is associated with the quality of one's life, especially in terms of moral and ethical decisions and actions. As described by Huitt (Chapter 1, this volume), character is one of two core elements that are dynamically related to both the personal and social aspects of one's life. That is, development in each of the ten identified domains and the other core element of self-view influences the development of one's moral character and this development, in turn, influences development in the ten domains and the other core element.

Berkowitz (2002) identified seven psychological components of the "moral anatomy," and urged scientists and educators to begin reconstructing the "complete moral person."

1. Moral behavior (prosocial, sharing, donating to charity, telling the truth)
2. Moral values (believe in moral goods)
3. Moral emotion (guilt, empathy, compassion)
4. Moral reasoning (about right and wrong)
5. Moral identity (morality as an aspect self-image)
6. Moral personality (enduring tendency to act with honesty, altruism, responsibility
7. "Metamoral" characteristics meaning they make morality possible even though they are not inherently moral.

Vessels (1998) divided cognition into moral knowing and moral reasoning. He addressed will or volition by examining the intersections between moral feeling and both thinking (empathy, motivation) and knowing (values, beliefs), and by defining moral behavior as intentional by definition. According to Vessels, the intersection of moral knowing, reasoning, feeling, and behaving yields conscience, which reflects one's (a) past thoughts, feelings, and behavior, (b) one's present thoughts and feelings, and (c) one's view of the future in terms of feeling compelled to act morally. He agreed with the other researchers in that moral character includes both personal and social aspects, which he describes as personal and social integrity.

There is a great deal of overlap among these psychological-component models of moral character, particularly the conceptual models of Berkowitz (1998), Damon (1988), Lickona (1991), Navarez and Rest (1995), and that described in this chapter. Their conceptual models bare some resemblance to those proposed by Plato, Confucius, and Freud (Vessels, 1998). Differences are largely a matter of emphasis rather than substance. It seems reasonable to conclude, therefore, that character is a multi-faceted psychological and behavioral phenomenon that involves the predictable co-occurrence and inter-connectedness of its many psychological and behavioral components with the level of character being determined by the consistency and strength with which these components co-occur in response to challenging life events.

Philosophical and Scientific Foundations

For centuries, philosophers have debated the proper focus of moral education and character education. Library shelves are filled with persuasive arguments about the proper focus: moral judgment, moral sensitivity, moral values, moral emotion, moral reasoning, moral intention, moral action. Each focus corresponds to a "school of thought" or cluster of psychological and philosophical explanations of morality and/or moral development. Each has a basic assumption about human nature (good, bad, neither good nor bad) and related prescriptions for social action and educating children. Reminiscent of Dewey (Gouinlock, 1994) and in keeping with Berkowitz's (1998) call for a re-constructive view of the complete moral person, Damon (2002) stated that it is time to move beyond the endless debates and ". . . take as our target of moral instruction the whole child—habit and reflection, virtue and understanding, and every system of judgment, affect, motivation, conduct, and self-identity that contributes to a child's present and future moral life" (p. xi). Similarly, Berkowitz said that we must ask how each theory advances our knowledge and not view them as incompatible or mutually exclusive.

The different philosophical positions led researchers to develop different hypotheses regarding moral character and its development and collect different types of data. This, in turn, has brought the field to its current state of development where it might appear to a naïve onlooker that there are an infinite variety of theoretical positions. However, from a sizeable collection of psychological, sociological, and psycho-physiological theories of morality and moral development, it is possible to extract four theory types: (1) *External/Social*, which includes *behaviorists* and *sociologists* who commonly view morality as a product of external imposition in the form of consequences and/or the intentional transmission of social rules and norms, respectively; (2) *Internal*, which includes *nativists* and *sociobiologists* who commonly focus on genetic and maturational influences; (3) *Interactional*, which is divided into subcategories of *instinctual* (psychoanalytic, psychosocial, and socio-analytic theories that view human nature as instinctual, undeveloped, and in need of control or socialization) and *maturational* (cognitive- and affective-developmental theories and social-learning theories that view human nature as good.); and (4) *Personality/Identity*, which includes theories that find virtue rooted in personality and personal identity. An overview of each of these categories is provided in the remainder of this section.

External/Social

There are two theories that view human nature as neutral (a blank slate) and subject to change by the environment. From an *operant conditioning* perspective (Skinner, 1971), all behavior, including moral behavior, is the result of the application of environmental consequences (Gerwitz & Peláez-Nogueras, 1991; Peláez-Nogueras & Gewirtz, 1995; Wynne, 1986). When parents, educators, or other social agents reward desired behavior, it increases; when they punish undesired behavior, it decreases. Strictly behavioral approaches focus on conduct rather than reasoning or other internal processes (Burton & Kunce, 1995). Reasoning, affect, volition, and other internal processes are thought to be determined by environmental influences on behavior. Wren (1991) criticizes the behavioral view for omitting human intention and moral agency, and for assuming that good character can be cultivated without considering and understanding agency and intention.

Sociologists also view the individual as a blank slate but see morality and character as being imbedded in society and culture. They focus more on the values, mores, norms, and moral exemplars in the environment rather than in the application of personal consequences. They emphasize the transmission of moral norms and expectations from one generation to the next (Haste, 1996) through modeling and explaining (Durkheim, 1961). An early study of moral character by Hartshorne and May (1928) confirmed the importance of the social environment and showed that the school as a whole has an impact on moral behavior through group norms. Shweder, Mahapatra, and Miller (1987) provide evidence that one's culture (a) supplies specific instances of moral behavior, and (b) influences how one thinks about moral events.

Berkowitz and Grych (1998) saw the family as the primary interpreter of culture, which implies that the transmission of moral values depends on parents knowing how to foster goodness in their children. Huxley (1990), Mische (2001), and Smith (1992) asserted that (a) cultures transmit values and (b) that religions are a central cultural force that should be acknowledged and supported. Mische advocated a dialogue among the world's religions with the purpose of identifying humankind's deepest universal values and beliefs so that they can be effectively transmitted to children and youth around the world. She stated that the world is transitioning to a more democratic nation-state system that will give way to a world "characterized by a greater sense of wholeness, interconnectedness, and mutuality in inter-human and human-Earth relations" (p. 16). Her major point was that human evolution is now more sociocultural than biological and that we can now construct cultures that will meet human needs.

Internal/Psychophysiological

There are two major theories that focus on genetic and maturational influences on character development: nativism and sociobiology. Nativists philosophers like Rousseau (1979) believe that human nature is essentially good and that unhealthy social influences should not be allowed to thwart the natural development of the child's predispositions to think, feel, and act morally. Constructivists today often present a nativistic misinterpretation of Piaget (1969; Piaget & Inhelder, 1966) by viewing heteronomy (externally imposed goodness) as an obstacle rather than an essential prerequisite to moral autonomy, as Piaget proposed (Vessels, 1998). A more accurate presentation of Piaget's views is presented below.

Sociobiology also focuses on genetic and maturational influences on morality (Miele, 1996). Clark and Grunstein (2000) and Plomin (1990) found that up to 50% of variance in behavior may be genetically determined. Clark and Grunstein stated that "behavior (just like anatomy and physiology) is in large part inherited and…every organism acts (consciously or not) to enhance its inclusive fitness--to increase the frequency and distribution of its selfish genes in future generations" (p. 43). Wilson's (1975, 1998) view is that our sense of right and wrong is the result of biological evolution interacting with culture and social convention. Killen and de Waal (2000) found that cooperation and conflict resolution are as much a part of our genetic heritage as competition and aggression. From a sociobiological position, human agency and intention are hardwired and difficult to modify; there is a corresponding belief that education has relatively little impact on a person's character. Critics like Wright (1994) disagree. He stated that "the uniquely malleable human mind, together with the unique force of culture, has severed our behavior from its evolutionary roots;...[and] there is no inherent human nature driving events...our essential nature is to be driven" (p. 5).

Another basically physiological theory focuses on an innate human cognitive processing ability and suggests that children develop a sense of right and wrong and moral values through an analysis of competing alternatives (Primack, 1986). Rational thought, to which all human beings are predisposed, is seen as the primary factor in acting morally. Proponents contend that changing times and conditions require the thoughtful application of principles to unique situations rather than "following the prescription." They propose teaching children to think critically about competing values and alternatives. Hard liners are now quite rare. In keeping with Aristotle (Kraut, 2001) and Havighurst (1953), and having departed from his earlier advocacy of values clarification, Kirschenbaum (1994; Simon, Howe, & Kirschenbaum, 1995), advocates that children need to be taught a specific code of conduct before engaging in critical thinking and moral reasoning. Even Kohlberg (1985) took a similar position near the end of his career. The shift in the thinking of these two influential figures is noteworthy and aligns them with earlier eclectics like Dewey (1975) and contemporary eclectics like Damon (1988).

Several researchers focus on innate human emotions as the foundation for moral character development. For example, Berkowitz (1998), Eisenberg (2000), Hoffman (1991, 2000), and Kagan (1984) identify several basic emotions that play a fundamental role in morality. These include compassion, empathy, guilt, shame, and sympathy. Hoffman (1991, 2000) provides substantial evidence that empathy should be considered an essential emotion for moral motivation. He suggested that empathy can be discerned in infants and that it develops in readily identifiable stages. He viewed the parents' use of guided induction of affective empathy and early perspective taking to deal with children's misconduct as essential for moral development. A careful look at the identified emotions reveals an internal/social distinction that is a recurring theme among authors who attempt to synthesize multiple theorists (Vessels, 1998). For example, guilt and shame are more intrapersonal, while empathy, sympathy, and compassion are more interpersonal.

Interactional

There are a variety of interactional theories that give different emphases to instincts, cognitions, affections, and social interactions. From the psychoanalytic perspective, human nature is instinctually anti-social and undeveloped and must be corrected and socialized (Freud, 1990). However, human intention and agency are the result of internal forces and unconscious intention. Therefore, moral character development is a constant struggle between biological predispositions to act selfishly and aggressively and social pressures to act in a prosocial manner. The similarity between Freud's id, ego, and superego and Plato's desire, spirit, and reason may not be coincidental. Adler (1995) suggested that in order to resolve the conflict between biology and social norms, the individual must acquire sound moral principles and direct his life according to these principles using reason.

Again, there seems to be a connection with the ideas of Plato and Aristotle (Vessels, 1998).

Erikson (1993) took exception to Freud's (1990) focus on biological instincts and proposed that personality was a product of social and emotional development with social demands posing a series of crises that must be resolved. For Erikson, the task of developing conscience and morals is primarily one of middle childhood. However, prerequisites include the development of a sense of trust, autonomy, initiative, and accomplishment with the corresponding virtues of hope, will, imagining, and skill. If there is insufficient resolution of one or more of these earlier crises, then the development of conscience becomes problematic.

Hogan and Emler's (1995) socio-analytic viewpoint places even more emphasis on the social context of moral development. The moral aspect of personality involves three milestones or psychological transformations in the individual/social relationship: (1) in early childhood, the child develops identification with parents and other persons of authority; (2) in middle childhood and early adolescence, the primary identification is with social groups; and (3) in later adolescence and young adulthood, the identification is with themes that define self as a result of assuming adult roles.

The cognitive-developmental theory of moral character development that dominated during the 1970s was based on the work of Piaget (1969) and Kohlberg (1984). It proposed that all children are predisposed to engage in moral and ethical thinking, feeling, choosing, and behaving. Morality was viewed as the result of the development of moral thinking based on a concept of justice. Moral schemas, which are cognitive structures that provide a way to organize important aspects of moral events or ideas, were thought to guide thinking about moral issues with thinking providing a guide to behavior. They acknowledged that a child's interactions with the environment are powerful influences yet proposed that thinking is the primary process that allows the child to move into the moral realm.

Piaget (1969) did a better job of accounting for emotion and will or volition by at least mentioning their importance than does Kohlberg (1984). But the attention he gave to affect falls far short of that given by Hoffman (1991), Kagan (1984), and others in the last two decades. Actually, Piaget's theory is much more elaborate than Kohlberg's in that it delineates stages or changes in children's (a) game play, (b) game rule practice, (c) dependence upon rules and authority in order to be good, (d) sense of justice, (e) ability to reason, and (f) conceptions of responsibility. Although not as thoroughly analyzed, he writes about a morality of good that emerges from mutual affection between child and parent and is initially manifest in children's sympathetic tendencies and affective reactions. Piaget says that the raw material for future moral behavior is present in these tendencies and reactions, which become moral when subjected to rules. Finally, he wrote that moral sentiments about right and wrong and moral motivation reflect the subordination of early sympathetic tendencies and affective reactions with will emerging as a permanent set of constructed values to which one is obligated to adhere. In many ways, Piaget anticipated the more elaborate moral-affective theories of Hoffman and Kagan.

Kohlberg (1984) proposed that moral thinking is based on an individual's thinking regarding justice, fairness, and equity. He stated that children's thinking about right and wrong begins with operant conditioning. As the child matures, he is able to think about right and wrong in terms of reciprocal activities and then progresses to conventional thinking where he begins to think in terms of important group members such as parents, teachers, or friends before moving to a society-maintaining orientation of following laws and regulations. Theoretically, some people move to post-conventional thinking where they accept principles in a contract and select their own moral principles. This theory is best described as social-cognitive because reasoning and concepts of justice evolve from a sequence of perspectives on the world: egocentric, individualistic, interpersonal, organizational, societal, and universal. At the early stages, it validated behavioral theories and moves the child through stages of extrinsic and then intrinsic motivation. What it lacks is any validation of affective processes other than motivation.

Gilligan (1977) asserted that Kohlberg's theory was developed using boys and men and that girls and women have a different basis for making moral decisions. She proposed that care is the central principle underlying female reasoning, not justice, and that girls and women score lower on Kohlberg's scale as a result. Hoffman (2000) synthesized these two positions by proposing that care and equity are two different forms of justice with a person's level of empathy providing a foundation for both.

A neo-Kohlbergian view developed by Rest and his associates (Narvaez & Rest, 1995; Rest, 1986; Rest, Narvaez, Bebeau, & Thoma, 1999) suggested there are three levels of moral judgment: (1) personal interest, (2) maintaining norms, and (3) post-conventional. They agreed that movement from a self-orientation to an other-orientation is brought about as the child develops a society-maintaining schema. They proposed that post-conventional thinking might be considered society-creating rather than society-maintaining. Individuals in the norm-maintaining stage will actively seek norms that are group-wide first and then seek norms that are society-wide. They seek uniform, categorical application of these norms and are oriented to fulfilling their social obligations or duties. Individuals in the post-conventional stage are more focused on the establishment of moral criteria and appealing to an abstract ideal that may not be found in present society. They also seek ideals that can be shared across cultures and societies and seek full reciprocity among the group members who establish those ideals.

Figure 10-1. Model of Moral Character Development

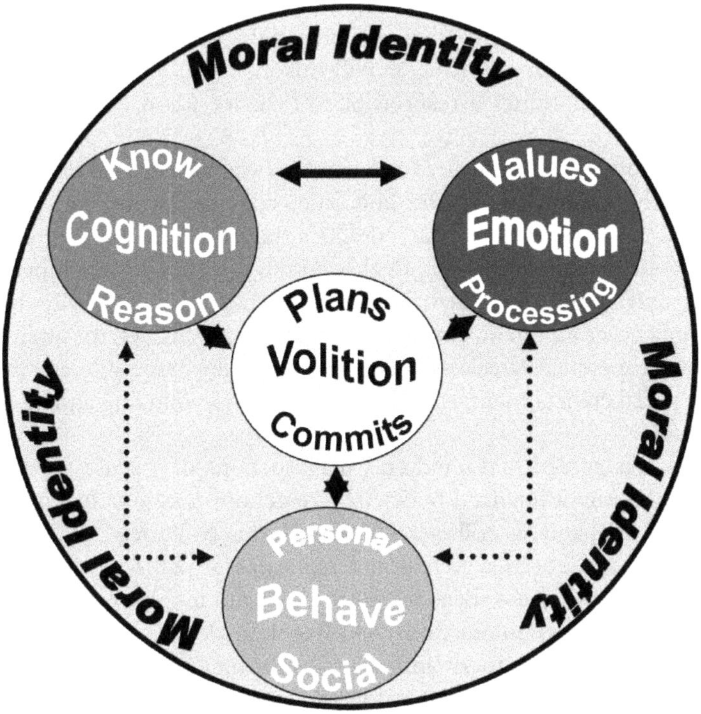

One of the newest viewpoints on moral character development that can be grouped in the interactional category is social cognition (Bandura, 1977, 1991b). This approach combines many of the assumptions of the blank slate, information processing, and affective approaches. A major difference is that it focuses on putting thoughts and values into action. It proposed a relationship of reciprocal determinism among the environment, overt behavior, and personal factors such as reasoning skills or level of empathy (See Figure 10-1). For example, not only do models, consequences, and other environmental influences have an impact on behavior, but behavior also has an impact on different aspects of the environment.

Another focus of the social-cognitive view is human agency or volition. Whereas Kohlberg (1984) and cognitive-structuralists concentrate on increased levels of moral reasoning, Bandura (1977, 1991b) focused more on self-regulation and self-efficacy. He proposed that moral development occurs gradually from transactions with environment, including the application of consequences, the observation of models, and acculturation by social agents. Most importantly it is the person's reflection on both external and internal factors that provides the crucial processes related to moral development. As such, the social cognition approach is more focused on the processes of moral development than on content (Thomas, 1997). Social-cognitive theorists generally focus on personal agency and the freedom to choose (Kurtines, Berman, Ittel, & Williamson, 1995). They proposed that with this freedom comes a responsibility to make good decisions and act morally.

An additional component of the psychosocial view is that development involves "the emergence of the linguistic, cognitive, communicative, *and* sociomoral competencies that define the interrelated domains of development by which the individual becomes a competent member of the social system" (Kurtines, Mayock, Pollard, Lanza, & Carlo, 1991, p. 309). This linguistic component emphasizes a need to consider the individual's language competencies because that is one way the person interacts morally with the social environment, especially in connecting thinking and intentions to behavior.

While it is agreed that children's constructions of a sense of right and wrong are heavily influenced by social interactions and a widening view of the world, Turiel and his colleagues (1983; Helwig & Turiel, 2002) proposed that morality and social convention have separate paths of development. They suggested that most social interactions do not involve moral issues and that success in these interactions involves knowledge and skills that are important on their own merit and not because they impact moral thinking. Turiel identified four major dimensions that separate universal morals from conventional valuing: *alterability*—moral principles do not change, conventions are changeable; *contingency*—morality is not contingent on authority, social practice, or group agreement whereas social conventions are based on rules established by an individual or group; *generality*—morality and what is considered moral behavior is universal, whereas social conventions are specific to group or society; *seriousness*—moral transgressions are seen as more serious than social convention transgressions. This is a topic that was discussed in more detail in the chapter on social development (Huitt & Dawson, Chapter 7, this volume).

Personality/Virtue

A final theoretical category is labeled the "virtues" approach. Proponents see virtues as combining (a) natural predispositions and (b) interactions with the environment that involve both reflection and commitment to moral values and behavior. As personality constructs, virtues are habitual ways of thinking, feeling, committing, and acting that reflect moral character. Erikson (1994) and Blasi (1993) suggested that virtues are the dominant aspect of moral identity.

Multiple authors have developed lists of critical virtues. Borba (2001) suggested empathy, respect, courtesy, kindness, tolerance, and fairness and confirms Hoffman's (2000) identification of empathy as a critical emotion in that it is foundational to the others. Kavelin-Popov, Popov, and Kavelin (1997) listed 52 virtues without any distinction of some as being more critical or how the virtues might be grouped. Huitt (2001b) identified 52 virtues which he categorized according to his Brilliant Star framework. Seligman (2002) identified 25 positive identity traits, which he labeled "signature strengths", and grouped them in five categories: wisdom and knowledge, courage, love and humanity, justice, temperance, and spirituality and transcendence. Even state departments of education have developed lists of values, virtues, and character traits that should be addressed in public schools (eg, Georgia Department of Education, 1997). Vessels (1998) divides his concept of personal integrity into four primary virtues, and his concept of social integrity into three. Additional virtues elaborate each of the seven and are incorporated into curricular objectives. With respect to personal integrity, Vessels stated that people with moral character are predisposed to: (1) show kindness and compassion with empathetic understanding; (2) show the courage to be honest and principled irrespective of circumstances; (3) acquire a wide range of abilities that enable them to independently resolve problems, analyze situations where moral values and principles may be in conflict, and adapt to change in a personally and socially constructive manner; and (4) display a high level of effort in their daily work, and a high level of commitment to individual and group goals and standards. With respect to social integrity, he stated that people with moral character are predisposed to (1) show an interest-in and concern-for others in the spirit of friendship and brotherhood and to act on these concerns routinely, (2) perform as responsible and other-directed team members within families and other groups, and (3) view the preservation of social institutions and improvement of both self and community as civic duties.

Walker (2002b) also identified clusters of attributes or themes that contribute to people's understanding of morality. The "principled-idealistic" theme concerns notions of justice, acting according to principle, and rationality; the "dependable-loyal" theme involves the development of interpersonal relations; the "caring-trustworthy" theme addresses interpersonal warmth; the "confidence" theme concerns the extent to which one demonstrates personal agency. This last theme is similar to that proposed by Bandura (1991a) in his focus on self-efficacy and self-regulation. Walker identified a relatively small set of moral attributes. The first cluster includes honesty, truthfulness, and trustworthiness; a second includes care, compassion, thoughtfulness, and considerateness. Finally, he suggested that integrity, or the connection of thought to action, should be emphasized.

Stilwell and her team (Stillwell, 1998; Stilwell, Galvin, Kopta, & Padgett, 1996; Stillwell, Galvin, Kopta, Padgett, & Holt, 1997) provided another multi-modal view. She focused on moral motivation and proposes that children develop it within four domains of human experience:

1. attachment bond with parents—children learn about compliance and respect;
2. moral-emotional responsiveness—children learn about the ways in which emotions regulate moral life, including reparation and healing responses after wrongdoing;
3. moral valuation—children learn about the developmental processes of deriving and justifying moral rules in the service of values; and
4. moral volition—children learn about the ways in which autonomy is used and will become associated with what should be done.

Like Vessels (1998), she suggested that development within these domains is synthesized into a supra-domain, labeled conscience. Reminiscent of Berkowitz (1998), she stated that this is a person's composite understanding of the moral system within the self, a moral identity that functions through the operation of the subdomains.

Colby and Damon (1992) proposed moral exemplars rather than virtues should function as a curricular centerpiece. They contended that exemplars provide an adequate guide for how to think, feel, commit, and act morally and identified several shared characteristics (which could be considered virtues) among moral exemplars:

1. a long-term commitment to moral ideals, including a general love of humanity;
2. a willingness to be socially influenced and to change;
3. the conscientious use of morally justifiable means to pursue moral goals;
4. a willingness to risk self-interest for the sake of moral goals;
5. a clear image of themselves and their ideals, including humility, optimism, faith, and a sense of spirituality.

Walker (2002a, 2002b) proposed that people's thinking about the attributes of exemplars can be classified on two continuums. The first he described as a self—other dimension. He proposed that moral people are thought to have a sense of personal agency (they are responsible for their own actions) and are considered to have a sense of responsibility for the care of others. The second was labeled internal—external. In this domain moral people are thought to be governed by their own conscience. However, they are also cognizant of shared norms. Walker suggested that the internal aspect requires autonomy, experience, and reflection; the external aspect requires sensitivity to expectations of others.

The variety of virtues or values or important attributes of moral individuals can be somewhat daunting to those interested in implementing a character development program. It is especially important to have agreement among critical stakeholders such as teachers, parents, and the community. To assist in this identification, Huitt (2003) developed a survey of 152 terms used by a variety of authors. Educators can have different constituencies complete the survey and then identify common qualities that will be the focus of their school program.

Summary

Any summary of extant theoretical positions requires a multi-modal or multi-dimensional perspective if one is attempting to convey the diversity of thought and research related to moral character development. The importance of thinking, both in terms of a knowledge base and reasoning or processing of information must be included, along with emotions, will or volition, and overt behavior. Moral identity, conscience, and virtues must also be considered as well as how biological factors and the social environment influence each component. Suffice it to say that if the radical sociobiological position is correct, there is no need for a discussion of educational programs as morality from that perspective is impervious to social influences. All of the other positions propose some sort of environmental influence, although there is enormous disagreement about exactly what that ought to be. The next section will make suggestions we believe incorporate major findings of the different positions.

Applications of Moral Character Development Theories

As one might expect, there are numerous approaches to implementing the diverse theories and research related to moral character development. However, there are a number of conclusions that can be drawn from previous work. One is that character education needs to be reflected in school- and community-wide programs. Another is that there are a variety of sound instructional methods that can be used by classroom teachers to engage students in character development.

Programs

The planning of programs should be guided by developmental characteristics of children and youth. It should yield a spiraling, developmentally-appropriate set of objectives and strategies for each age or age range. Program planners need to be cognizant of the fact that characteristic reasoning skills, values and empathy, volition and commitment to act, and skills at each age level influence each other in a reciprocal manner within a social context that can be constructed to promote growth. Therefore, they will likely need to consult other chapters in this volume that separately discuss cognitive, affective, conative, and social development as they prepare their approach to character development. We have prepared an overview of some of the major developmental milestones (see Table 10-1). Some general guidelines for program development may be in order. In order to promote optimum character growth, adults need to be aware of and responsive to children's needs and must develop authoritative relationships with them that combine love with much communication, guidance, structure, and firm yet fair discipline (Berkowitz, 2002). They should socially reward examples of appropriate behavior and provide developmentally appropriate explanations of why the behavior is appropriate. The emphasis on explanation should gradually shift from minimal during infancy through preschool to extensive from about age twelve since, as Piaget (1969) has so effectively explained, there needs to be a shift from expiatory or punitive sanctions (heteronomy) to reciprocity sanctions that focus on the impact on others and on relationships of inappropriate behavior, thereby fostering internalization, moral autonomy, and intrinsic motivation. Adults should have high expectations for moral maturity that are age-appropriate and should model the characteristics they want their children to develop (Bandura, 1991b; Baumrind, 1989; Damon, 1988).

Advocates of character education recognize that parents are critically important in the development of moral character (Berkowitz, 2002). Unfortunately, many parents have abandoned their responsibilities for moral and values education to the schools and the larger society through popular cultural outlets such as television and movies. Even those interested may not possess the training and experience necessary to follow the general guidelines listed above; therefore, school personnel will likely need to provide parent education programs that assist parents in developing the appropriate knowledge, dispositions, and skills to assist educators in this important work.

Table 10-1. Moral Development Milestones

Stage	Age	Domain	Developmental Standard
Infancy	Birth to 18/24 months	Cognitive/ Knowledge	Knowledge limited to interactions with immediate environment; organized and stored in sensory perceptions (ie, without language)
		Cognitive/ Reasoning	Object permanence—see people as separate
		Affective	Empathy—becomes upset when others are upset; later becomes aware and attempts to console
		Conative	Early display of will, use of "no"
		Social	Attachment—strong bond with at least one adult, generally primary caretaker
Toddler & Early Childhood	18/24 months to 7 years	Cognitive/ Knowledge	Beginning to form ideas about how the world works; begins to use language to organize knowledge
		Cognitive/ Reasoning	Egocentric to seeing other's perspective; beginning to use imagination
		Affective	Empathy—begins to use language to express connections of one's own feelings to those of others
			Shame—recognition of misbehavior; sense of regret and sorrow for inappropriate use of self-control
			Guilt—sorrow, remorse for behavior
		Conation	Self-control, Self-regulation—becomes increasingly able to direct and control ideas, emotions, behaviors, etc.; ability to delay gratification
		Social	Parallel play, role playing

Table 10-1. Moral Development Milestones (continued)

Stage	Age	Domain	Developmental Standard
Middle Childhood	7-12 years	Cognitive/ Knowledge	Begins to develop knowledge in academic disciplines: Language arts, mathematics, science, social studies, fine arts, etc.
		Cognitive/ Reasoning	Concrete operations, reversibility, rule-governed thinking; concrete examples of right and wrong govern thinking, first in self-orientation, then to other-orientation
		Affective	Empathy—develops capacity to feel empathy for another's life condition or experience
		Conative	Self-efficacy—develops ideas about what is possible and realistic to perform; self-regulation—more capable of developing weekly and longer goals and plans
		Social	Focus on group identity
Adolesc-ence	13-18 years	Cognitive/ Knowledge	Potential to develop competency as disciplined thinker
		Cognitive/ Reasoning	Potential for developing abstract symbolic thinking; abstract principles govern thinking of right and wrong
		Affective	Has the potential to show mature levels of empathy, emotional behavior, and emotional self-regulation
		Conative	Frontal lobe maturity allows making complex decisions
		Social	Development of moral identity, first in relation to others, then self-defined

In addition to parents and schools, religious organizations and other youth-serving agencies in the community also have an important impact on children's character development (Epstein, 1995; Epstein, Coates, Salinas, Sanders, & Simon, 1997). As communitarians such as Benson (1997) have so eloquently explained, everyone in the community bears some of the responsibility for raising good children who can responsibly assume the roles of student, parent, neighbor, friend, employee, supervisor, worker, service provider, citizen, spouse, and family member.

Acknowledging that parents and the community play important roles in the moral character development of children does not absolve educators of responsibility to be powerful advocates. Educators need to develop an atmosphere in the classroom and school that encourages character development (Dewey, 1975; Power, Higgins, & Kohlberg, 1989; Schaps, 2002; Vessels, 1998; Wynne & Ryan, 1997). This should be done with an explicit curriculum that focuses on the social skills, virtues, and moral principles that are also taught within homes and communities (excluding only the religious contents, contexts, and methodologies specific to a particular religion though including ecumenical concepts and principles such as the Golden Rule).

The most effective school-based character education programs promote the development of moral virtues, moral reasoning abilities, and other assets and qualities that make the will and ability to do what is right and good probable. They explicitly address issues of moral thinking, valuing, choosing, committing, and planning that indirectly impact moral behavior and character development while simultaneously focusing on moral behavior and responding appropriately to both moral and immoral behavior (Kirshenbaum, 1994; Narvaez, 2002; Power et al., 1989; Primack, 1986). These eclectic programs do this by combining direct instruction, modeling, reinforcement, and various community-building strategies such as class meetings, service learning, cooperative learning, intercultural exchange, social skills training, and caring interpersonal support (Huitt & Vessels, 2002). While maintaining active teaching and learning, students are encouraged to adhere to group norms and rules that are taught directly (Kirschenbaum, 1994; Ryan & Wynne, 1996). As Aristotle (Kraut, 2001) and many since him have explained, bringing behavior in line with adult expectations at an early age provides a foundation for building the internal processes necessary for autonomous selection of sound moral and ethical behavior.

Benninga et al. (1991) provided support for this eclectic approach. Their research showed that a traditional program emphasizing specific virtues and relying heavily on direct instruction and reinforcement successfully improved students' self-esteem while a more progressive program that promoted virtue through in-school service learning and other active community building strategies without teaching virtues directly successfully improved students' fairness, consideration, helpfulness, and social responsibility. Most experts in the field now believe that a blend of the two approaches is best at all levels but with an emphasis on the former with younger children, and an emphasis on the latter with students aged ten or eleven and above.

An eclectic approach is also implicit in the 11 Principles of Effective Character Education prepared by Lickona, Schaps and Lewis (2003):

1. Promote core ethical values as the basis of good character.
2. Define character comprehensively to include thinking, feeling, and behavior.
3. Promote core values intentionally and proactively through all parts of school life.
4. Are caring communities.
5. Give students opportunities for moral action.
6. Have meaningful and challenging academic curriculums that respect learners.
7. Develop students' intrinsic motivation.
8. Have professionals who exemplify core values and maintain a moral community.
9. Require moral leadership from educators and students.
10. Recruit parents and community members as full partners.
11. Evaluate school character, student character, and adults as character educators.

Many theorists previously mentioned have substantiated the necessity of building a foundation through external influences before developing a child's sense of moral autonomy. Constructivists erroneously claimed that Piaget saw heteronomy, or a morality of constraint, as an obstacle rather than a foundation (Vessels, 1998). However, the research and related theories of Hoffman (1991; 2000) and Kagan (1984), as well as others, indicated that this foundation is not only the product of external imposition but also the product of genetics and psychophysiology in the form of natural moral emotions that are evident in rudimentary forms at birth such as affective empathy.

Berkowitz (2002) and Bandura (1991b) emphasized the importance of adult modeling of the internal processing and behavior they desire in children and youth. The maxim "Your actions speak so loudly I can't hear what you say" is more correct for teaching virtues and other character qualities than it is for other types of behavior. Adults should verbally express their expectations of good behavior and provide many opportunities to practice good behavior and to be acknowledged for doing so. They need to provide age-appropriate opportunities for students to reason about, debate, and reflect on moral issues. This can and should be done in the course of academic instruction through (a) unit planning, (b) the use of teachable moments, and (c) taking time to discuss student interactions that occur as a normal part of life in the classroom. Such efforts at school can be extended to the family (1) by making sure that parents know that school personnel want students to become both good and smart, and (2) by including character themes and issues into (a) homework, (b) student performances that parents attend, (c) newsletters from the school and classroom, and (d) and conferences during home visits and parent-teacher conferences at the school. From the perspective of cognitive development and moral thinking, parents and educators should be aware-of and build-on students' changing conceptions of fairness, human welfare, human rights, and the application of these moral understandings to issues of everyday life (Damon, 1988; Nucci, 1989; Selman, 1971). Children and youth should be provided age-appropriate opportunities for participation, discussion, collaboration, and reflection on moral and ethical issues (Solomon, Watson, and Battistich, 2001). In order to achieve this outcome, educators and parents need to *gradually transition away from* (1) insisting that children learn and follow rules *through*: (a) direct instruction, (b) consequences, (c) authoritative relationships, and (d) disciplinary "inductions" (which foster the development of internal standards by taking advantage of children's natural capacity for affective empathy) *toward* (2) giving youth the opportunity to recognize or figure out what is right and to choose what is right (as a result of understanding, internalized standards, and mature empathy) *by*: (a) increasing the level of reciprocity in their dealings with youth and (b) the frequency with which they provide opportunities to discuss moral dilemmas and to challenge and replace the status quo within their relationships, groups, and communities (Berkowitz, 1998; Hoffman, 1991; Piaget, 1969; Vessels, 1998). This instructional transition neither precludes efforts to promote the moral autonomy and intrinsic motivation of young children nor requires abandoning efforts to teach right and wrong directly to older youth or to hold them accountable for immoral action through logical consequences. Rather, the transition involves a shift in emphasis. Vessels (1998) developed a character development curriculum that is developmentally-based and addresses both the content and processes that have been discussed. Curricular scope is achieved by addressing both content (virtues) and developmental processes related to conscience and moral reasoning (See Table 10-2).

Table 10-2. Vessel's Core Curriculum

Develop-mental Level (Grades)	Main Primary-Virtue Focus for Level	Other Targeted Primary and Elaborative Virtues	Targeted Psychological Processes
Pre-K & K	Kindness	**Kindness:** Nice, Loving, Gentle, Cheerful, Thankful, Friendly **Courage:** Honest, Exploring **Ability:** Attentive, Creative **Effort:** Hard-Working **Friendship:** Helpful, Sharing **Teamwork:** On-Task	Affective Empathy Initiative/ Just Do Things Conformity to Rules Non-selectively Sociable
First Second	Friendship	**Friendship:** Fair, Forgiving, Patient, Considerate **Kindness**: Comforting, Courteous **Courage:** Brave, Sorry **Ability:** Prepared, Skillful **Effort:** Energetic, Determined, Competitive **Teamwork:** Respectful **Citizenship:** Rule-Following	Authoritarian Conscience Fairness as Equality Competence / Do Things Well Unevenhanded Reciprocity in Friendships
Third Fourth Fifth	Teamwork	**Teamwork:** Cooperative, Positive, Productive, Responsible, Mediating, Punctual/Prompt **Kindness:** Sensitive, Interested **Courage**: Remorseful **Ability:** Knowledgeable, Organized, Realistic **Effort:** Self-Disciplined, Studious **Friendship:** Supportive **Citizenship:** Drug-Free, Health-Conscious, Law-Abiding	Beginning Rational Conscience Fairness as Equity/ Context-Dependent Justice True Perspective Taking/ Cognitive Part of Empathy

Table 10-2. Vessel's Core Curriculum (continued)

Developmental Level (Grades)	Main Primary-Virtue Focus for Level	Other Targeted Primary and Elaborative Virtues	Targeted Psychological Processes
Sixth Seventh Eighth	Courage	**Courage:** Independent, Decisive Risk-Taking, Assertive, Self-Disclosing, Self-Evaluating **Kindness:** Compassionate **Ability:** Flexible, Objective **Effort:** Ambitious, Dedicated **Friendship:** Understanding, Trustworthy, Devoted/Loyal **Teamwork**: Humble/modest, Genuine/sincere **Citizenship**: Health-conscious	Full Rational Conscience Early Autonomous Moral Reasoning Social Consciousness or Sense of Duty to Others Besides Peers & Friends Mutual Trust and Sharing in Personal Friendships
Ninth Tenth Eleventh Twelfth	Citizen-ship	**Citizenship:** Respecting rights, Educated, Employable, Patriotic, Historically and Culterally Literate, Family Valuing **Kindness:** Empathetic Courage: Persevering, Principled **Ability:** Deliberate, Prudent, Resourceful Effort: Optimistic, Idealistic, Persistent, Conscientious **Friendship:** Charitable, Altruistic **Teamwork:** Compromising, Temperate	Self-Directed, Principled and Self-Governing Autonomy Autonomous Critical Thinking About Moral Issues, Laws, and Social Conventions Integration of Roles, Values, Behaviors, and Attributes into Prosocial and Ethical Identity

In addition to authoritative relationships with children and the use of induction in disciplinary encounters with children, perhaps the best means of promoting the internalization of moral standards, the formation of conscience, and the emergence of moral autonomy is service learning (Hinck & Brandell, 1999; Howard, 1993; Muscott, 2001). Academic service learning may be the most effective instructional method at all age levels. Younger children can simply become involved in ongoing service projects initiated by adults or older students. Older students can take more initiative in creating and implementing a service learning project. In any case, students should be involved in deciding what to do and how to make the program work. This should include a discussion of values, alternative forms of service, potential impact, and how to measure success. Students should develop a plan of action, commit to it, carry it out as independently as possible, and reflect on the results. There is a wealth of good service learning materials for teachers to use, but none are better than those provided by the Giraffe Project (see http://www.giraffe.org/). This program defines Giraffes as those who show courage and caring by sticking out their necks to help others. They first learn about Giraffes, then look for Giraffes in their communities, and then plan a service project that enables them to be Giraffes.

Instructional Methods

As discussed previously, promising character education programs (a) focus on developing the internal processes of thinking, feeling, and committing, (b) teach the social skills needed for appropriate behavior, and (c) focus on developing a moral identity as a virtuous person. Each of the theories of moral development that have been described, compared, and contrasted provides something of value for those endeavoring to build character and/or plan effective programs in schools that extend into and connect with parallel efforts in homes and communities. Each corresponds to a set of instructional or facilitative strategies as revealed in the Vessels' chart below (see Table 10-3), and some provide useful specifics about the developmental characteristics of children at various age levels. It is our position that all theories and their related strategies are valid and valuable since these theories have been derived from extensive research and observation. We see no single correct theory or set of corresponding instructional strategies. All should be viewed by practitioners as complementary, and when drawn from freely, practitioners are very likely to access all avenues to learning.

Table 10-3. Instructional Strategies Organized by Theory and Learning Mode

Theory Category	Learning Mode	Instructional Strategies	
External/ Social	Develop-mentally Appropriate Discipline and Reinforcement	• increasing positive interactions with students • a new type of grading system • "critical contracts"	• self-improvement projects; awards for model citizenship • classroom management based on mutual respect & building intrinsic motivation
	Direct Instruction	• visual displays • literature; storytelling • social skills instruction • multicultural teaching • virtue of the week/month	• teaching parenting K-12 • high-school ethics courses • school behavior codes and pledges • character infusion across the curriculum
	Observation and Modeling	• teaching artists • adult mentoring • cross-grade tutors and buddies • direct and indirect exposure to "giraffes" or heroes	• "family heritage museums" and "grandparents gatherings" • teachers and parents modeling virtues and doing volunteer work
Internal/ Psycho-physiological	Unstructured Peer-group Interaction and Play	• camps • recess at school • parties with friends • overnight visits with friends	• center time in K-2 classrooms • socializing during school lunchtime • free play with siblings, other children, and others at recreational sites

Table 10-3. Instructional Strategies Organized by Theory and Learning Mode (continued)

Interactional	Interpersonal-Environmental Support	• a new-student welcoming committee • community support for parents to be • caring and democratic classrooms and schools	• caring and "authoritative" principals, teachers, and parents • school restructuring ideas that build community like looping
	Active Experiental Participation in Class and School Communities	• sociodrama • rule making • class captains • class meetings • student government • cooperative learning	• creative arts activities • extracurricular activities • student discipline panels • interpersonal problem solving class-to-class intercultural exchanges
Personality/ Virtue	Real-World Experiences in the Larger Community	• vacations • scouting • free reading • teen court work • cultural festivals • organized sports	• movies and plays • visiting museums • Internet exploration • teacher and parent-initiated service learning • church attendance, including cross-cultural church attendance

Vessels' (1998) referred to these theory-supported and strategically rich avenues to learning as learning modes, and, like Ryan and Bohlin (1999) identified about a half dozen. He referred to these as the five E's: experience, expectations, ethos, example, explanation. Vessels includes in his list developmentally-appropriate discipline and reinforcement, direct instruction, modeling and observation, unstructured peer-group interaction and play, interpersonal/environmental support, active experiential participation in class and school communities, and real-world experiences within the larger community. Although nearly every instructional strategy uses more than one learning mode, most use one more than the others. In Table 10-3, he aligned each learning mode with strategies that correspond.

Figure 10-2. The Intersection of Autonomy/Heteronomy and Individual/Community

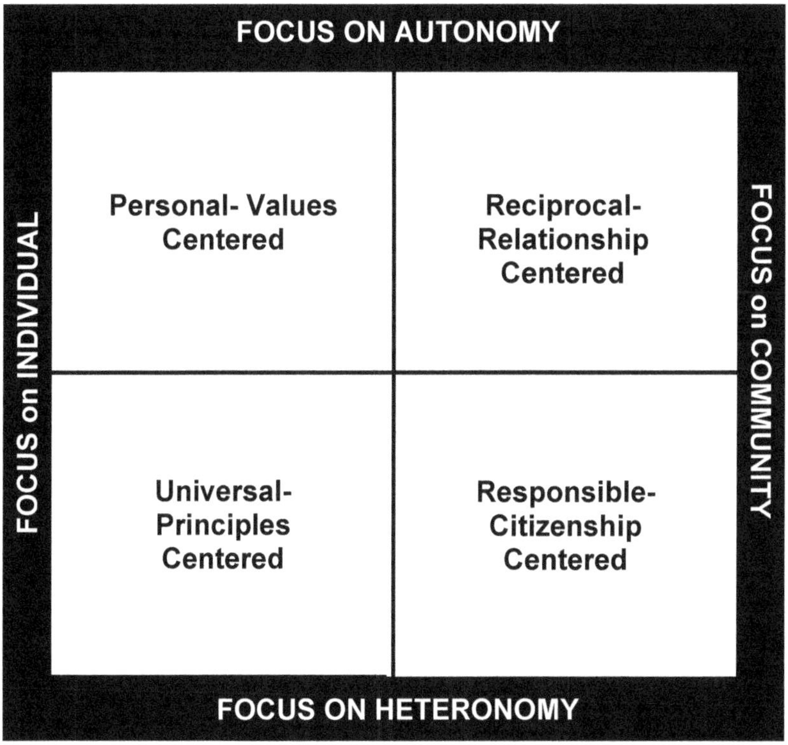

Another way to think about instructional strategies is to organize them in terms a combination of a focus on autonomy and heteronomy and a focus on the individual or community (Vessels, 1998). Vessels' categories are produced by the intersection of two dichotomies: a primary focus on the individual versus a primary focus on the community; an emphasis on individual autonomy versus an emphasis on heteronomy, that is, internally versus externally imposed goodness. This intersection produces four quadrants: (1) individual and autonomy, (2) individual and heteronomy, (3) community and autonomy, and (4) community and heteronomy (See Figure

10-2). While he found that some theories do not fit comfortably within a single quadrant, nearly all are more identifiable with one than the other three

Table 10-4. Types of Programs and Orientations Used in Different Orientations

Focus on Individual Beliefs & Autonomy • Academic and Creative Potential of Students • Fostered in a Competitive School & Classroom Climate • Non-Curricular/Incidental Moral Education and Socialization • Value and Responsibilities of Liberty and Individual Rights Discovered • Radical Constructivist, Student-Centered Instruction	Focus on Community, Service & Autonomy • Natural Development • Cooperative Learning • Daily Class Meetings • Experiential Learning • Looping • Mentoring • Interpersonal Support • Classroom Communities • Unstructured Social Play • Extracurricular Activities • Shared Decision Making • Guided Reflection
Focus on Individual Beliefs & Heteronomy • Maxims, Proverbs, Codes of Conduct, and Pledges • Great Moral Exemplars • Great Stories and Literature • Teaching Specific Virtues • Developing Good Habits • Teaching About Religions • Emotional Commitment • Discipline & Reinforcement • Morally and Ethically Rich Academic Content	Focus on Community, Service & Heteronomy • Teaching Duties, Obligations, Social Roles, and Responsibilities • Village Child Rearing • Service Learning • Intercultural Exchange • Student Government • Parenting Education K-12 • Rules and Consequences • Community Youth Programs

From this perspective there are orientations that can be used to develop a moral character education program. If the focus is on developing an autonomous individual, then the program would concentrate on a personal-values centered approach. If the focus is on the individual within society, then the program would concentrate on a universal-principles centered approach. Correspondingly, if the focus is on an autonomous person's relationship with the community, the program would concentrate on a reciprocal-relationship centered approach. Finally, if the focus is on the person's role within the community, the program would focus on a responsible-citizenship centered approach. An eclectic program would have elements of all approaches, although it is likely that each school's implementation would have one of the viewpoints as its primary interest. The types of program and instructional strategies most likely to be used in each of the orientations are shown in Table 10-4.

Children and youth are never too old to be encouraged to learn about, adopt, and display a set of specific virtues (Kavelin-Popov et al., 1997; Lickona, 1992; Seligman, 2002; Vessels, 1998). When selecting virtues to teach about and promote moral character, it is important to include a variety, perhaps using the categories of theories discussed above, the two types of virtues (personal and social) discussed by Vessels (1998), or the domains of the Brilliant Star (Huitt, Chapter 1, this volume). One way to practice this is to provide specific activities involving role playing with immediate encouragement and feedback. Another is to use narratives and personally-developed stories (Tappan & Brown, 1989) that are discussed in terms of the internal processes and overt behavior. Additionally, Kavelin-Popov et al, suggested that each virtue should be considered in terms of four questions: (1) What is it (knowledge); (2) Why practice it (valuing); (3) How do you practice it (volition and behavior); and (4) What are signs of success (reflection on behavior). This implies teaching the virtues as concepts, not as definitions. The dual focus on (a) the internal processes of understanding, valuing, and desiring, and (b) external behavior makes student learning deeper and better predictor of future behavior.

Assessment and Evaluation

Assessing or evaluating individual moral character, one or more of its components, or an entire school program is a challenge. Few research design and statistics specialists have been trained in program evaluation methods and exposed to the limited number of measurement instruments now available to educators who are seeking to build character. Their natural inclination is to minimize the value of qualitative methods that are especially valuable for evaluating process and implementation. But it makes little sense to evaluate outcomes such as moral thinking, moral feeling, moral behavior, moral intention, or school climate if there is no clear evidence that the program was implemented as planned, and no way of knowing where it was strong or weak and why. This situation led researchers to begin constructing instruments and studying and using qualitative evaluation methods. Qualitative methods are not limited to investigating hypotheses and outcomes but are open-ended and information rich; traditional quantitative methods are more likely tied to program hypotheses and the program plan, so they may not reflect unintended outcomes, both positive and negative.

Ideally, evaluation plans for character education programs should allow for (1) on-going monitoring which will detect immediate benefits and/or a breakdown in implementation, (2) the documentation of benefits that may emerge after a year or two as more and more students have multiple-year exposure to the program, and (3) an analysis of social indicators that may reflect long-term benefits such as dropout rates and rates of divorce and crime in your community. All evaluation plans (1) should be designed before program implementation, (2) should be consistent with the goals and objectives of your program, (3) should include a variety of measures (triangulation of instruments), (4) should include both quantitative and qualitative components, and (5) should use all possible informants including students, teachers, parents, and trained "third-person" observers from outside the school or school system if available (triangulation of data sources). Of course, teacher evaluations of attempts to impact moral character in the classroom may not involve such an extensive evaluation program. However, research suggests that such individual implementations are much less promising than school-wide programs involving educators, parents, and members of the community.

Because "moral" or "virtuous" behavior does not always indicate that moral feeling and thinking led to the behavior, or that the person had the necessary knowledge and social skills to behave similarly and independently in appropriate future situations without special incentives or prompting, one cannot always draw reliable inferences about "internal" moral states from observable behavior. Even when these internal states appear to be reliably reflected in such observable behaviors as crying, a gentle touch, a smile, a considerate statement, or a complex sequence of helpful actions, an undetectable lack of genuineness or a significant amount of imitation may preclude reliable and valid inferences with respect to the presence of relatively internal moral states and competencies. Conversely, moral feeling, reasoning, intent, and competence do not always lead to moral action as demonstrated by the Hartshorne and May (1928) studies decades ago. People sometimes engage in "right" behavior for purely selfish reasons, and they sometimes imitate such behavior without feeling or understanding. They also fail to do what they know and feel to be right and either suffer guilt or engage in bizarre rationalizations to protect their self-esteem as a result.

It seems reasonable to assume that in most cases, spontaneous "moral" behaviors justify the inference that moral affect, cognition, and competence preceded the behavior or co-occurred. This is more likely to be the case for upper elementary, middle, and high school students; younger children tend to imitate more and are primarily driven by anticipated consequences. Therefore, the assessment of spontaneous behaviors through systematic recording by trained observers should probably be the nucleus of all program evaluation plans, particularly for elementary school children who are not skilled at communicating feelings and thoughts through language. The evaluation plan could also include elicited or contrived behaviors. Both can be verbal (oral or written expression), nonverbal, or a combination of both. For older children, adolescents, and adults, the best way to get at moral affect, cognition, and knowledge (not social skill) is indirectly through questioning, although some surveys and questionnaires are available. It also seems reasonable to assume that the best way to measure the social skills necessary for moral behavior is directly through the observation of spontaneous behaviors and/or behaviors in contrived situations designed to elicit the verbal and nonverbal behaviors that occur naturally in social situations.

Ideally, therefore, an evaluation plan should include a combination of (1) direct observations of behaviors with a primary emphasis on naturally occurring or spontaneous behaviors, and (2) indirect observations of internal states (feeling, thoughts, knowledge) through questioning or elicited verbal responses, supplemented with data collected with valid and reliable instruments where available. Results from the latter will be invalid if the instruments or questions used are poor or the person fails to communicate the truth due to a lack of skill or will; therefore, one should use tested instruments if available and should take care to adapt to the limitations of the various age groups you are evaluating. Results from direct measures will be invalid if the behavior observed is not representative, if the recording devices are faulty, or if the observers are incompetent due to a lack of ability or training. Results from indirect measures or asking students about internal feelings, thoughts, and intentions will be invalid if students do not respond honestly each time questioned.

Time Sampling/Event Recording/Pre-Coded Observation Forms. Observing and recording specific behaviors can be done as they occur or later via (a) tape recording (video and/or audio), (b) the review of anecdotal notes, or (c) the recall of past experiences and observations. The most structured and reliable approach uses pre-coded observation forms. Pre-coded observation forms limit the amount of writing by using various combinations of letters, numbers, pluses, and minuses in place of words. For some low-frequency behaviors such as interpersonal conflicts, it may be possible to record every instance of the behavior during specified time periods. A partial-interval time-sampling system requires only a single occurrence of the behavior during the designated time interval (eg, five minute or one-half hour intervals). Other time-sampling options include "whole-interval," in which the behavior or type of behavior is recorded if it occurs throughout the chosen time interval (eg, social harmony in the classroom), and "momentary" in which the behavior or type of behavior is recorded if it is occurring at the end of each time interval (eg, at least one student in the room voluntarily assisting another). Vessels' (1998) Classroom Observation Form uses a combination of event recording (32 types of interpersonal interactions), quality ratings, and whole-interval time sampling for observable aspects of instruction.

School-climate and classroom-climate measures. School climate and classroom climate can be defined as the readily perceptible personality or atmosphere within a classroom or school. Measures of school and classroom climate can help to determine if your program is producing enough responsible, respectful, and caring behavior on the part of students, teachers, and administrators to change the total atmosphere. James Comer's School Development Program, Matthew Davidson, the Developmental Studies Center, and Gordon Vessels all have climate measures that are reliable and valid (Vessels, 1998). Vessels' school climate survey is specifically designed to assess the social-environmental effects of character education programs and whether or not critical elements of a character-building community are present. There is an emphasis on leadership and relationships among members of the school community. He also has created classroom-climate instruments for the elementary level.

Behavioral observations during contrived small group tasks. One way of judging whether students will behave prosocially in real world situations is to involve them with one another in contrived small-group tasks which seek to elicit the same array of interpersonal behaviors that occur naturally as they play and work with one another. Obviously, teachers use small-group tasks within their classrooms as an instructional method and/or a way of informally assessing whether students will behave prosocially as they have been taught to do. The created tasks must be interesting to students, sufficiently unique to do more than elicit well-rehearsed behaviors, and sufficiently open or ambiguous in terms of instructions (semi-structured rather than structured) that behaviors other than prosocial behaviors and various forms and degrees of prosocial behavior can occur (Tauber, Rosenberg, Battistich, & Stone, 1989). As with questionnaires and direct observation forms and procedures, the Developmental Studies Center (Battistich, Solomon, Watson, Solomon & Schaps, 1989) has led the way in developing small-group tasks that can be used to evaluate the internalized or conditioned effects of character education programs (K-6).

Teacher anecdotals, journals, diaries. Teachers' anecdotal notes can be used to help evaluate the effectiveness of a character education program if they are done consistently, and if they routinely include detailed descriptions of relevant interpersonal events. Guidelines such as asking teachers to record the three most significant interpersonal events each day, positive and/or negative, and to avoid referring to any one child more than once each week might make these notes a more reliable and valid indicator of program effectiveness.

Student diaries and journals*:* By the third or fourth grade, most students have developed writing skills to the point where they can convey their thoughts and feelings to others fairly well. Additionally, journal writing has become a rather common practice in elementary schools. Journals and diaries, therefore, provide a convenient and valuable source of information about moral affect, cognition, and knowledge, particularly if students are encouraged to recount and reflect upon interpersonal and moral problems they have encountered incidentally or by instructional design each day. Most elementary children will need considerable prompting in order to fully convey their feelings and thoughts.

Portfolios with follow-up visits by outside evaluation teams. The traditional "Values and Character Recognition Program" in the Fresno area initiated a voluntary evaluation program in 1988 which required each school to complete an application (Vessels, 1998). This application included five categories of questions about the school's character education program: school planning; instructional activities; school goals, standards, and procedures; opportunities for student involvement; and student recognition. A select committee from outside the participating schools and school systems evaluated the responses to these questions along with supportive documents including handbooks, school newspapers, and announcements for special activities, i.e., a portfolio of information.

Hypothetical problem situations presented by interview or essay. Constructed statements of hypothetical conflict situations and dilemmas have been used extensively. With this technique, students are presented with a hypothetical problem and asked what they would and/or should do if they were near or involved, and/or what others who are directly involved in the situation should do. These hypothetical situations have been presented orally through interviews and in writing through essays. The advantage of this technique is that students can convey their inner thoughts, feelings, needs, knowledge, opinions, beliefs, etc. freely and honestly provided they see no need to hide what they really think, feel, need, and know.

In the Measure of Moral Values (Hogan and Dickstein, 1972), students are presented with fifteen brief statements they hear in everyday conversation and are asked to write one-line reactions to each. These reactions are scored for (1) concern for the sanctity of the individual, (2) judgments based on the spirit rather than the letter of the law, (3) concern for the welfare of society as a whole, and (4) the capacity to see both sides of an issue. The Moral Judgment Interview (Kohlberg, 1979) presents dilemmas followed by a series of open-ended questions. Hoffman's (1970) approach presents students with story beginnings and asks them to write endings. Battistich et al. (1989) used an interview approach and pictures to present three conflict situations to kindergarten, second grade, and fourth grade children. These conflicts involved a focal child whose use of an object was interfered with by another child. The oral presentation was followed by a set of open-ended questions. The responses were scored for eight variables including (1) the interviewee's understanding of the thoughts and feelings of the conflict participants, (2) his or her belief that their actions will solve the problem, (3) means-ends thinking (planning, considering alternatives, anticipating obstacles and consequences), (4) the type of strategies suggested, and (5) the proportion of prosocial and antisocial strategies offered.

Presented statements: Choosing from ready-made responses. This technique involves the presentation of questions that have ready-made responses from which to choose. Students can be asked to choose the response that reflects their views, or they can be asked to rank the responses from most to least desirable. It is difficult to construct such instruments in a way that prevents students from choosing the alternative they believe their teachers and parents want them to choose. The temptation to choose an obviously "right" or "good" alternative, and the natural inclination for students to deceive themselves into thinking that they would act prosocially rather than selfishly in a given situation may pose insurmountable threats to validity. Several instruments have been developed using presented statements including the Kohlbergian Defining Issues Test (Rest, 1979).

Introspective questionnaires. Questionnaires that use students as respondents often include questions about classroom and school environments and questions that try to get at the various internal aspects of morality. They may provide the best tool for determining the existence and degree of moral feeling, thinking, and knowing. These "internal predictors" of moral behavior can only be determined indirectly through observational inferences or indirectly by asking students questions about what is going on "inside." The student questionnaires developed by the Developmental Studies Center (1993a, 1993b, 1994, 1995) include questions that concern individual character traits and related social skills. Vessels' early elementary (VSCQ-EE), late elementary (VSCQ-LE), and high school (VSCQ-HS) student character questionnaires (see Appendices in Vessels, 1998) attempt to assess all aspects of individual moral functioning including moral feeling, moral thinking, moral skills, moral behavior.

Unstructured/semi-structured interviews and related rating scales. Interviews were previously discussed as one of two ways to present hypothetical problems to students, but interviews can also be used in a less structured way to indirectly assess the degree of moral emotion that students experience (eg, empathy, guilt, obligation to share), the extent of their sociomoral knowledge (eg, what is considered morally right in a given situation), and the moral reasoning or thinking they engage in (eg, their conceptions of fairness) as they deal with everyday situations that have moral implications. Interviews can be semi-structured, which means that questioning is conversational but intended to elicit information that will allow for answering a few basic questions following the interview.

Summary and Conclusions

The purpose of this chapter has been to be suggestive and open-ended rather than definitive and conclusive. It is not our intention to describe in detail all aspects of theories of moral and character development or suggest a best approach to its maturation. However, we do believe there are some broad guidelines that can be followed and specific programs that can be emulated.

We share the conclusion drawn by other researchers such as Graham (1990) and Benson (1997) that experiential learning opportunities for moral action must be available to youth of all ages within schools and communities where all adults provide moral guidance. At a minimum we believe that character education programs should focus on the internal processes of knowing, thinking, and judging; feeling and expressing empathy and valuing; planning and committing to a set of ethical values or moral decisions; and explicitly putting knowledge, values, and commitments into action. We also suggest that encouraging a sense of moral identity, especially seeing oneself as a virtuous person, is important.

A values education program, or a moral judgment program, or a values analysis program isolated by itself is likely to be a disappointment to project developers. Merely incorporating a word of the week activity into a curriculum exclusively focused on raising test scores is to unlikely to have an impact unless the virtue is considered, valued, intentioned, and practiced. Working diligently on modifying student's behavior without considering the operation of the student's interaction with the adult world of the family, school, religious organization, and community is both naïve and counterproductive. Children and youth imitate and want to be a part of the adult world and that culture must consider that young people are watching and learning.

11

Self and Self-views[11]

William G. Huitt

While temperament and personality are important aspects of an individual (Rothbart, Ahadi, & Evans, 2000), the concepts of self and self-views are more relevant to education and schooling as they are more likely impacted through directed experiences (Swann, Chang-Schneider, & McClarty, 2007). A major challenge when considering the concept of self and self-views is that everyone has a subjective experience of one's self that can produce conflict when attempting to objectively investigate the topic. A second challenge is that one's mental representation of the world and one's initial starting point can have a substantial impact on one's conclusions (Huitt, Chapter 4, this volume). For example, a person adopting a secular/materialistic worldview would likely start with a scientific investigation and attempt to reconcile any subjective experiences with material written by others from that perspective. A person adopting a cosmic-spiritual worldview, on the other hand, might be more likely to turn inward, investigating the self through contemplative practice and then connecting with others who might have done similar inward-looking investigations. Finally, a person adopting a God-centered worldview might first look to scripture or the teachings of elders, connecting subjective experiences to those teachings. The major orientation of this chapter is a secular/materialistic worldview as that is in keeping with other chapters in the book. For those interested in investigating the cosmic-spiritual worldview and the reality of human beings from that perspective, McIntosh (2015) and Phipps (2012) both provide a good starting point. For those wishing to investigate the topic from a God-centered perspective, a compilation of quotations from major religions is available at http://www.edpsycinteractive.org/brilstar/quotes.html#Religious.

In a secular/materialistic investigation, the term self is generally used in reference to the conscious reflection of one's own being or identity, as an object separate from other or from the environment. There are a variety of ways to think about the self with self-concept and self-esteem as two of the

[11] The majority of this chapter first appeared as Huitt, W. (2011). Self and self-views. *Educational Psychology Interactive*. Valdosta, GA: Valdosta State University.

most widely used. Self-concept is often considered as the cognitive or thinking aspect of self (related to one's self-image) and generally refers to

> "the totality of a complex, organized, and dynamic system of learned beliefs, attitudes and opinions that each person holds to be true about his or her personal existence" (Purkey, 1988).

Self-esteem more often is used to refer to the affective or emotional aspect of self and generally alludes to how one feels about or how one values him- or herself. This is sometimes used as a synonym for self-worth, although some authors suggest self-worth is a more central concept (Crocker & Wolfe, 2001). Self-concept can also refer to the general idea we have of ourselves and self-esteem can refer to particular measures about components of self-concept.

Franken (1997) stated the importance of one's self-concept:

> "[T]here is a great deal of research which shows that the self-concept is, perhaps, the basis for all motivated behavior. It is the self-concept that gives rise to possible selves, and it is possible selves that create the motivation for behavior" (p. 443).

Additionally, Franken (1997) suggested that self-concept is related to self-esteem in that

> "people who have good self-esteem have a clearly differentiated self-concept.... When people know themselves they can maximize outcomes because they know what they can and cannot do" (p. 439).

It would seem, then, that one way to increase one's affective evaluation of one's self is to obey the somewhat outworn cliche of "Know thyself." One the other hand, Hansford and Hattie (1982) found that measures of self-views such as self-concept and self-esteem were only weakly correlated with each other ($r = 0.20$). [Note: r is a measure of the strength of relationship among two factors; an $r = 0.20$ signals a relatively week relationship.]

People develop and maintain their self-concepts through the process of taking action and then reflecting on what they have done and what others tell them about what they have done (Brigham, 1986). That is, self-views are not innate, but are constructed and developed by the individual through interaction with the environment and reflecting on that interaction. This reflection is based on actual and possible actions in comparison to one's own expectations and the expectations of others and to the characteristics and accomplishments of others.

James' (1890) developed the following formula for how self-esteem is constructed:

Self-esteem = Success / Pretensions.

Simply stated, the formula proposed that self-esteem will be created by the individual as he or she reflects on behavior as related to one's own and other's expectations. An important point is that two people can have exactly the same success but develop different levels of self-esteem because they or important people in their environments have different levels of expectations.

This dynamic aspect of self-concept (and, by corollary, self-esteem) is important because it indicates that it can be modified or changed. Franken (1997) stated

> "there is a growing body of research which indicates that it is possible to change the self-concept. Self-change is not something that people can will but rather it depends on the process of self-reflection. Through self-reflection, people often come to view themselves in a new, more powerful way, and it is through this new, more powerful way of viewing the self that people can develop possible selves" (p. 443).

There are several different components of self-concept for which measures have been developed: physical, academic, social, and transpersonal. The physical aspect of self-concept relates to that which is concrete: how one looks, his or her sex, gender, height, weight, etc.; what kind of clothes one wears; what kind of car one drives; what kind of home one lives in; and so forth. One's academic self-concept relates to how well the individual does in school or how well one demonstrates an ability to learn academic content. There are at least two levels: a general academic self-concept of how good one is overall and a set of specific content-related self-concepts that describe how good one is in math, science, language arts, social science, etc. The social self-concept describes how one relates to other people and the transpersonal self-concept describes how one relates to the supernatural or unknowns of the universe.

Swann et al. (2007) provided a review of the research on the relationship of a variety of self-measures. They showed that the relationships of self-concept to various measures of school achievement are very specific. They found that measures of non-academic aspects of self-concept are not related to measures of academic work. However, measures of general self-concept are related to general measures of academic achievement (eg, overall grade-point average), but only moderately. In fact, using linear discriminate analysis, Byrne (1990) found that academic self-concept was more effective than was academic achievement in differentiating between low-track and high-track students. Hamachek's (1995) review of research also demonstrated the complex relationships between self-concept and school achievement, especially that the relationship is reciprocal, with each influencing the other. On the other hand, specific measures of subject-related achievement are highly related to success in that content area. Bandura (1997) used the term self-efficacy for these specific measures. He provided evidence that self-efficacy or one's belief that he or she can perform a specific task is the best predictor for success on that task.

The major issue is, therefore, the strength and the direction of the relationship: does general or academic or subject-specific self-concept produce achievement or does achievement produce these various measures of self-concept. Gage and Berliner (1992) stated

> "the evidence is accumulating, however, to indicate that level of school success, particularly over many years, predicts level of regard of self and one's own ability (Bridgeman & Shipman, 1978; Kifer, 1975); whereas level of self-esteem does not predict level of school achievement. The implication is that teachers need to concentrate on the academic successes and failures of their students. It is the student's history of success and failure that gives them the information with which to assess themselves" (p. 159).

That is, increasing general measures of self-esteem does not impact future levels of school achievement; however, when academic achievement results in improvements relative to expectations and those expectations are considered via reflections, it is possible to further impact school achievement. From this perspective, Bandura's (1997) research on the importance of self-efficacy could be thought of as reflecting the importance of pretensions or expectations as he stated that one's mastery experiences related to success are the major influence on one's self-efficacy. Bandura showed that modeling and social persuasion (giving encouragement) can also be helpful, but not as much as being successful previously on the same or a similar task.

By rearranging the components of the equation created by James (1890), an interesting corollary can be produced stating that success is limited by pretentions or expectations and self-esteem:

Success = Pretensions * Self-esteem.

This equation states that success, especially the limits of one's success, can be improved by increasing expectations and/or self-esteem. However, as noted by Gage and Berliner (1992), the research on the relationship between self-esteem/self-concept and school achievement suggested that measures of general or even academic self-concept are not significantly related to school achievement. It is at the level of very specific subjects (eg, reading, mathematics, science) that there begins to be more than a moderate relationship between self-concept/self-esteem measures and academic success. The correlations are even stronger for self-efficacy as it relates to specific academic tasks (Parjares, 1996). Given the above formula, one could conclude that success in a particular subject area is not really changing one's self-concept (knowledge of one's self) or even self-esteem (one's subjective evaluation of one's value or worth), but rather is impacting one's expectations about future success based on one's past experience and reflections on that experience.

Summary and Conclusions

As self-efficacy and self-esteem are both constructed during one's conscious reflections, it is recommended that educators and parents provide experiences that allow learners to master relatively specific content and skills and have learners consciously reflect on those successes. Attempting to boost self-esteem directly through other means does not appear to have any impact (Swann et al., 2007). However, self-views should not be dismissed lightly, either. Hattie (as cited in Huitt, Huitt, Monetti, & Hummel, 2009) found that students' self-report of their previous grades, which can be thought of as a correlate of student self-efficacy, was the most powerful predictor of academic achievement (with an effect size of d = 1.44) when compared to the other 137 variables. [Note: A normal cutoff effect size to determine the practical importance of a relationship between two variables is d = 0.40 (Hattie, 2009) and only 66 of the 138 variables that Hattie highlighted in his investigation of 800 meta-analyses met this relatively stringent criteria.]

Seligman (1996) added to this body of work with his investigations of explanatory style; he proposed that the intervening variable connecting self-esteem and achievement is the student's level of "optimism" or the tendency to see the world as benevolent (good things will probably happen) or malevolent (bad things will probably happen).

Some additional "self" terms are self-direction (Smith, 1996) and self-determination (Ryan & Deci, 2000)--the extent to which one's aspirations, dreams, and goals are self-selected; self-regulation (Bandura, 1997; Behncke, 2002)--one's guidance of one's goal-directed thinking, attitudes, and behavior); and self-transcendence (Polanyi, 1970; Frankl, 1998)--going beyond or above the limitations of one's ego or creating meaningful connections to others, nature, universe, Creator, etc.). It is important that parents and educators address all of these constructions in a holistic manner in order to prepare children and youth for successful adulthood.

12

Developing Curriculum for Glocal Citizenship[12]

William G. Huitt

Parents, educators, and concerned citizens throughout the world are discussing ways to best prepare children and youth for successful adulthood in the global, digital, information-based context of the 21st century. Hudzik (as cited in Whitsed & Green, 2013) stated the task quite clearly: "[there is a need to produce] graduates who can live, work and contribute as productive citizens in an increasingly fluid and borderless global context" (para 4). Discussions on how to do this are often seen in their most concrete form in discussing curriculum. Huitt (2017c) discussed the issue of what is a human being and the necessity of education to develop potential into competence. This chapter will focus on four major issues that should be addressed when discussing curriculum for glocal (both global and local) citizenship:

1. What is curriculum?
2. What is the importance of glocal citizenship? Why should this be an issue of concern?
3. What should be the focus of a glocal citizen curriculum?
4. How should educators deal with the issue of "too much"?

These issues will be discussed individually and the chapter concludes with an overview of how these fit together in a decision-making process.

Curriculum Planning

Curriculum is traditionally defined in terms of courses or courses of study as demonstrated in the following definitions:

1. A course of study in one subject at a school or college; a list of all the courses of study offered by a school or college; any program or plan of activities. (Curriculum, 2009).

---

[12] Huitt, W. (2013). *Developing curriculum for global citizenship: What should be learned and why?* Revision of paper presented at the Alliance for International Education World Conference, Doha, Qatar, October 22.

2. The aggregate of courses of study given in a school, college, university, etc.; the regular or a particular course of study in a school, college, etc. (Curriculum, 2012a).
3. The courses offered by an educational institution; a set of courses constituting an area of specialization (Curriculum, 2012b).

Engaging in a curriculum development process using these definitions makes it difficult to consider how to change curriculum other than to change courses or create a new program of study. However, some curriculum experts suggested the focus should be on aims of learning (Cowan & Harding, 1986) or learning outcomes (Stefani, 2004-05). Stefani, building on the work of Cowan and Harding, showed how the different components of curriculum development are linked together. The model places learning outcomes at the center and includes 'why' in addition to 'what' and 'how', relating to assessment, learning and teaching (see Figure 12-1).

Figure 12-1. A Logical Model of Curriculum Development

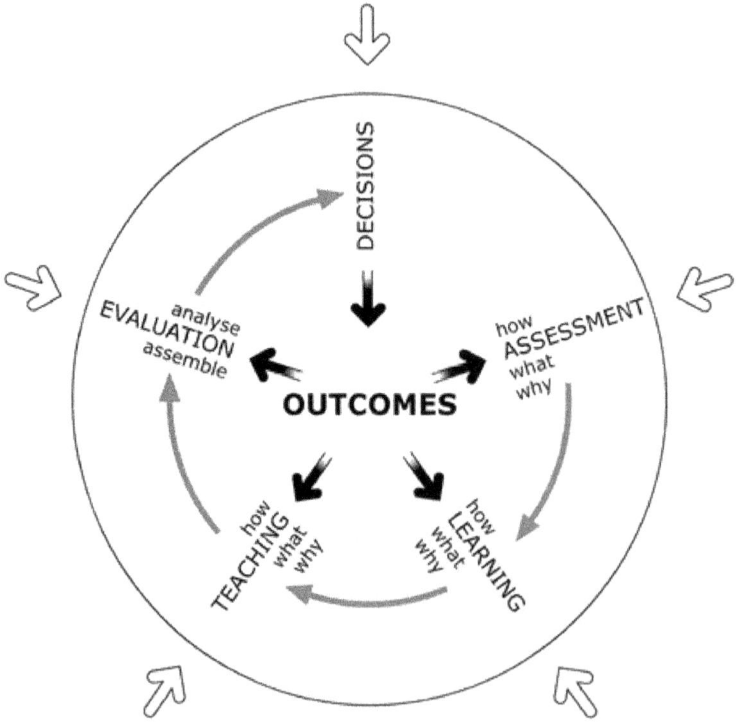

From this perspective, the identification of desired outcomes impacts all phases of curriculum design, implementation, and evaluation. For example, as one identifies desired knowledge, attitudes, and skills that learners should acquire, one also identifies possible assessments by addressing not only what should be assessed, but also how and why. The implication is that one would include in the developed curriculum only those items for which the program or institution is willing to hold itself accountable and which are addressed in the other components of curriculum development. As these two activities are completed educators focus on understanding how learners can acquire those outcomes and developing an organized sequence of means and methods by which learners will acquire them. Evaluation is then addressed by making judgments about the effectiveness of the teaching methods and learning processes used to guide learners to acquire the desired outcomes.

One activity that is not explicit in the model is that of deciding how to communicate results to interested stakeholders. However, the model does point to the need to make curriculum development a continuous process; as decisions are implemented new issues arise that require a new set of decisions be made about modifying any or all of the components of the curriculum. More detail of how this can work in practice is discussed below.

Of course, actual practice is much more fluid than this linear, serial description would imply. This is indicated by the internal and external arrows pointed to each of the components. New understandings or techniques might influence educators to make a change in one of the components and this would impact the other components in turn. Nevertheless, the attention to desired outcomes is always at the center of any changes in the curriculum as assessment, learning, teaching, and evaluation activities are designed and implemented.

Additionally, Ebert, Ebert, and Bentley (2011) defined curriculum development as the means and materials with which students interact for the purpose of achieving identified educational outcomes. Their classification of curriculum into four categories added additional complexity to the process of curriculum development:

1. Explicit (or intended) curriculum – refers to the stated knowledge, attitudes, and skills to be learned as well as the subjects to be taught.
2. Implicit (or hidden) curriculum – refers to knowledge, attitudes, behaviors that are learned as part of the culture or ethos of the learning environment but are not explicitly stated.
3. Null curriculum– what students are not offered or what knowledge, attitudes, or skills that are not explicitly or implicitly developed, but could be.
4. Extracurricular (also co-curricular) – school sponsored programs that supplement the otherwise explicit curriculum.

This classification warned educators that the explicit curriculum as stated in identified goals or standards does not address all learning that occurs within the school. Attention must also be paid to the social and cultural climate that evolves as part of the actions of those involved in the education process and the extra-curricular activities that the school sponsors. These can at times be even more meaningful to learners than the explicit curriculum (Frelin & Grannas, 2010). Additionally, the concept of the null curriculum signals a need to at least discuss what is possible even though it might not be practical at a particular point in time.

Hayden (2006) discussed curriculum in an important context for developing glocal citizens, specifically in the context of international schooling. She defined curriculum as "the means by which expectations of the various communities may be realized and to which they will relate in some way, whether by determining policy as to its nature, delivering it, experiencing it as a learner or taking it into account as a deciding factor in the choice of school" (p. 131). Hayden highlighted the importance of considering curriculum as a cultural process of selecting and emphasizing a list of priorities. The relationship of curriculum to the establishment of a school culture is vital as school culture is related to such factors as academic achievement (Rutter, Maughan, Mortimore, Ouston, & Smith, 1979), social and emotional development (Greenberg, Weissberg, O'Brien, Zins, Fredericks, Resnik, & Elias, 2003), and the acceptance of diversity within a school (Johnson, 2003). Hayden classified the explicit or intended curriculum into two categories:

1. Academic curriculum -- the academic content and skills in the curriculum.
2. Pastoral curriculum -- additional skills such as social skills, study skills, career and occupational counseling.

The consideration of the variety of views on curriculum emphasizes the need to consider the institutional climate when considering its creation. Of course, one can always import or adapt a curriculum that has already been developed, but that still requires an in-depth analysis to verify it meets the expectations of the school community and the needs of the students. Integrating these into a coherent, dynamic curriculum is one of the main challenges facing educators today (Oxley, 2008).

Backwards Planning or Understanding by Design

Fortunately, Wiggins and McTighe (2007, 2011), drawing from the early work on backwards planning (Case & Bereiter, 1984; Gagne, 1974), showed how consideration of these elements can be accomplished. These authors agreed with Stefani (2004-05) and stated that their three-stage understanding by design (UBD) process should start with stating desired results or outcomes. They then provided additional clarity for the various activities involved in curriculum development. The UBD model detailed how to develop statements of desired outcomes, consider assessment strategies for those outcomes, and design learning activities that create the learning experiences for guiding student learning.

1. State desired results:
   - Establish goals -- state the desired outcomes in broad terms as well as the standards that should be met.
   - Develop statements of understandings -- develop statements of big ideas that should be learned as well as the levels of understanding that are expected.
   - Develop essential questions -- create questions that promote inquiry and/or connections to prior learning.
   - Create learning objectives -- produce specific statements of what students should be able to do as a result of the learning experience.
2. Consider assessment evidence:
   - Performance tasks -- establish the performance tasks that will allow students to demonstrate learning as well as the standards that will be used; focus on the establishment of authentic tasks that are realistic and similar to what adults are expected to do.
   - Contextual analysis -- consider how data on performance tasks will be analyzed such as gains (pre-post), normative (individual/group), or degree of reliability (informal-formal).
3. Learning activities (WHERETO) -- the authors of understanding by design proposed seven principles that should guide lesson and unit development:
   - Make sure learners know ***Where*** the lesson is headed (goals and objectives) and ***Why***.
   - ***Hook*** learners at the beginning of the lesson (activate attention) and ***Hold*** learners throughout.
   - ***Equip*** learners with the prerequisite knowledge, attitudes, and skills that will allow them to meet the performance goals.
   - Provide learners opportunities in the learning process where they can ***Rethink***, ***Reflect***, and ***Revise*** their understandings and their work.
   - Provide opportunities for learners to ***Evaluate*** their progress towards the completion of desired goals and objectives.

- ***Tailor*** lessons as much as possible to reflect individual preferences, interests, needs, and different ways of expressing themselves.
- ***Organize*** the lessons and units in such a way as to promote elaboration and extension of concepts and principles to develop deep understanding at higher levels of knowledge (Krathwohl, 2002).

Notice that the step of identifying how learning will occur is not addressed in the UBD model. One reason is that the authors promote a constructivistic view of learning (Huitt, 2009a) so this issue is not explicitly addressed. However, the specific activities they suggested in the UBD model provide the level of guidance needed to actually produce units and lessons.

Views of the Learner

Educators should consider their theories of how to view a learner and the learning processes that students will use to acquire the desired outcomes. This is an important consideration as the learning theories provide the foundation for educators as they design instructional activities. As shown in Table 12-1, different learning theories have radically different views of how to describe the learner, and thus, the task of the teacher. Skipping the step of reflecting on how students learn can lead to designing instructional activities that do not fit well with the other components of curriculum development. For example, the behavioral view of how human beings learn leads to quite different teaching strategies than does the view of the learner provided by a cognitive constructivist view or a humanistic view. The teaching strategies advocated by an operant conditioning theorist would have the teacher carefully develop step-by-step learning activities with rewards associated with completion of each step and then assessing those individual skills. The cognitive constructivist would focus on the learner as an inquirer and assist the learner in constructing mental organizations as a result of a learning activity and then assess through projects. The humanist would more likely focus on the personal interests of the student and reflections on the personal feelings of the learner and assess through created products.

In summary, this brief overview of curriculum and curriculum development suggests that these are very complex issues that require considerable attention to both strategic analysis and detailed planning. The purpose of the next section is to emphasize the importance of considering the role of glocal citizenship in the process of curriculum development.

Table 12-1. Views of Learner Defined by Different Learning Theories

Learning Theory	View of the Learner	Task of the Teacher
Behaviorism	Reactive adaptor	Arrange the correct environment and provide the appropriate stimuli; in the case of operant conditioning this means applying the correct reinforcers and punishers.
Information Processing	Processor of information	Define levels of knowledge and/or knowing that learner should attain and arrange the correct environment so those levels will be attained.
Social Learning	Observer reactor	Model desired processes and skills and then use operant conditioning to modify those to the desired standard.
Social Constructivism	Apprentice	Model the desired process and skills and provide assistance to help the learner demonstrate task mastery (scaffolding). Then selectively withdraw the assistance until the learner can demonstrate mastery independently.
Cognitive Constructivism	Inquirer	Arrange the environment in such a way that independent and collective investigation can occur relatively uninterrupted by outside interference.
Humanistic	Autonomous agent	Assist the learner to develop an understanding of personal interests and goals and facilitate the actualization of personally-important capacities.

Table 12-1. Views of Learner Defined by Different Learning Theories (continued)

Social Cognition	Embedded agent	Facilitate the learner in adapting to socially-prescribed requirements as well as in establishing personal learning goals; facilitate the development of the knowledge, attitudes and skills necessary for meta-cognitive and self-regulation as the learner works to successfully master both sets of goals.
Connectivism	Networked life-long learner	Assist the learner to connect to various networks of knowers, inquirers, and knowledge bases; empower learners to be producers of knowledge that can be accessed throughout one's lifetime.

Importance of Glocal Citizenship

The rapid change in sociocultural context resulting from the spreading of industrialization, the movement to a digital, information-based economy, and the mass migrations of human beings has produced a keen interest in defining what it means to be a citizen (Huitt, 2015). There are at least three concepts that are related to a view of citizenship: identity (Banks, 2001; McIntyre-Mills, 2010), loyalty and responsibility (Hansen, 2010; Karlberg, 2008), and rights (Isin, 2009). These issues are discussed more extensively in Huitt (2015) and will not be repeated here. An important conclusion that can be drawn from this discussion is that the interconnection of levels of citizenship (eg, community, state, nation, international region) demands attention be paid to each of those in addition to the level of global citizenship.

As an example of how one's circumstances can impact one's concept of citizenship, think of various answers to these questions especially in relationship to one's identity and the related issues of loyalty, responsibility, and rights.

1. Where were you born?
2. Where were your parents born?
3. Where are you from?
4. Where do you live?

Think about people you know as well as their friends and acquaintances who would provide answers for questions two or three that are different from yours. Perhaps you might even know individuals who would provide different locations for all four of the questions. Now think of someone you know whose friends and acquaintances would provide the same answer to all four questions. Think about differentiating characteristics such as level of education; type of work; interest in local, national, or global affairs; amount of annual travel, political viewpoints; religion; etc. Are those people similar and/or different in significant or trivial ways? Do you believe that people who answer these questions differently would think and behave differently or have different values?

Here is another way of considering the importance of context and experience when discussing citizenship. Think about how you would answer the question of where are you from in these different circumstances:

1. You have a passport for the country in which you currently live and are attending a meeting in another country.
2. You have a passport from one country, are living in a different country, and attending a meeting in yet a third country.
3. You are talking with a colleague where both of you live in the same country for which you hold a passport and work for the same institution or company in a particular city?

The answers you provide to these questions are relative to the person who is asking, the location of the questioner, and your location at the time. You are embedded in all of these levels and you select the appropriate level for the circumstances. That is the essence of the concept of glocal citizenship.

As educators work to assist learners to develop an understanding of citizenship, the work of Blatt and Kohlberg (1975) should be considered. These researchers showed that children and youth could understand one level above their current level of thinking about moral issues and could readily differentiate their level from one below that. However, young people had difficulty explaining one level above even though they could understand it. Perry (1999) found a similar situation in his study of young adult's levels of knowing.

In this regard, Abrams and Primack (2011) advocated that the concept of cosmic citizenship adds to an understanding of citizenship in important ways. First, the solar system and planet are the result of approximately a 13.7-billion-year process that has resulted in one's human physical form being constructed from stars forming and exploding (Brown, 2007; Christian, 2011. Dowd (as cited in Huitt, 2017c) stated that "the simple act of breathing (taking in oxygen and nitrogen that originated when a red giant star collapsed billions of years ago) connects every human being to the cosmos." Abrams and Primack (2011) suggested there is a spiritual connection of humanity to the cosmos as "experiencing our true connection to all that exists" (p. 142) and an understanding of cosmic citizenship can provide the foundation for developing "a transculturally shared vision for how to solve global problems" (p. 143).

The notion of different levels of citizenship would imply that developing an understanding of glocal citizenship would necessitate providing children and youth with experiences at multiple levels, beginning with their own communities, and then having them reflect on those experiences. Additionally, it would seem that Townsend's (2009) admonition to both think and act locally and globally would need to be modified to include thinking and acting cosmically. But exactly what would that mean?

One part of the answer is to consider that, as far as is empirically known, human beings are the only creatures with a level of consciousness that allows them to be aware of themselves and their relationship to the cosmos. In this sense, human beings represent the cosmos becoming aware of itself (Abrams & Primack, 2011). Being aware of oneself as a cosmic citizen can impact one's identity as well as one's understanding of loyalty and responsibility at all less encompassing levels. This awareness creates the potential for a very different understanding of citizenship (Huitt, 2015).

Curriculum Focus

When considering the focus of the curriculum (ie, the identification of desired outcomes), there are at least three different starting points. First, one could consider different theories of human potential or intelligences and focus on developing those potentials. Second, one could focus on human needs, motives, and what it means to thrive and flourish and focus on those issues. Third, one could focus on identifying the demands of citizenship at a particular point in time such as the fast-paced, global, information-based twenty-first century society and focus on preparing children and young people to meet those demands. This section will provide an overview of what those different approaches might mean for curriculum development.

Defining Human Potential

Anyone who has engaged in even a cursory inquiry on the origins and display of human thought and behavior recognizes there are widely divergent views on human potential. Not only is the issue complicated because of different sources of information such as that derived from science, history, philosophy, the arts, and/or religion, there are disparate views within each of these. This discussion will focus on knowledge based on science, but other sources could easily be used. However, it should be recognized the issue of the source of knowledge must be considered as part of the discussion of curriculum development.

Figure 12-2. Domains of the Brilliant Star Framework

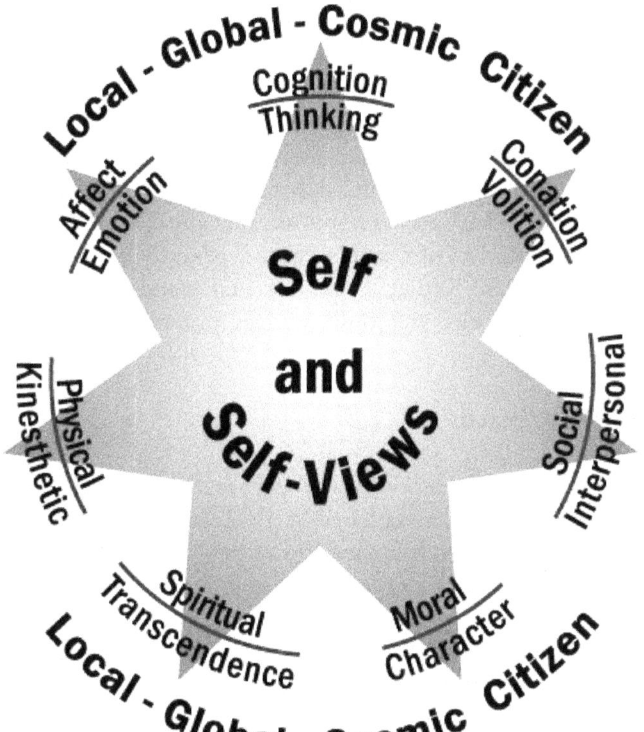

From the perspective of science, knowledge of human development within a specific context must provide the foundation for making decisions about curriculum (as well as instructional methods and materials, assessment, organization of schooling and education, and methods of communication with parents and community). The discussion of developing human ability often starts with a discussion of intelligence, especially cognitive intelligence (Adey, Csapo, Demetriou, Hautamaki, & Shayer, 2007). However, researchers such as Gardner (1983, 1999) and Sternberg (1985) have questioned traditional views of intelligence and provided alternatives to the study of human ability to learn and adapt to the environment. The Brilliant Star framework (see Figure 12-2) is a view of holistic development that encompasses multiple domains of human potential (Huitt, Chapter 1, this volume), including well-known aptitudes such as emotional intelligence (Mayer, Salovey, & Caruso, 2008) and social intelligence (Goleman, 2006). From this perspective, the development of successful citizenship depends on the development of competence and capability in each of the areas identified as encompassing a human potential.

There are a number of other well-known frameworks that take a holistic view of human potential such as the Learner Profile developed by the International Baccalaureate Organization (2010), the habits of mind (Costa & Kallick, 2000), the Integrated Ethics Education program (based on Kohlberg's theory of moral development; Narvaez and colleagues, 2001), and the list of developmental assets developed by the Search Institute (2017). An analysis of these different frameworks demonstrated that there is no framework that addresses all of the domains identified in the Brilliant Star framework (Huitt, 2011c). This is not to say that any one of these approaches is incorrect or not worthy of consideration in identifying desired outcomes for children and youth. Rather it suggests that merely adopting any single one of these frameworks will omit human potential identified through scientific research.

Defining Human Needs

As with defining human potential, there are a variety of frameworks and theories related to defining human needs. Perhaps the most well-known was the hierarchy of human needs developed by Maslow (1954, 1971). He described four deficiency needs (physiological. safety and security, belongingness and love, esteem) and two growth needs (self-actualization and transcendence). He also described the first two levels of self-actualization as the need to know and understand and the need of beauty or aesthetics.

Pink (2009) developed a theory of adult motivation in which he identified three basic drives: autonomy, mastery, and purpose. This is similar to the psychological needs proposed in self-determination theory (Ryan & Deci, 2000, 2008).

Seligman (2011) provided another framework that focused on demonstrating a high level of well-being that he labeled flourishing: positive emotions, engagement, positive relationships, meaning and purpose, and accomplishment or achievement (PERMA). In a similar framework, Diener and Biswas-Diener (2008) described how a measure of life satisfaction (focused on being engaged and interested) and measures of psychological and emotional well-being can make clear what it means to live the "good life."

As in the previous analysis, a comparison of these five frameworks showed that no single one fully addressed the domains identified by others as indicating human potential (Huitt, 2011d). Again, this does not mean that each of these frameworks is not providing valuable information; rather it means that those involved in identifying desired outcomes for children and youth will need to analyze multiple options in some detail in order to make a determination of the outcomes that should be the focus of the curriculum.

Demands of Citizenship in the 21st Century

Using research and theory to identify human potential and needs seems quite reasonable given that human beings have been anatomically stable for at least 40,000 years and likely hundreds of thousands of years before then (Huitt, 2017b). However, the context of the twenty-first century is dramatically different and raises the issue of how that might impact the knowledge, attitudes, and skills that need to be developed for successful adulthood (Huitt, 2017a).

Tapscott (2000, 2008, 2010) suggested that the movement from an analog reality to one that is founded on the digitalization of information is a significant shift in human history. Perhaps the most important is that the human brain is actually changing as a result of interaction with this digital environment (Small & Vorgan, 2008).

Figure 12-3. The Age of Transition

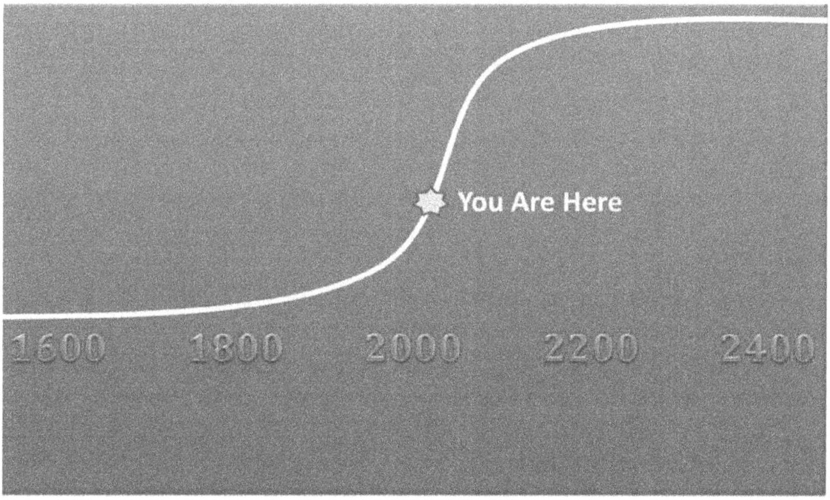

Others have described this shift as the information age (Toffler, 1970) or the conceptual age (Pink, 2005), but Wallerstein (2000) stated that the industrial and digital-information-conceptual ages combined should more rightly be consider as the age of transition. The "S" curve shown in Figure 12-3 maps any number of phenomena, from number of people on earth, to number of miles traveled, to new inventions, etc. On almost any metric the rate of change in human lifestyle is unlike anything ever experienced. About 300 years ago, philosophers and theologians began to think differently about reality and role of humanity (Wallerstein, 2000). That change in thinking led to new scientific insights which, in turn, resulted in a hundred years of transition in Europe that dramatically changed normative patterns of working and living. That process was replicated in the USA where almost 50% of the population still worked in agriculture in the 1860s; that number has dropped dramatically until today only 3 to 5 percent of the population is employed in agriculture (Huitt, 2007). This pattern is quite similar to what is seen in China today (National Bureau of Statistics, 2005).

About 60 years ago, humanity began to experience the beginnings of the digital age and information revolution and the rate of change is now unequivocally exponential. In fact, Kurzweil (2003) stated that "it is not the case that we will experience a hundred years of progress in the twenty-first century; rather we will witness on the order of twenty thousand years of progress (at *today's* rate of progress, that is)." The implication of this trend is that humanity will experience a rate of change beyond anything currently imagined by even the most far-sighted and intuitive thinkers and writers. This rate of change will lead to increasing instabilities, at least for the next several hundred years. Parents and educators must assist children and youth to be prepared for successful adulthood while at the same time adapting to changes around them.

There is a positive aspect to this changing sociocultural context. The reality is that for most of human history, humanity, like all organisms, had to adapt to a relatively hostile environment. During the twentieth century increasing numbers of people had to learn to adapt to a fast-changing, though relatively less hostile environment, that has led to the opportunity for more and more people to thrive and flourish. One might think of this change in developing human potential as different stages of humanity, first in infancy (hunter/gatherer) and childhood (agriculture), and now in its adolescence (industrial) and emerging adulthood (digital and information/conceptual), preparing to enter adulthood as a species. Presently, there is the possibility of first imagining and then creating an environment to which future generations of children and youth will more readily adapt. This is the issue to which those who focus on the demands of the 21st century are applying their imaginations and efforts.

One of the most recognized attempts to define the knowledge, attitudes, and skills necessary to flourish in this century, at least in the USA, was developed by the Partnership for 21st Century Skills (2009). It built upon earlier work done in the early 1990s under the guidance of the Secretary of Labor titled the SCANS report (Huitt, 1997). More recently, Fullan and his colleagues (Fullan, 2017; Fullan & Langworthy, 2013; Fullan, Quinn, & McEachen, 2017) adapted the Partnership's list and identified six competencies they believe should be the focus of developing children and youth—character, citizenship, collaboration, communication, creativity, and critical thinking. While these sets of knowledge and skills specified are quite remarkable, they completely omit any reference to affect/emotional development, as well as issues related to meaning and purpose. A strength of the Partnership framework is that it described in depth issues dealing with citizenship such as starting and maintaining a family, starting and maintaining a career, becoming financially independent, and participating in civic society. The importance of these issues cannot be overstated as anyone who has worked in K-12 education can attest. For example, the family is the smallest unit of society and the child's first school (Barton & Cooley, 2007; Goode, 1982). Although it seems as if the family has come under attack in recent decades, the U. S. Census Bureau (2005) found that by age 60, 95% of Americans had been married at some point in their lives. One can imagine the statistics are similar for most places around the world. Moreover, marriage has positive benefits in terms of people's happiness and well-being (Waite & Gallagher, 2001). Additionally, facilitating parents to prepare their children for the benefits of schooling are quite well known, if not always implemented (Binford & Newell, 1991).

The importance of preparing young people for the world of work is shown dramatically in countries that are experiencing high levels of unemployment at the same time that middle class jobs for those with relatively low educational levels are disappearing (Diehm & Hall, 2013). The reality is that most new jobs in the coming decades will be in career specialties that have not yet been established (Clark, 2006). Moreover, in countries where high numbers of individuals work in the service and information sectors of the economy, most people will have seven jobs in three different careers throughout their working lives (Polachek & Siebert, 1993). This challenge is demonstrated by the fact that, although unemployment is less for individuals earning a 4-year degree, many college graduates do not get their first job in the field for which they were prepared (Sum & McLaughlin, 2008).

The issue of finances is closely related to the issue of work and career. Kiyosaki and Lechter (2000) proposed there are four career categories when thinking about creating financial wealth: (1) employee, (2) self-employed, (3) entrepreneur, and (4) investor. A major distinction among these categories is how income is generated. An employee essentially trades time for dollars and income is dependent on the amount of dollars paid per hour. As there is a limit on the number of hours any individual can work, that sets an upper limit on income. An individual who is self-employed with no employees is in the same situation. However, the self-employed person has the opportunity to hire employees and then collect income based on their productivity. This is essentially the case for the entrepreneur with the addition that the income generation can be enhanced by having multiple divisions or locations for generating income. The investor has the potential to have passive income and cut the ties between time spent and income. The widening gap between the very wealthy and everyone else seen in today's modern economy (see Wikinson & Pickett, 2009, for a discussion of this phenomena and its social implications) is a result of an uneven ability of some individuals to take advantage of the opportunities provided by a changing economic structure to engage in entrepreneurship and investing while others can only demand relatively low wages for the time they spend working as employees (Huitt, 2008). This is a significant issue that must be addressed in the K-12 curriculum.

Ramsey (2008) stated that saving and staying out of debt are just as important as earning. In fact, he suggested that anyone with only an average income in a developed country such as the USA is able to become very wealthy simply living on substantially less than earned income and beginning a savings program in his or her early twenties. The key is delayed gratification, which is not an easy attitude to develop or skill to learn. Fortunately, there are standards for financial literacy (Council for Economic Education, 2013; Jump$tart Coalition for Personal Financial Literacy, 2007) and a wide variety of materials available on personal finance that could easily be incorporated into the K-12 curriculum (eg, http://www.econedlink.org/).

Another issue discussed by the Partnership for 21st Century Skills (2009) is related to sociocultural knowledge and responsibilities that allow one to fully participate in a society. In addition to family literacy and skills, they specifically addressed environmental literacy, media literacy, information and communication technologies (ICT) literacy, and the valuing and participation in social structures. Their basic advocacy is that children and youth need to be prepared to participate in social and cultural activities without restrictions.

Wagner (2008, 2012) also created a list, though less detailed, of attributes necessary for adult success that he identified through extensive interviews with leaders in business, government, and industry. Wagner's (2012) work on developing the attributes related to creativity and innovation is especially interesting as those are the skills that are difficult to develop using the industrial-age K-12 schooling system that is focused on increasing scores on standardized tests of basic skills (Robinson, 2011).

Huitt (2012c) provided an analysis of the Partnership for 21st Century skills, the Deep Learning Competencies developed by Fullan and his colleagues, and those suggested by Wagner. As in the other analyses, there were human potentials not addressed by these perspectives.

Summary

All of the frameworks discussed have some legitimacy and should be considered as educators make decisions about how to develop individual human capacities that will allow children and youth to meet their needs and grow and develop their competencies in order to thrive and flourish in the sociocultural context of the 21st century. Huitt (2012b) provided a spreadsheet comparing all of the frameworks discussed in this essay.

One of the most interesting results is that only the IBO Learner Profile (International Baccalaureate Organization, 2010) advocated the need for children and youth to develop the ability to think like an artist, historian, mathematician, scientist, etc. rather than simply demonstrating mastery in those content areas. Gardner (2000b) discussed this idea extensively and this supports Wiggins and McTighe's (2007) advocacy of teaching for understanding.

Another domain that did not get extensive attention by the majority of the frameworks is the importance of physical health and the development of a healthy lifestyle. Given that obesity is one of the primary challenges that face children and youth (as well as adults) today (Trost, 2009), it would seem that this issue should receive substantial support in any curriculum development efforts.

This overall comparison substantiates the finding that no single framework or theory provides a complete list of the abilities, needs, or skills that might provide the foundation for a curriculum for global citizenship. Therefore, parents, educators, and concerned citizens need to consider some basic principles of that preparation such as:

1. Provide a process for making decisions about curriculum for global citizenship.
2. Derive knowledge from each and all of the multiple sources that identify potentials, needs, or necessary knowledge, attitudes, and skills.
3. Provide for personal and societal development -- increased differentiation and integration (unity with diversity).

4. Integrate academic standards with those considered to be more holistic in nature.
5. Define certain levels of academic knowledge that are necessary for global citizenship by looking at the roles, responsibilities, and rights of citizenship.

Too Much

At this point, most people are probably thinking, "My school cannot address all those capacities, needs, knowledge, attitudes, and skills." In my opinion, that is absolutely correct. No single institution can be everything for all learners. As a result, there is a need to differentiate curriculum and to make choices. Two points should be considered in this process:

1. Not all people, groups, communities, societies, nations will make the same decisions.
2. "People take different roads seeking fulfillment and happiness. Just because they're not on your road does not mean they've gotten lost." The Dalai Lama, quoted by H. Jackson Browne, Jr. (1991)

Categories of Decisions

The decision of what to leave out of the stated curriculum (ie, the null curriculum) is just as important as what to include (ie, the explicit curriculum). Thus, I suggest there are three primary categories that can be used to sort desired outcomes, standards, objectives, etc.

- Justified – minimum knowledge, attitudes, and skills needed for individual to participate in social and cultural activities at that person's desired level of activity.
- Just-in-case – knowledge, attitudes, and skills necessary to be involved successfully in a personally-desired activity (eg, go to college, obtain a job in a specific industry, etc.)
- Just-in-time – knowledge or skills necessary to participate in a specific learning experience (.g, a specific problem-based or project-based learning activity; a cooperative learning assignment, a specific game or PE activity) or work task (use a particular computer program, lead group discussion, etc.)

Those items in the justified category might seem to be relatively stable given the plethora of state and national curricula and standardized tests. However, I suggest that if the criteria are the minimum knowledge, attitudes, and skills necessary to participate in a global society then the justified curriculum might be different than the academic knowledge needed to obtain access to ever higher levels of formal schooling. For example, almost all adults will at some point spend time in a committed relationship, will be involved in raising children, and will need to acquire enough financial wealth to support themselves after they reach retirement age. Should the knowledge, attitudes, and skills necessary to engage successfully in those activities become part of the justified curriculum? Are the knowledge, attitude, and skills necessary to do that more or less important than those developed in second year algebra or an advanced course in a nation's literature?

Those items in the just-in-case category will also depend on a number of factors. For example, if one desires to attend an elite university and major in computer science, an AP calculus course might be considered to be part of a justified curriculum whereas this might be part of a just-in-case curriculum for those who plan to enroll in a local community college with an undetermined major. The same might be said for many of the Advance Placement or even honors courses in the traditional academic disciplines. For some students, courses that would allow dual enrollment in a technical college might be more justified. The challenge is, of course, how to work with young people and their parents so as to optimize the choices that will be available to the student after high school graduation. Offering a variety of experiences that allows learners to engage in authentic work-related experiences is certainly a significant part of this process. Also, providing individuals an opportunity to make a change in direction with a minimal loss of academic credit should be considered.

The most varied category will be the just-in-time category. Items in this category might be prerequisite knowledge and/or skills that were supposed to be learned previously (ie, they are part of the justified curriculum in an earlier grade) or can be taught quickly with a minimum of effort and are needed for a specific learning experience. For example, a science teacher might have a problem-based learning experience requiring learners to solve a quadratic equation. The teacher could prepare or find an online lesson covering that topic that would provide enough instruction so that students either remember how to do this task or have just enough information that they can participate in the activity. The students could complete the lesson in the previous day's class or as a homework assignment before engaging in the problem-based learning activity. Or the teacher might want students to engage in a lesson that requires them to use a specific component of a presentation program such as Power Point. Again, the teacher could cover that quickly or develop a homework lesson before having learners engage in the activity. The latter activity is the method used in a flipped classroom approach to learning (Huitt & Vernon, 2015).

The most important issue is that each school must determine how it can best meet the needs of their particular students. Simply attempting to cover every activity in a textbook or systematically addressing every standard in a specific curriculum is not likely to meet all students learning needs. Rather teachers can use published curricula and textbooks as guides for making decisions about topics to be taught that are specific to the needs and learning experiences of their particular students.

Summary and Conclusions

In summary, while there is much discussion regarding philosophy, development and learning theory, projected needs for adult success in the 21st century, assessment practices, and a myriad of other issues, these are all made practicable in a stated curriculum. Most people recognize that what has been done in the past, while it might have been very effective for that time period, will need to be modified or perhaps totally discarded in the process of developing updated curricula as well as pedagogy, assessments, and methods of communication with parents and other interested stakeholders. It must be recognized that it is not necessary to be absolutely correct in every decision made, but rather to have a framework in place that can be used in an iterative manner to adjust those decisions going forward. A framework that addresses the issues discussed in this chapter will also provide the opportunity for educators to discuss the rationale for their decisions and to share what they find that works and what does not.

Table 12-2 provides a summary of the components of curriculum development shown in Figure 12-1 above and how one's view of the learner impacts each component of the curriculum. Educators should think first of their views learners, major topics to be addressed, and some alternative generic assessment processes that would match the first two. For example, if one thinks of the learner as a reactive observer, as one would do from an operant conditioning perspective, one would identify specific skills that need to be developed and would assess each one of those independently as the learning process proceeds. The curriculum would be developed inductively, connecting specific skills into more complex tasks.

Or if the learner is viewed as an inquirer, as advocated by cognitive constructivists, one would identify mental models that students use to interact with the natural, built, and social environment, and would develop tasks that would create disequilibrium on the part of learners. The assessment would be comprised of a variety of tasks that would allow learners to demonstrate the construction of new mental structures that can be used in a wide variety of situations. Or if learners are viewed as networked life-

Table 12-2. Analysis of Components of Curriculum Development

	Learning and Developmental Theories							
	Behaviorism & Operant Conditioning	**Cognition & Information Processing**	**Social Learning**	**Constructivism**		**Human-istic**	**Social Cognitive**	**Connect-ivism**
				Social	Cognitive			
View of the Learner	Reactive Observer	Information Processor	Observer Reactor	Apprentice	Inquirer	Agent		Networked life-long learner
						Autono-mous	Embedded	
Curric-ulum	Prescribed skills as overt behavior	Prescribed knowledge at different levels	Pre-scribed modeled behaviors	Socially relevant knowledge and skills	Cognitive processes and mental models for creative interaction with the environ-ment	Individ-ually establish-ed through personal interests and goals	Individ-ually-established and socially-prescribed knowledge, attitudes, and skills	Individually -established and socially-prescribed knowledge, attitudes, and skills that exist in networks
Assess-ment	Specific assessment of taught content and skills	Generic and sampled assessment of stated content objectives	Observe modeled behavior	Skilled inquiry processes, content, or skills taught and ability to creatively adapt	Personal displays of adaptive mental structures	Display the authen-tic self	Self-regulation towards personally- and environ-mentally-set goals	Socially constructed authentic knowledge products

Table 12-2. Analysis of Components of Curriculum Development (continued)

	Learning and Developmental Theories							
	Behaviorism & Operant Conditioning	**Cognition & Information Processing**	**Social Learning**	**Constructivism**		**Human-istic**	**Social Cognitive**	**Connect-ivism**
				Social	**Cognitive**			
Pedagogy	Scripted Lessons	Direct Instruction	Modeling	Demons-trations and guided practice	Guided inquiry projects and challeng-ing problems	Self-organized learning activities	Activities designed to address environ-mentally- and person-ally-set goals	Learners connect to various networks of knowers and knowledge and contribute to the production of knowledge.
Commun-ication	Assessment scores; Curriculum checklists	Assessment scores; written documents; presenta-tions	Check-lists; videos of perfor-mances	Group participa tion; Authen-tic products	Projects; Portfolios	Originally -designed projects, art, and innova-tions	Body of work over time; Portfolios	Body of networks utilized and con-structed over time

long learners, the curriculum would comprise knowledge, attitudes, and skills that would allow individuals to connect with networks of databases and people and engage in authentic tasks that would create something of value to the network. The assessment would address connecting to the network (or perhaps even developing a new one) and creating a valued product.

The critical feature of curriculum development at the building level is to have multiple, deep discussions about all of the components in the framework and arrive at some agreements about each component. It is really too much to expect complete agreement among all parties, but it certainly is reasonable to expect that everyone is able to articulate and implement a view that is compatible with the school's stated mission and vision. While diversity of views and practices can contribute to a rich and lively learning culture at a school, too much diversity can be detrimental to the school's meeting its mission and attaining its vision.

Finally, it is important that school and classroom practices address desired outcomes as created by the school (or adopted from national or state curricula, as is the case in many school systems) and that institutions hold themselves accountable for their actions. There are a variety of aspects to this. Alton-Lee and Nuthall (1992) advocated that schools and classrooms should be evaluated on their providing an opportunity to learn which includes specific instruction on valued knowledge and skills (Cohen, 1995; Cooley and Leinhardt, 1980). In fact, these researchers found that this factor overwhelmed the amount of variance explained by all other variables, including the instructional practices of the teacher. At the same time, Hattie (as cited in Huitt, Huitt, Monetti, & Hummel, 2009), in a meta-analysis of 800 meta-analyses, identified seven school-level factors, fourteen curricular options, fourteen teaching strategies, and eight specific teaching events that were related to improved student learning. In the end, however, it is the overall coherence of the instructional program, not the individual parts, that results in learning improvement that can be sustained over a significant period of time (Fullan & Quinn, 2016; Oxley, 2008). Having just read a somewhat brief overview of research relating to the process of actualizing capacities, a parent or educator might ask the question: "What are we supposed to do?" In my opinion the more fundamental question is: "What goals or desired outcomes do we have for our children and youth?" I agree with such authors as Park (2003) who believe a wider variety of outcomes must be explicitly stated. The aspirations adults have for young people can be summarized in four categories: to become good, smart, happy, and healthy. Parents and educators also want young people to be prepared to provide service to others, recognizing that doing good is just as important as doing well (Coplin 2000). Sternberg (2004) said something quite similar in his advocacy for the development of wisdom as a primary goal of one's life.

> Wisdom is the use of one's intelligence and experience as mediated by values toward the achievement of a common good through a balance among (1) intrapersonal, (2) interpersonal, and (3) extrapersonal interests, over the (1) short and (2) long terms, to achieve a balance among (1) adaptation to existing environments, (2) shaping of existing environments, and (3) selection of new environments (p. 164).

As educators consider the appropriate role for schools in the development of children and youth, approaches to curricula, classroom practice, and assessment instruments and methods can be summarized in terms of four major categories. The first is an "Academics and/or Technical Skills Only" category which considers the school as the place for the development of knowledge and skills related to academic disciplines (eg, Hirsch, 1996) or vocational/technical skills (eg, Losh, 2000). Educators and parents who adopt this approach are quite comfortable with only using standardized tests of basic skills or standardized protocols for technical/vocational skills as ways to measure school success. Huitt et al. (2009) provided an overview of research that can provide a framework for action for educators with a basic academic skills perspective. Gemici and Rojewski (2007) and Lewis (2008) report on similar efforts in the area of vocational-technical skills development. The appropriateness of any school-based activities related to the development of capacities discussed in the present chapter would be judged in terms of the influence they might have on the improvement of academic test scores or demonstrations of vocational-technical skills. While educators with this perspective might agree that the development of additional capacities is important, they would leave that to parents and religious or other organizations.

A second category might be labeled "Academics/Technical Skills Plus". Educators adopting this approach hypothesize that academic success can be developed through instruction directly focused on the desired academic knowledge and skills, but additional gains can be obtained through addressing cognitive processing skills with the goal of developing disciplined minds (Gardner, 2000b). The programs developed by Feuerstein et al. (1980), Sternberg and his colleagues (Sternberg, 1996; Sternberg et al., 2000; Sternberg & Grigorenko, 2000), or Wegener (2005) are examples of programs developed within this approach. Each provides specific recommendations, including materials and teacher training, that address the cognitive processing skills used in learning academic content. Again, the development of capacities in additional domains would be left to others.

A third category might be labeled "Partial Holistic". Educators adopting this approach recognize the importance of the knowledge and skills associated with achievement in the academic disciplines but believe the research on developing competencies in additional domains warrants that school resources be devoted to actualizing potential in at least one domain in addition to the cognitive domain. The Habits of Mind (Costa and Kallick, 2008), SEL (eg, CASEL, 2003, 2007), or moral character (eg, Narvaez, 2006, 2007, 2008a, 2008b) programs will likely meet the goals of such educators. The advantage of these approaches is that they simultaneously focus on actualizing cognitive, emotional, conative, and social intelligences as defined in this chapter. CASEL's and Narvaez's approaches have the added bonus of focusing on developing moral intelligence. The programs focused on emotional development (eg, Deham (1998), Saarni, 2007), subjective well-being (eg, Park et al., 2004), self-regulation (eg, Debrowski et al., 2001; Zimmerman, 2002), movement education (eg, Dobbins et al, 2001, 2009), and spiritual development (Kessler, 2000) can also be considered as belonging within this category.

The fourth category might be labeled "Holistic" in that educators adopting this perspective focus on actualizing a majority of the capacities described in this chapter. Examples of such programs can be found in Reggio Emilia (eg, Caldwell, 1997; Kinney & Wharton, 2008), Montessori (eg, Cossentino, 2009; Hainstock, 1997), Waldorf (see https://waldorfeducation.org/), the International Primary Curriculum (see http://www.internationalprimarycurriculum.com/), and the three International Baccalaureate programs (see http://www.ibo.org/). Additionally, the Asset Development framework advocated by the Search Institute (Benson, Galbraith, & Espeland, 1994; Lerner & Benson, 2003; Roehlkepartain et al., 2003) fits well within this perspective. Each of these programs has a different focus or emphasis, yet they separate themselves from others by implementing a whole-school, integrated approach to holistic development of children or youth.

Table 12-3 provides a brief of overview of the types of school-based curricula and programs that might be found in each category.

Getting Started

In a review of research related to improving scores on standardized tests of basic skill, Huitt et al. (2009) recommended that the first step was the formation and development of high functioning faculty teams using the work of Losada (2008a & b) as a basic component of developing a learning organization (Senge, 1990). The same first step applies to using the research outlined in this chapter. A major difference would be that the teams must first consider, with guidance from the administration, the possibility of revisiting the worldview, vision, and mission statements of the school. If these statements of the school are congruent with an "Academics and/or Technical Skills Only" approach to schooling, leading to a coherence among academic goals, curriculum, instructional practices, and traditional assessments, then the teams would begin by reviewing the research synthesized by Hattie (2009) and summarized by Huitt et al., the more recent work by Hattie and Donoghue (2016) on the development of learning strategies, as well as the research on improving vocational/technical skills instruction (Kyei-Blankson & Ntuli, 2014; Stone, 2017).

Table 12-3. Categories of Curricula and Approaches to Schooling

Category	Desired Outcomes	Examples
Academics and/or Technical Skills Only	Academic Knowledge and/or Technical Skills	Most state- or nationally-mandated curricula focused on reading/language arts, mathematics, science, and social studies; vocational-technical curricula focus on specific job-related skills
Academics and/or Technical Skills Plus	Academics Knowledge and/or Technical Skills plus Cognitive Processing Skills	Instrumental Enrichment, Sternberg's Analytic, Creative, and Practical Intelligence, Wegner's Process Skills
Partial Holistic	Academics and Cognitive Processing plus at least one additional focus	Habits of Mind, Emotional Development, Moral Character, Social Emotional Learning, Subjective Well-Being, Self-Regulation, Movement Education, Pathways to the Soul
Holistic	Academics plus a majority of the Brilliant Star domains	Reggio Emilia, Waldorf, International Primary Curriculum, International Baccalaureate (PYP, MYP, DP), Search Institute's External and Internal Asset Development

However, if there is a desire to begin addressing the capacities identified in this book, it might best be coordinated at the district level. If it does not seem possible to adopt one of the holistic programs discussed above, it might be best to adopt one of the Habits of Mind, SEL, or moral character programs discussed previously. Alternatively, a district might selectively focus on actualizing different capacities at different grade levels. For example, the PreK through second grades might focus on integrating emotional and physical/kinesthetic competencies with academic competence and helping students to make explicit their physical and academic self-views. At the upper elementary (grades three through five), teachers might focus on additionally integrating the development of cognitive processing skills and continue to emphasize their students' academic and physical/kinesthetic self-views. At the middle school level, teachers might focus on integrating social and conative/volitional/self-regulation competencies with academic work. Social self-views would be integrated with previously held academic and physical self-views. Finally, at the high school level, teachers could focus on integrating the development of moral and spiritual competencies into either the academic or vocational/technical curriculum, and help students integrate different aspects of their personalities and self-views.

Given that actualizing cognitive intelligence accounts for at best a third of the variance related to adult life success (Gardner, 1995; Goleman, 1998; Sternberg, Wagner, Williams, & Horvath, 1995), schools need to provide leadership in developing the whole person if they are to accept their responsibilities for preparing children and youth for successful adulthood. However, there are legitimate reasons why parents would want a school to adopt less than a holistic approach, especially if they believe competencies in the other domains are adequately addressed through home and community activities. Ideally, schools would not only provide directed learning experiences that match the desired outcomes parents have for their children and youth but would also coordinate with families and community to provide a holistic education to all young people. That is, if all children and youth are to be provided an excellent education, they need to develop capacities, acquire virtues, and provide service as they prepare to be good, smart, happy, and healthy adults regardless of whether or not these are addressed directly in a school's curriculum. It is also necessary to revisit the school curriculum and classroom practices on a regular basis as young people live in a rapidly changing physical and sociocultural environment that is recognized as increasingly global in scope.

The idea of having different school curricula and programs available to students on demand might sound utopian, but this is the foundation of the school choice (Huitt, 2006b) and school self-management (Caldwell, 2004) movements that are rapidly gaining wider acceptance. In a fast-paced, quickly-changing global environment educators, parents, and concerned members of the community must work together to provide the resources children and youth need as they develop towards adulthood (Benson et al., 1994; Coleman, 1988; Lerner & Benson, 2003). This will only happen if parents and the community agree substantially with the worldview, vision, mission, and curricula as well as the instructional and assessment practices of the school. The task is difficult, but doable, and one that the world's children and youth desperately need for the adults in their lives to accomplish.

References

Abbot, B. (2002). *Human memory*. Fort Wayne, IN: Indiana University-Purdue University at Fort Wayne, Psychology Department. Retrieved from http://users.ipfw.edu/abbott/120/LongTermMemory.html

Abelson, R. (1981). Psychological status of the script concept. *American Psychologist, 36*(7), 715-729.

Abrams, N., & Primack, J. (2011). *The new universe and the human future: How a shared cosmology could transform the world*. New Haven, CT: Yale University Press. (See http://new-universe.org/TerryLectures.html)

Adey, P., Csapo, B., Demetriou, A., Hautamaki, J., & Shayer, M. (2007). Can we be intelligent about intelligence? Why education needs the concept of plastic general ability. *Educational Research Review, 2*, 75–97. Retrieved from http://www.edu.u-szeged.hu/~csapo/publ/AdeyCsapoDemetriouHautamakiShayer.pdf

Adler, A. (1980). *What life should mean to you*. London, UK: George Allen & Unwin. [Originally published in 1932].

Adler, M. (1995). *What man has made of man: A study of the consequences of Platonism and positivism in psychology*. Somerset, NJ: Transaction Publishers. [Originally published in 1937].

Adrienne, C. (1998). *The purpose of your life*. New York, NY: Eagle Book.

Ai, A., Kastenmüller, A., Tice, T., Wink, P., Dillon, M., & Frey, D. (2014). The Connection of Soul (COS) Scale: An assessment tool for afterlife perspectives in different worldviews. *Psychology of Religion and Spirituality, 6*(4), 316-329.

Ainsworth, M., Blehar, M., Waters, E., & Wall, S. (2015). *Patterns of attachment: A psychological study of the strange situation*. New York, NY: Routledge. [Originally published in 1978].

Albrecht, K. (2005). *Social intelligence: The new science of success*. San Francisco, CA: Jossey-Bass.

Alford, B., & Beck, A. (1998). *The integrative power of cognitive therapy*. New York, NY: Guilford Press.

Alton-Lee, A., & Nuthall, G. (1992). Children's learning in classrooms: Challenges in developing a methodology to explain "opportunity to learn." *Journal of Classroom Interaction, 27*(2), 1-2.

American Fitness Alliance. (2001). *Physical best: Discover how you can implement health-related physical education effectively*. Champaign, IL: Human Kinetics Publishers. Retrieved from http://www.americanfitness.net/Physical_Best/

American Heart Association (2004). *Dietary guidelines for American children.* Retrieved from http://www.americanheart.org

Ames, C. (1988). Achievement goals in the classroom: Students' learning strategies and motivation processes. *Journal of Educational Psychology; 80*(3), 260-267.

Ames, C. (1992). Classrooms: Goals, structures, and student motivation. *Journal of Educational Psychology, 84*(3), 261-271.

Amram, Y. (2007). *The seven dimensions of spiritual intelligence: An ecumenical grounded theory.* Paper presented at the 115th Annual Conference of the American Psychological Association, San Francisco, CA, August. Retrieved from http://www.yosiamram.net/docs/7_Dimensions_of_SI_APA_confr_paper_Yosi_Amram.pdf

Amram, Y., & Dryer, (2008). *The Integrated Spiritual Intelligence Scale (ISIS): Development and preliminary validation.* Paper presented at the 116th Annual Conference of the American Psychological Association, Boston, MA. August 14-17. Retrieved from http://www.yosiamram.net/docs/ISIS_APA_Paper_Presentation_2008_08_17.pdf

Amsel, A. (1992). Confessions of a neobehaviorist. *Integrative Physiological and Behavioral Science, 27*(4), 336-346.

Anderson, J., & Bower, G. (1973). *Human associative memory.* Washington, D.C.: Winston.

Anderson, L., & Krathwohl, D. (Eds.). (2000). *A taxonomy for learning, teaching, and assessing: A revision of Bloom's taxonomy of educational objectives.* Boston, MA: Longman.

Ardelt, M. (2008). Wisdom, religiosity, purpose in life, and attitudes toward death. In A. Tomer, G. T. Eliason, & P. T. P. Wong (Eds.), *Existential and spiritual issues in death attitudes* (pp. 139-158). Mahwah, NJ: Lawrence Erlbaum.

Aronson, E. (2000). *Nobody left to hate: Teaching compassion after Columbine.* New York. NY: W. H. Freeman.

Aronson, E. (2007). *The social animal* (10th ed.). New York, NY: Worth Publishers.

Aspinwall, L. (1998). Rethinking the role of positive affect in self-regulation. *Motivation and Emotion, 22,* 1–32.

Atkinson, J., & Birch, D. (1978). *An introduction to motivation* (rev. ed.). New York, NY: Van Nostrand.

Atkinson, R., & Shiffrin, R. (1968). Human memory. A proposed system and its control processes. In K. Spence & J. Spence (Eds.), *The psychology of learning and motivation.* Princeton, NJ: Van Nostrand.

Atkinson, R., & Shiffrin, R. (1971). The control processes of short-term memory. *Scientific American, 224,* 82-90.

Atman, K. (1987). The role of conation (striving) in the distance learning enterprise. *The American Journal of Distance Education, 1*(1), 14-28.

REFERENCES

Bagozzi, R. (1992). The self-regulation of attitudes, intentions, and behavior. *Social Psychology Quarterly, 55*(2), 178-204.

Bailey, B. (2001). *Conscious discipline: 7 basic skills for brain smart classroom management.* Ovledo, FL: Loving Guidance, Inc.

Baker, J. (1992). *Paradigms: The business of discovering the future.* New York: HarperBusiness.

Bandura, A. (1965). Influence of models' reinforcement contingencies on the acquisition of imitative response. *Journal of Personality and Social Psychology, 1,* 589-595.

Bandura, A. (1977). *Social learning theory.* Englewood Cliffs, NJ: Prentice-Hall.

Bandura, A. (1986). *Social foundations of thought and action: A social-cognitive theory.* Upper Saddle River, NJ: Prentice-Hall.

Bandura, A. (1989). The concept of agency in social-cognitive theory. *American Psychologist, 44,* 1175-1184.

Bandura, A. (1991a). Self-regulation of motivation through anticipatory and self-reactive mechanisms. In R. A. Dienstbier (Ed.), *Perspectives on motivation. Nebraska Symposium on Motivation* (Vol. 38, pp. 69-164). Lincoln, NE: University of Nebraska Press.

Bandura, A. (1991b). Social cognitive theory of moral thought and action. In W. Kurtines & J. Gewirtz (Eds.), *Handbook of moral behavior and development* (Vol. 1, 45-103). Hillsdale, NJ: Erlbaum.

Bandura, A. (1994). Self-efficacy. In V. S. Ramachaudran (Ed.), *Encyclopedia of human behavior* (Vol. 4, pp. 71-81). New York: Academic Press. (Reprinted in H. Friedman [Ed.], *Encyclopedia of mental health.* San Diego, CA: Academic Press, 1998).

Bandura, A. (1997). *Self-efficacy: the exercise of control.* New York, NY: Freeman.

Bandura, A. (1999). A social cognitive theory of personality. In L. Pervin & O. John (Eds.), *Handbook of personality* (2nd ed., pp. 154-196). New York: Guilford Publications. (Reprinted in D. Cervone & Y. Shoda [Eds.], *The coherence of personality.* New York: Guilford Press.) Retrieved from http://www.uky.edu/~eushe2/BanduraPubs/Bandura1999HP.pdf

Bandura, A. (2001a). Social cognitive theory: An agentic perspective. *Annual Review of Psychology, 52,* 1-26.

Bandura, A. (2001b). Social cognitive theory of mass communications. In J. Bryant, & D. Zillman (Eds.). *Media effects: Advances in theory and research* (2nd ed., 121-153). Hillsdale, NJ: Lawrence Erlbaum.

Bandura, A. (2002). Social cognitive theory in cultural context. *Journal of Applied Psychology: An International Review, 51,* 269-290. Retrieved from http://www.uky.edu/~eushe2/Bandura/Bandura2002AP.pdf

Banks, J. (2001). Citizenship education and diversity: Implications for teacher education. *Journal of Teacher Education, 52*(5), 5-16. doi: 10.1177/0022487101052001002

Barell, J. (1995). *Critical issue: Working toward student self-direction and personal efficacy as educational goals.* Oak Brook, IL: North Central Regional Educational Laboratory. Retrieved from http://www.lupinworks.com/glit6756/onlineArticles/Barell.html

Bar-On, R., Maree, J., & Elias, M. (Eds.). (2007). *Educating people to be emotionally intelligent.* Westpoint, CT: Praeger.

Barrett, D. B., Kurian, G., & Johnson, T. (2001). *World Christian encyclopedia* (2nd ed.). Oxford, UK: Oxford University Press.

Barro, R., Hwang, J., & McCleary, R. (2010). Religious conversion in 40 countries. *Journal of the Scientific Study of Religion, 49*(1), 15-36.

Bartlett, F. (1995). *Remembering: A study in experimental and social psychology.* Cambridge, UK: Cambridge University Press. [Originally published in 1932].

Barton, P., & Coley, R. (2007). *The family: America's smallest school.* Princeton, NJ: Educational Testing Service. Retrieved from http://www.ets.org/Media/Education_Topics/pdf/5678_PERCReport_ School.pdf

Bartsch, K., & Estes, D. (1996). Individual differences in children's developing theory of mind and implications for metacognition. *Learning and Individual Differences, 8*(4). 281-304.

Bateson, G. (1987). *Steps to an ecology of mind: Collected essays in anthropology, psychiatry, evolution, and epistemology.* New York, NY: Jason Aronson.

Battistich, V. (2003). Effects of a school-based program to enhance prosocial development on children's peer relations and social adjustment. *Journal of Research in Character Education, 1*(1), 1–16.

Battistich, V., Solomon, D., Watson, M., Solomon, J., & Schaps, E. (1989). Effects of an elementary school program to enhance prosocial behavior on children's cognitive-social problem-solving skills and strategies. *Journal of Applied Developmental Psychology, 10*, 147-169.

Baumeister, R., Bratslavsky, E., Muraven, M., & Tice, D. (1998). Ego depletion: Is the active self a limited resource? *Journal of Personality and Social Psychology, 74*(5), 1252-1265.

Baumeister, R., Campbell, J., Krueger, J., & Vohs, K. (2003). Does high self-esteem cause better performance, interpersonal success, happiness, or healthier lifestyles? *Psychological Science in the Public Interest, 4*, 1–44.

Baumeister, R., & Vohs, K. (Eds.). (2007). *Handbook of self-regulation: Research, theory, and applications.* New York, NY: Guilford Press.

Baumrind, D. (1989). Rearing competent children. In W. Damon (Ed.), *Child development today and tomorrow* (pp. 349-378). San Francisco, CA: Jossey-Bass.

REFERENCES

Baumrind, D. (1993). The average expectable environment is not good enough: A response to Scarr. *Child Development, 64*, 1299-1317.

Beck, A. (1976). *Cognitive theory and emotional disorders*. New York, NY: International Universities Press.

Beck, P., & Walters, A. (1977). *The sacred: Ways of knowledge, sources of life.* Tsaile, AZ: Navajo Community College.

Behncke, L. (2002). Self-regulation: A brief review. *Athletic Insight, 14*(1). Retrieved from http://www.athleticinsight.com/Vol4Iss1/SelfRegulation.htm

Benavot, A., & Resnik, J. (2007). Lessons from the past: A comparative socio-historical analysis of primary and secondary education. In A. Benavot, J. Resnik, and J. Corrales, *Global educational expansion: Historical legacies and historical obstacles.* Cambridge, MA: American Academy of Arts and Sciences. Retrieved from http://www.amacad.org/publications/Benavot.pdf

Bencivenga, E. (2012). Fuzzy reasoning. *Common Knowledge, 18*(2), 229-238. doi:10.1215/0961754X-1544914

Ben-Hur, M. (2000). *Feuerstein's Instrumental Enrichment: Better learning for better students.* Baltimore, MD: John Hopkins University.

Bennett, W. (1993, April 7). Is our culture in decline? *Education Week, 12*(28), 32.

Benninga, J., Tracz, S., Sparks, R., Solomon, D., Battistich, V., Delucchi, K., Sandoval, R., & Stanley, B. (1991). Effects of two contrasting school task and incentive structures on children's social development. *The Elementary School Journal, 92*(2), 149-167.

Benson, P. (1997). *All kids are our kids.* San Francisco, CA: Jossey-Bass.

Benson, P., Galbraith, J., & Espeland, P. (1994). *What kids need to succeed: Proven, practical ways to raise good kids.* Minneapolis, MN: Free Spirit Publishing.

Berg, G. (1997). *Living waters spiritual assessment software.* St. Cloud, MN: Living Water Software.

Bergin, C., & Bergin, D. A. (1999). Classroom discipline that promotes self-control. *Journal of Applied Developmental Psychology, 20,* 189-206.

Berkowitz, M. (1998). The education of the complete moral person. In L. Nucci (webmaster), *Studies in Moral Development and Education.* Chicago, IL: University of Illinois.

Berkowitz, M. (2002). The science of character education. In W. Damon (Ed.), *Bringing in a new era in character education* (pp. 43-63). Stanford, CA: Hoover Institute Press.

Berkowitz, M. (2007). *Social and emotional learning: The true purpose of education.* Seattle, WA: Committee for Children.

Berkowitz, M., & Grych, J. (1998). Fostering goodness: Teaching parents to facilitate children's moral development. *Journal of Moral Education, 27*(3), 371-391. Retrieved from http://parenthood.library.wisc.edu/Berkowitz/Berkowitz.html

Bertrand, J. M. (2007). *Rethinking worldview: Learning to think, love, and speak in this world.* Wheaton, IL: Crossway Books.

Bierman, K. L. (2004). *Peer rejection: Developmental processes and intervention.* New York, NY: Guilford Press.

Binford, V., & Newell, J. (1991). Richmond, Virginia's two decades of experience with Ira Gordon's approach to parent education. *The Elementary School Journal, 91*(3), 233-237.

Black, J., & McClintock, R. (1995). An interpretation construction approach to constructivivist design. In B. Wilson (Ed.), *Constructivist learning environments.* Englewood Cliffs, NJ: Educational Technology Publications.

Blakey, E., & Spence, S. (1990). *Developing metacognition.* Syracuse, NY: ERIC Clearinghouse on Information Resources. Retrieved from https://www.ericdigests.org/pre-9218/developing.htm

Blasi, A. (1993). The development of identity: Some implications for moral functioning. In G. Naom, & T. Wren (Eds.), *The moral self* (99-122). Cambridge, MA: MIT Press.

Blatt, M. M., & Kohlberg. L. (1975). The effects of classroom moral discussion upon children s level of moral judgment. *Journal of Moral Education, 4*(2), 129-161.

Bloom, B., Englehart, M., Furst, W., Hill, W., & Krathwohl, D. (1956). *Taxonomy of educational objectives: The classification of educational goals. Handbook I: Cognitive domain.* Boston, MA: Addison-Wesley.

Blumenfeld-Jones, D. (2009). Bodily-kinesthetic intelligence and dance education: Critique, revision, and potentials for the democratic ideal. *Journal of Aesthetic Education, 43*(1), 59-76.

Bodine, R., & Crawford, D. (1999). *The handbook of conflict resolution education: A guide to building quality programs in schools.* San Francisco, CA: Jossey-Bass.

Boekaetrs, M., Pintrich, P., and Zeidner, M. (2000). *Handbook of self-regulation.* San Diego, CA: Academic Press.

Bohr, N. (1949). Discussions with Einstein on epistemological problems with atomic physics. In N. Bohr, *Albert Einstein: Philosopher-scientist.* Cambridge, UK: Cambridge University Press. Retrieved from https://www.marxists.org/reference/subject/philosophy/works/dk/bohr.htm

Bono, G. & Froh, J. (2009). Gratitude in school: Benefits to students and schools. In R. Gilman, E, Huebner, & M. Furlong (Eds.), *Handbook of positive psychology in the schools* (pp. 77-88). New York, NY: Routledge.

REFERENCES

Booth, F., Chakravarthy, M., & Spangenburg, E. (2002). Exercise and gene expression: physiological regulation of the human genome through physical activity. *Journal of Physiology 543*(2), 399-411.

Borba, M. (2001). *Building moral intelligence: The seven essential virtues that teach kids to do the right thing.* San Francisco, CA: Jossey-Bass.

Bowen, M. (1994). *Family therapy in clinical practice.* Oxford, UK: Roman & Littlefield. [Originally published in 1978].

Bowlby, J. (1982). *Attachment and loss: Vol. 1. Attachment.* New York, NY: Basic Books. [Originally published in 1969].

Bowlby, J. (1988). *A secure base: Parent-child attachment and healthy human development.* New York, NY: Basic Books.

Bransford, J. (1979). *Human cognition: Learning, understanding, and remembering.* Belmont, CA: Wadsworth Publishing Company.

Bransford, J. (1985). Schema activation and schema acquisition. In H. Singer & R. B. Ruddell (Eds.), *Theoretical models and processes of reading* (3rd ed., pp. 385-397). Newark, DE: International Reading Association.

Braun, H. (2004, January 5). Reconsidering the impact of high-stakes testing. *Education Policy Analysis Archives, 12*(1). Retrieved from https://epaa.asu.edu/ojs/article/view/157/283

Bridges, W. (1994). *JobShift: How to prosper in a workplace without jobs.* Reading, MA: Addison-Wesley.

Brigham, J. (1986). *Social psychology.* Boston, MA: Little, Brown & Co.

Broadbent, D. (1975). The magic number seven after 15 years. In A. Kennedy and A. Wilkes (Eds.), *Studies in long term memory* (3-18). New York., NY: Wiley.

Broderick, P., & Blewitt, P. (2010). *The life span: Human development for helping professionals* (3rd ed.). Upper Saddle River, NJ: Pearson.

Bronfenbrenner, U. (1979). *The ecology of human development.* Cambridge, MA: Harvard University Press.

Bronson, M. (2000). *Self-regulation in early childhood: Nature and nurture.* New York, NY: Guilford Press.

Brooks, J., & Brooks, M. (2000). *In search of understanding: The case for constructivist classrooms.* Upper Saddle River, NJ: Prentice-Hall.

Brooks-Gunn, J., Berlin, L., & Fuligni, A. (2000). Early childhood intervention programs: What about the family? In J. Shonkoff, & S. Meisels (Eds.), *Handbook of early childhood intervention* (2nd ed., pp. 549-588). New York, NY: Cambridge University Press.

Brophy, J. (1981) Teacher praise: A functional analysis. *Review of Educational Research, 51*, 5-32.

Brown, C. S. (2007). *Big history: From the big bang to the present.* New York, NY: W. W. Norton.

Brown, K., & Ryan, R. (2003). The benefits of being present: Mindfulness and its role in psychological well-being. *Journal of Personality and Social Psychology, 84*(4), 822-848.

Browne, H. J., Jr. (1991). *Life's little instruction book: 511 suggestions, observations, and reminders on how to live a happy and rewarding life.* Nashville, TN: Thomas Nelson.

Bruer, J. (1997, November). Education and the brain. *Educational Researcher, 26*(8), 4-16. Retrieved from https://www.jsmf.org/about/j/education_and_brain.pdf

Bruner, J. (1977a). *A study of thinking.* Malaban, FL: Krieger Publishing.

Bruner, J. (1977b). *The process of education.* Cambridge, MA: Harvard University Press. [Originally published in 1960].

Bruner, J. (1986). *Actual minds, possible worlds.* Cambridge, MA: Harvard University Press.

Bruner, J. (1990). *Acts of meaning.* Cambridge, MA: Harvard University Press.

Brunstein, J., & Gollwitzer, P. (1996). Effects of failure on subsequent performance: The importance of self-defining goals. *Journal of Personality and Social Psychology, 70*, 395-407.

Brynjolfsson, E., & McAfee, A. (2011). *Race against the machine: How the digital revolution is accelerating innovation, driving productivity, and irreversibly transforming employment and the economy.* Lexington, MA: Digital Frontier Press.

Bub, K. (2009). Testing the effects of classroom support on children's social and behavioral skills at key transition points using latent growth modeling. *Applied Developmental Science, 13*(3), 130-148.

Buckley, M., & Saarni, C. (2009). Emotion regulation: Implications for positive youth development. In R. Gilman, E, Huebner, & M. Furlong (Eds.), *Handbook of positive psychology in the schools* (pp. 107-118). New York, NY: Routledge.

Buckley, M., Storino, M., & Saarni, C. (2003). Promoting emotional competence in children and adolescents: Implications for school psychologists. *School Psychology Quarterly, 18,* 177-191.

Bufford, R., Paloutzian, R., & Ellison, C. (1991). Norms for the spiritual well-being scale. *Journal of Psychology and Theology, 19*, 56-70.

Bures, V., & Tucnik, P. (2014). Complex agent-based models: Application of a constructivism in the economic research. *Economics & Management, XVII*(1), 152-168 . doi:10.15240/tul/001/2014-3012

Burton, R., & Kunce, L. (1995). Behavioral models of moral development: A brief history and integration. In W. Kurtines & J. Gewirtz (Eds.), *Moral development: An introduction* (141-171). Needham Heights, MA: Allyn & Bacon.

Bushaw, W., & Gallup, A. (2008). Americans speak out—Are educators and policy makers listening? The 40th annual Phi Delta Kappan/Gallup Poll on the public's attitudes toward public schools. *Phi Delta Kappan, 90*(1), 9-20.

Byrne, B. (1990). Self-concept and academic achievement: Investigating their importance as discriminators of academic track membership in high school. *Canadian Journal of Education, 15*(2), 173-182.

Caldarella, P., & Merrell, K.W. (1997). Common dimensions of social skills of children and adolescents: A taxonomy of positive behaviors. *School Psychology Review, 26*, 264–278.

Caldwell, B. (2004). *Re-imagining the self-managing school.* London, UK: Specialist Schools Trust.

Caldwell, L. (1997). *Bringing Reggio Emilia home: An innovative approach to early childhood education.* New York, NY: Teachers College Press.

Campbell, C. (1999). Action as will power. *The Sociological Review, 47*(1), 48-61.

Campbell, J. (1972). *The hero with a thousand faces.* Princeton, NJ: Princeton University Press.

Campbell, J. D. (1990). Self-esteem and clarity of the self-concept. *Journal of Personality and Social Psychology, 59*(3), 538-549.

Campbell, J. J. (1972). *The hero with a thousand faces.* Princeton, NJ: Princeton University Press.

Campos, J., Mumme, D., Kermoian, R. & Campos, R. (1994). A functionalist perspective on the nature of emotion. *Monographs of the society for research in child development, 59*, 284-303.

Caprara, G., Barbanelli, C., Pastorelli, C., Bandura, A., & Zimbardo, P. (2000). Prosocial foundations of children's academic achievement. *Psychological Science, 11*, 302-306.

Carney, D., Jost, J., Gosling, S., & Potter, J. (2008). The secret lives of liberals and conservatives: Personality profiles, interaction styles, and things they leave behind. *Political Psychology, 29*(6), 807-840.

Carney, M. & Jordan, D. (1976). *Affective competence.* Amherst, MA: Anisa Publications.

Carroll, J. (1963). A model of school learning. *Teachers College Record, 64*, 723-733.

Carter, J., Wiecha, J., Peterson, K., Nobrega, S., & Gortmaker, S. (2007). *Planet health: An interdisciplinary curriculum for teaching middle school nutrition and physical activity* (2nd ed.). Champaigne, IL: Human Kinetics. (see http://www.planet-health.org/)

Carter, R. (1998). *Mapping the mind.* Berkeley, CA: University of California Press.

Case, R. (1978). Intellectual development from birth to adulthood: A neo-Piagetian interpretation. In R. Siegler (Ed.), *Children's thinking: What develops?* Hillsdale, NJ: Erlbaum.

Case, R. (1985). *Intellectual development: Birth to adulthood.* San Diego, CA: Academic Press.

Case, R., & Bereiter, C. (1984). From behaviorism to cognitive behaviorism to cognitive development: Steps in the evolution of instructional design. *Instructional Science, 13*, 141- 158.

Center on Education Policy. (2007). *Choices, changes and challenges: Curriculum and instruction in the NCLB era.* Washington, DC: Author.

Centers for Disease Control and Prevention (2000). *Promoting better health for people through physical activity and sports: A report to the President from the Department of Health and Human Services and the Secretary of Education.* Atlanta, GA: U.S. Department of Health and Human Services, Centers for Disease Control and Prevention, National Center for Chronic Disease Prevention and Health Promotion.

Central Intelligence Agency. (2013). *The world factbook 2013-14: Religions.* Washington, DC: Author. Retrieved https://www.cia.gov/library/publications/the-world-factbook/fields/2122.html

Chan, D., Ramey, S., Ramey, C., & Schmitt, N. (2000). Modeling intraindividual changes in children's social skills at home and at school: A multivariate latent growth approach to understanding between-settings differences in children's social development. *Multivariate Behavioral Research, 35*(3), 365-396.

Chee, K. (2002, July). *The heart of leaders: Spirituality in educational administration.* Paper presented at the Linking Research to Educational Practice II symposium at the University of Calgary.

Chi, M. T. H. (1978). Knowledge structures and memory development. In R. Siegler (Ed.), *Children's thinking: What develops?* Hillsdale, NJ: Erlbaum.

Christian, B. M., Miles, L. K., Hoi Kei Fung, F., Best, S., & Macrae, C. N. (2013). The shape of things to come: Exploring goal-directed prospection. *Consciousness and Cognition, 22*(2), 471-478.

Christian, D. (2011). *Maps of time: An introduction to big history.* Berkeley, CA: University of California Press.

Clark, H. (2006, May 23). Jobs of the future. *Forbes*. Retrieved from http://www.forbes.com/2006/05/20/jobs-future-work_cx_hc_06work_0523jobs.html

Clark, W., & Grunstein, M. (2000). *Are we hardwired? The role of genes in human behavior.* New York: Oxford University Press.

Clark, J. M. & Paivio, A. (1991). Dual coding theory and education. *Educational Psychology Review, 3*(3), 149-170.

Clayton, P. (2012). *Religion and science: The basics.* New York, NY: Routledge.

Cleary, T., & Zimmerman, B. (2004). Self-regulated empowerment program: A school-based program to enhance self-regulated and self-

motivated cycles of student learning. *Psychology in the Schools, 41*(5), 537-550.
Cohen, J. (2006). Social, emotional, ethical, and academic education: Creating a climate for learning, participation in democracy, and well-being. *Harvard Educational Review, 76(2),* 201–237.
Cohen, S. A. (1995). Instructional alignment. In J. Block, S. Evason, & T. Guskey (Eds.), *School improvement programs: A handbook for educational leaders* (pp. 153-180). New York, NY: Scholastic.
Colby, A., & Damon, W. (1992). *Some do care: Contemporary lives of moral commitment.* New York, NY: Free Press.
Cole, J., Dodge, K., & Coppotelli, H. (1982). Dimensions and types of social status: A cross-age perspective. *Developmental Psychology, 18*, 557-570.
Cole, M., & Wertsch, J. (1996). Beyond the individual-social antimony in discussions of Piaget and Vygotsky. *The Virtual Faculty.* Palmerston North, New Zealand. Massey University, Retrieved from http://www.massey.ac.nz/~alock//virtual/colevyg.htm
Coleman J. S. (1969). A brief summary of the Coleman Report. In Editorial Board of Harvard Educational Review (Ed.), *Equal Educational Opportunity* (pp. 253-260). Cambridge, MA: Harvard University Press.
Coleman J. S. (1988). Social capital in the creation of human capital. *American Journal of Sociology, 95*, S95–120.
Coleman, J., Campbell, E., Hobson, C., McPartland, J. Mood, A., Weinfeld, F., & York, R. (1966). *Equality of educational opportunity.* Washington, DC: U.S. Government Printing Office.
Coles, R. (1990). *The spiritual life of children.* Boston, MA: Houghton Mifflin.
Coles, R. (1996). *The moral life of children.* New York, NY: Atlantic Monthly Press.
Coles, R. (1998). *The moral intelligence of children: How to raise a moral child.* New York, NY: Plume.
Collaborative for Academic, Social, and Emotional Learning (CASEL). (2003). *Safe and sound: An educational leader's guide to evidence-based social and emotional learning programs.* Chicago, IL: Author.
Collaborative for Academic, Social, and Emotional Learning (CASEL). (2007). *What is SEL? Skills and competencies.* Retrieved from https://casel.org/core-competencies/
Collins, A., & Loftus, J. (1975). Spreading Activation Theory of semantic processing. *Psychological Review, 82*, 407-428.
Collins, A., & Quillian, M. (1969) Retrieval time from semantic memory. *Journal of Verbal Learning and Verbal Behavior, 8*, 240-247.
Collins, G. (1998). *The soul search: A spiritual journey to an authentic intimacy with God.* Nashville, TN: Thomas Nelson Publishers.

Common Core State Standards Initiative. (2018). *Common core state standards for English language arts & literacy in history/social studies, science, and technical subjects*. Washington, DC: National Governors Association. Retrieved from http://www.corestandards.org/wp-content/uploads/ELA_Standards1.pdf

Conway, P. (1975). Volitional competence and the process curriculum of the Anisa model. In P. Conway (Ed.), *Development of volitional competence: Selected readings*. New York, NY: MSS Information Corporation. Retrieved from http://www.edpsycinteractive.org/anisa/development/volitional_competence.pdf

Conway, P. (1981). Volitional competence: Attention. In D. Jordan (Ed.), *The Anisa process curriculum* (Vol. I). Escondido, CA: Anisa Publications. Retrieved from http://www.edpsycinteractive.org/anisa/curriculum/process_volition_attention.pdf

Conway, P., & McCullough, L. (1981). Volitional competence: Goal setting. In D. Jordan (Ed.), *The Anisa process curriculum* (Vol. I). Escondido, CA: Anisa Publications. Retrieved from http://www.edpsycinteractive.org/anisa/curriculum/process_volition_goals.pdf

Cook-Cottone, C., Casey, C., Feeley, T., & Baran, J. (2009). A meta-analytic review of obesity prevention in the schools: 1997-2008). *Psychology in the Schools, 46*(8), 695-719.

Cooley, W.W., & Leinhardt, G. (1980). The instructional dimensions study. *Educational Evaluation and Policy Analysis, 2*, 7-25.

Cooper Institute, The. (2001). *FitnessGram*. Dallas TX: Author. Retrieved from http://www.cooperinstitute.org/fitnessgram

Cooper, A., & Holmes, L. (2006). *Lunch lessons: Changing the way we feed our children*. New York, NY: HarperCollins (see http://www.chefann.com)

Cooper, J., Masi, R., & Vick, J. (2009). *Social-emotional development in early childhood: What every policymaker should know*. New York, NY: National Center for Children in Poverty (NCCP). Retrieved from http://www.nccp.org/publications/pdf/text_882.pdf

Cooper, K. (1991). *The aerobics program for total well-being: Exercise, diet, emotional balance* (Reissue ed.). New York, NY: Bantam. [Originally published in 1983].

Cooper, K. (1999). *Fit kids! The complete shape-up program from birth though high school.* Nashville, TN: Broadman and Holman Publishers.

Cooper, P. A., (1993, May). Paradigm shifts in designed instruction: From behaviorism to cognitivism to constructivism. *Educational Technology, 33*(5), 12-19.

Cooper, S. (1997). *The clinical use and interpretation of the Wechsler Intelligence Scale for children* (3rd ed.). Springfield, IL: Charles C. Thomas Publisher.

Copan, P. (2001). *That's just your interpretation: Responding to skeptics who challenge your faith.* Holland, MI: Baker Book House.

Coplin, W. (2000). *How you can help: An easy guide to doing good deeds in your everyday life.* New York, NY: Routledge.

Corcoran, J. (2012). Schema. In E. Zalta (Ed.), *Stanford Encyclopedia of Philosophy.* Stanford, CA: The Metaphysics Research Lab, Stanford University. Retrieved from http://plato.stanford.edu/entries/schema/

Corey, G. (1996). *Theory and practice of counseling and psychotherapy* (5th ed.). Pacific Grove, CA: Brooks/Cole Publishing.

Corno, L. (1989) Self-regulated learning: A volitional analysis. In J. Zimmerman and D. Schunk (Eds.), *Self-regulated learning and academic achievement: Theory, research and practice.* New York, NY: Spinger-Verlag.

Corno , L. (1992). Encouraging students to take responsibility for learning and performance. *Elementary School Journal, 93*(1), 69-83.

Corno, L. (1993). The best-laid plans: Modern conceptions of volition and educational research. *Educational Researcher, 22*, 14-22.

Cossentino, J. (2009). Culture, craft, and coherence: The unexpected vitality of Montessori teacher training. *Journal of Teacher Education, 60*(5), 520-527

Costa, A. (Ed.). (2009). *Habits of mind across the curriculum: Practical and creative strategies for teachers.* Alexandria, VA: Association for Supervision and Curriculum Development.

Costa, A. L., & Kallick, B. (2000). *Habits of mind: A developmental series.* Alexandria, VA: Association for Supervision and Curriculum Development.

Costa, A., & Kallick, B. (2008). *Learning and leading with habits of mind: 16 essential characteristics for success.* Alexandria, VA: Association for Supervision and Curriculum Development.

Council for Economic Education. (2013). *National standards for financial literacy.* New York, NY: Author. Retrieved May 2013, from https://www.councilforeconed.org/wp-content/uploads/2013/02/national-standards-for-financial-literacy.pdf

Covey, S., Merrill, A. R., & Merrill, R. (1994). *First things first: To live, to love, to learn, to leave a legacy.* New York, NY: Simon & Schuster.

Cowan, J., & Harding, A. (1986). A logical model for curriculum development. *British Journal of Educational Technology, 17*(2), 103-109.

Craik, F., & Lockhart, R. (1972). Levels of processing: A framework for memory research. *Journal of Verbal Thinking and Verbal Behavior, 11*, 671-684.

Crocker, J., & Wolfe, C. T. (2001). Contingencies of self-worth. *Psychological Review, 108*, 593-623.

Crowell, S. (2015). Existentialism. In E. Zalta (Ed.), *The Stanford Encyclopedia of Philosophy*. Stanford, CA: The Metaphysics Research Lab, Stanford University. Retrieved from http://plato.stanford.edu/archives/spr2015/entries/existentialism

Csikszentmihalyi, M. (1991). *Flow: The psychology of optimal experience*. New York, NY: HarperCollins.

Csikszentmihalyi, M. (1998). *Finding flow: The psychology of engagement with everyday life*. New York, NY: Basic Books.

Curriculum. (2009). *Collins English Dictionary*. Complete and Unabridged 10th ed. Retrieved from http://dictionary.reference.com/browse/curriculum

Curriculum. (2012a). *Dictionary.com*. Retrieved February 2018 from http://dictionary.reference.com/browse/curriculum

Curriculum. (2012b). *Merriam-Webster Online Dictionary*. Retrieved from http://www.merriam-webster.com/dictionary/curriculum

Cummings, K., Kaminski, R., & Merrell, K. (2008). Advances in the assessment of social competence: Findings from a preliminary investigation of a general outcome measure for social behavior. *Psychology in the Schools, 45*(10), 930-946.

Daly, H., & Farley, J. (2011). *Ecological economics: Principles and applications*. Washington, DC: Island Press.

Damasio, A. (1999). *The feeling of what happens: Body and emotion in the making of consciousness*. New York, NY: Harcourt Brace & Company.

Damon, W. (2004). What is positive youth development? *Annals of the American Academy of Political and Social Science, 591*, 13-24.

D'Andrade, R. (1995). *The development of cognitive anthropology*. New York, NY: Cambridge University Press.

Danesh, H. B. (2001). *The psychology of spirituality* (Revised ed.). Victoria, Canada: Paradigm Publishing, Ottawa, Canada: Nine Pines Publishing.

Daniels, S., Jacobson, M., McCrindle, B., Eckel, R., & Sanner, B. (2009). American Heart Association childhood obesity research summit report. *Circulation, 119*, e489-e517. Retrieved from http://circ.ahajournals.org/cgi/reprint/CIRCULATIONAHA.109.192216

Darwin, C. (1998). *The expression of the emotions in man and animals* (3rd ed.). Oxford, UK: Oxford University Press. [Originally published in 1872].

Dempster, F. (1981). Memory span: Sources of individual and developmental differences. *Psychological Bulletin, 89*(1), 63-100.

Debowski, S., Wood, R., & Bandura, A. (2001). Impact of guided exploration and enactive exploration on self-regulatory mechanisms and information acquisition through electronic search. *Journal of Applied Psychology, 86*, 1129–1141.

Deci, E., & Ryan, R. (1985). *Intrinsic motivation and self-determination in human behavior.* New York, NY: Plenum Press.

Denham, S. (1986). Social cognition, social behavior, and emotion in preschoolers: Contextual validation. *Child Development, 57,* 194-201.

Denham, S. (1998). *Emotional development in young children.* New York, NY: Guilford Press.

Denham, S., Blair, K., DeMulder, E., Levitas, J., Sawyer, K., Auerbach-Major, S., & Queenan, P. (2003). Preschool emotional competence: Pathway to social competence? *Child Development, 74,* 238-256.

Denham, S., & Couchoud, E. (1991). Social-emotional contributors to preschoolers' responses to an adult's negative emotions. *Journal of Child Psychology and Psychiatry, 32,* 595-608.

Denham, S., McKinley, M., Couchoud, E., & Holt, R. (1990). Emotional and behavioral predictors of peer status in young preschoolers. *Child Development, 61,* 1145-1152.

Denham, S., & Weissberg, R. (2003). Socio-emotional learning in early childhood: What we know and where do we go from here. In E. Chesebrough, P. King, T. Gullotta. & M. Bloom (Eds.), *A blueprint for the promotion of prosocial behavior in early childhood* (pp. 13-50). New York, NY: Kluwer/Academic Publishers.

Dent, H., Jr. (2014). *The demographic cliff: How to survive and prosper during the great deflation of 2014-2019.* New York, NY: Portfolio/Penguin.

Derryberry, D., & Reed, M. (1994). Temperament and the self-organization of personality. *Development and Psychopathology, 6*(3), 653-676.

Desetta, A., & Wolin, S. (Eds.). (2000). *The struggle to be strong: True stories by teens about overcoming tough times.* Minneapolis, MN: Free Spirit Publishing

Devaney, E., O'Brien, M., Tavegia, M., & Resnik, H. (2005, Winter). Promoting children's ethical development through social and emotional learning (SEL). *New directions for youth development, 108,* 107-116.

Developmental Studies Center. (1993a). *Student questionnaire: Spring 1993, Part II, Grade 4.* Oakland, CA: Author.

Developmental Studies Center. (1993b). *Student questionnaire: Spring 1993, Part II, Grade 5.* Oakland, CA: Author.

Developmental Studies Center. (1994). *Student questionnaire: Spring 1994, Part II, Grade 6.* Oakland, CA: Author.

Developmental Studies Center. (1995). *Student questionnaire: Spring 1995, Part I.* Oakland, CA: Author.

Dewey, J. (1944). *Democracy and education: An introduction to the philosophy of education.* New York, NY: MacMillan. [Originally published in 1916]. Retrieved from http://en.wikisource.org/wiki/Democracy_and_Education

Dewey, J. (1975). *Moral principles in education.* Carbondale, IL: Southern Illinois University Press. [Originally published 1909].

Dewey, J. (1991). *School and society* and *The child and the curriculum* (Reissue edition). Chicago: University of Chicago Press. [Originally published in 1896 and 1902].

Dewey, J. (1997). *Experience and education.* New York: Macmillan. [Originally published in 1938].

Dewey, J. (1998). *How we think* (Rev. ed.). Boston, MA: Houghton Mifflin Company. [Originally published in 1933].

DeWitt, R. (2010). *Worldviews: An introduction to the history and philosophy of science* (2nd ed.). Chichester, West Sussex, UK: Wiley-Blackwell.

De Wolff, M., & van IJzendoorn, M. (1997). Sensitivity and attachment: A meta-analysis on parental antecedents of infant attachment. *Child Development, 68*(4), 571-591. doi: 10.1111/j.1467-8624.1997.tb04218.x

Diamandis, P., & Kotler, S. (2012). *Abundance: The future is better than you think.* New York, NY: Free Press.

Diamandis, P., & Kotler, S. (2015). *Bold: How to go big, create wealth and impact the world.* New York, NY: Simon & Schuster.

Diener, E. (1984). Subjective well-being. *Psychological Bulletin, 95*(3), 542-575.

Diener, E. (2012). New findings and future directions for subjective well-being. *American Psychologist, 67*(8), 590-597.

Diener, E., & Biswas-Diener, R. (2008). *Happiness: Unlocking the mysteries of psychological wealth.* Malden, MA: Blackwell Publishing.

Diener, E., & Dierner, R. (2008). *Happiness: Unlocking the mysteries of psychological wealth.* Malden, MA: Blackwell Publishing.

Diener, E., Suh, E., Lucas, R., & Smith, H. (1999). Subjective well-being: Three decades of progress. *Psychological Bulletin, 125*(2), 276-302.

Dietel, R., Herman, J., & Knuth, R. (1991). *What does research say about assessment?* Naperville, IL: North Central Regional Educational Laboratory (NCREL).

Dobbins, M, DeCorby, K., Robeson, P., Hussen, H., & Tinlis, D. (2009). School-based physical activity programs for promoting physical activity and fitness in children and adolescents aged 6-18. *Cochrane Database of Systematic Reviews*, Issue 1.

Dodge, K., Schlundt, D., Schocken, I., & Delugach, J. (1983). Social competence and children's sociometric status: The role of peer group entry strategies. *Merrill-Palmer Quarterly, 29*, 309-336.

Donagan, A. (1987). *Choice, the essential element in human action.* London, UK: Routledge & Kegan Paul.

Dossey, L. (2002). How healing happens: Exploring the nonlocal gap. *Alternative Therapies in Health and Medicine, 8*(2), 12-16+

Driscoll, M. (2001). *Psychology of learning for assessment* (2nd ed). Boston, MA: Allyn and Bacon.

Dunbar, R. (1998). The social brain hypothesis. *Evolutionary Anthropology, 6,* 178–90. Retrieved from http://psych.colorado.edu/~tito/sp03/7536/Dunbar_1998.pdf
Duncan, R. (2012). *The new depression: The breakdown of the paper money economy.* New York, NY: Wiley.
Durkheim, E. (1961). *Moral education* (trans. Everett K. Wilson and Herman Schaurer). New York, NY: The Free Press.
Durlak, J., Weissberg, R., Dymnicki, A., Taylor, R., & Schellinger, L. (2011). The impact of enhancing students' social and emotional learning: A meta-analysis of school-based universal interventions. *Child Development, 82*(1), 405-432. doi: 10.1111/j.1467-8624.2010.01564.x
Dweck, C. (1986). Motivational processes affecting learning. *American Psychologist, 41*(10), 1040-1048.
Dweck, C. (2000). *Self-theories: Their role in motivation, personality, and development.* New York, NY: Routledge.
Ebert, E. II, Ebert, C., & Bentley, M. (2011). Curriculum definition. In *The educator's field guide: From organization to assessment* (pp. 102-106). [excerpt]. Thousand Oaks, CA: Corwin. Retrieved from http://www.education.com/reference/article/curriculum-definition/
Eck, D. (2001). *A new religious America: How a 'Christian' country has now become the world's most religiously diverse nation.* San Francisco, CA: HarperSanFrancisco.
Edlin, G., Golanty, E., & Brown, K. (2002). *Health and wellness* (7th ed.). Sudbury, MA: Jones & Bartlett.
Edwards, J., Lanning, K., & Hooker, K. (2002). The MBTI and social information processing: An incremental validity study. *Journal of Personality Assessment, 78*(3), 432-450.
Eisenberg, N. (2000). Emotion, regulation, and moral development. *Annual Review of Psychology.* Washington, DC: American Psychological Association.
Ekman, P., & Davidson, R. (Eds.). (1994). *The nature of emotion: Fundamental questions.* New York, NY: Oxford University Press.
Ekman, P., & Rosenberg, E. (Eds.) (1997). *What the face reveals.* New York, NY: Oxford University Press.
Elam, S., Rose, L., & Gallup, A. (1992). The 24th Annual Gallup/Phi Delta Kappa Poll of the Public's Attitudes Toward the Public Schools. *Phi Delta Kappan, 74*(1), 41-53.
Elam, S., Rose, L., & Gallup, A. (1993, October). The 25th annual Phi Delta Kappa/Gallup poll of the public's attitudes toward the public schools. *Phi Delta Kappan, 75*, 137-152.

Elias, M. J., & Arnold, H. (Eds.). (2006). *The educator's guide to emotional intelligence and academic achievement: Social emotional learning in the classroom.* Thousand Oaks, CA: Corwin Press.

Elias, M., Zins, J., Graczyk, P., & Weissberg, R. (2003). Implementation, sustainability, and scaling up of social-emotional and academic innovations in public schools. *School Psychology Review, 32*(3), 303-319.

Elias, M., Zins, J., Weissberg, R., Frey, K., Greenberg, M., Haynes, N., Kessler, R., Schwab-Stone, M., & Shriver, T. (1997). *Promoting social and emotional learning: Guidelines for educators.* Alexandria, VA. Association for Supervision and Curriculum Development.

Eliasmith, C. (Ed.) (2001). Memory. *Dictionary of philosophy of mind.* Pullman, WA: Washington State University. Retrieved from https://sites.google.com/site/minddict/memory

Elkind, D., & Sweet, F. (2004). *How to do character education.* San Francisco, CA: Live Wire Media. Retrieved from http://www.goodcharacter.com/Article_4.html

Elliott, S. N., & Gresham, F. (2007). *Social Skills Improvement System (SSIS) classwide intervention program.* Upper Saddle River, NJ: Pearson Assessments.

Emmons, R. (1986). Personal strivings: An approach to personality and subjective well-being. *Journal of Personality and Social Psychology, 51*, 1058-1068.

Emmons, R. (2000). Is spirituality an intelligence? Motivation, cognition, and the psychology of ultimate concern. *The International Journal for the Psychology of Religion, 10*(1), 3-26.

Engels, R., Finkenaur, C., Meeus, W., & Dekovic, M. (2005). Parental attachment and adolescents' emotional adjustment: The associations with social skills and relational competence. *Journal of Counseling Psychology, 48*(4), 428-439.

Epstein, J. (1995). School/family/community partnerships: Caring for the children we share. *Phi Delta Kappan, 76*(9), 701-712.

Epstein, J., Coates, L., Salinas, K., Sanders, M., & Simon, B. (1997). *School, family, community partnerships: Your handbook for action.* Thousand Oaks, CA: Corwin.

Epstein, J., & Sanders, M. (2000). Connecting home, school, and community: New directions for social research. In M. Hallinan (Ed.), *Handbook of the sociology of education* (pp. 285-306). New York, NY: Klower Academic/Plenum Publishers.

Epstein, M. H., Harniss, M. K., Pearson, N., & Ryser, G. (1999). The behavioral and emotional rating scale: Test-retest and inter-rater reliability. *Journal of Child and Family Studies, 8,* 319-327.

Epstein, M., & Sharma, J. (1998). *Behavioral and emotional rating scale: A strength-based approach to assessment.* Austin, TX: PRO-ED.

REFERENCES

Epstein, S. (1990). Cognitive-experiential self-theory. In L. Pervin (Ed.), *Handbook of personality: Theory and research* (pp. 165-191). New York, NY: Guilford Press.

Erikson, E. (1993). *Childhood and society*. New York, NY: Norton. [Originally published in 1950].

Erikson, E. (1994). *Insight and responsibility*. New York, NY: Norton. [Originally published in 1964].

Erskine, R. (Ed.). 2010). *Life scripts: A transactional analysis of unconscious relational patterns*. London, UK: Karnac.

Ertmer, P., & Newby, T. (1993). Behaviorism, cognitivism, constructivism: Comparing critical features from an instructional design perspective. *Performance Improvement Quarterly, 6*(4), 50-72.

Eshel, Y., & Kohavi, R. (2003). Perceived classroom control, self-regulated learning strategies, and academic achievement. *Educational Psychology, 23*, 249-260.

Eylon, B., & Linn, M. (1988). Learning and instruction: An examination of four research perspectives in science education. *Review of Educational Research, 58*(3), 251–301.

Festinger, L. (1957). *A theory of cognitive dissonance*. Evanston, IL: Row, Peterson.

Festinger, L. (1962). Cognitive dissonance. *Scientific American, 207*(4), 93-107. doi:10.1038/scientificamerican1062-93

Feuerstein, R. (1979). *The dynamic assessment of retarded performers*. Baltimore, MD: University Park Press.

Feuerstein, R., Rand, Y., Hoffman, M., & Miller, R. (1980). *Instrumental enrichment: An intervention program in cognitive modifiability*. Baltimore, MD: University Park Press.

Fitchett, G. (1993). *Assessing spiritual needs: A guide for caregivers*. Minneapolis, MN: Augsburg.

Flavell, J. (1963). *The developmental psychology of Jean Piaget*. New York, NY: D. Van Nostrand.

Flavell, J., Miller, P., & Miller, S. (2002). *Cognitive development* (4th ed.). Upper Saddle River, NJ: Prentice-Hall.

Flory, K., Lynam, D., & Milich, R. (2002). The relations among personality, symptoms of alcohol and marijuana abuse, and symptoms of comorbid psychopathology: Results from a community sample. *Experimental and Clinical Psychopharmacology, 10*, 425-434.

Fogel, A., Nwokah, E., Dedo, J. Messinger, D., Dickson, K. L., Matusov, E., & Holt, S. (1992) Social process theory of emotion: A dynamic systems approach. *Social Development, 1*, 122-142.

Ford, J. (1987, November). Whither volition? *American Psychologist*, 1030-1032.

Fowler, J. (1995). *Stages of faith: The psychology of human development and the quest for meaning.* San Francisco, CA: Harper and Rowe. [Originally published in 1981].

Fox, L., Dunlap, G., Hemmeter, M. L., Joseph, G., & Strain, P. (2003, July). The teaching pyramid: A model for supporting social competence and preventing challenging behavior in young children. *Young Children, 58*(4), 48-52. Retrieved from http://csefel.vanderbilt.edu/modules/module4/handout7.pdf

Franken, R. (1997). *Human motivation* (4th ed.). Pacific Grove, CA: Brooks/Cole.

Frankfurt, H. (1982). Freedom of the will and the concept of a person. In G. Watson (Ed.), *Free will* (pp. 96-110). Oxford, UK: Oxford University Press.

Frankl, V. (1997). *Man's search for ultimate meaning.* New York, NY: Insight Books.

Frankl, V. (1998). *Man's search for meaning* (Rev. ed.). New York, NY: Washington Square Press. [first published in Germany in 1946].

Fredericks, L. (2003). Making the case for social and emotional learning, and service-learning. *Collaborative for Academic, Social, and Emotional Learning (CASEL),* 1-14. Retrieved February 2018 from https://casel.org/wp-content/uploads/2016/08/PDF-8-making-the-case-for-social-and-emotional-learning-and-service-learning.pdf

Freiberg, H. (2002). Essential skills for new teachers. *Educational Leadership, 59*(6), 56-60.

Frelin, A., & Grannas, J. (2010). Negotiations left behind: In-between spaces of teacher-student negotiation and their significance for education. *Journal of Curriculum Studies, 42*(3), 353-369.

Freud, S. (1960). *The psychopathology of everyday life.* (A. Tyson, trans.). New York, NY: Norton. [Originally published in 1901].

Freud, S. (1990). *The ego and the id.* (Published in J. Strachey (Ed), J. Riviere (trans.). *The standard edition of the complete psychological works of Sigmund* Freud). New York, NY: W. W. Norton. (Originally written in 1923).

Froh, J., Miller, D., & Snyder, S. (2007). Gratitude in children and adolescents: Development, assessment, and school-based intervention. *School Psychology Forum, 2,* 1-13.

Froh, J., Sefick, W.J., & Emmons, R.A. (2008). Counting blessings in early adolescents: An experimental study of gratitude and subjective well-being. *Journal of School Psychology.46,* 213-233.

Fullan, M. (2017, May). *Global competencies: The 6C's.* Ontario, CA: The Learning Exchange. Retrieved from http://thelearningexchange.ca/videos/global-competencies-the-6cs/

Fullan, M., & Langworthy, M. (2013, June). *Towards a new end: New pedagogies for deep learning: An invitation to partner.* Seattle, WA: Collaborative

Impact. Retrieved from https://michaelfullan.ca/wp-content/uploads/2013/08/New-Pedagogies-for-Deep-Learning-An-Invitation-to-Partner-2013-6-201.pdf

Fullan, M., & Quinn, J. (2016). *Coherence: The right drivers in action for schools, districts, and systems.* Thousand Oaks, CA: Corwin.

Fullan, M., Quinn, J., & McEachen, J. (2017). *Deep learning: Engage the world to change the world.* Thousand Oaks, CA: Corwin.

Funk, K. (2001). *What is a worldview?* Corvallis, OR: Oregon State University. Retrieved from http://web.engr.oregonstate.edu/~funkk/Personal/worldview.html

Gage, N., & Berliner, D. (1992). *Educational psychology* (5th ed.). Boston, MA: Houghton Mifflin.

Gagne, R. (1974). *Essentials of learning from instruction.* Hinsdale, IL: Dryden.

Gallup International. (2017). Religion. *News.* Omaha, NE: Author. Retrieved from http://news.gallup.com/poll/1690/religion.aspx

Gallup, G. (1975, December). The seventh annual Gallup Poll of public attitudes toward public schools. *Phi Delta Kappan, 57*, 227-241.

Gallup, G. (1980, September). The twelfth annual Gallup Poll of public attitudes toward public schools. *Phi Delta Kappan, 62*, 39.

Gallup, G. (1993). *Religion in America.* Princeton, NJ: Princeton Religious Research Center.

Garamszegi, L. (2011). Information-theoretic approaches to statistical analysis in behavioural ecology: An introduction. *Behavioral Ecological and Sociobiology, 65*(1), 1-11. doi:10.1007/s00265-010-1036-7

Garcia, T., & Pintrich, P. (1996). Assessing students' motivation and learning strategies in the classroom context: The Motivated Strategies for Learning Questionnaire. In M. Brienbaum & F. Duchy (Ed.), *Alternatives in assessment of achievement, learning process and prior knowledge* (pp. 319-364). Hinghma, MA: Kluwer Academic Publishers.

Gardner, H. (1983). *Frames of mind: The theory of multiple intelligences.* New York, NY: Basic.

Gardner, H. (1995). Cracking open the IQ box. In S. Fraser (Ed.), *The bell curve wars* (pp. 23-35). New York, NY: Basic Books.

Gardner, H. (1999). *Intelligence reframed: Multiple intelligences for the 21st century.* New York, NY: Basic Books.

Gardner, H. (2000a). A case against spiritual intelligence. *The International Journal for the Psychology of Religion, 10*(1), 27-34.

Gardner, H. (2000b). *The disciplined mind: Beyond facts and standardized tests: The K-12 education that every child deserves.* New York, NY: Penguin.

Gardner, H. (2004). *Changing minds: The art and science of changing our own and other people's minds.* Boston, MA: Harvard Business School Press.

Gardner, H. (2006). *Multiple intelligences: New horizons in theory and practice.* New York, NY: Basic Books.

Gathman, A. & Nessan, C. (1997). Fowler's stages of faith development in an honors science-and-religion seminar. *Zygon: Journal of Religion and Science, 32*(3). 407-414.

Gay, P. (Ed.). (1989). *The Freud reader.* New York, NY: W. W. Norton.

Gemici, S., & Rojewski, J. (2007). Evaluating research in career and technical education using scientifically-based research standards. *Career and Technical Education Research, 32*(3), 145-159.

Georgia Department of Education. (1997). *Values education implementation guide.* Atlanta, GA: Office of Instructional Services, Georgia Department of Education. Retrieved from http://www.edpsycinteractive.org/topics/affect/valuesga.html

Gerwitz, J., & Peláez-Nogueras, M. (1991). Proximal mechanisms underlying the acquisition of moral behavior patterns. In W. Kurtines & J. Gewirtz (Eds.), *Handbook of moral behavior and development* (Vol. 1, 153-182). Hillsdale, NJ: Erlbaum.

Gewertz, C. (2003, September 3). Hand in hand. *Education Week, 23*(1), 38-42.

Ghassemi, M., & Kern, D. (2014, August, 25). *Effectiveness of school-based physical activity interventions in children and youth: Rapid review of the evidence.* Peel, Ontario, Canada: Regional Municipality of Peel. Retrieved from https://www.peelregion.ca/health/library/pdf/school-pa-interventions.pdf

Gibson, J. (1979). *The ecological approach to visual perception.* Boston, MA: Houghton Mifflin.

Gilligan, C. (1977). In a different voice: Women's conceptions of self and morality. *Harvard Educational Review, 47*(4), 481-517.

Gilovich, T., Keltner, D., & Nisbett, R. (2006). *Social psychology.* New York, NY: W. W. Norton & Company, Inc.

Ginsburg, A., & Hanson, S. (1986). *Gaining ground: Values and high school success.* Washington, DC: U. S. Department of Education.

Glasser, W. (1998). *Choice theory: A new psychology of personal freedom.* New York, NY: HarperCollins.

Goldin, C., & Katz, L. (1999). The shaping of higher education: The formative years in the United States, 1890-1940. *Journal of Economic Perspectives, 13*(1), 37-62.

Goldstein, A., & Michaels, G. (1985). *Empathy: development, training, and consequences.* Hillsdale, NJ: Lawrence Earlbaum Associates.

Goleman, D. (1995). *Emotional intelligence: Why it can matter more than IQ for character, health and lifelong achievement.* New York, NY: Bantam.

Goleman, D. (1998). *Working with emotional intelligence.* New York, NY: Bantam.

Goleman, D. (2006). *Social intelligence: The revolutionary new science of human relations.* New York, NY: Bantam.

Gollwitzer, P. (1990). Action phases and mind-sets. In E. Higgins & R. Sorrentino (Eds.), *Handbook of motivation and cognition* (Vol 2, pp. 53-92). New York, NY: Guilford Press.

Gollwitzer, P., & Bargh, J. (Eds.) (1996). *The psychology of action: Linking cognitions and motivation to behavior.* New York, NY: Guilford Press.

Goode, W. (1982). The theoretical importance of the family. *The Family*, 1-14. Retrieved from http://www.socqrl.niu.edu/Forest/SOCI454/Goode1.pdf

Gooden, W. (2000). Confidence under pressure: How faith supports risk taking. In R. Banks & K. Powell (Eds.) *Faith in leadership: How leaders live out their faith in their work and why it matters.* San Francisco, CA: Jossey-Bass.

Goodyear, R. (1997). Psychological expertise and the role of individual differences: An exploration of issues. *Educational Psychology Review, 9*(3), 251-265.

Gosling, D. (2011). Darwin and Hindu tradition: "Does what goes around come around?" *Zygon, 46*(2), 345-369.

Gottman, J. (1997). *Raising an emotionally intelligent child.* New York, NY: Simon & Schuster.

Gottman, J., Katz, L., & Hooven, C. (1997). *Meta-emotion: How families communicate emotionally.* Mahwah, NJ: Lawrence Elbaum.

Gouinlock, J. (Ed.). (1994). *The moral writings of John Dewey* (rev. ed.). Del Mar, CA: Prometheus Books.

Graham, G. (2015). Behaviorism. In E. Zalta (Ed.), *The Stanford Encyclopedia of Philosophy.* Stanford, CA: The Metaphysics Research Lab, Stanford University. Retrieved from http://plato.stanford.edu/entries/behaviorism/

Graham, J. (1990). *It's up to us: The Giraffe heroes program for teens.* Langley, WA: The Giraffe Project.

Green, S., & Gredler, M. (2002). A review and analysis of constructivism for school-based practice. *School Psychology Review, 31*(1), 53.

Greenberg, L., Rice, L., & Elliot, R. (1993). *Facilitating emotional change: The moment-by-moment process.* New York, NY: The Guilford Press.

Greenberg, M., Weissberg, R., O'Brien, M., Zins, J., Fredericks, L., Resnik, H., & Elias, M. (2003). Enhancing school-based prevention and youth development through coordinated social, emotional, and academic learning. *American Psychologist, 58*(6-7), 466-474. doi: 10.1037/0003-066X.58.6-7.466

Greeno, J. (1989). A perspective on thinking. *American Psychologist, 44*, 134-141.

Greenspan, S. (1997). *The growth of the mind: And the endangered origins of intelligence.* Reading, MA: Addison-Wesley Publishing.

Greenspan, S., & Greenspan, N. T. (1985). *First feelings.* New York, NY: Penguin Books.

Greer-Chase, M., Rhodes, W., & Kellam, S. (2002). Why the prevention of aggressive
disruptive behaviors in middles school must begin in elementary school. *The Clearing House, 75*(5), 242-245.

Gregory, R. (1998). *Foundations of intellectual assessment: The Wais-III and other tests in clinical practice.* Boston, MA: Allyn & Bacon.

Gresham, F. (1983). Social validity in the assessment of children's social skills: Establishing standards for social competency. *Journal of Psychoeducational Assessment, 1*(3), 299-307.

Gresham, F., & Elliott, S. (1990). *Social Skills Rating System manual.* Circle Pines, MN: AGS.

Gresham, F., & Elliott, S. (2009). *Social Skills Improvement System: Teacher rating scales.* Bloomington, MN: Pearson Assessments.

Gresham, F., Sugai, G., & Horner, R. (2001). Interpreting outcomes of social skills training for students with high-incidence disabilities. *Exceptional Children, 67*(3), 331-344.

Guessoum, N. (2010). Science, religion, and the quest for knowledge and truth: An Islamic perspective. *Cultural Studies of Science Education, 5*(1), 55-69.

Hainstock, E. (1997). *The essential Montessori: An introduction to the woman, the writings, the method, and the movement* (Rev ed.). New York, NY: Plume. [Originally published in 1978].

Hamachek, D. (1995). Self-concept and school achievement: Interaction dynamics and a tool for assessing the self-concept component. *Journal of Counseling & Development, 73*(4), 419-425.

Hamachek, D. (2000). Dynamics of self-understanding and self-knowledge: Acquisition, advantages, and relation to emotional intelligence. *Journal of Humanistic Counseling, Education & Development, 38*(4), 230-243.

Hamilton, D., and Jackson, M. (1998). Spiritual development: Paths and processes. *Journal of Instructional Psychology, 25*(4), 262-270.

Hansen, D. (2010). Chasing butterflies without a net: Interpreting cosmopolitanism. *Studies in Philosophy and Education, 29*(2), 151-166. doi: 10.1007/s11217-009-9166-y

Hansford, B., & Hattie, J. (1982). The relationship between self and achievement/performance measures. *Review of Educational Research, 52*(1), 123-142.

Harrison, P. (2010). A scientific Buddhism. *Zygon, 45*(4), 861-869.

Harshorne, H., & May, M. A. (1928). *Studies in the nature of character. Vol. 1. Studies in deceit.* New York, NY: Macmillan.

Harter. S. (1999). *The construction of self: A developmental perspective.* New York, NY: Guilford Press.

Hartmann-Boyce, J., Jebb, S., Fletcher, B., & Aveyard, P. (2015). Self-help for weight loss in overweight and obese adults: Systematic review and meta-analysis. *American Journal of Public Health, 105*(3), e43-e57. doi:10.2105/AJPH.2014.302389

Hartup, W. (1992). *Having friends, making friends, and keeping friends: Relationships as educational contexts.* ERIC Digest. Champaign, IL: ERIC Clearinghouse on Elementary and Early Childhood Education. ED 345 854. Retrieved from https://files.eric.ed.gov/fulltext/ED345854.pdf

Haste, J. (1996). Communitarianism and the social construction of morality. *Journal of Moral Education, 25*(1), 47-55.

Hattie, J. (2009). *Visible learning: A synthesis of over 800 meta-analyses relating to achievement.* London, UK & New York, NY: Routledge.

Hattie, J., & Donoghue, G. (2016). Learning strategies: A synthesis and conceptual model. *npj Science of Learning, 1*, 1-13. doi:10.1038/npjscilearn.2016.13

Hauser, M. (2006). *Moral minds: How nature designed our universal sense of right and wrong.* New York, NY: Ecco.

Havighurst, R. (1953). *Developmental tasks and education.* White Plains, NY: Longmans.

Hay, D. (2007). *Something there: The biology of the human spirit.* Rednor, PA: Templeton Press.

Hay, D., with Nye, R. (1998). *The spirit of the child.* London, UK: Fount.

Hayamizu, T. & Weiner, B. (1991) A test of Dweck's model of achievement goals as related to perceptions of ability. *Journal of Experimental Education, 59*, 226-234.

Heckhausen, J., & Dweck, C. (Eds.). (1998). *Motivation and self-regulation across the life span.* New York, NY: Cambridge University Press.

Hegyi, G., & Garamszegi, L. (2011). Using information theory as a substitute for stepwise regression analysis in ecology and behavior. *Behavioral Ecological and Sociobiology, 65*(1), 69-71. doi:10.1007/s00265-010-1036-7

Helminiak, D. (1996). *The human core of spirituality: Mind as psyche and spirit.* Albany, NY: State University of New York Press.

Helmstetter, S. (1987). *The self-talk solution.* New York, NY: William Morrow & Co.

Helwig, C., & Turiel, E. (2002). Children's social and moral reasoning. In P. Smith & C. Hart (Eds.), *Handbook of social development* (475-490). Malden, MA: Blackwell.

Hemmeter, M., Ostrosky, M., & Fox, L. (2006). Social and emotional foundations for early

learning: A conceptual model for intervention. *School Psychology Review, 35*(4),
583-601.
Henderson, A., & Mapp, K. (2002). *A new wave of evidence: The impact of school, family, and community connections on school achievement.* Austin, TX: National Center for Family & Community Connections with Schools, Southwest Educational Development Laboratory. Retrieved from http://www.sedl.org/connections/resources/evidence.pdf
Herbert-Myers, H., Guttentag, C., Swank, P., Smith, K., & Landry, S. (2006). The importance of language, social, and behavioral skills across early and later childhood as predictors of social competence with peers. *Applied Developmental Science, 10*(4), 174-187.
Herman, J. (1990). Action plans to make your vision a reality. *NASSP Bulletin, 74*(523). 14-17.
Hershberger, W. (1987, November). Of course there can be an empirical science of volitional action. *American Psychologist, 42*, 1032-1033.
Hershberger, W. (1988). Psychology as a conative science. *American Psychologist, 43*(10), 823-824.
Hibberd, F. (2014). The metaphysical basis of process psychology. *Journal of Theoretical and Philosophical Psychology, 34*(3), 161-186.
Hickman, C. (2003). *Live on purpose.* Enumclaw, WA: Pleasant Word.
Hilgard, E. R. (1980). The trilogy of mind: Cognition, affection, and conation. *Journal of the History of the Behavioral Sciences, 16*, 107-117.
Hinck, S., & Brandell, M. E. (1999). Service learning: Facilitating academic learning and character development. *NAASP Bulletin, 83*(609), 16-24,
Hirsch, E. D., Jr. (1996). *The schools we need and why we don't have them.* New York, NY: Doubleday.
Hirt, E. R., Levine, G. M., McDonald, H. E., & Melton, R. J. (1997). The role of mood in quantitative and qualitative aspects of performance: Single or multiple mechanisms? *Journal of Experimental Social Psychology, 33,* 602–629.
Hodge, D. (2001). Spiritual assessment: A review of major qualitative methods and a new framework for assessing spirituality. *Social Work, 46*(3), 203-214.
Hoffman, M. (1970). Moral development. In P. Mussen (Ed.), *Charmichael's manual of child psychology* (3rd ed., 251-359). New York, NY: Wiley.
Hoffman, M. (1991). Empathy, social cognition, and moral action. In W. Kurtines & J. Gewirtz (Eds.), *Handbook of moral behavior and development* (Vol. 1, 275-301). Hillsdale, NJ: Erlbaum.
Hoffman, M. (2000). *Empathy and moral development: The implications for caring and justice.* Cambridge, UK: Cambridge University Press.
Hofstede, G. (2001). *Culture's consequences: Comparing values, behaviors, institutions and organizations across nations.* Thousand Oaks, CA: Sage.

Hogan, R., & Dickstein, E. (1972). A measure of moral values. *Journal of Consulting and Clinical Psychology, 39*(2), 210-214.
Hogan, R., & Emler, N. (1995). Personality and moral development. In W. Kurtines & J. Gewirtz (Eds.), *Moral development: An introduction* (209-227). Needham Heights, MA: Allyn & Bacon.
Holt, D. (1993). Cooperative learning for students from diverse language background: An introduction. In D. Holt (Ed.). *Cooperative learning: A response to linguistic and cultural diversity* (pp. 1-8). McHenry, IL: Center for Applied Linguistics and Delta Systems. Retrieved from https://files.eric.ed.gov/fulltext/ED355813.pdf
Hout, M., & Fischer, C. (2002). Why more Americans have no religious preference: Politics and generations. *American Sociological Review, 67*(2), 165-190.
Howard, G., & Conway, C. (1987, November). The next step toward a science of agency. *American Psychologist*, 1034-1036.
Howard, M. (1993). Service learning: Character education applied. *Educational Leadership, 51*(3), 42-44.
Howes, C. (1987). Social competence with peers in young children: Developmental sequences. *Developmental Review, 7*(3), 252-272.
Huddleston, J. (1993). Perspectives, purposes, and brotherhood: A spiritual framework for a global society. In S. Bushrui, I. Ayman, & E. Laszlo, *Transition to a global society* (pp. 142-150). Oxford, England: Oneworld Publications Ltd.
Huitt, W. (1988). Personality differences between Navajo and non-Indian college students: Implications for instruction. *Equity & Excellence, 24*(1), 71-74. Retrieved from http://www.edpsycinteractive.org/papers/1988-huitt-mbti.pdf
Huitt, W. (1992). Problem solving and decision making: Consideration of individual differences using the Myers-Briggs Type Indicator. *Journal of Psychological Type, 24*, 33-44. Retrieved from http://www.edpsycinteractive.org/papers/1992-huitt-mbti-problem-solving.pdf
Huitt, W. (1997). *The SCANS report revisited.* Paper delivered at the Fifth Annual Gulf South Business and Vocational Education Conference, Valdosta State University, Valdosta, GA, April 18. Retrieved from http://www.edpsycinteractive.org/papers/scanspap.pdf
Huitt, W. (2000). The spiritual nature of a human being. *Educational Psychology Interactive.* Valdosta, GA: Valdosta State University. Retrieved from http://www.edpsycinteractive.org/topics/spiritual/spirit.html
Huitt, W. (2001a). Becoming a Brilliant Star activity. *Educational Psychology Interactive.* Valdosta, GA: Valdosta State University. Retrieved from http://www.edpsycinteractive.org/brilstar/BrilStaract.pdf

Huitt, W. (2001b). Becoming a Brilliant Star; Attributes, values, and virtues: Selections from the Bahá'í writings. *Educational Psychology Interactive.* Valdosta, GA: Valdosta State University. Retrieved from http://www.edpsycinteractive.org/brilstar/quotes/brilstar-bahai.pdf

Huitt, W. (2003). Important values for school-aged children and youth: A preliminary report. *Educational Psychology Interactive.* Valdosta, GA: Valdosta State University. Retrieved from http://www.edpsycinteractive.org/brilstar/valuesreport.html

Huitt, W. (2004). Moral and character development. *Educational Psychology Interactive.* Valdosta, GA: Valdosta State University. Retrieved February 2018 from http://www.edpsycinteractive.org/topics/morchr/morchr.html

Huitt, W. (2005). Becoming a Brilliant Star: "Thought for the Day" activity. *Educational Psychology Interactive.* Valdosta, GA: Valdosta State University. Retrieved from http://www.edpsycinteractive.org/brilstar/quotes/BrilStarThought.html

Huitt, W. (2006a). *Becoming a Brilliant Star: An introduction.* Paper presented at the International Networking for Educational Transformation (iNet) conference, Augusta, GA, April 23-27. Retrieved from http://www.edpsycinteractive.org/brilstar/brilstarintro_s.pdf

Huitt, W. (2006b, June 25). *Educational accountability in an era of global decentralization.* Paper presented at the International Networking for Educational Transformation (iNet) Conference, Augusta, GA. Retrieved from http://www.edpsycinteractive.org/papers/edaccount.pdf

Huitt, W. (2007, October 26). *Success in the conceptual age: Another paradigm shift.* Paper presented at the annual meeting of the Georgia Educational Research Association, Savannah, GA. Retrieved from http://www.edpsycinteractive.org/papers/conceptual-age.pdf

Huitt, W. (2008, November). A successful lifestyle: The relationship of time and money. *Educational Psychology Interactive.* Valdosta: GA: Valdosta State University. Retrieved from http://www.edpsycinteractive.org/topics/citizen/finances.html

Huitt, W. (2009a). Constructivism. *Educational Psychology Interactive.* Valdosta, GA: Valdosta State University. Retrieved from http://www.edpsycinteractive.org/topics/cognition/construct.html

Huitt, W. (2009b). Individual differences: The 4MAT system. *Educational Psychology Interactive.* Valdosta, GA: Valdosta State University. Retrieved from http://www.edpsycinteractive.org/topics/instruct/4mat.html

Huitt, W. (2009c). Integrating physical activity and academic objectives. *Educational Psychology Interactive.* Valdosta, GA: Valdosta State University. Retrieved from http://www.edpsycinteractive.org/brilstar/integrative/physical/index.html

Huitt, W. (Ed.). (2009d, March). The Brilliant Star Integrative Reading Project (Grades 3-5). *Educational Psychology Interactive*. Valdosta, GA: Valdosta State University. Retrieved from http://www.edpsycinteractive.org/brilstar/integrative/upelem/index.html

Huitt, W. (Ed.). (2010a, November). The Brilliant Star Integrative Reading Project (PreK-2). *Educational Psychology Interactive*. Valdosta, GA: Valdosta State University. Retrieved from http://www.edpsycinteractive.org/brilstar/integrative/index.html

Huitt, W. (2010b, May). The mind. *Educational Psychology Interactive*. Valdosta, GA: Valdosta State University. Retrieved from http://www.edpsycinteractive.org/topics/self/mind.html

Huitt, W. (2011a). Analyzing paradigms used in education and schooling. *Educational Psychology Interactive*. Valdosta, GA: Valdosta State University. Retrieved from http://www.edpsycinteractive.org/topics/intro/paradigm.html

Huitt, W. (2011b). Bloom et al.'s taxonomy of the cognitive domain. *Educational Psychology Interactive*. Valdosta, GA: Valdosta State University. Retrieved from http://www.edpsycinteractive.org/topics/cognition/bloom.html

Huitt, W. (2011c). Comparison of attributes for five approaches to defining the whole student. *Educational Psychology Interactive*. Valdosta, GA: Valdosta State University. Retrieved from http://www.edpsycinteractive.org/brilstar/CurrMap/ltr/comparison-of-attributes-5-whole-student.pdf

Huitt, W. (2011d). Comparison of five different views of human domains. *Educational Psychology Interactive*. Valdosta, GA: Valdosta State University. Retrieved from http://www.edpsycinteractive.org/brilstar/CurrMap/ltr/Compare-Huitt-Maslow-Pink-Seligman.pdf

Huitt, W. (2011e). Motivation to learn: An overview. *Educational Psychology Interactive*. Valdosta, GA: Valdosta State University. Retrieved from http://www.edpsycinteractive.org/topics/motivation/motivate.html

Huitt, W. (2012a). A systems approach to the study of human behavior. *Educational Psychology Interactive*. Valdosta, GA: Valdosta State University. Retrieved February 2018. from http://www.edpsycinteractive.org/materials/sysmdlo.html

Huitt, W. (2012b). Comparisons of attributes across frameworks of possible curricula. *Educational Psychology Interactive*. Valdosta, GA: Valdosta State University. Retrieved from http://www.edpsycinteractive.org/brilstar/CurrMap/ltr/comparison-of-frameworks.xlsx

Huitt, W. (2012c). Comparison of attributes for defining success in the 21st century. *Educational Psychology Interactive.* Valdosta, GA: Valdosta State University. Retrieved from http://www.edpsycinteractive.org/brilstar/CurrMap/ltr/compare-brilstar-21st-century-fullan-wagner.pdf

Huitt, W. (2015). Citizenship. *Cosmic-Citizenship.* Atlanta, GA: Community Development through Academic Service Learning. Retrieved from http://www.cosmic-citizenship.org/index.html

Huitt, W. (2017a, June). A phase change: Forces, trends, and themes in the human sociocultural milieu (revised). *Educational Psychology Interactive.* Valdosta, GA: Valdosta State University. Retrieved from http://www.edpsycinteractive.org/papers/2017-huitt-a-phase-change.pdf

Huitt, W. (2017b). What is a human being and why is education necessary. *Educational Psychology Interactive.* Valdosta, GA: Valdosta State University. Retrieved from http://www.edpsycinteractive.org/topics/intro/human.html

Huitt, W. (2018). Phasing-in: Exploring necessary capacities and implications for success in the next three decades. *Educational Psychology Interactive.* Valdosta, GA: Valdosta State University. Retrieved from http://www.edpsycinteractive.org/papers/2018-huitt-phasing-in-exploring-necessary-capacities-rev.pdf

Huitt, W., Caldwell, J., Traver, P., & Graeber, A. (1981). Collecting information on student engaged time. In D. Helms, A. Graeber, J. Caldwell, & W. Huitt (Eds.). *Basic skills instructional improvement program: Leader's guide for student engaged time.* Philadelphia: Research for Better Schools, Inc.

Huitt, W., Huitt, M., Monetti, D., & Hummel, J. (2009). *A systems-based synthesis of research related to improving students' academic performance.* Paper presented at the 3rd International City Break Conference sponsored by the Athens Institute for Education and Research (ATINER), October 16-19, Athens, Greece. Retrieved from http://www.edpsycinteractive.org/papers/improving-school-achievement.pdf

Huitt, W., & Hummel, J. (2003). Piaget's theory of cognitive development. *Educational Psychology Interactive.* Valdosta, GA: Valdosta State University. Retrieved from http://www.edpsycinteractive.org/topics/cognition/piaget.html

Huitt, W., Monetti, D., & Hummel, J. (2009). Designing direct instruction. Prepublication version of chapter published in C. Reigeluth and A. Carr-Chellman, *Instructional design theories and models: Volume III, Building a common knowledgebase* (pp. 73-97). Mahwah, NJ: Lawrence Erlbaum Associates. Retrieved from http://www.edpsycinteractive.org/papers/designing-direct-instruction.pdf

Huitt, W., & Vernon, K. (2015). *The flipped classroom and project-based learning: Theory and practice.* Presentation at the European Council for International Schools (ECIS), Barcelona, Spain, November 21. Retrieved from http://edpsycinteractive.org/edpsyppt/Presentations/flipped-classroom-and-pbl.html

Huitt, W., & Vessels, G. (2002). Character education. In J. Gutherie (Ed.), *Encyclopedia of education* (2nd ed., pp. 259-263). New York, NY: Macmillan.

Hummel, J., & Huitt, W. (1994, February). What you measure is what you get. *GaASCD Newsletter: The Reporter*, 10-11. Retrieved from http://www.edpsycinteractive.org/papers/wymiwyg.html

Humphreys, M. S., Bain, J. D., & Pike, R. (1989). Different ways to cue a coherent memory system: A theory for episodic, semantic, and procedural tasks. *Psychological Review, 96*(2), 208-233. doi:10.1037/0033-295X.96.2.208

Husman, J., McCann, E., & Crowson, H. M. (2000). Volitional strategies and future time perspective: Embracing the complexity of dynamic interactions. *International Journal of Educational Research, 33*(7-8), 777-799.

Huxley, A. (1990). *The perennial philosophy.* New York, NY: HarperCollins. [Originally published in 1972].

Hyson, M. (2003). *The emotional development of young children: Building an emotion-centered curriculum* (2nd ed.). New York, NY: Teachers College Press.

Ibarra, H. (2015). *Act like a leader, Think like a leader.* Boston, MA: Harvard Business Review Press.

Ihanus, J. (2014). Putin's macho pose: On masculinity and psychopolitics. *The Journal of Psychohistory, 42*(2), 110-129.

International Baccalaureate Organization. (2010). *IB learner profile.* Cardiff, Wales, UK: Author. Retrieved from http://www.ibo.org/globalassets/publications/recognition/learnerprofile-en.pdf

Irvine, D. (2003). *Becoming real, journey to authenticity.* Stanford, FL: DC Press.

Isen, A. (2008). Some ways in which positive affect influences decision making and problem solving. In M. Lewis & J. Haviland-Jones, *Handbook of emotions* (3rd ed.) (pp. 548-573). New York, NY: Guilford Press.

Isen, A. M. (1993). Positive affect and decision making. In M. Lewis & J. M. Haviland (Eds.), *Handbook of emotions* (pp. 261–277). New York, NY: Guilford Press.

James, W. (1884). What is an emotion? *Mind, 9*, 188-205.

James, W. (1890). *Principles of psychology*. New York, NY: Henry Holt.

Jenkins, J. M., Oatley, K, & Stein, N. L. (1998). History and culture. In J. M. Jenkins, K. Oately, & N. L. Stein (Eds.), *Human emotions: A reader* (pp. 7-12). Malden, MA: Blackwell Publishers.

Jensen, A. (2002). Psychometric g: Definition and substantiation. In R. Sternberg, & E. Grigorenko (Eds.). *The general factor of intelligence: How general is it?* (pp. 39–53). Mahwah, NJ: Lawrence Erlbaum.

Johnson, L. (2003). The diversity imperative: Building a culturally responsive school ethos. *Intercultural Education, 14*(1), 17-30.

Johnson-Laird, P. (1983). *Mental models: Towards a cognitive science of language, inference, and consciousness*. Cambridge, MA: Harvard University Press.

Jones, B., Valdez, G., Nowakowski, J., & Rasmussen, C. (1995). *Plugging in: Choosing and using educational technology*. Washington, DC: Council for Educational Development and Research, and North Central Regional Educational Laboratory. Retrieved from https://eric.ed.gov/?id=ED415837

Joo, Y., Bong, M., & Choi, H. (2000). Self-efficacy for self-regulated learning, academic self-efficacy and internet self-efficacy in web-based instruction. *Educational Technology Research and Development, 48,* 5–17.

Judge, T., Bono, J., Ilies, R., & Gerhardt, M. (2002). Personality and leadership: A qualitative and quantitative review. *Journal of Applied Psychology, 87*(4), 765-780.

Jump$tart Coalition for Personal Finance Literacy. (2007). *National standards in K-12 personal finance* (3rd ed.). Washington, DC: Author. Retrieved from http://www.jumpstart.org/assets/files/standard_book-ALL.pdf

Juneer, J. (2000). Spiritual intelligence or spiritual consciousness? *The International Journal for the Psychology of Religion, 10*(1), 47-56.

Juneer, J., & Salovey, P. (1997). What is emotional intelligence. In P. Salovey D. Sluyter (Eds.), *Emotional development and emotional intelligence: Educational implications* (pp. 3-31). New York, NY: Basic Books.

Jung, C. (1981). *The structure and dynamics of the psyche*. Princeton, NJ: Princeton University Press. CW *8*. (First published in 1960.)

Jung, K. (1971). *Psychological types*. Princeton, NJ: Princeton University Press. [Originally published in 1921].

Jusczyk, P. (1997). *The discovery of spoken language*. Cambridge, MA: MIT Press.

Kagan, J. (1984). *The nature of the child.* New York, NY: Basic Books.

Kagan, J. (1994). *Galen's prophecy: Temperament in human nature*. New York, NY: Basic Books.

Kagan, S. (1991). *Cooperative learning resources for teachers*. San Juan Capistrano, CA: Resources for Teachers.

Kane, R. (1985). *Free will and values*. Albany, NY: State University of New York Press.

Kant, J. (1993). *Critique of pure reason: A revised and expanded translation based on Meiklejohn*. London, UK: Everyman's Library. [Originally published in 1781].

Karlberg, M. (2008). Discourse, identity, and global citizenship. *Peace Review: A Journal of Social Justice, 20*(3), 310-320. doi: 10.1080/10402650802330139 Retrieved from http://myweb.facstaff.wwu.edu/karlberg/articles/DiscourseIdentityGC.pdf

Kaschub, M. (2002). Defining emotional intelligence in music education. *Arts Education Policy Review, 103*(5), 9-15.

Kass, J. (2007). Spiritual maturation: A developmental resource for resilience, well-being, and peace. *Journal of Pedagogy, Pluralism and Practice, 3*(4), article 13.

Kass, J. & Kass, L. (2000). *The spirituality and resilience assessment packet*. Cambridge, MA: Institute for Contemplative Education. Retrieved from http://www.spiritualityhealth.com/newsh/items/selftest/item_234.html

Katz, D. (2005). Competing dietary claims for weight loss: Finding the forest through the truculent trees. *Annual Review of Public Health, 26*, 61-88.

Kavanaugh, D., & Bower, G. (1985). Mood and self-efficacy: Impact of job and sadness on perceived capabilities. *Cognitive Therapy and Research, 9*, 507-525.

Kavelin-Popov, L., Popov, D., & Kavelin, J. (1997). *The family virtues guide: Simple ways to bring out the best in our children and ourselves*. Toronto, Ontario, CA: Penguin Books of Canada.

Kazdin, A. (1985). *Treatment of antisocial behavior in children and adolescents*. Homewood, IL: Dorsey Press.

Kearsley, G. (2001a). Constructivist theory. *Theory Into Practice*. Jacksonville, FL: Jacksonville State University. Retrieved from http://www.instructionaldesign.org/theories/constructivist.html

Kearsley, G. (2001b). Dual coding theory (A. Paivio). *Theory Into Practice*. Jacksonville, FL: Jacksonville State University. Retrieved from http://www.instructionaldesign.org/theories/dual-coding.html

Kearsley, G. (2001c). Levels of processing. *Theory Into Practice*. Jacksonville, FL: Jacksonville State University. Retrieved from http://www.instructionaldesign.org/theories/levels-processing.html

Kearsley, G. (2001d). Social development theory. *Theory Into Practice.* Jacksonville, FL: Jacksonville State University. Retrieved from http://www.instructionaldesign.org/theories/social-development.html

Kearsley, G. (2001e). Triarchic theory (R. Sternberg). *Theory Into Practice.* Jacksonville, FL: Jacksonville State University. Retrieved from http://www.instructionaldesign.org/theories/triarchic-theory.html

Keirsey, D. (1998). *Please understand me II: Temperament, character, intelligence.* Del Mar, CA: Prometheus Nemesis Book Company.

Keller, J.M. (1987, November-December). The systematic process of motivational design. *Performance and Instruction Journal,*1-8.

Kennedy, R. B., & Kennedy, D. A. (2004). Using the Myers-Briggs Type Indicator® in career counseling. *Journal of Employment Counseling, 41*(1), 38-44.

Kernis, M. H. (2003). Toward a conceptualization of optimal self-esteem. *Psychological Inquiry, 14,* 1–26.

Kessler, R. (2000). *The soul of education: Helping students find connection, compassion, and character in school.* Alexandria, VA: Association for Supervision and Curriculum Development.

Killen, M., & de Waal, F. (2000). The evolution and development of morality. In F. Aureli and F. de Waal (Eds.), *Natural conflict resolution.* Berkeley, CA: University of California Press.

Kilpatrick, W. (1992). *Why Johnny can't tell right from wrong.* New York, NY: Touchstone Books.

Kinney, L., & Wharton, P. (2008). *An encounter with Reggio Emilia: Children's early learning made visible.* New York, NY: Routledge.

Kirshenbaum, H. (1994). *100 ways to enhance values and morality in schools and youth settings.* Boston, MA: Allyn & Bacon.

Kivinen, K. (2003). *Assessing motivation and the use of learning strategies by secondary school students in three international schools.* [Unpublished Dissertation]. Tampere, Finland: University of Tampere.

Kiyosaki, R., & Lechter, S. (2000). *Rich dad, poor dad: What the rich teach their kids about money--That the poor and middle class do not.* New York, NY: Warner.

Klatzky, R. (1980). *Human memory* (2nd ed.). New York, NY: Freeman.

Klontz, B., Saay, M., Sullivan, P. & Canale, A. (2015). The wealthy: A financial psychological profile. *Consulting Psychology Journal: Practice and Research, 67*(2), 127-143. doi:10.1037/cpb0000027

Kluge, I. (2003). The Aristotelian substratum of the Bahá'í Writings. *Lights of Irfan* (Book IV). Evanston, IL: Bahá'í National Curriculum. Retrieved from http://irfancolloquia.org/pdf/lights4_kluge_aristotle.pdf

Knitzer, J., & Lefkowitz, J. (2005). *Resources to promote social and emotional health and school readiness in young children and families.* New York, NY: National Center for Children in Poverty, Columbia University.

REFERENCES

Koenig, H. (1999). *The healing power of faith.* New York, NY: Simon & Schuster.

Koenig, H. (2002). *Spirituality in patient care: Why, how, when, and what.* Radnor, PA: Templeton Foundation Press.

Koenig, H., McCullough, M., Larson, D. (2001). *Handbook of religion and health.* New York, NY: Oxford University Press.

Kogan, S. (2004). *Step by step: A complete movement education curriculum* (2nd ed.). Champaign, IL: Human Kinetics.

Kohlberg, L. (1979). *The meaning and measurement of moral development.* Heinz Werner Memorial Lecture. Worcester, MA: Clark University Press.

Kohlberg, L. (1984). *Essays on moral development: The psychology of moral development.* Vol. 2. San Francisco, CA: Harper & Row.

Kohlberg, L. (1985). A current statement on some theoretical issues. In S. Modgil and C. Modgil (Eds.). *Lawrence Kohlberg: Consensus and controversy* (485-546). Philadelphia, PA: The Falmer Press, Taylor & Francis.

Kolbe, K. (1990). *The conative connection.* Reading, MA: Addison-Wesley Publishing Company, Inc.

Koltko-Rivera, M. (2004). The psychology of worldviews. *Review of General Psychology, 8*(3), 3-58.

Kong, D. (1999, November 9). Exercise seen boosting children's brain function. *The Boston Globe,* A1.

Koonce, R. (1996). Emotional IQ, a new secret of success? *Training & Development, 50*(2), 19-25.

Kosko, B. (1993). *Fuzzy thinking: The new science of fuzzy logic.* New York, NY: Hyperion.

Kozulin, A., Gindix, B., Ageyev, V., & Miller, S. (2003). Introduction: Sociocultural theory and education: Students, teachers, and knowledge. In A. Kozulin, B. Gindis, V. Ageyev, & S. Miller (Eds.), *Vygotsky's educational theory in cultural context.* Cambridge, UK: Cambridge University Press. Retrieved from http://catdir.loc.gov/catdir/samples/cam041/2002042902.pdf

Krathwohl, D. (2002). A revision of Bloom's taxonomy: An overview. *Theory Into Practice, 41*(4), 212-218.

Krathwohl, D. R. Bloom, B. S., & Masia, B. B. (1964). *Taxonomy of educational objectives, the classification of educational goals, handbook II: Affective domain.* New York, NY: David McKay Co., Inc.

Kraut, R. (2001). Aristotle's ethics. In E. Zalta (Ed.), *Stanford Encyclopedia of Philosophy.* Stanford, CA: The Metaphysics Research Lab, Stanford University. Retrieved from http://plato.stanford.edu/entries/aristotle-ethics/

Kroeger, O., & Thuesen, J. (1989). *Type talk: The 16 personality types that determine how we live, love, and work.* New York, NY: Dell.

Kuhn, T. S. (1970). *The structure of scientific revolutions* (2nd ed.). Chicago: University of Chicago Press.

Kurtines, W., Berman, S., Ittel, A., & Williamson, S. (1995). Moral development: A co-constructivist perspective. In W. Kurtines & J. Gewirtz (Eds.), *Moral development: An introduction* (337-376). Needham Heights, MA: Allyn & Bacon.

Kurtines, W., Mayock, E., Pollard, S., Lanza, T., & Carlo, G. (1991). Social and moral development from the perspective of psychosocial theory. In W. Kurtines & J. Gewirtz (Eds.), *Handbook of moral behavior and development* (Vol. 1, 303-333). Hillsdale, NJ: Erlbaum.

Kurz, T. (1994). *Stretching scientifically* (3rd ed). Island Pond, VT: Stadion Publishing Company, Inc.

Kurzweil, R. (2001). The law of accelerating returns. *The Singularity.* Retrieved from http://www.kurzweilai.net/the-law-of-accelerating-returns

Kurzweil, R. (2003, April 9). *The societal implications of nanotechnology.* Testimony presented April 9, 2003 at the Committee on Science, U.S. House of Representatives Hearing to examine the societal implications of nanotechnology and consider H.R. 766, The Nanotechnology Research and Development Act of 2003. Retrieved from http://www.kurzweilai.net/testimony-of-ray-kurzweil-on-the-societal-implications-of-nanotechnology

Kyei-Blankston, L., & Ntuli, E. (2014). *Practical applications and experiences in K-20 blended learning environments.* Hershey, PA: Information Science Reference.

Laino, C. (2003, June 16). One in three kids will develop diabetes. *WebMD.* Retrieved https://www.webmd.com/diabetes/news/20030616/one-in-three-kids-will-develop-diabetes#1

Larson, E., & Witham, L. (1998). Leading scientists still reject God. *Nature,* 394, 313.

Lau, A., Wang, S.-W., Fung, J., & Namikoshi, M. (2014). What happens when you "Can't read the air?" Cultural fit and aptitude by values interactions on social anxiety. *Journal of Social & Clinical Psychology, 33*(10), 853-866.

Lawrence, G. (1984). A synthesis of learning style research involving the MBTI. *Journal of Psychological Type, 8*, 2-15.

Lazarus, A. (1991). Cognition and motivation in emotion. *American Psychologist, 46*, 352-367.

Lazarus, R. (1991). *Emotion and adaptation.* New York, NY: Oxford U Press.

Lazarus, R. (1999). The cognition-emotion debate: A bit of history. In T. Dalgleish & M. Power (Eds.), *Handbook of cognition and emotion* (pp. 3-20). New York, NY: Wiley.

LeDoux, J. (1996). *The emotional brain: The mysterious underpinnings of emotional life.* New York, NY: Simon and Schuster.

Leondari, A. Syngollitou, E., & Kiosseoglou, G. (1998). Academic achievement, motivation and future selves. *Educational Studies, 24*(2), 153-163.

Lepper, M. (1988). Motivational considerations in the study of instruction. *Cognition and Instruction,* 5, 289-309.

Lerner, R., & Benson, P. (Eds.). (2003). *Developmental assets and asset-building communities: Implications for research, policy, and practice.* New York, NY: Springer.

Levenson, D. (1978). *The seasons of a man's life.* New York, NY: Ballantine.

Levin, J. (2001). *God, faith, and health.* New York, NY: John Wiley & Sons.

Levine, M. (1997). Pantheism. In E. Zalta, *Stanford Encyclopedia of Philosophy.* Stanford, CA: Stanford University. Retrieved from http://plato.stanford.edu/entries/pantheism/

Lewis, C., McTigue, K., Burke, L., Poirier, P., Eckel, R., Howard, B., Allison, D., Kumanyika, S., & Pi-Sunyer, F. X. (2009). Mortality, health outcomes, and body mass index in the overweight range: A science advisory from the American Heart Association. *Circulation, 119,* 3263-3271. Retrieved from http://circ.ahajournals.org/cgi/reprint/CIRCULATIONAHA.109.192574

Lewis, M., Haviland-Jones, J., & Barrett, F. (Eds). (2008). *Handbook of emotions* (3nd ed.). New York, NY: Guilford Press.

Lewis, M. V. (2008). Effectiveness of previous initiatives similar to programs of study: Tech Prep, career pathways, and youth apprenticeships. *Career and Technical Education Research, 33*(3), 165-188.

Lickona, T. (1991). *Educating for character: How our schools can teach respect and responsibility.* New York, NY: Bantam.

Lickona, T., Schaps, E., & Lewis, C. (2003). *Character Education Partnership's eleven principles of effective character education.* Washington, DC: Character Education Partnership. Retrieved from http://www.character.org/uploads/PDFs/Eleven_Principles.pdf

Liu, E., & Noppe-Brandon, S. (2009). *Imagination first: Unlocking the power of possibility.* San Francisco, CA: Jossey-Bass.

Liu, Y., & Ipe, M. (2010). How do they become nodes? Revisiting team member network centrality. *The Journal of Psychology, 144*(3), 243-258.

Logan, G., Taylor, S., & Etherton, J. (1999). Attention and automaticity: Toward a theoretical integration. *Psychological Research, 62*(2-3), 165-181.

Long, J., & Perry, P. (2011). *Evidence of the afterlife: The science of near-death experiences.* New York, NY: HarperOne.

Losada, M. (2008a, December 8). Want to flourish: Stay in the zone. *Positive Psychology News Daily*. Retrieved from http://positivepsychologynews.com/news/marcial-losada/200812081289

Losada, M. (2008b, December 9). Work teams and the Losada line: New results. *Positive Psychology News Daily*. Retrieved from http://positivepsychologynews.com/news/marcial-losada/200812091298

Losh, C. (2000). Using skill standards for vocational-technical education curriculum development. Columbus, OH: ERIC Clearinghouse on Adult, Career, and Vocational Education. Retrieved from https://eric.ed.gov/?id=ED440295

Lucas, C. (1999). Spirit of complexity. *Dynamical Psychology*. Retrieved from http://goertzel.org/dynapsyc/1999/spirit.htm

Lumsden, L. (1994). *Student motivation to learn.* Retrieved from http://www.edpsycinteractive.org/files/stdtmotv.html

Lyubomirsky, S. (2007). *The how of happiness: A scientific approach to getting the life you want.* New York, NY: Penguin Press.

Maag, J. (2006). Social skills training for students with emotional and behavioral disorders: A review of reviews. *Behavioral Disorders, 32*(1), 5-17.

Malecki C., & Elliot, S. (2002). Children's social behaviors as predictors of academic achievement: A longitudinal analysis. *School Psychology Quarterly, 17*(1), 1-23.

Malinowski, B. (2014). *A scientific theory of culture.* Boulder, CO: Marcel Press. [Originally published in 1941].

Markham, A. B. (1999). *Knowledge representation.* Mahwah NJ: Lawrence Erlbaum Associates.

Markus, H., & Nurius, P. (1986). Possible selves. *American Psychologist, 41*, 954-969.

Marler, P., & Hadaway, K. (2002). "Being religious" or "being spiritual" in America: A zero-sum proposition? *Journal for the Scientific Study of Religion, 41*(2), 289-300.

Marlowe, B., & Page, M. (1998). *Creating and sustaining the constructivistic classroom.* Thousand Oaks, CA: Corwin Press.

Marsh, H. W., & Hattie, J. (1996). Theoretical perspectives on the structure of self-concept. In B. A. Bracken (Ed.), *Handbook of self-concept* (pp. 38–90). New York, NY: Wiley.

Martin, B. L., & Briggs, L. J. (1986). *The affective and cognitive domains: Integration for instruction and research.* Englewood Cliffs, NJ: Educational Technology Publications.

Martin, D. G. (1999). *Counseling and therapy skills* (2nd ed.). Prospect Heights, IL: Waveland Press.

Maslow, A. (1954). *Motivation and personality*. New York, NY: Harper.
Maslow, A. (1971). *The farther reaches of human nature*. New York, NY: The Viking Press.
Maslow, A. (1983). *Farther reaches of human nature*. Magnolia, MA: Peter Smith Publishers.
Matthews, G., Emo, A., Roberts, R., & Zeidner, M. (2006). What is this thing called emotional intelligence? In K. Murphy (Ed.), *A critique of emotional intelligence: What are the problems and how can they be fixed?* (pp. 3-35). Mahwah, NJ: Lawrence Erlbaum.
Matthews, G., Roberts, R. D. & Zeidner, M, (2004). Seven myths about emotional intelligence. *Psychological Inquiry, 15(3)*, 179-196.
Maurer, M., & Brackett, M. A., & Plain, F. (2004). *Emotional literacy in the middle school: A six-step program to promote social, emotional, and academic learning*. Portchester, NY: National Professional Resources.
Maxwell, G. (2016). *The dynamics of transformation: Tracing an emerging world view*. Nashville, TN: Persistent Press.
Maxwell, J. (2013). *Conceptual framework design: An interactive approach* (3rd ed.). Los Angeles, CA: Sage.
May, R. (1958). The origins and significance of the existential movement in psychology. In R. May, E. Angel, & H. E Ellenberger (Eds.), *Existence: A new dimension in psychiatry and psychology* (pp. 3-36). New York, NY: Simon & Schuster.
Mayer, J. D., Salovey, P., & Caruso, D. R. (2008). Emotional intelligence: New ability or eclectic traits? *American Psychologist, 63*, 503–517.
McCarthy, B. (2000). *About teaching: 4MAT in the classroom*. Wauconda, IL: About Learning.
McCleary, R., & Barro, R. (2006). Religion and political economy in an international panel. *Journal for the Scientific Study of Religion, 45*(2), 149-175.
McClellan, B. (1992). *Schools and the shaping of character: Moral education in America, 1607-present*. Bloomington, IN: ERIC Clearinghouse for Social Studies/Social Science Education and the Social Studies Development Center, Indiana University.
McClelland, D. (1985). *Human motivation*. Glenview, IL: Scott, Foresman.
McClelland, D. (1992). *Achievement motive*. New York, NY: Irvington Publishers.
McClelland, J. (1995). A connectionist perspective on knowledge and development. In T. Simon & G. Halford (Eds.), *Developing cognitive competence: New approaches to process modeling* (pp. 157-204). Hillsdale, NJ: Lawrence Erlbaum.

McClelland, J., & Rumelhart, D. (1981) An interactive activation model of context effects in letter perception. Part I: An account of basic findings. *Psychological Review, 88*, 375-407.

McClelland, J., & Rumelhart, D. (1986). *Parallel distributed processing. Explorations in the microstructure of cognition: Vol. 2. Psychological and biological models.* Cambridge, MA: MIT Press.

McCombs, B. (1991). Motivation and lifelong learning. *Educational Psychologist, 26*(2), 117-128.

McCombs, B., & Whisler, J. (1989). The role of affective variables in autonomous learning. *Educational Psychologist, 24*(3), 277-306.

McCrae, R., & Costa, P., Jr. (1997). Personality trait structure as a human universal. *American Psychologist, 52,* 509-516.

McCraty, R., Atkinson, M., Tomasino, D., Goelitz, J., & Mayrovitz, H. H, (1999). The impact of an emotional self-management skills course on psychosocial functioning and autonomic recovery to stress in middle school children. *Integrative Physiological and Behavioral Science, 34,* 246-269.

McCurry, M., & Hunter Revell, S. (2015). Partners in family caregiving: A conceptual framework. *Journal of Theory Construction & Testing, 19*(1), 21-25.

McFadden, S. & Gerl, R. (1990). Approaches to understanding spirituality in the second half of life. *Generations, 14*(4), 35-45.

McFarland, R. (1997). An overview of the adult technology-based learning environment. *Assessment and Accountability Forum, 7*(2), 1-5.

McGreevy, A., & Copley, S. (1998, December/1999, January). Spirituality and education: Nurturing connections in schools and classrooms. *Classroom Leadership Online, 2*(4). Retrieved from http://www.ascd.org/publications/classroom-leadership/dec1998/Spirituality-and-Education.aspx

McIntosh, S. (2015). *The presence of the infinite: The spiritual experience of beauty, truth, and goodness*. Wheaton, IL: Quest Books.

McIntyre-Mills, J. (2010). Constructing citizenship and transnational identity: Participatory policy to enhance attachment and involvement. *Systemic Practice and Action Research, 23*(1), 1-19. doi: 10.1007/s11213-009-9143-y

McKown, C., Gumbiner, L., Russo, N., & Lipton, M. (2009). Social-emotional learning skill, self-regulation, and social competence in typically developing and clinic-referred children. *Journal of Clinical Child & Adolescent Psychology, 38*(6), 858-871.

McMahon, M., & Luca, J. (2001). *Assessing students' self-regulatory skills.* Retrieved from http://ro.ecu.edu.au/cgi/viewcontent.cgi?article=5839&context=ecuworks

McMullin, R.E. (1986). *Handbook of cognitive therapy techniques*. New York, NY: W.W. Norton and Company.

McRae, K., Misra, S., Prasad, A., Pereira, S., & Gross, J. (2012). Bottom-up and top-down emotion generation: Implications for emotion regulation. *Social Cognitive & Affective Neuroscience, 7*(3), 254-262. doi:10.1093/scan/nsq103

McSherry, E. (1987). The need and appropriateness of measurement and research in chaplaincy: Its criticalness for patient care and chaplain department survival post 1987. *Journal of Health Care Chaplaincy, 1*(1), 3-41.

Merrell, K. (1993). Using behavior rating scales to assess social skills and antisocial behavior in school settings. *School Psychology Review, 22*(1), 115-133.

Merrell, K. (2008). *School social behavior scales: User's guide* (2nd ed.). Baltimore, MD: Brooks Publishing.

Merrell, K., & Caldarella, P. (2008). *Home & community social behavior scales (HCSBS): Users guide*. Baltimore, MD: Brooks Publishing.

Merrell, K., & Guelder, B. (2010). *Social and emotional learning in the classroom: Promoting mental health and academic success*. New York, NY: Guilford Press.

Merrill, K., Streeter, A., Boelter, E., Caldarella, P., & Gentry, A. (2001). Validity of the home and community social behavior scales: Comparisons with five behavior-rating scales. *Psychology in the Schools, 38*(4), 313-325.

Mervis, C. B., & Rosch, E. (1981). Categorization of natural objects. *Annual Review of Psychology, 32*, 89-115. doi:10.1146/annurev.ps.32.020181.000513

Mesle, R. (1993). *Process theology: A basic introduction*. St. Louis, MO: Chalice Press.

Miele, F. (1996). The (im)moral animal: A quick & dirty guide to evolutionary psychology & the nature of human nature. *Skeptic, 4*(1), 42-49. Retrieved from http://www.skeptic.com/04.1.miele-immoral.html

Miller, A. (1991). Personality types, learning styles and educational goals. *Educational Psychology, 11*(3-4), 217-238.

Miller, A., & Hom, H., Jr. (1990). Influence of extrinsic and ego incentive value on persistence after failure and continuing motivation. *Journal of Educational Psychology, 82*(3), 539-545.

Miller, G., Galanter, E., & Pribram, K. (1960). *Plans and the structure of behavior*. New York, NY: Holt, Rinehart, & Winston.

Miller, J., & Page, S. (2007). *Complex adaptive systems: An introduction to computational models of social life*. Princeton, NJ & Oxford, UK: Princeton University Press.

Miller, R., Greene, B., Montalvo, G., Ravindran, B., & Nichols, J. (1996). Engagement in academic work: The role of learning goals, future consequences, pleasing others, and perceived ability. *Contemporary Educational Psychology, 21*(4), 388- 422.

Millman, D. (1993). *The life you were born to live: A guide to finding your life purpose*. Tiburon, CA: H J Kramer.

Mische, P. (2001). Toward a civilization worthy of the human person. In P. Mische & M. Merkling (Eds.), *Toward a global civilization? The contributions of religions*. New York, NY: Peter Lang.

Mischel, W. (1996). From good intentions to willpower. In P. Gollwitzer & J. Bargh (Eds.), *The psychology of action* (pp. 197-218). New York, NY: Guilford Press.

Model. (2012). *Merriam-Webster Online Dictionary*. Retrieved from http://www.merriam-webster.com/dictionary/model

Moody, H., & Carroll, D. (1998). *The five stages of the soul: Charting the spiritual passages that shape our lives*. New York, NY: Doubleday.

Moody, R. (2001). *Life after life: The investigation of a phenomenon-survival after death*. New York, NY: HarperSanFrancisco. [Originally published in 1975].

Moore, K., Lippman, L., & Brown, B. (2004). Indicators of child well-being: The promise of positive youth development. *Annals of the American Academy of Political and Social Science, 591*, 125-145.

Moshman, D. (1982). Exogenous, endogenous, and dialectical constructivism. *Developmental Review, 2*, 371-384.

Mueller, C., & Dweck, C. (1998). Praise for intelligence can undermine children's motivation and performance. *Journal of Personality & Social Psychology, 75*(1), 33-52.

Murray, H. A. (1938). *Explorations in personality*. New York, NY: Oxford University Press.

Murray, N., Sujan, H., Hirt, E. R., & Sujan, M. (1990). The influence of mood on categorization: A cognitive flexibility interpretation. *Journal of Personality and Social Psychology, 59*, 411–425.

Muscott, H. (2001). Service learning and character education as "antidotes" for children with egos that cannot perform. *Reclaiming Children and Youth, 10*(2), 91-99.

Myers, D. (2000). *The American paradox: Spiritual hunger in an age of plenty*. New Haven, CT: Yale University Press.

Myers, I. B. (1995). *Gifts differing: Understanding personality type*. Mountain View, CA: Davies-Black Publishing. [Originally published in 1980].

Nagel, T. (2012). *Mind and cosmos: Why the materialist neo-Darwinian conception of nature is almost certainly false.* New York, NY: Oxford University Press.

Narvaez, D. (2002). The expertise of moral character. *Education Matters, VIII*(6), 1, 6. Retrieved from http://www.aaeteachers.org/newsletters/julyaugustnews.pdf

Narvaez, D. (2006). Integrative ethical education. In M. Killen & J. Smetana (Eds.), *Handbook of moral development* (pp. 703-733). Mahwah, NJ: Erlbaum. Retrieved from http://www.nd.edu/~dnarvaez/Narvaez%20HMD%2009.14.pdf

Narvaez, D. (2007). How cognitive and neurobiological sciences inform values education for creatures like us. In D. Aspin & J. Chapman (Eds.), *Values education and lifelong learning: Philosophy, policy, practices.* Cham, Switzerland: Springer Press International. Retrieved from http://www.nd.edu/~dnarvaez/documents/NARVAEZCreatureslikeus.pdf

Narvaez, D. (2008a). Human flourishing and moral development: Cognitive and perspectives of virtue development. In L. Nucci & D. Narvaez, *Handbook of moral and character education* (pp. 310-327). New York, NY: Routledge.

Narvaez, D. (2008b). Triune ethics: The neurobiological roots of our multiple moralities. *New Ideas in Psychology, 26,* 95-119. Retrieved from http://www.nd.edu/~dnarvaez/documents/TriuneEthicsTheory0725071.pdf

Narvaez, D. & colleagues. (2001). *Community voices and character education: Curriculum materials.* Notre Dame, IN: Collaboration for Ethical Education, University of Notre Dame. Retrieved from http://cee.nd.edu/curriculum/curriculum1.shtml

Narvaez, D. & Rest, J. (1995). The four components of acting morally. In W. Kurtines & J. Gewirtz (Eds.), *Moral development: An introduction* (385-400). Needham Heights, MA: Allyn & Bacon.

Nathanson, D. (1992). *Shame and pride: Affect, sex, and the birth of the self.* New York, NY: W.W. Norton & Company.

National Bureau of Statistics. (2005). *China Statistical Yearbook, 2005. Table 5-2.* Beijing, Peoples Republic of China: Author. Retrieved from http://www.gerhard-k-heilig.com/cp/data/fig_employment_1.htm

National Center for Chronic Disease Prevention and Health Promotion. (2004). *Body mass index calculator.* Atlanta, GA: Centers for Disease Control and Prevention (CDC). Retrieved from http://www.cdc.gov/nccdphp/dnpa/bmi/calc-bmi.htm

National Commission on Excellence in Education, The. (1983). *A nation at risk: The imperative for educational reform.* Washington, DC: U.S.

Department of Education. Retrieved from http://www2.ed.gov/pubs/NatAtRisk/index.html

Neber, H., & Schommer-Aikins, M. (2002). Self-regulated science learning with highly gifted students: The role of cognitive, motivational, epistemological, and environmental variables. *High Ability Studies, 13*, 59-74.

Neisser, E. (1967). *Cognitive psychology*. New York, NY: Appleton-Century-Crofts

Nelson, A., Cleary, T., & Platten, P. (2008). Effectiveness of the self-regulation empowerment program with urban high school students. *Journal of Advanced Academics, 20*(1), 70-107.

Newberg, A., D'Aquili, E., & Rause, V. (2001). *Why God won't go away*. New York, NY: Ballantine Books.

New York Online Access to Health. (2004). *Ask NOAH about: Physical fitness and exercise*. Retrieved from http://www.noah-health.org/english/wellness/healthyliving/exercise.html

Nicholl, T. (1998). Vygotsky. *The virtual faculty*. Palmerston North, New Zealand: Massey University, Retrieved from http://www.massey.ac.nz/~alock//virtual/trishvyg.htm

Niehoff, D. (1999). *The biology of violence: How understanding the brain, behavior, and the environment can break the vicious circle of aggression*. New York, NY: The Free Press.

Nino, A. (1997). Assessment of spiritual quests in clinical practice. *International Journal of Psychotherapy, 2*(2), 192-212.

Norris, J. (2003). Looking at classroom management through a social and emotional learning lens. *Theory into Practice, 42*(4), 313-318. doi:10.1207/s15430421tip4204_8

Novick, B., Kress, J., & Elias, M. J. (2002). *Building learning communities with character: How to integrate academic, social and emotional learning*. Alexandria, VA: Association for Supervision and Curriculum Development.

Nucci, L. (Ed.). (1989). *Moral development and character education: A dialogue*. Berkley, CA: McCutchan.

Oakland, T., & Joyce, D. (2004). Temperament-based learning styles and school-based applications. *Canadian Journal of School Psychology, 19*(1-2), 59-74.

Oakland, T., Stafford, M., Horton, C., & Glutting, J. (2001). Temperament and vocational preferences: Age, gender, and racial-ethnic comparisons using the Student Styles Questionnaire. *Journal of Career Assessment, 9*(3), 297-314.

Oatley K., & Johnson-Laird P. N. (1995). The Communicative Theory of emotion: Empirical tests, mental models, and implications for social interaction. In L. L. Martin and A. Tesser (Eds.), *Striving and feeling:*

Interactions among goals, affect and self-regulation (pp. 363-393). Hillsdale, NJ: Erlbaum.

Oliver, J. (2009). *Jamie's food revolution: Rediscover how to cook simple, delicious, affordable meals.* New York, NY: Hyperion.

Omdahl, B. (1995). *Cognitive appraisal, emotion and empathy.* Mahwah, NJ: Lawrence Erlbaum Associates.

Orlich, D. (2000). Education reform and limits to student achievement. *Phi Delta Kappan, 81*(6), 468.

Ornish, D. (2007). *The spectrum: A scientifically proven program to feel better, live longer, lose weight, and gain health.* New York, NY: Ballantine Books

Ortney, A., Clore, G. L., & Collins, A. (1988). *The cognitive structure of emotions.* Cambridge, UK: Cambridge University Press.

Oxley, D. (2008). Creating instructional program coherence. *Principal's Research Review, 3*(5), 1-7. Retrieved from http://educationnorthwest.org/webfm_send/620

Page, D., & Wong, P. T. P. (2013). *A conceptual framework for measuring servant-leadership.* Retrieved from http://www.drpaulwong.com/wp-content/uploads/2013/09/Conceptual-Framework.pdf

Paivio, A. (1971). *Imagery and verbal pro*cesses. New York, NY: Hotel, Rinehart, and Winston.

Paivio, A. (1986). *Mental representations: A dual coding approach.* New York, NY: Oxford University Press.

Pajares, F. (1996). *Assessing self-efficacy beliefs and academic outcomes: The case for specificity and correspondence.* Paper presented at the annual meeting of the American Educational Research Association, New York. Retrieved from https://www.uky.edu/~eushe2/Pajares/aera2.html

Pajares, F., & Graham, L. (1999). Self-efficacy, motivation constructs, and mathematics performance of entering middle school students. *Contemporary Educational Psychology, 24*, 124-139.

Palmer, P. (1998/1999). Evoking the spirit in public education. *Educational Leadership, 56*(4), 6-11. Retrieved from http://www.couragerenewal.org/parker/writings/evoking-the-spirit

Palmer, P. (2003). Teaching with heart and soul: Reflections on spirituality in teacher education. *Journal of Teacher Education, 54*(5), 376-385. Retrieved from http://www.couragerenewal.org/parker/writings/heart-and-soul

Paloutzian, R., & Ellison, C. (1982). Loneliness, spiritual well-being, and the quality of life. In Peplau, L. A., & Perlman, D. (Eds.), *Loneliness: A sourcebook of current theory, research and therapy.* New York, NY: Wiley.

Parent, S., Normandeau, S., & Larivee, S. (2000). A quest for the holy grail in the new millennium: in search of a unified theory of cognitive development. *Child Development, 71*(4), 860-861.

Pargament, K. (1997). *The psychology of religion and coping.* New York, NY: Guilford Press.

Pargament, K., & Mahoney, A. (2002). Spirituality: Discovering and conserving the sacred. In C. Snyder and S. Lopez (Eds.), *Handbook of positive psychology* (pp. 646-659). New York, NY: Oxford University Press.

Park, N. (2003). Character strengths and positive youth development. *Annals of the American Academy of Political and Social Science, 591*, 40-54.

Park, N., Peterson, C., & Seligman, M. E. P. (2004). Strengths of character and well-being. *Journal of Social and Clinical Psychology, 23*, 603-619.

Parke, R. & Buriel, R. (2006). Socialization in the family: Ethnic and ecological perspectives. In N. Eisenberg (Ed.), *The handbook of child psychology: Social, emotional, and personality development* (6th ed., Vol. 3, pp. 429-504). New York, NY: Wiley.

Parkinson, B., & Manstead, A. S. R. (1992). Appraisal as a cause of emotion. In Clark, M. S. (1992). *Emotion* (pp. 125-126). Newbury Park, CA: Sage Publications, Inc.

Parks, S. (1992). *Inside HELP-Hawaii Early Learning Profile administration and reference manual.* Palo Alto, CA: VORT.

Partnership for 21st Century Skills. (2004). *The MILE guide: Milestones for improving learning and education.* Retrieved from http://science.nsta.org/enewsletter/2004-06/P21_MILE_Guide.pdf

Partnership for 21st Century Skills. (2009). P21 framework definitions. Washington, DC: Author. Retrieved from http://www.p21.org/our-work/p21-framework

Patrikakou, E., & Weissberg, R. (2007). School-family partnerships to enhance children's social, emotional, and academic learning. In R. Bar-on, J. Maree, & M. Elias, Educating people to be emotionally intelligent (pp. 49-77). Westport, CT: Praeger Publishers

Payton, J., Weissberg, R., Durlak, J., Dymnicki, A., Taylor, R., Schellinger, K., & Pachan, M. (2008). The positive impact of social and emotional learning for kindergarten to eighth-grade students: Findings from three scientific studies. [Executive Summary]. Chicago, IL: Collaborative for Academic, Social, and Emotional Learning (CASEL). Retrieved from https://files.eric.ed.gov/fulltext/ED505370.pdf

Peck, M. S. (1998a). *Further along the road less traveled: The unending journey towards spiritual growth* (2nd ed.). New York, NY: Touchstone.

Peck. M. S. (1998b). *The road less traveled: A new psychology of love, traditional values, and spiritual growth* (2nd ed.). New York, NY: Simon & Schuster.

Peil, K. (2000). *Mastering emotional intelligence.* Seattle, WA: EFS International.

Peláez-Nogueras, M., & Gewirtz, J. (1995). The learning of moral behavior: A behavior-analytic approach. In W. Kurtines & J. Gewirtz (Eds.),

Moral development: An introduction (173-199). Needham Heights, MA: Allyn & Bacon.

Pelicano, E. (2010). Individual differences in executive function and central coherence predict developmental changes in theory of mind in Autism. *Developmental Psychology, 46*(2), 530-544.

Pepper, S. C. (1942). *World hypotheses: A study in evidence.* Berkeley: University of California Press.

Pepper, S. C. (1967). *Concept and quality: A world hypothesis.* Chicago, IL: Open Court Publishing.

Perels, F., Guertler, T., & Schmitz, B. (2005). Training of self-regulatory and problem-solving competence. *Learning and Instruction, 15*(2), 123-139.

Perry, N. E. (1999). Young children's self-regulated learning and contexts that support it. *Journal of Educational Psychology, 90*, 715-729.

Perry, W., Jr. (1999). *Intellectual and ethical development in the college years: A scheme.* San Francisco, CA: Jossey-Bass. [Originally published in 1970].

Peterson, C., Park, N., & Seligman, M. E. P. (2005). Orientations to happiness and life satisfaction: The full life versus the empty life. *Journal of Happiness Studies, 6*, 25-41.

Peterson, C., & Seligman, M. E. P. (2004). *Character strengths and virtues: A handbook and classification.* Washington, DC: American Psychological Association.

Phelps, S. (2009, July). *The Bahá'í Faith and atheism.* Revised and edited transcripts of two talks at the Swedish Bahá'í Summer School, Lundsbrunn, Sweden. Retrieved from https://bahaiwritings.files.wordpress.com/2011/03/the-bahai-faith-and-atheism-by-dr-steven-phelps.pdf

Phillips, D. (Ed.). (2000). *Constructivism in education: Opinions and second opinions on controversial issues.* Chicago, IL: The National Study for the Study of Education.

Phipps, C. (2012). *Evolutionaries: Unlocking the spiritual and cultural potential of science's greatest idea.* New York, NY: HarperCollins.

Piaget, J. (1952). Jean Piaget. In E. Boring, H. Langfeld, H. Werner, & R. Yerkes (Eds.), *History of psychology in autobiography* (Vol. IV, pp. 237-256). Worcester, MA: Clark University Press.

Piaget, J. (1969). *The moral judgment of the child.* Glencoe, IL: Free Press. [Originally published 1932].

Piaget, J. (2000). Piaget's theory. In K. Lee (Ed.), *Childhood cognitive development: The essential readings* (pp. 33-47). Malden, MA, Oxford, UK: Blackwell Publishing.

Piaget, J. (2001). *The psychology of intelligence* (2nd ed.). London, UK: Routledge. [Originally published in 1950].

Piaget, J., & Inhelder, B. (1966). *The psychology of the child.* (Translated 1968). New York, UK: Basic Books.
Pink, D. (2005). *A whole new mind: Moving from the Information Age to the Conceptual Age.* New York, NY: Riverhead Hardcover.
Pink, D. (2009). *Drive: The surprising truth about what motivates us.* New York, NY: Riverhead Books.
Pinker, S. (1997). *How the mind works.* New York, NY: W.W. Norton.
Plaud, J., Plaud, D., & von Duvillard, S. (1999). Human behavioral momentum in a sample of older adults. *Journal of General Psychology, 126*(2), 165-175.
Plomin, R. (1990). *Nature and nurture: An introduction to human behavioral genetics.* New York, NY: Wadsworth Publishing.
Plutchik, R. (1980) *Emotion: A psychoevolutionary synthesis.* New York, NY: Harper and Row.
Plutchik, R. (2001). The nature of emotions. *American Scientist, 89,* 344-350.
Polachek, S., & Siebert, W. S. (1993). *The economics of earnings.* New York, NY: Cambridge University Press.
Polanyi, M. (1970). Transcendence and self-transcendence. *Soundings, 53*(1), 88-94.
Polkinghorne, J. (2011). *Science and religion in quest for truth.* New Haven, CT & London, UK: Yale University Press.
Ponton, M., & Carr, P. (2000). Understanding and promoting autonomy in self-directed learning. *Current Research in Social Psychology, 5*(19), 281-284. Retrieved from https://uiowa.edu/crisp/volume-5-issue-19-september-15-2000
Postman, N. (1995) *The end of education: Redefining the value of school.* New York, NY: Alfred A. Knopf.
Power, F. C., Higgins, A., & Kohlberg, L. (1989). *Lawrence Kohlberg's approach to moral education.* New York, NY: Columbia University Press.
Prawat, R. (1985). Affective versus cognitive goal orientations in elementary teachers. *American Educational Research Journal, 22*(4), 587-604.
Price, E. (1998, Nov-Dec). Instructional systems design and the affective domain. *Educational Technology, 38*(6), 17-28.
Primack, R. (1986). No substitute for critical thinking: A response to Wynne. *Educational Leadership, 43,* 12-13.
Pritchard, I. (1988). Character education: Research prospects and problems. *American Journal of Education, 96*(4), 469-495.
Pruyser, P. (1976). *The minister as diagnostician: Personal problems in pastoral perspective,* Philadelphia, PA: The Westminster Press.
Purkey, W. (1988). An overview of self-concept theory for counselors. *ERIC Clearinghouse on Counseling and Personnel Services,* Ann Arbor, Mich. (An ERIC/CAPS Digest: ED304630). Retrieved from http://www.edpsycinteractive.org/files/selfconc.html

Purpel, D., & Ryan, K. (Eds.). (1976). *Moral education...It comes with the territory.* Berkeley, CA: McCutchan.

Pylyshyn, Z. (2002). Mental imagery: In search of a theory. *Behavior and Brain Sciences.* Retrieved http://ruccs.rutgers.edu/images/personal-zenon-pylyshyn/docs/bbs2002_reprint.pdf

Quinn, M., Kavale, K., Mathur, S., Rutherford , R., & Forness, S. (1999). A meta-analysis of social skill interventions for students with emotional or behavioral disorders. *Journal of Emotional and Behavioral Disorders, 7*(1), 54.

Ramsey, D. (2008). *The total money makeover: A proven plan for financial fitness* (3rd ed.). Nashville, TN: Thomas Nelson.

Rebora, A. (2004). No child left behind. *Education Week on the Web.* Retrieved from http://www.edweek.org/context/topics/issuespage.cfm?id=59

Renner and others. (1976). *Research, teaching, and learning with the Piaget model.* Norman, OK: University of Oklahoma Press.

Rest, J. (1979). *Manual for the Defining Issues Test: An objective test of moral judgment development* (Rev. ed.). Minneapolis, MN: University of Minnesota Press.

Rest, J. (1986). *Moral development: Advances in research and theory.* New York, NY: Praeger.

Rest, J., Narvaez, D., Bebeau, M., & Thoma, S. (1999). *Postconventional moral thinking: A neo-Kohlbergian approach.* Nahwah, NJ: Lawrence Erlbaum.

Richardson, R. (2000). Teaching social and emotional competence. *Children and Schools, 22,* 246-251.

Ries, A., & Trout, J. (1993). *The 22 immutable laws of marketing: Violate them at your own risk.* New York, NY: HarperCollins Publishers.

Rimmer, J. H. (1994). *Fitness and rehabilitation programs for special populations.* Dubuque, IA: Brown & Benchmark Publishers.

Ringwalt, S. (Compiler). (2008). *Developmental screening and assessment instruments with an emphasis on social and emotional development for young children ages birth to five.* Chapel Hill, NC: The National Early Childhood Technical Assistance Center (NECTAC). Retrieved from http://www.nectac.org/~pdfs/pubs/screening.pdf

Robinson, K. (2011). *Out of our minds: Learning to be creative* (Rev. ed.). Chichester, West Sussex, UK: Capstone Publishing, Ltd.

Roebben, B. (1995). Catching a glimpse of the palace of reason: The education of moral emotions. *Journal of Moral Education, 24,* 185-198.

Roehlkepartain, E., Benson, P., & Sesma, A. (2003). *Signs of progress in putting children first: Developmental assets among youth in St. Louis Park, 1997-2001.* Minneapolis, MN: Search Institute.

Roehlkepartain, E., Ebstyne, P., Wagener, L., & Benson, P. (Eds.). (2006). *The handbook of spiritual development in childhood and adolescence.* Thousand Oaks, CA: Sage Publications.

Roehlkepartain, E., Scales, P., Roehlkepartain, J., Rude, S. (2002). *Building strong families: Highlights from a preliminary survey on what parents need to succeed.* Chicago, IL and Minneapolis, MN: YMCA of the USA and Search Institute.

Rogers, C. (2003). *Client-centered therapy: Its current practice, implications, and theory.* London, UK: Constable. [Originally published in 1951].

Rosch, E., Mervis, C., Gray. W., Johnson, D., & Boyes-Braem, P. (1976). Basic objects in natural categories. *Cognitive Psychology, 8*, 382-439.

Rosenthal, J., & Kaye, N. (2005). *State approaches to promoting young children's healthy mental development: A survey of Medicaid, maternal and child health, and mental health agencies.* Portland, ME: National Academy of State Health Policy.

Rossi, E. L. (1993). *The psychobiology of mind-body healing: New concepts of therapeutic hypnosis* (Rev. ed.). New York, NY: W.W. Norton.

Rothbart, M., Ahadi, S., & Evans, D. (2000). Temperament and personality: Origins and outcomes. *Journal of Personality and Social Psychology, 78*(1), 122-135. doi:10.103/#0022-3514.78.1.122

Rothbart, M. K., & Hwang, J. (2005). Temperament and the development of competence and motivation. In A. Elliot, & C. Dweck (Eds.), *Handbook of competence & motivation* (pp. 167-184). New York, NY: Guilford Press.

Rousseau, J. (1979). *Emile* (A. Bloom, Trans.). New York, NY: Basic Books. (Original work published in 1762).

Rumelhart, D. (!980). Schemata: The building blocks of cognition. In R. Spiro, B. Bruce, & W. Brewer (Eds.), *Theoretical issues in reading comprehension.* Hillsdale, NJ: Erlbaum.

Rumelhart, D., & McClelland, J. (1986). *Parallel distributed processing. Explorations in the microstructure of cognition: Vol.1. Foundations.* Cambridge, MA: MIT Press.

Rushkoff, D. (2014). *Present shock: When everything happens now.* New York, NY: Current/Penguin.

Russ, S. (1999). (Ed.), *Affect, creative experience, and psychological adjustment.* Philadelphia, PA: Brunner/Mazel.

Russek, L., & Schwartz, G. (1997). Perceptions of parental caring predict health status in midlife: A 35-year follow-up of the Harvard Mastery of Stress Study. *Psychosomatic Medicine, 59*, 144-149.

Rutter, M., Maughan, B., Mortimore, P., Ouston, J, and Smith, A. (1979). *Fifteen thousand hours: Secondary schools and their effects on children.* Cambridge, MA: Harvard University Press.

Ryan, A., & Patrick, H. (2001). The classroom social environment and changes in adolescents' motivation and engagement during middle school. *American Educational Research Journal, 38*(2), 437-460. doi: 10.3102/0002831203800243

Ryan, K., & Bohlin, K. (1999). *Building character in schools.* San Francisco, CA: Jossey-Bass.

Ryan, K., & Wynne, E. (1996). *Reclaiming our schools: Teaching character, academics, and discipline* (2nd ed.). Upper Saddle River, NJ: Prentice-Hall.

Ryan, R., & Deci, E. (2000). Self-determination theory and the facilitation of intrinsic motivation, social development, and well-being. *American Psychologist, 55*, 68-78. Retrieved from http://www.psych.rochester.edu/SDT/documents/2000_RyanDeci_SDT.pdf

Ryan, R., & Deci, E. (2008). A self-determination theory approach to psychotherapy: The motivational basis for effective change. *Canadian Psychology, 49*(3), 186-193.

Saarni, C. (1999). *The development of emotional competence.* New York, NY: Guilford Press.

Saarni, C. (2007). The development of emotional competence: Pathways for helping children to become emotionally intelligent. In R. Bar-On, J. Maree, & M. Elias. (Eds.), *Educating people to be emotionally intelligent* (pp. 15-35). Westpoint, CT: Praeger.

Salovey, P. & Juneer, J. D. (1990). Emotional intelligence. *Imagination, Cognition, and Personality, 9*, 185-211.

Salovy, P., & Sluyter, D. (Eds.). (1997). *Emotional development and emotional intelligence - educational implications.* New York, NY: Basic Books.

Salti, M., El Karoui, I., Maillet, M., & Naccache, L. (2014). Cognitive dissonance resolution is related to episodic memory. *PLoS ONE 9*(9): e108579. doi:10.1371/journal.pone.0108579

Samuelson, P., & Nordhaus, W. (2009). *Economics* (19th ed.). New York, NY: McGraw-Hill Education.

Sansone, C., & Harackiewicz, J. (1996). "I don't feel like it"; The function of self interest in self-regulation. In L. Martin & A. Tesser (Eds.), *Striving and feeling: Interactions among goals, affect, and self-regulation* (203-228). Mahwah, NJ: Erlbaum.

Sartre, J. P. (1993). *Being and nothingness.* (Trans. H. Barnes). New York, NY: Washington Square Press. [Originally published *as L'Etre et le neant* in 1943].

Savery, J., & Duffy, T. (1996). Problem based learning: An instructional model and its constructivist framework. In B. Wilson (Ed.), *Constructivist learning environments: Case studies in instructional design* (pp. 135-148). Englewood Cliffs, NY: Educational Technology Publications.

Scales, P. C., Benson, P. L. Roehlkepartain, E. C., Sesman, A., & van Dulmen, M. (2006). The role of developmental assets in predicting academic achievement: A longitudinal study. *Journal of Adolescence, 29*(5), 692–708.

Scarr, S. (1993). Biological and cultural diversity: The legacy of Darwin for development. *Child Development, 64*, 1333-1353.

Schank, R. C., & Abelson, R. P. (1977) *Scripts, plans, goals and understanding: An inquiry into human knowledge structures.* Hillsdale, NJ: Lawrence Erlbaum.

Schaps, E. (2002). *Community in school: Central to character formation and more.* Paper presented at the White House Conference on Character and Community, June 19. Retrieved https://www2.ed.gov/admins/lead/safety/character/schaps.pdf

Schlegel, A., & Barry, H. III. (1980). The evolutionary significance of adolescent initiation ceremonies. *American Ethologist, 7*, 696-715.

Schlitz, M., Vieten, C., & Amorok, T. (2008). *Living deeply: The art and science of transformation in everyday life.* Oakland, CA: New Harbinger, Institute of Noetic Sciences.

Schneider, W., Korkel, J., & Weinert, F. (1989). Domain-specific knowledge and memory performance: A comparison of high- and low-aptitude children. *Journal of Educational Psychology, 81*, 306-312.

Schoell, W., & Guiltman, J. (1992). *Marketing: Contemporary concepts and practices.* Boston, MA: Allyn and Bacon.

Schunk, D. (2000). *Learning theories: An educational perspective* (2nd ed.). Upper Saddle River, NJ: Merrill.

Schunk, D., & Zimmerman, B. (Ed.). (1994). *Self-regulation of learning and performance: Issues and educational applications.* Hillsdale, NJ: Erlbaum.

Schunk, D., & Zimmerman, B. (Eds.). (1998). *Self-regulated learning: From teaching to self-reflective practice.* New York, NY: Guilford Press

Schutz, (1967). *The phenomenology of the social world.* (Trans. G. Walsh & F. Lehnert). Chicago, IL: Northwestern University Press. [Originally published as *Der sinnhafte Aufbau der sozialen Welt* in 1932].

Schwartz, J., & Begley, S. (2002). *The mind and the brain: Neuroplasticity and the power of mental force.* New York: HarperCollins.

Search Institute. (2017). *The Developmental Assets® framework.* Minneapolis, MN: Author. Retrieved from https://www.search-institute.org/our-research/development-assets/developmental-assets-framework/

Segars, M., & Jelen, T. (1998). *A wall of separation? Debating the public role of religion.* London, UK: Rowman & Littlefield Publishers.

Seijts, G., Meertens, R., & Kok, G. (1997). The effects of task importance and publicness on the relation between goal difficulty and performance. *Canadian Journal of Behavioural Science, 29*(1), 54-62.

Seligman, M. E. P. (1990). *Learned optimism.* New York, NY: Alfred A. Knopf.

Seligman, M. E. P. (1996) *The optimistic child: How learned optimism protects children from depression.* New York, NY: Houghton Mifflin.

Seligman, M. E. P. (2002). *Authentic happiness: Using the new positive psychology to realize your potential for lasting fulfillment.* New York: Free Press.

Seligman, M. E. P. (2011). *Flourish: A visionary new understanding of happiness and well-being.* New York, NY: Free Press.

Seligman, M. E. P., Railton, P., Baumeister, R., & Sripada, C. (2013). Navigating the future or driven by the past. *Perspectives on Psychological Science, 8*(2), 119-141. doi:10.1177/174569161247317

Selman, R. (1971). The relation of role taking to the development of moral judgment in children. *Child Development, 42*, 79-91.

Senge, P. (1990). *The fifth discipline: The art & practice of the learning organization.* New York, NY: Doubleday/Currency.

Senge, P., Scharmer, C. O., Jaworski, J., & Flowers, B. S. (2004). *Presence: Human purpose and the field of the future.* New York, NY: Doubleday.

Sheldon, K., & Elliot, A. (1999). Goal striving, need satisfaction, and longitudinal well-being: The self-concordance model. *Journal of Personality and Social Psychology, 76*(3), 482-497.

Sheldon, K., & Schmuck, P. (2001). Suggestions for healthy goal striving. In P. Schmuck and K. Sheldon (Eds.), *Life goals and well-being: Towards a positive psychology of human striving.* Seattle, WA: Hogrefe & Huber Publishers.

Shields, A., & Cicchetti, D. (1997). Emotion regulation in school-aged children: The development of a new criterion Q-sort scale. *Developmental Psychology, 33*, 906-916.

Shonkoff, J. (2000). Science, policy and practice: Three cultures in search of a shared mission. *Child Development, 71*(1), 181-187.

Shweder, R., Mahapatra, M., & Miller, J. (1987). Culture and moral development. In J. Kagan & S. Lamb (Eds.), *The emergence of morality in young children* (1-82). Chicago, IL: University of Chicago Press.

Siegler, R. (1991). *Children's thinking* (2nd ed.). Upper Saddle River, NJ: Prentice-Hall.

Sigelman, C., & Rider, E. (2006). *Human growth and development across the lifespan* (5th ed.). Belmont, CA: Thompson Corporation.

Simon, S., Howe, L., & Kirschenbaum, H. (1995). *Values clarification* (rev. ed.). New York, NY: Warner Books.

Sire, J. (2010). *Naming the elephant: Worldview as a concept* (2nd ed.). Downers Grove, IL: InterVarsity Press.

Sisson, M. (2013). *The primal blueprint: Reprogram your genes for effortless weight loss, vibrant health, and maximum longevity.* (rev.). Malibu, CA: Primal Nutrition.

Skinner, B. F. (1953). *Science and human behavior.* New York, NY: The Free Press.

Skinner, B. F. (1971). *Beyond freedom and dignity.* New York, NY: Knopf.

Slavin, R. (1994). *Cooperative learning: Theory, research, and practice* (2nd ed.). Boston, MA: Allyn & Bacon.

Small, G., & Vorgan, G. (2008). *iBrain: Surviving the technological alteration of the modern mind.* New York, NY: HarperCollins.

Smeyers, P. (1992). The necessity for particularity in education and child-rearing. [Special Issue: The moral issue]. *Journal of Philosophy of Education, 26,* 63-73.

Smith, D. W. (2013). Phenomenology. In E. Zalta (Ed.), *The Stanford Encyclopedia of Philosophy* Stanford, CA: The Metaphysics Research Lab, Stanford University. Retrieved from http://plato.stanford.edu/archives/win2013/entries/phenomenology

Smith, E., Shoben, E., & Rips, L. (1974). Structure and process in semantic memory: A featural model for semantic discussion. *Psychological Review, 81,* 214-241.

Smith, G. (2008). *The Jamie Oliver effect: The man, the food, the revolution* (2nd ed.). London, UK: Andre Deutsch.

Smith, H. (1992). *The world's religions: Our great wisdom traditions.* New York, NY: HarperCollins.

Smith, M. (1996). Self-direction in learning. *The Encyclopedia of Informal Education.* London, UK: YMCA George Williams College. Retrieved from http://infed.org/mobi/self-direction-in-learning/

Snow, R. (1989). Toward assessment of cognitive and conative structures in learning. *Educational Researcher, 18*(9), 8-14.

Snow, R., & Swanson, J. (1992). Instructional psychology: Aptitude, adaptation, and assessment. *Annual Review of Psychology, 43,* 583-626.

Solomon, D., Watson, M., & Battistich, V. (2001). Teaching and schooling effects on moral/pro-social development. In V. Richardson (Ed.), *Handbook of research on teaching* (4th ed.) (566-603). Washington, DC: Association for Supervision and Curriculum Development.

Solomon, R. (1980). The opponent-process theory of acquired motivation: The costs of pleasure and the benefits of pain. *American Psychologist, 8,* 691-712.

Solomon, R. (2002). *Spirituality for the skeptic: The thoughtful love of life.* Oxford, UK: Oxford University Press.

Sommers, C. (2002). How moral education is finding its way back into America's schools. In W. Damon, (Ed.), *Bringing in a new era in character education* (23-41). Stanford, CA: Hoover Institute Press.

Sonnier, I. L. (ed.) (1989). *Affective education: Methods and techniques.* Englewood Cliffs, NJ: Educational Technology Publications.

Sosna, T., & Mastergeorge, A. (2005). *Compendium of screening tools for early childhood social and emotional development.* Sacramento, CA: The Infant, Preschool, Family Mental Health Initiative, California Institute for Mental Health.

South Carolina Department of Education. (2018). *South Carolina physical education curriculum standards.* Columbia, SC: Author. Retrieved from https://ed.sc.gov/instruction/standards-learning/physical-education/

Speicker, B. (1988). Education and the moral emotions. In B. Speicker & R. Straughan (Eds), *Philosophical issues in moral education and development* (pp. 43-63). Maidenhead, UK: Open University Press.

Sroufe, L. (1996). *Emotional development: The organization of emotional life in the early years.* New York, NY: Cambridge University Press.

Sroufe, L., Egeland, B., Carlson, E., & Collins, W. (2005). *Minnesota Study of Risk and Adaptation from birth to maturity: The development of the person.* New York, NY: Guilford Press.

Stack, D., Serbin, L., Enns, L., Ruttle, P., & Barrieau, L. (2010). Parental effects on children's emotional development over time and across generations. *Infants and Young Children, 23*(1), 52-69.

Stanton, W. (1993). A cognitive development framework. *Current Psychology, 12*(1), 26-47.

Stefani, L. (2004-05). Assessment of student learning: Promoting a scholarly approach. *Learning and Teaching in Higher Education, 1*, 51-66. Retrieved from http://www2.glos.ac.uk/offload/tli/lets/lathe/issue1/articles/stefani.pdf

Sternberg, R. (1985). *Beyond IQ: A triarchic theory of human intelligence.* New York, NY: Cambridge University Press.

Sternberg, R. (1988). *The triarchic mind: A new theory of human intelligence.* New York, NY: Penguin Books.

Sternberg, R. (1996). *Successful intelligence: How practical and creative intelligence determine success in life.* New York, NY: Simon & Schuster.

Sternberg, R. (2003). *Wisdom, intelligence, and creativity synthesized.* Cambridge, MA: Cambridge University Press.

Sternberg, R. (2004). What is wisdom and how can we develop it? *Annals of the American Academy of Political and Social Science, 591*, 164-174.

Sternberg, R., & Grigorenko, E. (2000). *Teaching for successful intelligence.* Arlington Heights, IL: Skylight Training and Publishing Inc.

Sternberg, R., Forsythe, G., Hedlund, J., Horvath, J., Wagner, R., Williams, W., Snook, S., & Grigorenko, E. (2000). *Practical intelligence for everyday life.* New York, NY: Cambridge University Press.

Sternberg, R., Wagner, T., Williams, W., & Horvath, J. (1995). Testing common sense. *American Psychologist, 50*(11), 912-927.

Stiggins, R. (June, 2002). Assessment crisis: The absence of assessment for learning. *Phi Delta Kappan, 83*(10), 758. Retrieved from http://www.electronicportfolios.org/afl/Stiggins-AssessmentCrisis.pdf

Stilwell, B. (1998, February). Moral volition: The fifth and final domain leading to an integrated theory of conscience understanding. *Journal of the American Academy of Child and Adolescent Psychiatry.*

Stilwell, B., Galvin M, Kopta S., & Padgett, R. (1996). Moral valuation: A third domain of conscience functioning. *Journal of the American Academy of Child and Adolescent Psychiatry, 35*, 230-239

Stilwell, B., Galvin, M, Kopta, S., Padgett, R., & Holt, J. (1997). Moralization of attachment: A fourth domain of conscience functioning. *Journal of the American Academy of Child and Adolescent Psychiatry, 36*, 1140-1147.

Stone, J. R. III. (2017). Introduction to pathways to a productive adulthood: The role of CTE in the American high school. *Peabody Journal of Education, 92*(2), 155-165. doi:10.1080/0161956X.2017.1302207

Stonehouse, C. (1998). *Joining children on the spiritual journey: Nurturing a life of faith.* Grand Rapids, MI: Baker Book House.

Strauss, W., & Howe, N. (1997). *The fourth turning: An American prophecy - What the cycles of history tell us about America's next rendezvous with destiny.* New York, NY: Broadway Books.

Strayer, J. (1980). A naturalistic study of empathic behaviors and their relation to affective states and perspective-taking skills in preschool children. *Child Development, 51,* 815-822.

Suizzo, M.A. (2000, July/August). The social-emotional and cultural contexts of cognitive development: Neo-Piagetian perspectives. *Child development, 71*(4), 846-849.

Sullivan, E. (1993). The importance of the human spirit in self-care for older adults. *Generations, 17*(3), 33-37.

Sullivan, H. S. (1968). *The interpersonal theory of psychiatry.* New York, NY: W. W. Norton.

Sum, A., & McLaughlin, J. (2008). *Out with the young and in with the old: U.S. labor markets 2000-2008 and the case for an immediate jobs creation program for teens and young adults.* Boston, MA: Center for Labor Market Studies Publications. Retrieved from http://hdl.handle.net/2047/d20000601

Swann, W., Chang-Schneider, C., & McClarty, K. (2007). Do people's self-views matter? *American Psychologist, 62*(2), 84-94.

Tafarodi, R., & Vu, C. (1997). Two-dimensional self-esteem and reaction to success and failure. *Personality & Social Psychology Bulletin, 23*(6), 626-635.

Tallon, A. (1997). *Head and heart: Affection, cognition, and volition as triune consciousness.* New York, NY: Fordham University Press.

Tappan, M., & Brown, L. (1989). Stories told and lessons learned: Toward a narrative approach to moral development and moral education. *Harvard Educational Review, 59*(2), 182-206.
Tapscott, D. (2000). *Growing up digital: The rise of the net generation.* Cambridge, MA: Harvard Business Press.
Tapscott, D. (2008) *Grown up digital: How the net generation is changing the world.* New York, NY: McGraw-Hill.
Tapscott, D. (2010). *Grown up digital and the transformation of learning.* Presentation at the annual ASCD conference. Retrieved from http://dontapscott.com/2011/03/grown-up-digital-and-the-transformation-of-learning/
Tate, N. (2008). *What do children in the 21st century really need to learn?* Presentation at the International Primary Curriculum Conference, International School of Geneva, October 4.
Taub, J. (2001). Evaluation of the Second Step Violence Prevention Program at a rural elementary school. *School Psychology Review, 31*(2),186-200.
Tauber, M., Rosenberg, M., Battistich, V., & Stone, C. (1989). Procedures for assessing children's social behavior: Four-person tasks. *Moral Education Forum, 14*(1), 1-11.
Taylor, E. (1994). Desperately seeking spirituality. *Psychology Today, 27*, 54ff.
Ten Dam, G., & Volman, M. (2007). Educating for adulthood or for citizenship: Social competence as an educational goal. *European Journal of Education, 42(*2), 281-298.
Thomas, R. M. (1997). *Moral development theories—Secular and religious: A comparative study.* Westport, CT: Greenwood Press.
Tisdell, E. (2001). *Spirituality in adult and higher education.* (Contract No. ED-99-CO-0013). U.S. Department of Education. (ERIC Document Reproduction Service No. ED459370).
Toffler, A. (1970). *Future shock.* New York, NY: Bantam Books.
Toffler, A., & Toffler, H. (1995). *Creating a new civilization.* New York, NY: Turner Publishing.
Tolan, S. (2002). *Spirituality and the highly gifted adolescent.* Charlotte, NC: Author. Retrieved from http://www.stephanietolan.com/spirituality.htm
Tomkins, S. (1991). *Affect, imagery, consciousness: The negative affects: Anger and fear.* London, UK: Gaunt, Inc.
Tompkins, S. (1979). Script theory: Differential magnification of affects. In H. Howe, Jr. & R. Dienstbier (Eds.), *Nebraska symposium on motivation* (Vol. 26, pp. 201-236). Lincoln, NE: University of Nebraska Press.
Tompkins, S. (1987). Script theory. In J. Aronoff, A. Rabin, & R. Zucker (Eds), *The emergence of personality* (pp. 147-216). New York, NY: Springer.

Tosun, L., & Lajunen, T. (2009). Why do young adults develop a passion for internet activities? The associations among *personality*, revealing "true self" on the internet, and passion for the internet. *CyberPsychology & Behavior, 12*(4), 401-406.

Townsend, T. (2009). Third millennium leaders: Thinking and acting both locally and globally. *Leadership and Policy in Schools, 8*(4), 355-379. doi: 10.1080/157007/60802535278

Trost, S. (2009). *Active education: Physical education, physical activity, and academic performance.* San Diego, CA: Active Living Research. Retrieved from https://activelivingresearch.org/sites/default/files/ALR_Brief_Active Education_Summer2009.pdf

Tulving, E. (1972). Episodic and semantic memory. In E. Tulving, & W. Donaldson (Eds.), *Organization and memory.* New York, NY: Academic Press.

Turiel, E. (1983). *The development of social knowledge: Morality and convention.* Cambridge, MA: Cambridge University Press.

Ulanowicz, R. (2009). *A third window: Natural life beyond Newton and Darwin.* West Conshohocken, PA: Templeton University Press.

Urdan, T., & Maehr, M. (1995). Beyond a two-goal theory of motivation and achievement: A case for social goals. *Review of Educational Research, 65*(3), 213-243.

U.S. Census Bureau. (2005, February 10). *Table 1. Marital history for people 15 years and over, by age, sex, race, and hispanic origin: 2001.* Washington, DC: Author. Retrieved from http://www.census.gov/population/socdemo/marital-hist/p70-97/tab01.pdf

U.S. Department of Agriculture. (1995). *Nutrition and your health: Dietary guidelines for Americans.* Washington, DC: Author. Retrieved from https://www.cnpp.usda.gov/sites/default/files/dietary_guidelines_for_americans/1995DGConsumerBrochure.pdf

U.S. Department of Education. (2001). *Fact sheet on the major provisions of the Conference Report to H.R. 1, the No Child Left Behind Act.* Washington, DC: Author. Retrieved from http://www2.ed.gov/nclb/overview/intro/factsheet.html

U.S. Department of Education. (2009, July 24). *President Obama, U.S. Secretary of Education Duncan announce national competition to advance school reform.* Washington, DC: Author. Retrieved from http://www2.ed.gov/news/pressreleases/2009/07/07242009.html

U.S. Department of Health and Human Services. (2001). *The Surgeon General's call to action to decrease overweight and obesity.* Rockville, MD: U.S. Department of Health and

Van Belle, H. (2013). *Explorations in the history of psychology: Persisting themata and changing paradigms.* Sioux Center, IA: Dordt College Press.

Vanderstraeten, R. & Biesta, G. (1998). *Constructivism, educational research, and John Dewey*. Paper presented at the Twentieth World Congress of Philosophy, Boston, MA, August 10-15. Retrieved from http://www.bu.edu/wcp/Papers/Amer/AmerVand.htm

Vernon, A. (1999). *Counseling children and adolescents* (2nd ed.). Denver, CO: Love Publishing Company.

Vessels, G. (1998). *Character and community development: A school planning and teacher training handbook*. Westport, CT: Praeger Publishers.

Vessels, G., & Boyd, S. (1996). Public and constitutional support for character education. *NASSP Bulletin, 80*(579), 55-63.

Visser, B., Ashton, M., & Vernon, P. (2008). What makes you think you're so smart: Measured abilities, personality, and sex differences in relation to self-estimates of multiple intelligences. *Journal of Individual Differences, 29*(1), 35-44.

Vygotsky, L. (1978). *The mind in society: The development of higher psychological processes* (edited by M. Cole, V. John-Steiner, S. Scribner, & E. Souberman). Cambridge, MA: Harvard University Press.

Wagner, T. (2008). *The global achievement gap: Why even our best schools don't teach the new survival skills our children need—and what we can do about it.* New York, NY: Basic Books.

Wagner, T. (2012). *Creating innovators: The making of young people who will change the world.* New York, NY: Scribner.

Waite, L, & Gallagher, M. (2001). *The case for marriage: Why married people are happier, healthier, and better off financially*. New York, NY: Broadway.

Waitley, D. (1996). *The new dynamics of goal setting: Flextactics for a fast-changing world.* New York, NY: William Morrow.

Walker, L. (2002a). *The character of moral exemplars*. Paper presented at the White House Conference on Character and Community, June 19. Retrieved https://www2.ed.gov/admins/lead/safety/character/walker.pdf

Walker, L. (2002b). Moral exemplarity. In W. Damon (Ed.), *Bringing in a new era in character education* (65-83). Stanford, CA: Hoover Institute Press.

Wallerstein, I. (2000). Globalization or the Age of Transition?: A long-term view of the trajectory of the world-system. *International Sociology, 15*(2), 251-267.

Walsh, K., King, M., Jones, L., Tookman, A., & Blizard, R. (2002). Spiritual beliefs may affect outcome of bereavement: Prospective study. *British Medical Journal, 324*(7353), 1551-1554.

Wang, M., Haertel, G., & Walberg, H. (1990). What influences learning? A content analysis of review literature. *Journal of Educational Research, 84*(1), 30-34.

Warnes, E., Sheridan, S., Geske, J., & Warnes, W. (2005). A contextual approach to the assessment of social skills: Identifying meaningful behaviors for social competence. *Psychology in the Schools, 42*(2), 173-187. doi: 10.1002/pits.20052

Warren, R. (2002). *The purpose-driven life: What on earth am I here for?* Grand Rapids, MI: Zondervan.

Weare, K. (2010). Mental health and social and emotional learning: Evidence, principles, tensions, balances. *Advances in School Mental Health Promotion, 3*(1), 5-17.

Weaver II, R. & Cotrell, H. (1992). A nonreligious spirituality that causes students to clarity their values and to respond with passion. *Education, 112*(3), 426-435.

Webb, E. (2009). *Worldview and mind: Religious thought and psychological development.* Columbia, MO & London, UK: University of Missouri Press.

Webster, R. S. (2004). An existential framework of spirituality. *International Journal of Spirituality, 9*(1), 7-19.

Wegener, D. (2005). *The learning ladder: Escalating student achievement with deep alignment and process skills.* Phoenix, AZ: Learning 24/7.

Werker, J., & Tees, R. (1999). Influences on infant speech processing: Toward a new synthesis. *Annual Review of Psychology, 50*, 509-535.

White, S., Keonig, K. and Scahill, L. (2007) Social skill development in children with Autism Spectrum Disorder: A review of intervention research. *Journal of Autism and Developmental Disorders. 37*, 1858-1868.

Whitsed, C., & Green, W. (2013, January 26). Internationalisation begins with the curriculum. *University World News, 256.* Retrieved from http://www.universityworldnews.com/article.php?story=20130123121225469

Wiggins, G., & McTighe, J. (2007). *Understanding by design* (Expanded 2nd ed.). Alexandria, VA: Association for Supervision and Curriculum Development (ASCD).

Wiggins, G., & McTighe, J. (2011). *The understanding by design guide to creating high-quality units.* Alexandria, VA: ASCD.

Wikeley, F., Bullock, K., Muschamp, Y., & Ridge, T. (2007). *Educational relationships outside school: Why access is important.* York, UK: Joseph Rowntree Foundation.

Wilkens, S., & Sanford, M. (2009). *Hidden worldviews: Eight cultural stories that shape our lives.* Downers Grove, IL: InterVarsity Press.

Willett, W. (2001). Food pyramids: What should we really eat? *Eat, drink and be healthy.* New York, NY: Simon & Schuster.

Willett, W., Skerrett, P., & Giovannucci, E. (2001). *Eat drink and be healthy: The Harvard Medical School guide to healthy eating.* New York, NY: Simon & Schuster.

Williams, W., Blythe, T., Li, J., White, N., Sternberg, R., & Gardner, H. (1997). *Practical intelligence for school.* Boston, MA: Allyn & Bacon.
Williams, W., Markle, F., Brigockas, M., & Sternberg, R. (2002). *Creative intelligence for schools (CIFS). 21 lessons to enhance creativity in middle and high school students.* Boston, MA: Allyn and Bacon.
Wilson, A. (2000). *Affirming public meaning in a pluralistic world.* Paper presented at the Second Biannual International Conference on Personal Meaning, Vancouver, BC, July 18-21.
Wilson, A. (Ed.). (1991). *World scripture: A comparative anthology of sacred texts.* New York, NY: Paragon House.
Wilson, E. (1975). *Sociobiology: The new synthesis.* Cambridge, MA: Harvard University Press.
Wilson, E. (1998). *Consilience: The unity of knowledge.* New York, NY: Knopf.
Wink, J., & Putney, L. (2002). *A vision of Vygotsky.* Boston, MA: Allyn & Bacon.
Winn, W., & Snyder, D. (2001). Mental representation. *The Handbook of Research for Educational Communications and Technology* (chap. 5). Bloomington, IN: The Association of Educational Communications and Technology.
Winner, M. (2007). *Thinking about you, Thinking about me: Philosophy and strategies for facilitating the development of perspective taking for students with cognitive deficits* (2nd ed.). New York, NY: Jessica Kingsley Publishers.
Wolin, S. J., & Wolin, S. (1993). *The resilient self: How survivors of troubled families rise above adversity.* New York, NY: Villard.
Wong, P. T. P. (2012). *The human quest for meaning: Theories, research, and applications* (2nd ed.). New York, NY: Routledge.
Wongchai, S. (2003). *The ability of the Kolbe A index action modes to predict learners' attitudes and achievements within a web-based training context.* [Unpublished Dissertation]. College Station, TX: Texas A & M University.
Woods, S., & Schwartz, M. (2000). Food intake and the regulation of body weight. *Annual Review of Psychology, 51*, 255-277.
World Health Organization. (2010). *A conceptual framework for action on the social determinants of health.* Geneva, CH: Author.
Wren, T. (1991). *Caring about morality: Philosophical perspectives in moral psychology.* Cambridge, MA: MIT Press.
Wright, R. (1994). *The moral animal: The new science of evolutionary psychology.* New York, NY: Vintage.
Wynne, E. (1986). The great tradition in education: Transmitting moral values. *Educational Leadership, 43*, 4-9.
Wynne, E., & Ryan, K. (1997). *Reclaiming our schools: A handbook on teaching character, academics, and discipline* (2nd ed.). New York, NY: Merrill.

Wynne, E., & Walberg, H. (Eds.). (1984). *Developing character: Transmitting knowledge*. Posen, IL: ARL.
Yackinous, W. (2015). *Understanding complex ecosystem dynamics: A systems and engineering perspective*. London, UK & San Diego, CA: Academic Press.
Yap, M., Allen, N., Leve, C., & Katz, L. (2008). Maternal meta-emotion philosophy and socialization of adolescent affect: The moderating role of adolescent temperament. *Journal of Family Psychology, 22*(5), 688-700.
Yates, T., Ostrosky, M., Cheatham, A., Fettig, A., Shaffer, L., & Santos, R. (2008). *Research synthesis on screening and assessing social-emotional competence*. Nashville, TN: The Center on the Social and Emotional Foundations for Early Learning (CSEFEL). Retrieved from http://csefel.vanderbilt.edu/documents/rs_screening_assessment.pdf
Yerkes, R., & Dodson, J. (1908). The relation of strength of stimulus to rapidity of habit formation. *Journal of Comparative Neurology and Psychology, 18*, 459-482.
Youth Communication. (2004). *Who we are: Youth Communication mission statement*. New York, NY: Author.
Zajonc, R. (1984). On the primacy of affect. *American Psychologist, 39*(2), 117-123.
Ziglar, Z. (1994). *Over the top: Moving from survival to stability, from stability to success, from success to significance*. Nashville, TN: Thomas Nelson Publishers.
Zimmerman, B. (1989). A social cognitive view of self-regulated academic learning. *Journal of Educational Psychology, 81*(3), 329-339.
Zimmerman, B. (1998). Developing self-fulfilling cycles of academic regulation: An analysis of exemplary instructional models. In D. Schunk & B. Zimmerman (Eds.), *Self-regulated learning* (pp. 1–19). New York, NY: Guilford.
Zimmerman, B. (2002). Becoming a self-regulated learner: An overview. *Theory Into Practice, 41*(2), 64-70.
Zimmerman, B., Bonner, S., & Kovach, R. (1996). *Developing self-regulated learners: Beyond achievement to self-efficacy*. Washington, DC: American Psychological Association.
Zinn, L. (1997). Spirituality in adult education. *Adult Learning 8*(5/6), 26-30.
Zins, J., Payton, J., Weissberg, R., & O'Brien, M. (2007). Social and emotional learning for successful school performance. In G. Matthews, M. Zeidner, & R. D. Roberts (Eds.), *The science of emotional intelligence: Knowns and unknowns* (pp. 376-395). New York, NY: Oxford University Press.
Zins, J., Weissberg, R., Wang, M., & Walberg, H. (Eds.). (2004). *Building academic success on social and emotional learning: What does the research say?* New York, NY: Teachers College Press.

Zion, E., & Jenvey, V. (2006). Temperament and social behavior at home and school among typically developing children and children with an intellectual disability. *Journal of Intellectual Disability, 50*(6), 445-456.
Zohar, D., & Marshall, I. (2000). SQ: *Spiritual intelligence: The ultimate intelligence.* New York, NY: Bloomsbury USA.

Index

www.ingramcontent.com/pod-product-compliance
Lightning Source LLC
Chambersburg PA
CBHW070908030426
42336CB00014BA/2331
9781732606807